Cracking Programming Interviews
500 Questions with Solutions

Sergei Nakariakov

©2014 Sergei Nakariakov

All Rights Reserved.

This publication is protected by copyright unless stated otherwise, and permission must be obtained from the author prior to any prohibited reproduction, storage in a retrieval system, or transmission in any form or by any means, electronic, mechanical, photocopying, recording, or likewise.

For more information, feedback, suggestions and comments, please contact
sergei.nakariakov.5@gmail.com

ISBN-13: 978-1495459801
ISBN-10: 1495459802

Preface

This book contains **500** programming questions most frequently asked in technical interviews in top technical companies including Facebook, Microsoft, Google, Apple, Yahoo and others. Detailed solutions are provided for all of these including tips and techniques for solving similar problems.

For suggestions, feedback and comments, please contact :
sergei.nakariakov.5@gmail.com

Sergei Nakariakov
Senior Scientist(Defence Lab)
USA

List of Chapters

Preface i

List of Programs xi

I Algorithms and Data Structures   2

1 Fundamentals   4
   1.1   Approximating the square root of a number   4
   1.2   Generating Permutation Efficiently   7
   1.3   Unique 5-bit Sequences   11
   1.4   Select Kth Smallest Element   12
   1.5   The Non-Crooks Problem   23
   1.6   Is this (almost) sorted?   25
   1.7   Sorting an almost sorted list   31
   1.8   The Longest Upsequence Problem   34
   1.9   Fixed size generic array in C++   38
   1.10 Seating Problem   41
   1.11 Segment Problems   45
   1.12 Exponentiation   48
   1.13 Searching two-dimensional sorted array   49
   1.14 Hamming Problem   64
   1.15 Constant Time Range Query   66
   1.16 Linear Time Sorting   68
   1.17 Writing a Value as the Sum of Squares   68
   1.18 The Celebrity Problem   70
   1.19 Transport Problem   77
   1.20 Find Length of the rope   82
   1.21 Switch Bulb Problem   84
   1.22 In, On or Out   85
   1.23 The problem of the balanced segments   88
   1.24 The problem of the most isolated villages   89

2 Arrays   95
   2.1   The Plateau Problem   95
   2.2   Searching in Two Dimensional Sequence   97
   2.3   The Welfare Crook Problem 104
   2.4   2D Array Rotation 106
   2.5   A Queuing Problem in A Post Office 108
   2.6   Interpolation Search 111
   2.7   Robot Walk 114
   2.8   Linear Time Sorting 118

- 2.9 Write as sum of consecutive positive numbers 119
- 2.10 Print 2D Array in Spiral Order 120
- 2.11 The Problem of the Circular Racecourse 122
- 2.12 Sparse Array Trick 124
- 2.13 Bulterman's Reshuffling Problem 126
- 2.14 Finding the majority 128
- 2.15 Mode of a Multiset 131
- 2.16 Circular Array 132
- 2.17 Find Median of two sorted arrays 133
- 2.18 Finding the missing integer 134
- 2.19 Finding the missing number with sorted columns 139
- 2.20 Re-arranging an array 142
- 2.21 Switch and Bulb Problem 144
- 2.22 Compute sum of sub-array 147
- 2.23 Find a number not sum of subsets of array 147
- 2.24 K^{th} Smallest Element in Two Sorted Arrays 148
- 2.25 Sort a sequence of sub-sequences 150
- 2.26 Find missing integer 151
- 2.27 Inplace Reversing 151
- 2.28 Find the number not occurring twice in an array 152

3 Trees   154
- 3.1 Lowest Common Ancestor(LCA) Problem 154
- 3.2 Spying Campaign 167

4 Dynamic Programming   170
- 4.1 Stage Coach Problem 171
- 4.2 Matrix Multiplication 174
- 4.3 TSP Problem 175
- 4.4 A Simple Path Problem 175
- 4.5 String Edit Distance 176
- 4.6 Music recognition 183
- 4.7 Max Sub-Array Problem 185

5 Graphs   199
- 5.1 Reliable distribution 199
- 5.2 Independent Set 200
- 5.3 Party Problem 202

6 Miscellaneous   206
- 6.1 Compute Next Higher Number 206
- 6.2 Searching in Possibly Empty Two Dimensional Sequence 212
- 6.3 Matching Nuts and Bolts Optimally 216
- 6.4 Random-number generation 231
- 6.5 Weighted Median 234
- 6.6 Compute a^n 238
- 6.7 Compute a^n revisited 239
- 6.8 Compute the product $a \times b$ 239
- 6.9 Compute the quotient and remainder 240
- 6.10 Compute GCD 240
- 6.11 Computed Constrained GCD 241
- 6.12 Alternative Euclid' Algorithm 242
- 6.13 Revisit Constrained GCD 243
- 6.14 Compute Square using only addition and subtraction 244
- 6.15 Factorization 244

	6.16	Factorization Revisited 245
	6.17	Decimal Representation 246
	6.18	Reverse Decimal Representation 246
	6.19	Solve Inequality 246
	6.20	Solve Inequality Revisited 247
	6.21	Print Decimal Representation 248
	6.22	Decimal Period Length 249
	6.23	Sequence Periodicity Problem 249
	6.24	Compute Function 250
	6.25	Emulate Division and Modulus Operations 251
	6.26	Sorting Array of Strings : Linear Time 252
	6.27	LRU data structure 253
	6.28	Exchange Prefix and Suffix 255

7 Parallel Algorithms 258
 7.1 Parallel Addition 258
 7.2 Find Maximum 259
 7.3 The Parallel Prefix Problem 260
 7.4 Finding Ranks in Linked Lists 262
 7.5 Finding the kth Smallest Element on a Tree 264

8 Low Level Algorithms 269
 8.1 Introduction 269
  8.1.1 Manipulating Rightmost Bits 269
   8.1.1.1 Extending De Morgan's Laws 270
   8.1.1.2 Compute Next higher number with same number of 1-bits 271
 8.2 Bit Counting Algorithms 276
  8.2.1 Counting 1-Bits 276
   8.2.1.1 Counting the 1-bits in an Array 281
  8.2.2 Computing Parity of a word 286
  8.2.3 Counting Leading 0's 289
  8.2.4 Counting Trailing 0's 296
 8.3 Rearranging Algorithms 302
  8.3.1 Bit Reversal 302
  8.3.2 Bit Shuffling 305
 8.4 Computing Functions 308
  8.4.1 Integer Square Root 308
   8.4.1.1 Newton's Method 308
  8.4.2 Integer Exponentiation : Compute x^n 310
 8.5 Miscellaneous 311
  8.5.1 LRU Algorithm : Reference Matrix 312
  8.5.2 Find Shortest String of 1-Bits 315
  8.5.3 Fibonacci words 318
  8.5.4 Computation of Power of 2 321
   8.5.4.1 Round to a known power of 2 321
   8.5.4.2 Round to Next Power of 2 322
  8.5.5 Efficient Multiplication by Constants 325
  8.5.6 Bit-wise Rotation 328
  8.5.7 Gray Code Conversion 330
  8.5.8 Average of Integers without Overflow 330
  8.5.9 Double Linked List with One Pointer Field 331
  8.5.10 Least Significant 1 Bit 331
  8.5.11 Most Significant 1 Bit 331
  8.5.12 Swap Values Without a Temporary 332

8.5.13 Next bit Permutation 332
8.5.14 Compute Modulus Division 332
8.5.15 Conditionally set or clear bits without branching 333
8.5.16 Conditionally negate a value without branching 333

II C++   335

9 General   337

10 Constant Expression   410

11 Type Specifier   422

12 Namespaces   429

13 Misc   447

14 Classes   467

15 Templates   491

16 Standard Library   496

Index   501

List of Algorithms

1	Computing Square Root Program	7
2	Unique 5-bit Sequence Program	12
3	Maximum of a sequence	13
4	Generic Kth Select Minimum	19
5	Partitioning a sequence	20
6	Randomized Partition Algorithm	20
7	Randomized Quicksort Algorithm	21
8	Randomized Kth Min Select Algorithm	21
9	Iterative Version of Quick Select Algorithm	23
10	The Non-Crooks Program	24
11	Binary Search on unsorted list	26
12	is almost sorted	26
13	Sort Almost Sorted Algorithm	34
14	The Longest Upsequence Program	37
15	Seat Algorithm	42
16	ReSeat Algorithm	42
17	ReSeat Linear Time Algorithm	44
18	All Zeros Program	47
19	Exponentiation	48
20	Exponentiation Revisited	49
21	Efficient Exponentiation	49
22	Saddleback Search Algorithm	52
23	Saddleback Search Algorithm in practice	53
24	Saddleback Search Algorithm : Find First Occurrence	55
25	Saddleback Search Algorithm : Find All Occurrences	57
26	Saddleback Count Algorithm : Initial Approach	60
27	Saddleback Count : Correct Algorithm	62
28	Hamming Problem	66
29	Counting Sort Algorithm	67
30	Radix Sort Algorithm	68
31	Writing a Value as the Sum of Squares	69
32	Writing a Value as the Sum of Squares	70
33	Celebrity Algorithm	73
34	Celebrity Algorithm Brute Force	74
35	Celebrity Algorithm Optimized	75
36	Transport Algorithm	78
37	triangle analysis	86
38	The Plateau Problem	96
39	The Plateau Problem Revisited	97
40	Searching in a 2D Array	101
41	Searching in a 2D Array : Another Program	103
42	Searching in a 2D Array : Another Program(Simplified)	103

List of Chapters

43	The Welfare Crook Program	105
44	The Welfare Crook Program Simplified	105
45	Interpolation Search Algorithm	112
46	Robot Walk Algorithm	118
47	Write as sum of consecutive positive numbers	120
48	Circular Racecourse Program	124
49	Bulterman's Reshuffling Problem	128
50	Find Majority Simple Algorithm	129
51	Find Majority Algorithm Revisited	130
52	Find Majority Algorithm Simplified	130
53	Find Majority Algorithm Final	131
54	Circular Array Algorithm	132
55	Find Median of two sorted array	134
56	Median Search	134
57	Re-arranging an array	143
58	Re-arranging an array revisited	144
59	Switches and Bulbs	146
60	Find a number not sum of subsets of array	148
61	K^{th} Smallest Element in Two Sorted Arrays	149
62	Reversing an array inplace	152
63	Kadane's 1D Algorithm	186
64	Kadane's 1D Algorithm : Find Indices	188
65	Maximum sub-array sum using prefix array	197
66	K-Maximum sub-array sum using prefix array	198
67	Independent Set on trees	202
68	Searching in a possibly empty 2D Array	215
69	Partitioning a sequence	220
70	Quicksort to sort a sequence	223
71	Randomized Partition Algorithm	226
72	Randomized Quicksort Algorithm	227
73	Selecting a c-approximate median of X with O(n) complexity	230
74	Back-Tracking	230
75	Finding Misplaced Nuts and Bolts	231
76	Random number generation using binary search	232
77	Random number generation : Preprocess	233
78	Random number generation	233
79	Weighted Median	235
80	Linear Time Weighted Median	236
81	Compute a^n program	238
82	Compute a^n alternative program	239
83	Compute a^n program revisited	239
84	Compute the product $a \times b$	240
85	Compute the quotient and remainder	240
86	Compute GCD	241
87	Compute GCD : Euclid's Algorithm	241
88	Computed Constrained GCD	242
89	Alternative Euclid' Algorithm	243
90	Compute Square using only addition and subtraction	244
91	Factorization Program	245
92	Factorization Alternative Program	245
93	Factorization Program Revisited	245
94	Decimal Representation	246
95	Reverse Decimal Representation	246
96	Solve Inequality Program	247
97	Solve Inequality Revisited	248

98	Print Decimal Representation	249
99	Decimal Period Length	249
100	Sequence Periodicity Problem	250
101	Compute Function	251
102	Emulate Division and Modulus Operations	251
103	LRU Data Structure : Drop program	254
104	LRU Data Structure : Use program	254
105	LRU Data Structure : Insert program	255
106	Exchange Prefix and Suffix	256
107	Parallel Prefix Algorithm	261
108	Parallel Prefix : Efficient Algorithm	262
109	List Rank Algorithm	264

List of Programs

1.1	generate efficient permutation	9
1.2	Finding Maximum in an integer array	13
1.3	Finding First Maximum in an integer array	13
1.4	Finding First Maximum Satisfying Predicate	14
1.5	Finding First Minimum in an integer array	14
1.6	Ordering Equivalence	14
1.7	Finding Last Maximum in an integer array	14
1.8	Finding Last Minimum in an integer array	15
1.9	Another Ordering Equivalence	15
1.10	C++ Implementation of first min and first max	16
1.11	first_min_last_max_element	18
1.12	Generic Kth Select Minimum	19
1.13	Randomized version of Kth Select Minimum	21
1.14	generic array in C++	38
1.15	Saddleback search in C++11	53
1.16	Using Saddleback Search	54
1.17	Saddleback Search : First Occurrence	55
1.18	Using Saddleback Search : First Occurrence	56
1.19	Saddleback Find All	57
1.20	Using Saddleback Find All	58
1.21	Another Usage of Saddleback Find All	59
1.22	Continue Using Saddleback Find All	59
1.23	Saddleback Count : Initial Approach	61
1.24	Using Saddleback Count	61
1.25	Using Saddleback Count : Count of 6 should be 6	61
1.26	Implementing Saddleback Count	62
1.27	Using Saddleback Count	63
1.28	another Usage of Saddleback Count	63
1.29	Finding Celebrity Program	76
2.1	searching 2D Array	101
2.2	Search for 6 : yields a : 2 2	102
2.3	C++11 Version : Searching 2D Array	103
2.4	Usage : C++11 Version : Searching 2D Array	104
2.5	rotate 2D array	106
2.6	Interpolation Search	113
2.7	Print 2D Array in Spiral Order	120
2.8	Find the missing integer	151
2.9	Find the number not occurring twice in an array	152
3.1	Simple n-ary tree	156
3.2	Compute LCA : C++ : Stack Based	159
3.3	Compute LCA : C++ : Level Based	161
4.1	Simple Implementation : Levenshtein edit distance	179

List of Programs

xii

4.2	Improved Implementation : Levenshtein edit distance	180
4.3	Boost Implementation : Levenshtein edit distance	181
4.4	Implementing Kadane's Algorithm	186
4.5	Implementing Kadane's Algorithm	187
4.6	Implementing Kadane's Algorithm : Finding Indices	188
4.7	Using Kadane's Algorithm : Finding Indices	189
4.8	Finding sum closest to zero	192
6.1	C++ Implementation : Find the next higher permutation	207
6.2	next_permutation	208
6.3	reversing a sequence	209
6.4	C++ Implementation of prev_permutation	211
6.5	Usage of previous permutation	211
6.6	Searching 2D Array	215
6.7	Search for 6 : yields a 2 2	215
6.8	Partitioning in C++	220
6.9	STL style implementation of partition	221
6.10	std::partition	222
6.11	quicksort in C++	223
6.12	STL style implementation of quicksort	224
6.13	Implementing quicksort	225
6.14	randomized partition in C++	226
6.15	randomized quicksort in C++	227
8.1	*Next higher number with same number of 1-bits*	273
8.2	*Counting 1-Bits, divide and conquer*	277
8.3	*Counting 1-Bits in a word, divide and conquer improved*	277
8.4	*Counting 1-Bits in a word, HAKMEM Algorithm*	278
8.5	*Counting 1-Bits in a word, Variation of HAKMEM Algorithm*	278
8.6	*Counting 1-bits in a sparsely populated word*	279
8.7	*rotate*	279
8.8	*Two similar bit-counting algorithms*	280
8.9	*Determines which word has the larger population count*	280
8.10	*Counting the 1-bits in an Array*	281
8.11	*parity algorithms*	287
8.12	*Counting Leading zeros algorithms*	289
8.13	*Counting Trailing zeros algorithms*	296
8.14	*Integer Square Root : Newton's Method*	308
8.15	*Integer square root : binary search for first guess*	309
8.16	*Integer square root : simple binary search*	310
8.17	*Computing x^n by binary decomposition of n*	311
8.18	*Greatest power of 2 less than or equal to x, branch free*	323
8.19	*Least power of 2 greater than or equal to x*	324
8.20	*Gray Code Conversion*	330
8.21	*Most Significant 1 Bit*	331
8.22	*Swap Values Without a Temporary*	332
8.23	*Next bit Permutation : Faster*	332
8.24	*Next bit Permutation*	332
8.25	*Compute modulus division by $(1 \ll s)$ without a division operator*	332
8.26	*Compute modulus division by $(1 \ll s) - 1$ without a division operator*	333
8.27	*Conditionally set or clear bits without branching*	333
8.28	*Conditionally negate a value without branching*	333
9.1	Bit-fields and Concurrency	337
9.2	Bit-fields and Concurrency	337

List of Programs

9.3	Distinct Address Location	338
9.4	Temporary and Conversions	339
9.5	evaluation of expressions	340
9.6	trigraph sequences	340
9.7	replacing trigraph sequences	341
9.8	increment operator	341
9.9	user defined literal	342
9.10	Declaration vs Definition	343
9.11	Sample Class	343
9.12	Compiler Generated Member Functions	345
9.13	Compiler Generated Member Functions	346
9.14	ODR vs Default Constructor	346
9.15	ODR vs Default Constructor	347
9.16	Understanding Point of Declaration	347
9.17	class scope variables	348
9.18	namespace scope variables	349
9.19	Unqualified Name Lookup	351
9.20	Unqualified Name Lookup	352
9.21	Unqualified Name Lookup	353
9.22	Unqualified Name Lookup	354
9.23	Friend member function and Name Lookup	355
9.24	namespace extern and look-up	356
9.25	ADL	357
9.26	ADL	358
9.27	ADL	359
9.28	Basic Look-up	359
9.29	Basic Look-up	360
9.30	Basic Look-up	361
9.31	destructor and typedef	361
9.32	multiple declarations are ok	365
9.33	multiple declarations are ok	365
9.34	non-type name and namespace	366
9.35	declaration and nested namespace	367
9.36	declaration and nested namespace	368
9.37	declaration and nested namespace	368
9.38	injected class name	370
9.39	static and std::atexit	372
9.40	std::atexit and static	373
9.41	std::atexit and static	374
9.42	two std::atexit	374
9.43	non-const to const conversion	378
9.44	xvalue rvalue	379
9.45	valid usage of this pointer	380
9.46	sizeof	380
9.47	lambda and sorting	381
9.48	return type of lambda	382
9.49	lambda and default argument	382
9.50	nested lambda expressions	383
9.51	type of decltype((x))	384
9.52	brace initializer list as subscript	384
9.53	Pseudo Destructor	385
9.54	Dynamic Cast vs Base/Derived	386
9.55	Understanding Dynamic Cast	387
9.56	Understanding Dynamic Cast	388
9.57	typeid and const/volatile	390

List of Programs

9.58	static cast and base/derived	390
9.59	static cast and base/derived	391
9.60	static cast and base/derived	392
9.61	static cast to and fro	392
9.62	type of base class member	393
9.63	counting types	393
9.64	placement operator	395
9.65	illegal casting	396
9.66	mutable and const	397
9.67	relational operator and void *	397
9.68	Pointers to Members Comparison	399
9.69	brace initializer list and assignment	400
9.70	comma operator and argument	400
9.71	constexpr constructor	401
9.72	translation vs runtime	402
9.73	literal class and integral constant	402
9.74	scope of conditional variable	403
9.75	scope of conditional variable	404
9.76	simulation of while loop	405
9.77	return brace-init-list	407
9.78	specifying attributes	407
10.1	constexpr function example	414
10.2	constexpr function and substitution	415
10.3	revise constexpr function	416
10.4	revise constexpr constructor	417
10.5	constexpr and literal type	418
10.6	constexpr and constructor	419
11.1	const/volatile qualifier	422
11.2	decltype	423
11.3	friend template parameter	425
11.4	friend template parameter	426
11.5	auto type specifier	426
11.6	auto type specifier vs template argument deduction	427
11.7	scoped enumerator	427
12.1	using unnamed namespace	430
12.2	function definition and unnamed namespace	430
12.3	friend functions and namespace	431
12.4	namespace alias	432
12.5	redeclare namespace alias	433
12.6	redeclare namespace alias	433
12.7	redefinition namespace alias	433
12.8	using declaration	434
12.9	using declaration and base class	435
12.10	using declaration and template-id	435
12.11	using declaration and member declaration	436
12.12	using declaration and referring members	437
12.13	multiple using declaration	437
12.14	availability of using declaration	438
12.15	using declaration and same functions	439
12.16	hide/override and using declaration	441
12.17	using declaration and ambiguous base	442
12.18	using declaration and accessibility rules	443
12.19	using directive	443
13.1	nested linkage specifications	447
13.2	noreturn attribute	449

List of Programs

- 13.3 pointers 452
- 13.4 types 454
- 13.5 pointers to members 454
- 13.6 arrays and sizeof 455
- 13.7 typedef and function definition 457
- 13.8 typedef and const volatile function 457
- 13.9 default argument 459
- 13.10 default argument and local variables 460
- 13.11 explicitly defaulted functions 460
- 13.12 prevent new instance of class 462
- 13.13 noncopyable (aka moveonly) class 462
- 13.14 deleted function and inline 463
- 13.15 static member initialization scope 464
- 13.16 initializer list and map 465
- 13.17 initializer list and constructor 465
- 14.1 scope of static member 468
- 14.2 member name lookup 469
- 14.3 non-static member lookup 471
- 14.4 member lookup and virtual base 472
- 14.5 virtual function 473
- 14.6 virtual function and final 475
- 14.7 virtual function and override 476
- 14.8 access default template argument 476
- 14.9 access to virtual function 477
- 14.10 new and dangling reference 478
- 14.11 user defined conversion 479
- 14.12 conversion by constructor 479
- 14.13 destructor 480
- 14.14 delete and virtual 482
- 14.15 base class initializer 483
- 14.16 initializer and this 485
- 14.17 dynamic_cast and construction 486
- 14.18 hiding 488
- 14.19 hiding operators 488
- 15.1 template argument and type-id 492
- 15.2 virtual member function template 493

Part I

Algorithms and Data Structures

Chapter 1

Fundamentals

1.1 Approximating the square root of a number

Problem Description

Write a program that, given a fixed integer $n \geq 0$, establishes the truth of

$$R : 0 \leq a^2 \leq n < (a+1)^2$$

Solution

Taking the square root of all terms in R, we find that R is equivalent to $0 \leq a \leq \sqrt{n} < a+1$. Hence, a is the largest integer that is at most $\sqrt{n}$. The first step is to rewrite R as a set of conjuncts:

$$R : 0 \leq a^2 \wedge a^2 \leq n \wedge n < (a+1)^2$$

Deleting the third conjunct of R yields a possible invariant:

$$P : 0 \leq a^2 \leq n.$$

Because $n \geq 0$, P can be established by the assignment $a \leftarrow 0$. For the condition of the loop, use the complement of the deleted conjunct, so that when the loop terminates because the condition is false, the deleted conjunct is true. This yields the almost completed program :

```
1: a ← 0
2: while (a + 1)² ≤ n do
3:     ?
4: end while
```

The purpose of the command of the loop is to progress towards termination. Clearly, if the condition of the loop is true then a is too small, so that progress can be made by increasing a. Since a is bounded above by $\sqrt{n}$, a possible bound function is $t = \lceil \sqrt{n} \rceil - a$. Using the easiest way to increase a, incrementing by 1, yields the program

1.1. Approximating the square root of a number

```
1: a ← 0
2: while (a + 1)² ≤ n do
3:     a ← a + 1
4: end while
```

We show that P is indeed an invariant of the loop:
$$P \wedge B = 0 \le a^2 \le n \wedge (a+1)^2 \le n = 0 \le (a+1)^2 \le n$$
The execution time of the program is proportional to $\sqrt{n}$. This program is developed by deleting the conjunct $n < (a+1)^2$. Now let us try using the method of replacing a constant by a variable.

First try replacing the expression $a + 1$ by a fresh variable b to yield
$$a^2 \le n < b^2$$
Clearly, b must be greater than a if this predicate is to be true. Moreover, the predicate can be established by executing $a \leftarrow 0$ and $b \leftarrow n + 1$. Hence, b is bounded by $a + 1$ and $n + 1$, and the invariant is
$$P : a < b \le n + 1 \wedge a^2 \le n < b^2$$
The condition B for the loop, obtained by investigating $P \wedge \neg B \implies R$, is $a + 1 \ne b$. Thus far, the program is

```
1: a ← 0
2: b ← n + 1
3: while a + 1 ≠ b do
4:     ?
5: end while
```

Since P indicates that $a + 1 \le b$ and the loop should terminate with $a + 1 = b$, the task of each iteration is to bring a and b closer together, i. e. to decrease the value of $b - a$. Execution should continue until $b - a = 1$. Hence a possible bound function t is $b - a - 1$.

The size of the interval (a, b) could be decreased by one at each iteration, but perhaps a faster technique exists. Perhaps the interval could be halved, by setting either a or b to the midpoint $\frac{(a+b)}{2}$. If so, the command of the loop could have the form

```
1: if ? then
2:     a ← (a+b)/2
3: else if ? then
4:     b ← (a+b)/2
5: end if
```

Each command must maintain the invariant P. To find a suitable condition for the first command, first calculate
$$\tfrac{(a+b)}{2} < b \le n + 1 \wedge (\tfrac{(a+b)}{2})^2 \le n \wedge b^2 > n$$
The precondition will be the invariant together with the condition of the loop
$$P \wedge a + 1 \ne b$$

1.1. Approximating the square root of a number

The extra condition needed is $(\frac{(a+b)}{2})^2 \leq n$, so we take it as the condition for the first command. In a similar fashion, the condition for the second command is found to be $(\frac{(a+b)}{2})^2 > n$. Introducing a fresh variable d to save local calculations, we arrive at the program

---

1: $a \leftarrow 0$
2: $b \leftarrow n+1$
3: $Invariant : P : a < b \leq n+1 \wedge a^2 \leq n < b^2$
4: $bound\ t : b - a + 1$
5: **while** $a + 1 \neq b$ **do**
6:     $d \leftarrow \frac{(a+b)}{2}$
7:     **if** $d \times d \leq n$ **then**
8:         $a \leftarrow d$
9:     **else if** $d \times d > n$ **then**
10:         $b \leftarrow d$
11:     **end if**
12: **end while** $\triangleright\ a^2 \leq n < (a+1)^2$

It may seem that the technique of halving the interval was pulled out of a hat. It is simply one of the useful techniques that programmers must know about, for its use often speeds up programs considerably. The execution time of this program is proportional to $\log n$, while the execution time of the program developed earlier is proportional to $\sqrt{n}$.

This program illustrates another reason to introduce a variable : d has been introduced to make a local optimization. The introduction of d not only reduces the number of times the expression $\frac{(a+b)}{2}$ is evaluated, it also makes the program more readable.

Note that no definition is given for d. Variable d is essentially a constant of the loop body. It is assigned a value upon entrance to the loop body, and this values is used throughout the body. It carries no value from iteration to iteration. Moreover, d is used only in two adjacent lines, and its use is obvious from these two lines. A definition of d would belabor the obvious and is therefore omitted.

If the difference $b - a$ is always even, then d can be calculated using

$$d \leftarrow a + \frac{(b-a)}{2}$$

Therefore, let us attempt to deal with the difference, say c, between b and a and to keep this difference even. This will be easiest if c is always a power of 2. Thus we have:

$$b = a + c$$
$$d = a + c/2$$
$$p : 1 \leq p : c = 2^p \implies c \text{ is even.}$$

Because b and d are defined in terms of a and c, we may be able to write the program using only a and c. Thus, we try the loop invariant and bound function

$$P : a^2 \leq n < (a+c)^2 \wedge (p : 1 \leq p : c = 2^p)$$
$$t : c + 1$$

1.2. Generating Permutation Efficiently

The initialization will require a loop to establish P, since c must be a power of 2. The rest of the program is derived from the previous program. essentially by deleting the assignments to b and d and transforming the other commands into commands involving c:

Algorithm 1 Computing Square Root Program

1: $a \leftarrow 0$
2: $c \leftarrow 1$
3: **while** $c^2 \leq n$ **do**
4:    $c \leftarrow 2 \times c$
5: **end while** $\triangleright P$
6: **while** $c \neq 1$ **do**
7:    $c \leftarrow \frac{c}{2}$
8:    **if** $(a+c)^2 \leq n$ **then**
9:       $a \leftarrow a + c$
10:    **else if** $(a+c)^2 > n$ **then**
11:       skip
12:    **end if**
13: **end while** $\triangleright a^2 \leq n < (a+1)^2$

1.2 Generating Permutation Efficiently

Problem Description

Design a program that will generate the n! permutations of the values from 0 through n-1 in such an order that the transition from one permutation to the next is always performed by exactly one swap of two neighbors.

Solution

Reduction Approach(*to inversion*)

In a permutation each pair of values such that the larger value precedes the smaller one, presents a so-called *inversion*. In particular: the one and only permutation with zero inversions is the one in which the values are placed in monotonically increasing order.

The notion of inversions can be expected to be relevant here because the swapping of two neighbors changes the total number of inversions : i.e. the number of pairs in the wrong order: by (plus or minus) 1, and it is, therefore, suggested to

characterize each permutation by its inversions.

This can be done by introducing n inversion counters inversion[i] for $0 \leq i < n$, where inversion[i] equals the number of inversions between the value i and the values smaller than i.

In other words, inversion[i] equals the number of numbers $< i$, that are placed at *the wrong side* of i, so we can say that

inversion[i] = the number of inversions between the value i and smaller values.

From this definition

$$0 \leq inversion[i] \leq i$$

1.2. Generating Permutation Efficiently

follows;

> *the total number of inversions of a permutation is the sum of the corresponding inversion[i] values.*

i.e., The total number of inversions of the permutation is the sum of all the inversion[i] values.

So it is obvious that:

1. Each permutation defines the inversion[i] values uniquely, and
2. The inverse[i] define the permutation uniquely.

The second point above is easily seen by considering the algorithm constructing the permutation from the inversion[i] values, thus processing these values in the order of increasing i.

So there is a one-to-one correspondence between the n! possible inversion values and the n! permutations. With this insight, the original problem is reduced to the following problem :

which modifications of the inversion value correspond to a swap of neighbors

Each swap of two neighbors changes exactly one inversion[i] value by 1, viz. with i = the larger of the two values swapped. The value of inversion[i] is to be increased if the swap increases the number of inversions; otherwise it is to be decreased.

A feasible sequence of inversion values to be generated is now reasonably obvious: it is the generalization of the Grey-code. For n = 4 it would begin

inversion[0]	inversion[1]	inversion[2]	inversion[3]
0	0	0	0
0	0	0	1
0	0	0	2
0	0	0	3
0	0	1	3
0	0	1	2
0	0	1	1
0	0	1	0
0	0	2	0
0	0	2	1
0	0	2	2
0	0	2	3
0	1	2	3
0	1	2	2
⋮	⋮	⋮	⋮

Algorithm

The logic is simple: a number is changeable when

1. it may be increased by 1 $\implies$ if the sum of the numbers to its left is even and it has not reached its maximum value.
2. it may be decreased by 1 $\implies$ if the sum of the numbers to its left is odd and it has not reached its minimum value zero.

1.2. Generating Permutation Efficiently

Please note that at each step, always the right-most changeable number is changed. It is not difficult to see that in the permutation, the value i is, indeed, swapped with a smaller value.

After having established the value i, such that inversion[i] has to be changed, and, also, whether the value i has to be swapped with its predecessor in the permutation (corresponding to an increase of inversion[i]) or with its successor in the permutation (corresponding to a decrease of inversion[i]), we have to establish the place c in the permutation, where the value i is located, because $\forall j > i$, inversion[j] has an extreme value, c is given by:

$$c = i - inversion[i] + (\text{the number of values } j \mid j > i \ \&\& \ inversion[j] = j)$$

Reason is simple : i is its original position, inversion[i] is the number of smaller elements to the right of it; we have to add to it the number of larger elements in front of the section with *elements* $\leq i$.

C++ Implementation

Putting this algorithm in C++ code is easy now:

Program 1.1: generate efficient permutation

```cpp
#include <iostream>
#include <algorithm>

bool odd(int i)
{
    return i & 1;
}

bool even(int i)
{
    return !odd(i);
}

int main()
{
    const int n = 4;

    int permuted_array[n], inversion[n];
    bool ready;
    int total_inversion, i, c, sum_left_inversion;
    i = 0;

    while (i < n)
    {
        permuted_array[i] = i;
        inversion[i] = 0;
        ++i;
    }

    inversion[0] = -2;

    ready = false;
    total_inversion = 0;

    while (!ready)
    {
        for(auto e : permuted_array)
            std::cout << e << '\t';
```

1.2. Generating Permutation Efficiently   10

```cpp
            std::cout << std::endl;

            i = n - 1;
            c = 0;
            sum_left_inversion = total_inversion - inversion[
                i];

            while ((inversion[i] == i) && even(
                sum_left_inversion))
            {
                c = c + 1;
                i = i - 1;
                sum_left_inversion = sum_left_inversion -
                    inversion[i];
            }

            while ((inversion[i] == 0) && odd(
                sum_left_inversion))
            {
                i = i - 1;
                sum_left_inversion = sum_left_inversion -
                    inversion[i];
            }

            c = c + i - inversion[i];

            if (even(sum_left_inversion) && i > 0)
            {
                inversion[i] = inversion[i] + 1;
                total_inversion = total_inversion + 1;
                std::swap(permuted_array[c-1], permuted_array
                    [c]);
            }
            else if(odd(sum_left_inversion) && i > 0)
            {
                inversion[i] = inversion[i] - 1;
                total_inversion = total_inversion - 1;
                std::swap(permuted_array[c], permuted_array[c
                    + 1]);
            }
            else if(i == 0)
            {
                ready = true;
            }
        }
}
```

In the program given above, inversion[0], which should be constantly 0, has been assigned the funny value -2; this is the usual, mean, little coding trick, in order to let the search for the right-most changeable inversion[i] value terminate artificially when there is no more such an inversion[i] value. The value *total_inversion* records the total number of inversions in the array *permuted_array*, that is used to record the permutation; the variable *sum_left_inversion* records the sum of the (non-funny) inversion[j] values to the left of inversion[i] (i.e. with j < i).

1.3 Unique 5-bit Sequences

Problem Description

Consider sequences of 36 bits. Each such sequence has 32 $5-bit$ sequences consisting of *adjacent bits*. For example, the sequence 1101011... contains the $5-bit$ sequences 11010, 10101, 01011, ... Write a program that prints all $36-bit$ sequences with the two properties:

1. The first 5 bits of the sequence are 00000.
2. No two $5-bit$ subsequences are the same.

Call a sequence of zeros and ones that begins with 0000, i.e. 4 zeros, and satisfy property (2) a *good sequence*. Call a sequence with k bits a *k-sequence*.

Define an ordering among good sequences as follows:

- Sequence s_1 is less than sequence s_2, written as

  $s_1. < .s_2$, if, when viewed as decimal numbers with the decimal point to the extreme left, s_1 is less than s_2.

  For example, $101. < .1011$ because $.101 < .1011$.

- In a similar manner, we write $101. = .101000$, because $.101 = .101000$. Appending a *zero* to a sequence yields an equal sequence; appending a *one* yields a larger sequence.

- Any *good* sequence s to be printed satisfies $0. < .s. < .00001$, and must begin with 00000.

The program below iteratively generates, in order, all *good* sequences satisfying $0. \leq .s. \leq .00001$, printing the $36-bit$ ones as they are generated. The sequence currently under consideration will be called s. There will be no variable s; it is just a name for the sequence currently under consideration. s always contains at least 5 bits. Further, to eliminate problems with equal sequences, we will always be sure that s is the longest *good* sequence equal to itself.

$P_1 : good(s) \land \neg good(s \mid 0) \land 5 \leq \mid s \mid \land 0. \leq .s. \leq .00001 \land$ *All good sequences* $. < .s$ *are printed.*

Sequence s with n bits could be represented by a bit array. However, it is better to represent s by an integer array $c[4..n-1]$, where $c[i]$ is the decimal representation of the $5-bit$ subsequence of s ending in bit i. Thus, we will maintain as part of the invariant of the main loop the assertion

$$P_2 : 5 \leq n = \mid s \mid \leq 36 \land c[i] =$$
$$s[i-4] \times 2^4 + s[i-3] \times 2^3 + s[i-2] \times 2^2 + s[i-1] \times 2 + s[i], \text{ for } 4 \leq i < n$$

Further, in order to keep track of which $5-bit$ subsequence s contains, we use a Boolean array $in[0..31]$:

$$P_3 : i : 0 \leq i < 32 : in[i] = (i \in c[4..n-1])$$

1.4. Select Kth Smallest Element

With this introduction, the program should be easy to follow.

Algorithm 2 Unique 5-bit Sequence Program

1: $n \leftarrow 5$
2: $c[4] \leftarrow 0$
3: $in[0] \leftarrow T$
4: $in[1..31] \leftarrow F$ $\triangleright$ s = (0, 0, 0, 0, 0)
5: $invariant : P_1 \wedge P_2 \wedge P_3 \wedge \neg good(s \mid 0)$
6: **while** $c[4] \neq 1$ **do**
7:    **if** $n == 36$ **then**
8:       *Print sequence s*
9:    **else if** $n \neq 36$ **then**
10:       *skip*
11:    **end if**
12:    *Change s to next higher good sequence:*
13:    **while** $in[(c[n-1] \times 2 + 1) \mod 32]$ **do** $\triangleright$ i.e. $\neg good(s \mid 1)$
14:       *Delete ending 1's from s:*
15:       **while** $odd(c[n-1])$ **do**
16:          $n \leftarrow n - 1$
17:          $in[c[n]] \leftarrow F$
18:       **end while**
19:       *Delete ending 0:*
20:       $n \leftarrow n - 1$
21:       $in[c[n]] \leftarrow F$
22:    **end while**
23:    *Append 1 to s:*
24:    $c[n] \leftarrow (c[n-1] \times 2 + 1) \mod 32$
25:    $in[c[n]] \leftarrow T$
26:    $n \leftarrow n + 1$
27: **end while**

1.4 Select Kth Smallest Element

Problem

Design and implement an efficient algorithm to select the Kth Smallest Element of an array.

Basic Analysis

Simultaneous Min-Max Algorithm

Before embarking on this selection problem, let us work out a general scheme of finding maximum and minimum of the input sequence. Min-max algorithms are ubiquitous in various applications specially geometric ones. In this section we will revisit several versions with primary focus being finding the most efficient one.

Design an efficient algorithm to find the minimum and maximum of an integer sequence simultaneously.

Let us revisit a typical set-up for finding the maximum of an integer sequence where we end up examine each element of the sequence in turn along with keeping track of the largest element seen so far.

1.4. Select Kth Smallest Element

Algorithm 3 Maximum of a sequence

1: **function** MAXVAL(a, l, r)
2:     $0 \leq n$
3:     $a[k] \geq a[0..n-1]$
4:     $i \leftarrow 1$
5:     $k \leftarrow 0$
6:     **while** $0 \leq n$ **do**
7:         **if** $a[i] \leq a[k]$ **then**
8:             *do nothing*
9:         **else if** $a[i] \geq a[k]$ **then**
10:            $k \leftarrow i$
11:         **end if**
12:         $i \leftarrow i + 1$
13:     **end while**
14:     **return** k
15: **end function**

Program 1.2: Finding Maximum in an integer array

```cpp
#include <vector>
#include <algorithm>
#include <cassert>

template <typename T>
size_t maxValArray(std::vector<T> & v)
{
    size_t i = 1, k = 0;
    size_t n = v.size();

    while(i <= n)
    {
        if(v[i] >= v[k]) k = i;
        ++i;
    }

    assert(v[k] == *std::max_element(v.begin(),
                                     v.end()));
    return k;
}

int main()
{
    std::vector<int> v {10, 12, 2, 8, 5, 20, 7};
    maxValArray(v);
}
```

As can be seen that this doesn't address the scenario in presence of multiple occurrences. Let us put forth obvious solutions.

Program 1.3: Finding First Maximum in an integer array

```cpp
template <typename ForwardIterator>
ForwardIterator first_max_element(
    ForwardIter first, ForwardIter last)
{
    if (first == last) return last;
    ForwardIter max_result = first;
    while (++first != last)
```

1.4. Select Kth Smallest Element

```
8    {
9        if (*max_result < *first)
10           max_result = first;
11   }
12   return max_result;
13 }
```

Program 1.4: Finding First Maximum Satisfying Predicate

```
1 #include <boost/iterator_adaptors.hpp>
2
3 template <typename ForwardIterator,
4           typename Predicate>
5 ForwardIterator
6 first_max_element_if(ForwardIter first,
7                      ForwardIter last,
8                      Predicate pred)
9 {
10    return first_max_element(
11        boost::make_filter_iterator(first, last,
12                                     pred),
13        boost::make_filter_iterator(last, last,
14                                     pred)
15    );
16 }
```

Program 1.5: Finding First Minimum in an integer array

```
1 template <typename ForwardIterator>
2 ForwardIterator first_min_element(
3     ForwardIter first, ForwardIter last)
4 {
5     if (first == last) return last;
6     ForwardIter min_result = first;
7     while (++first != last)
8     {
9         if (*first < *min_result)
10            min_result = first;
11    }
12    return min_result;
13 }
```

Please note that :

Program 1.6: Ordering Equivalence

```
1 std::min_element(v.begin(), v.end(),
2                  std::less<int>())
3 ==
4 std::max_element(v.begin(), v.end(),
5                  std::greater<int>())
```

Program 1.7: Finding Last Maximum in an integer array

```
1 template <typename ForwardIterator>
2 ForwardIterator last_max_element(
3     ForwardIter first, ForwardIter last)
4 {
```

1.4. Select Kth Smallest Element

```
    if (first == last) return last;
    ForwardIter max_result = first;
    while (++first != last)
    {
        if (*first < *max_result)
            max_result = first;
    }
    return max_result;
}
```

Program 1.8: Finding Last Minimum in an integer array

```
template <typename ForwardIterator>
ForwardIterator last_min_element(
    ForwardIter first, ForwardIter last)
{
    if (first == last) return last;
    ForwardIter min_result = first;
    while (++first != last)
    {
        if (*min_result < *first)
            min_result = first;
    }
    return min_result;
}
```

Please note that:

Program 1.9: Another Ordering Equivalence

```
std::reverse_iterator(
    first_min_element(v.begin(), v.end(),
                      std::less<int>()))
==
last_max_element(v.rbegin(), v.rend(),
                 std::greater<int>())
```

All of these algorithms work in similar way requiring $n - 1$ comparisons in worst case.

How about simultaneously finding maximum and minimum of the sequence? Naively, we can get this done in two passes : once for finding maximum and another for finding minimum : total of $2n - 2$ comparisons. But we can definitely do better if we confine ourselves to a single pass and reply on maintaining maximum and minimum elements seen so far. Instead of picking one element and probing it against the current maximum or minimum, we can rather examine two elements at a time treating them as pairs. The process goes like this:

1. Maintain the minimum and maximum of elements seen so far.

2. Don't compare each element to the minimum and maximum separately, which requires two comparisons per element.

3. Pick up the elements in pairs.

4. Compare the elements of a pair to each other.

5. Then compare the larger element to the maximum so far, and compare the smaller element to the minimum so far.

1.4. Select Kth Smallest Element

The above requires only three comparisons per two elements. Setting up the initial values for the min and max depends on whether n is odd or even.

- If n is even, compare the first two elements and assign the larger to max and the smaller to min.

  This needs one initial comparison and then $\frac{3(n-2)}{2}$ more comparisons. Thus total number of comparisons =
  $1 + \frac{3(n-2)}{2}$
  $= 1 + \frac{3n-6)}{2}$
  $= 1 + \frac{3n}{2} - 3$
  $= \frac{3n}{2} - 2.$

  Then process the rest of the elements in pairs.

- If n is odd, set both min and max to the first element. Then process the rest of the elements in pairs. This needs a total of $\frac{3(n-1)}{2}$ comparisons.

Program 1.10: C++ Implementation of first min and first max

```cpp
template <typename ForwardIterator>
std::pair<ForwardIterator, ForwardIterator>
first_min_first_max_element(
    ForwardIterator first,
    ForwardIterator last)
{
    if (first == last)
        return std::make_pair(last, last);

    ForwardIterator min_result,
                    max_result = first;

    // if only one element
    ForwardIterator second = first; ++second;

    if (second == last)
    return std::make_pair(min_result,
                          max_result);

    // treat first pair separately
    //(only one comparison for
    //first two elements)
    ForwardIterator
       potential_min_result = last;

    if (*first < *second) max_result = second;
    else
    {
        min_result = second;
        potential_min_result = first;
    }

    // then each element by pairs,
    // with at most 3 comparisons per pair
    first = ++second;

    if (first != last) ++second;

    while (second != last)
    {
```

1.4. Select Kth Smallest Element

```
            if (*first < *second)
            {
                if (*first < *min_result)
                {
                    min_result = first;
                    potential_min_result = last;
                }

                if (*max_result < *second)
                    max_result = second;
            }
            else
            {
                if (*second < *min_result)
                {
                    min_result = second;
                    potential_min_result = first;
                }

                if (*max_result < *first)
                    max_result = first;
            }

            first = ++second;

            if (first != last) ++second;
        }
        // if odd number of elements,
        //treat last element
        if (first != last)
        { // odd number of elements
            if (*first < *min_result)
            {
                min_result = first;
                potential_min_result = last;
            }
            else if (*max_result < *first)
                max_result = first;
        }

        // resolve min_result being incorrect
        // with one extra comparison
        // (in which case potential_min_result
        // is necessarily the
        // correct result)
        if (potential_min_result != last &&
            !(*min_result < *potential_min_result))
            min_result = potential_min_result;

        return
            std::make_pair(min_result, max_result);
    }
```

Please note that only one comparison is required for first two elements(aka first pair). The above requires at most three comparisons per pair.

In similar spirit, there are multiple combinations possible like:

- first_min_first_max_element

1.4. Select Kth Smallest Element

- first_min_last_max_element
- last_min_first_max_element
- last_min_last_max_element

Let us look at the implementation of
first_min_last_max_element as inspiration.

Program 1.11: first_min_last_max_element

```cpp
template <typename ForwardIterator>
std::pair<ForwardIterator, ForwardIterator>
first_min_last_max_element(
    ForwardIterator first,
    ForwardIterator last)
{
    if (first == last)
        return std::make_pair(last, last);

    ForwardIterator min_result,
                    max_result = first;

    ForwardIterator second = ++first;

    if (second == last)
    return std::make_pair(min_result,
                          max_result);

    if (*second < *min_result)
        min_result = second;
    else max_result = second;

    first = ++second;

    if (first != last) ++second;

    while (second != last)
    {
        if (!(*second < *first))
        {
            if (*first < *min_result)
                min_result = first;
            if (!(*second < *max_result))
                max_result = second;
        }
        else
        {
            if (*second < *min_result)
                min_result = second;
            if (!(*first < *max_result))
                max_result = first;
        }

        first = ++second;

        if (first != last) ++second;
    }

    if (first != last)
    {
        if (*first < *min_result)
```

1.4. Select Kth Smallest Element

```
52          min_result = first;
53      else if (!(*first < *max_result))
54          max_result = first;
55  }
56  return std::make_pair(min_result, max_result);
57 }
```

Generic Select

Selection can be reduced to sorting by sorting the sequence and then extracting the sought after element. This method is more efficient when many selections need to be made from a sequence, in which case only one initial, so-called expensive sort is needed, followed by many relatively less expensive extraction operations, usually in amortized constant time. In general, this method requires $O(n \log n)$ time, where n is the length of the sequence.

Let us try using similar ideas as in finding minimum and maximum of a given sequence for finding the kth smallest or k^{th} largest element in a sequence.

Algorithm 4 Generic Kth Select Minimum

1: **function** GENERIC-KTH-MIN-SELECT(a, l, r, k)
2:     $numElements \leftarrow r - l + 1$
3:     **for** $i \leftarrow 1, k$ **do**
4:         $minIndex \leftarrow i$
5:         $minVal \leftarrow a[i]$
6:         **for** $j \leftarrow i + 1, numElements$ **do**
7:             **if** $a[j] < minVal$ **then**
8:                 $minIndex \leftarrow j$
9:                 $minVal \leftarrow a[j]$
10:             **end if**
11:         **end for**
12:         $swap(a[i], a[minIndex])$
13:     **end for**
14:     **return** $a[k]$
15: **end function**

Program 1.12: Generic Kth Select Minimum

```cpp
#include <algorithm>
#include <utility>
#include <vector>
#include <cassert>

int generic_kth_minselect(std::vector<int>& a,
                          size_t k)
{
    size_t minIndex = 0;
    size_t minVal = a[0];

    size_t numElements = a.size();

    for(size_t i = 0; i < k; ++i)
    {
        minIndex = i;
        minVal = a[i];
```

1.4. Select Kth Smallest Element

```
19            for(size_t j = i + 1;
20                j < numElements; ++j)
21            {
22                minIndex = j;
23                minVal = a[j];
24            }
25            std::swap(a[i], a[minIndex]);
26        }
27        return a[k - 1];
28 }
29
30
31 int main()
32 {
33     std::vector<int> v {1, 23, 12, 9, 30, 2, 50};
34
35     int fourth_min = generic_kth_minselect(v, 4);
36
37     assert(fourth_min == 12);
38 }
```

As can be seen that time complexity of this inefficient selection algorithm is $O(kn)$, where n is the length of the sequence, which is acceptable when k is small enough. It works by simply finding the most minimum element and moving it to the beginning until we reach our desired index, i.e., k. It resembles a *partial selection sort*.

Randomized Quick Select Algorithm

Let us recall RANDOMIZED-PARTITION and RANDOMIZED-QUICKSORT algorithms to help us build an efficient selection algorithm.

Algorithm 5 Partitioning a sequence

1: **function** PARTITION(a, l, r)
2:   $p \leftarrow a[r]$
3:   $i \leftarrow l - 1$
4:   **for** $j \leftarrow l, r - 1$ **do**
5:     **if** $a[j] \leq p$ **then**
6:       $i \leftarrow i + 1$
7:       $swap(a[i], a[j])$
8:     **end if**
9:   **end for**
10: **return** $i + 1$
11: **end function**

Algorithm 6 Randomized Partition Algorithm

1: **function** RANDOMIZED-PARTITION(a, l, r)
2:   $i \leftarrow random(l, r)$
3:   $swap(a[r], a[i])$
4:   **return** PARTITION(a, l, r)
5: **end function**

1.4. Select Kth Smallest Element

Algorithm 7 Randomized Quicksort Algorithm
1: **function** RANDOMIZED-QUICKSORT(a, l, r)
2: $\quad p \leftarrow$ RANDOMIZED-PARTITION(a, l, r)
3: $\quad$ RANDOMIZED-QUICKSORT$(a, l, p - 1)$
4: $\quad$ RANDOMIZED-QUICKSORT$(a, p + 1, r)$
5: **end function**

Let us model the algorithm *randomized-select* based on *randomized-quicksort*, but unlike quicksort, which involves partitioning the input array followed by processing both sides of the partition recursively, *randomized-select* works on only one side of the partition, thus throwing away the other partition.

Algorithm

Algorithm 8 Randomized Kth Min Select Algorithm
1: **function** RANDOMIZED-KTH-MIN-SELECT(a, l, r, k)
2: $\quad p \leftarrow$ RANDOMIZED-PARTITION(a, l, r)
3: $\quad pdist \leftarrow p - l + 1$
4: $\quad$ **if** k == mid **then**
5: $\quad\quad$ **return** $a[p]$
6: $\quad$ **else if** k < pdist **then**
7: $\quad\quad$ **return** RANDOMIZED-KTH-MIN-SELECT$(a, l, p - 1, k)$
8: $\quad$ **else if** k > pdist **then**
9: $\quad\quad$ **return** RANDOMIZED-KTH-MIN-SELECT$(a, p + 1, r, k - pdist)$
10: $\quad$ **end if**
11: **end function**

And it is not that difficult to see that average case time complexity of the algorithm RANDOMIZED-KTH-MIN-SELECT is $\Theta(n)$ and worst case time complexity is $\Theta(n^2)$, assuming that the elements are distinct.

C++11 Implementation

Program 1.13: Randomized version of Kth Select Minimum

```
#include <utility>
#include <cassert>
#include <cstdlib>

int partition(int a[], int l, int r)
{
    int p = a[r];
    int i = l - 1;

    for(int j = l; j <= r - 1; j++)
    {
        if(a[j] <= p)
        {
            i = i + 1;
            std::swap(a[i], a[j]);
        }
    }
```

1.4. Select Kth Smallest Element

```cpp
        std::swap(a[i + 1], a[r]);

        return i + 1;
}


int randomized_partition(int a[], int l, int r)
{
    int i = l + std::rand() % (r - l + 1);
    std::swap(a[r], a[i]);
    return partition(a, l, r);
}


int randomized_select(int a[], int l, int r,
                      size_t k)
{
    int p, pdist;
    if(l < r)
    {
        p = randomized_partition(a, l, r);

        pdist = p - l + 1;

        if(k == pdist) // pivot is the element
            return a[p];
        else if(k < pdist)
            return randomized_select(
                        a, l, p - 1, k);
        else // k > pdist
            return randomized_select(
                        a, p + 1, r, k - pdist);
    }
}


int main()
{
    int a[] = {8, 1, 6, 4, 0, 3, 9, 5};

    int sixth_min =
        randomized_select(a, 0, 7, 6);

    assert(sixth_min == 8);
}
```

RANDOMIZED-KTH-MIN-SELECT differs from
RANDOMIZED-QUICKSORT because it recurses on one side of the partition only.
After the call to RANDOMIZED-PARTITION, the sequence $a[l..r]$ is partitioned
into two sub-sequences $a[l..p-1]$ and $a[p+1..r]$, along with a pivot element
$a[p]$.

- The elements of sub-sequence $a[l..p-1]$ are all $\leq a[p]$.

- The elements of sub-sequence $a[p+1..r]$ are all $> a[p]$.

- The pivot element is the $pdist^{th}$ element of the sub-sequence $a[l..r]$, where $pdist = p-l+1$.

- If the pivot element is the kth smallest element (i.e., k = pdist), return A[p].

- Otherwise, recurse on the sub-sequence containing the kth smallest element.
    - If $k < pdist$, this sub-sequence is $a[l..p-1]$ and we want the kth smallest element.
    - If $k > pdist$, this sub-sequence is $a[p+1..r]$ and, since there are $pdist$ elements in $a[l..r]$ that precede $a[p+1..r]$, we want the $(k-pdist)^{th}$ smallest element of this sub-sequence.

It resembles a *partial quicksort*, generating and partitioning only $O(\log n)$ of its $O(n)$ partitions. This simple algorithm has expected linear performance, and, like quicksort, has quite good performance in practice. It is also an *in-place* algorithm, requiring only constant memory overhead, since the tail recursion can be eliminated with an equivalent iterative version as shown in the next section. In a *tail recursion*, the call is always the last action in an algorithm. A tail-recursive algorithm can always be transformed into an equivalent iterative algorithm with a *while* loop as shown ahead.

Iterative Version of Quick Select Algorithm

Algorithm 9 Iterative Version of Quick Select Algorithm

```
 1: function RANDOMIZED-KTH-MIN-SELECT(a, l, r, k)
 2:     while l < r do
 3:         p ← RANDOMIZED-PARTITION(a, l, r)
 4:         pdist ← p − l + 1
 5:         if k == mid then
 6:             return a[p]
 7:         else if k < pdist then
 8:             r ← p − 1
 9:         else if k > pdist then
10:             l ← p + 1
11:             k ← k − pdist
12:         end if
13:     end while
14: end function
```

1.5 The Non-Crooks Problem

Problem Description

Array $f[0..F-1]$ contains the names of people who work at Cornell, in alphabetical order. Array $g[0..G-1]$ contains the names of people on welfare at Ithaca, in alphabetical order. Thus, neither array contains duplicates and both arrays are monotonically increasing:

$$f[0] < f[1] < f[2] < \ldots < f[F-1]$$
$$g[0] < g[1] < g[2] < \ldots < g[G-1]$$

Count the number of people who are presumably not crooks: those that appear in at least one array but not in both.

1.5. The Non-Crooks Problem

Solution

The result assertion is

$$R : c = (i : 0 \le i < F : f[i] \notin g[0..G-1]) + (j : 0 \le j < G : g[j] \notin f[0..F-1])$$

We would expect to write a program that sequences up the two arrays together, in some synchronized fashion, performing a count as it goes. Thus, it makes sense to develop an invariant by replacing the two constants F and G of R as follows:

$$0 \le h \le F \wedge 0 \le k \le G \wedge c = (i : 0 \le i < h : f[i] \notin g[0..G-1]) + (j : 0 \le j < k : g[j] \notin f[0..F-1])$$

Now, consider execution of $h \leftarrow h + 1$. Under what conditions does its execution leave p true? The condition for this command must obviously imply $f[h] \notin g[0..G-1]$, but we want the condition to be simple. As it stands, this seems out of the question.

Perhaps strengthening the invariant will allow us to find a simple job. One thing we have not tried to exploit is moving through the arrays in a synchronized fashion, the invariant does not imply this at all. Suppose we add to the invariant the conditions $f[h-1] < g[k]$ and $g[k-1] < f[h]$, this might provide the synchronized search that we desire. That is, we use the invariant

$$P : 0 \le h \le F \wedge 0 \le k \le G \wedge f[h-1] < g[k] \wedge g[k-1] < f[h]$$
$$c = (i : 0 \le i < h : f[i] \notin g[0..G-1]) + (j : 0 \le j < k : g[j] \notin f[0..F-1])$$

Then the additional condition $f[h] < g[k]$ yields

$$g[k-1] < f[h] < g[k]$$

so that $f[h]$ does not appear in G, and increasing h will maintain the invariant. Similarly the condition for $k \leftarrow k+1$ will be $g[k] < f[h]$.

This gives us our program, written below. We assume the existence of virtual values $f[-1] = g[i-1] = -\infty$ and $f[F] = g[G] = +\infty$; this allows us to dispense with worries about boundary conditions in the invariant.

Algorithm 10 The Non-Crooks Program

1: $h \leftarrow 0, k \leftarrow 0, c \leftarrow 0$
2: $invariant : P, bound : F - p + G - q$
3: **while** $f \ne F \wedge g \ne G$ **do**
4:    **if** $f[h] < g[k]$ **then**
5:       $h \leftarrow h + 1$
6:       $c \leftarrow c + 1$
7:    **else if** $f[h] == g[k]$ **then**
8:       $h \leftarrow h + 1$
9:       $k \leftarrow k + 1$
10:   **else if** $f[h] > g[k]$ **then**
11:      $k \leftarrow k + 1$
12:      $c \leftarrow c + 1$
13:   **end if**
14: **end while**
15: *Add to c the number of unprocessed elements of f and g:*
16: $c \leftarrow c + F - h + G - k$

1.6 Is this (almost) sorted?

Harry Potter, the child wizard of Hogwarts fame, has once again run into trouble. Professor Snape has sent Harry to detention and assigned him the task of sorting all the old homework assignments from the last 200 years. Being a wizard, Harry waves his wand and says, *ordinatus sortitus*, and the papers rapidly pile themselves in order.

Professor Snape, however, wants to determine whether Harry's spell correctly sorted the papers. Unfortunately, there are a large number n of papers and determining whether they are in perfect order takes $\Omega(n)$ time.

Professor Snape instead decides to check whether the papers are almost sorted. He wants to know whether 90% of the papers are sorted: is it possible to remove 10% of the papers and have the resulting list be sorted?

In this problem, we will help Professor Snape to find an algorithm that takes as input a list A containing n distinct elements, and acts as follows:

- If the list A is sorted, the algorithm always returns true.
- If the list A is not 90% sorted, the algorithm returns false with probability at least $\frac{2}{3}$.

1. Professor Snape first considers the following algorithm:

   Repeat k times:

   a) Choose a paper i independently and uniformly at random from the open interval $(1, n)$. (That is, $1 < i < n$.)

   b) Compare paper $A[i-1]$ and $A[i]$. Output *false* and halt if they are not sorted correctly.

   c) Compare paper $A[i]$ and $A[i+1]$. Output *false* and halt if they are not sorted correctly.

   Output *true*.

   Show that for this algorithm to correctly discover whether the list is almost sorted with probability at least $\frac{2}{3}$ requires $k = \Omega(n)$. *Hint*: Find a sequence that is not almost sorted, but with only a small number of elements that will cause the algorithm to return *false*.

2. Imagine you are given a bag of n balls. You are told that at least 10% of the balls are *blue*, and no more than 90% of the balls are *red*. Asymptotically (for large n) how many balls do you have to draw from the bag to see a blue ball with probability at least $\frac{2}{3}$? (You can assume that the balls are drawn with replacement.)

3. Consider performing a *binary search* on an unsorted list:

1.6. Is this (almost) sorted?

Algorithm 11 Binary Search on unsorted list

```
1: function BINARY-SEARCH(A, key, left, right)         ▷ Search for key in A[left..right].
2:     if left == right then
3:         return left
4:     else
5:         mid ← ⌈(left+right)/2⌉
6:         if key < A[mid] then
7:             return BINARY-SEARCH(A, key, left, mid − 1)
8:         else
9:             return BINARY-SEARCH(A, key, mid, right)
10:        end if
11:    end if
12: end function
```

Assume that a binary search for key_1 in A (even though A is not sorted) returns slot i. Similarly, a binary search for key_2 in A returns slot j. Explain why the following fact is true: if $i < j$, then $key_1 \leq key_2$. Draw a picture. *Hint*: First think about why this is obviously true if list A is sorted.

4. Professor Snape proposes a randomized algorithm to determine whether a list is 90% sorted. The algorithm uses the function RANDOM(1, n) to choose an integer independently and uniformly at random in the closed interval $[1, n]$. The algorithm is presented below.

Algorithm 12 is almost sorted

```
1: function IS-ALMOST-SORTED(A, n, k)         ▷ Determine if A[1..n] is almost sorted
2:     for r ← 1 to k do
3:         i ← RANDOM(1, n)         ▷ Pick i uniformly and independently
4:         j ← BINARY-SEARCH(A, A[i], 1, n)
5:         if i ≠ j then
6:             return false
7:         end if
8:     end for
9:     return true
10: end function
```

Show that the algorithm is correct if k is a sufficiently large constant. That is, with k chosen appropriately, the algorithm always outputs true if a list is correctly sorted and outputs false with probability at least $\frac{2}{3}$ if the list is not 90% sorted.

5. Imagine instead that Professor Snape would like to determine whether a list is $1 - \epsilon$ sorted for some $0 < \epsilon < 1$. (In the previous parts $\epsilon = 0.10$) For large n, determine the appropriate value of k, asymptotically, and show that the algorithm is correct. What is the overall running time?

Solution

1. We show that Snape's algorithm does not work by constructing a counter example that has the following two properties:

1.6. Is this (almost) sorted?

- A is not 90% sorted.
- Snape's algorithm outputs false with probability $\frac{2}{3}$ only if $k = \Omega(n)$.

In particular, we consider the following counter-example:

$$A = [\lfloor \frac{n}{2} \rfloor + 1, \ldots, n, 1, 2, 3, \ldots, \lfloor \frac{n}{2} \rfloor]$$

Lemma 1

A is not 90% sorted.

Proof Assume, by contradiction, that the list is 90% sorted. Then, there must be some 90% of the elements that are correctly ordered with respect to each other. There must be one of these correctly ordered elements in the first half of the list, i.e., with index $i \leq \lfloor n2 \rfloor$. Also, there must be one of these correctly ordered elements in the second half of the list, i.e. with index $j > \lfloor \frac{n}{2} \rfloor$. However, $A[i] > A[j]$, by construction, which is a contradiction. Therefore A is not 90% sorted.

Lemma 2

Snape's algorithm outputs false with probability $\frac{2}{3}$ only if $k = \Omega(n)$.

Proof Notice that on each iteration of the algorithm, there are only two choices that allow the algorithm to detect that the list is not sorted: $i = \lfloor \frac{n}{2} \rfloor$ or $i = \lfloor \frac{n}{2} \rfloor + 1$. Define indicator random variables as follows:

$$X_l = \begin{cases} 1, & \text{if } i = \lfloor \frac{n}{2} \rfloor + 1 \text{ on iteration l}, \\ 0, & \text{otherwise.} \end{cases} \quad (1.1)$$

Notice then, that $Pr\{X_l = 1\} = \frac{2}{n}$ and $Pr\{X_l = 0\} = \left(1 - \frac{2}{n}\right)$. Therefore, the probability that Snape's algorithm *does not* output false for all k iterations (i.e., that Snape's algorithm does not work) is:

$$= \prod_{l=1}^{k}(X_l = 0)$$
$$= \left(1 - \frac{2}{n}\right)^k$$

We want to determine the minimum value of k for which Snape's algorithm works, that is, the minimum value of k such that the probability of failure is no more than $\frac{1}{3}$:

$$\left(1 - \frac{2}{n}\right)^k \leq \frac{1}{3}$$

Solving for k, we determine that:

$$k \geq \frac{\log_e \frac{1}{3}}{\log_e \left(1 - \frac{2}{n}\right)}$$

We now recall the following math fact

$$\left(1 - \frac{1}{x}\right)^x \leq \frac{1}{e}$$

From this, we calculate that:

$$\log_e\left(1 - \tfrac{1}{x}\right) \leq -\tfrac{1}{x}$$

We then conclude the following:

$$k \geq \frac{\log_e \tfrac{1}{3}}{\log_e\left(1 - \tfrac{2}{n}\right)}$$

$$k \geq \frac{\log_e \tfrac{1}{3}}{-\tfrac{2}{n}}$$

$$k \geq \frac{n \log_e 3}{2}$$

We conclude that Snape's algorithm is correct only if $k = \Omega(n)$.

2. Since the question only asked the asymptotic number of balls drawn, $\Theta(1)$ (plus some justification) is a sufficient answer. Below we present a more complete answer.

   Assume you draw k balls from the bag (replacing each ball after examining it).

Lemma 3

For some constant k sufficiently large, at least one ball is blue with probability $\tfrac{2}{3}$.

Proof Define indicator random variables as follows:

$$X_i = \begin{cases} 1, & \text{if ball } i \text{ is blue,} \\ 0, & \text{if ball } i \text{ is red.} \end{cases} \quad (1.2)$$

Notice, then, that $\Pr\ X_i = 1 = \tfrac{1}{10}$ and $\Pr\ X_i = 0 = \tfrac{9}{10}$. We then calculate the probability that at least one ball is blue:

$$= 1 - \prod_{i=1}^{k} Pr\left(X_i = 0\right)$$
$$= 1 - \left(\tfrac{9}{10}\right)^k$$
$$\geq \tfrac{2}{3}$$

Therefore, if $k = \frac{\log_e\left(\tfrac{1}{3}\right)}{\log_e 0.9}$, the probability of drawing at least one blue ball is at least $\tfrac{2}{3}$.

3. An example of a binary-search decision tree of an unordered array:

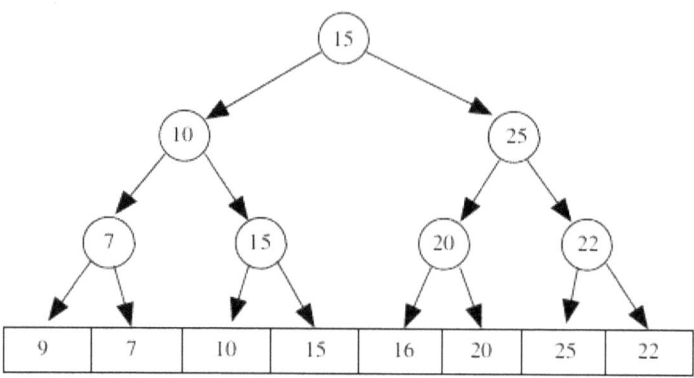

For the purpose of understanding this problem, think of the decision-tree version of the binary search algorithm. (Notice that unlike sorting algorithms, the decision tree for binary search is relatively small, i.e., $O(n)$ nodes.)

Consider the example in the figure provided earlier, in which a binary search is performed on the unsorted array [9 7 10 15 16 20 25 22]. Assume $key_1 = 20$ and $key_2 = 25$. Both 20 and 25 are ≥ 25, and choose the right branch from the root. At this point, the two binary searches diverge: $20 < 25$ and $25 \geq 25$. Therefore key_1 takes the left branch and key_2 takes the right branch. This ensures that eventually key_1 and key_2 are ordered correctly.

We now generalize this argument. For key_1, let $x_1, x_2, \ldots, x_k$ be the k elements that are compared against key_1 in line 6 of the binary search (where $k = O(\log n)$). (In the example, $x_1 = 15, x_2 = 25, and x_3 = 20$.) Let $y_1, y_2, \ldots, y_t$ be the t elements compared against key_2. We know that $x_1 = y_1$. Let l be the smallest number such that $x_l \neq y_l$. (In particular, $l > 1$.) Since $i < j$, by assumption, we know that key_1 cannot branch right while key_2 simultaneously branches left. Hence we conclude that

$$key_1 < x_{l-1} = y_{l-1} \leq key_2$$

(Note that a relatively informal solution was acceptable for the problem, as we simply asked that you *explain why* this is true. The above argument can be more carefully formalized.)

4. Overview: In order to show the algorithm correct, there are two main lemmas that have to be proved:

   a) If the list A is sorted, the algorithm always returns *true*;
   b) If the list A is not 90% sorted, the algorithm returns false with probability at least $\frac{2}{3}$.

We begin with the more straightforward lemma, which essentially argues that binary search is correct. We then show that if the list is not 90% sorted, then at least 10% of the elements fail the *binary search test*. Finally, we conclude that for a sufficiently large constant k, if the list is not 90% sorted, then the algorithm will output false with probability at least $\frac{2}{3}$.

Lemma 4

If the list A is *sorted*, the algorithm always returns *true*.

Proof This lemma follows from the correctness of binary search on a sorted list, which was shown in recitation one. The invariant is that key is in array A between *left* and *right*.

For the rest of this problem, we label the elements as *good* and *bad* based on whether they pass the binary sort test.

$$label(i) = \begin{cases} good, & \text{if } i = \text{BINARY-SEARCH}(A, A[i], 1, n), \\ bad, & \text{if } i \neq \text{BINARY-SEARCH}(A, A[i], 1, n). \end{cases} \quad (1.3)$$

Notice that it is not immediately obvious which elements are good and which elements are bad. In particular, some elements may appear to be sorted correctly, but be bad because of other elements being missorted. Similarly, some elements may appear entirely out of place, but be good because of other misplaced elements. A key element of the proof is showing that a badly sorted list has a lot of bad elements.

Lemma 5

If the list A is not 90% *sorted*, then at least 10% of the elements are *bad*.

Proof Assume, by contradiction, that fewer than 10% of the elements are bad. Then, at least 90% of the elements are good. Recall the definition of a 90% sorted list: if 10% of the elements are removed, then the remaining elements are in sorted order. Therefore, remove all the bad elements from the array. We now argue that the remaining elements are in sorted order. Consider any two of the remaining good elements, key_1 and key_2, where key_1 is at index i and key_2 is at index j. If $i < j$, then solution to third part shows that $key_1 \leq key_2$. Similarly, if $j < i$, then third part shows that $key_2 \leq key_1$. That is, the two elements are in correctly sorted order. Since all pairs of elements are in sorted order, the array of good elements is in sorted order. Once we have shown that there are a lot of bad elements, it remains to show that we find a bad element through random sampling.

Lemma 6

If the list A is not 90% sorted, the algorithm returns *false* with probability at least $\frac{2}{3}$.

Proof From Lemma 5, we know that at least 10% of the elements are bad. From second part, we know that if we choose $k > \frac{\log(\frac{1}{3})}{\log 0.9}$, then with probability $\frac{2}{3}$ we find a bad element. Therefore, we conclude that the algorithm returns *false* with probability at least $\frac{2}{3}$.

5. Lemma 4 is the same as in fourth part. A simple modification of Lemma 5 shows that if the array is not $(1-\epsilon)$-sorted, then there must be at least ϵn bad elements; otherwise, the remaining $(1-\epsilon)n$ elements would form a $(1-\epsilon)$-sorted list. Finally, it remains to determine the appropriate

value of k.

In this case, we want to choose k such that

$$(1-\epsilon)^k \leq \tfrac{1}{3}$$

We choose $k = \tfrac{c}{\epsilon}$, then we can conclude that

$$(1-\epsilon)^k \leq \left((1-\epsilon)^{\frac{1}{\epsilon}}\right)^c$$
$$(1-\epsilon)^k \leq \left(\tfrac{1}{e}\right)^c$$

We therefore conclude that if $k = \Theta\left(\tfrac{1}{\epsilon}\right)$, the algorithm will find a bad element with probability at least $\tfrac{2}{3}$. The running time of the algorithm is $O\left(\tfrac{\log n}{\epsilon}\right)$.

1.7 Sorting an almost sorted list

Problem

On his way back from detention, Harry runs into his friend Hermione. He is upset because Professor Snape discovered that his sorting spell failed. Instead of sorting the papers correctly, each paper was within k slots of the proper position. Hermione immediately suggests that insertion sort would have easily fixed the problem. In this problem, we show that Hermione is correct (as usual). As before, $A[1..n]$ in an array of n distinct elements.

1. First, we define an *inversion*. If $i < j$ and $A[i] > A[j]$, then the $pair(i, j)$ is called an inversion of A. What permutation of the array $\{1, 2, \ldots, n\}$ has the most inversions? How many does it have?

2. Show that, if every paper is initially within k slots of its proper position, insertion sort runs in time $O(nk)$. *Hint*: First, show that INSERTION-SORT(A) runs in time $O(n + I)$, where I is the number of inversions in A.

3. Show that sorting a list in which each paper is within k slots of its proper position takes $\Omega(n \log k)$ comparisons. *Hint*: Use the decision-tree technique.

4. Devise an algorithm that matches the lower bound, i.e., sorts a list in which each paper is within k slots of its proper position in $\Theta(n \log k)$ time.

Solution

1. The permutation $\{n, n-1, \ldots, 2, 1\}$ has the largest number of inversions. It has $n = \tfrac{n(n-1)}{2}$ inversions.

2. *Overview*: First we show that INSERTION-SORT(A) runs in time $O(n+I)$, where I is the number of inversions, by examining the insertion sort algorithm. Then we count the number of possible inversions in an array in which every element is within k slots of its proper position. We show that there are at most $O(nk)$ inversions.

Lemma 7

INSERTION-SORT(A) runs in time $O(n + I)$, where I is the number of inversions in A.

Proof

Consider an execution of INSERTION-SORT on an array A. In the outer loop, there is $O(n)$ work. Each iteration of the inner loop fixes exactly one inversion. When the algorithm terminates, there are no inversions left. Hence, there must be I iterations of the inner loop, resulting in $O(I)$ work. Therefore the running time of the algorithm is $O(n + I)$.

We next count the number of inversions in an array in which every element is within k slots of its proper position.

Lemma 8

If every element is within k slots of its proper position, then there are at most $O(nk)$ inversions.

Proof

We provide an upper bound on the number of inversions. Consider some particular element, $A[i]$. There are at most $4k$ elements that can be inverted with $A[i]$, in particular those elements in the range $A[i-2k..i+2k]$. Therefore, i is a part of at most $4k$ inversions, and hence there are at most $4nk$ inversions.

From this we conclude that the running time of insertion sort on an array in which every element is within k slots of its proper position is $O(nk)$.

As a side note, it seems possible to prove this directly, without using inversions, by showing that the inner loop of insertion sort never moves an element more than k slots. However, this is not as easy as it seems: even though an element is always begins within k slots of its final position, it is necessary to show that it never moves farther away. For example, what if it moves $k + 2$ slots backwards, and then is later moved 3 slots forward? However, perhaps one can show that an element never moves more than $4k$ slots.

3. We already know that sorting the array requires $\Omega(n \log n)$ comparisons. If $k > n/2$, then $n \log n = \Omega(n \log k)$, and the proof is complete. For the remainder of this proof, assume that $k \leq \frac{n}{2}$.

   Our goal is to provide a lower-bound on the number of leaves in a decision tree for an algorithm that sorts an array in which every element is within k slots of its proper position. We therefore provide a lower bound on the number of possible permutations that satisfy this condition.

   First, break the array of size n into $\lfloor \frac{n}{k} \rfloor$ blocks, each of size k, and the remainder of size $n(mod\,k)$. For each block, there exist $k!$ permutations, resulting in at least $(k!)^{\lfloor \frac{n}{k} \rfloor}$ total permutations of the entire array. None of these permutations move an element more than k slots.

   Notice that this undercounts the total number of permutations, since no element moves from one k-element block to another, and we ignore permutations of elements in the remainder block.

   We therefore conclude that the decision tree has at least $(k!)^{\lfloor \frac{n}{k} \rfloor}$ leaves.

1.7. Sorting an almost sorted list

Since the decision tree is a binary tree, we can then conclude that the height of the decision tree is

$$\geq \log\left((k!)^{\lfloor \frac{n}{k} \rfloor}\right)$$
$$\geq \lfloor \tfrac{n}{k} \rfloor \log(k!)$$
$$\geq \lfloor \tfrac{n}{k} \rfloor (c_1 k \log k)$$
$$\geq c_1(n-k)\log k$$
$$\geq \tfrac{c_1 n \log k}{2}$$
$$= \Omega(n \log k)$$

(The last step follows because of our assumption that $k \leq \tfrac{n}{2}$.)

4. For the solution to this problem, we are going to use a heap. We assume that we have a heap with the following subroutines:

   - MAKE-HEAP() returns a new empty heap.
   - INSERT(H, key, value) inserts the key/value pair into the heap.
   - EXTRACT-MIN(H) removes the key/value pair with the smallest key from the heap, returning the value.

   First, consider the problem of merging t sorted lists. Assume we have lists $A_1, \ldots, A_t$, each of which is sorted. We use the following strategy (pseudocode below):

   a) Make a new heap, H.

   b) For each of the t lists, insert the first element into the list. For list i, perform INSERT($H, A_t[1], i$).

   c) Repeat n times:

      i. Remove the smallest element from the heap using EXTRACT-MIN(H). Let v be the value returned, which is the identity of the list.

      ii. Put the extracted element from list v in order in a new array.

      iii. Insert the next element from the list v.

   The key invariant is to show that after every iteration of the loop, the heap contains the smallest element in every list. (We omit a formal induction proof, as the question only asked you to devise an algorithm.) Notice that each EXTRACT-MIN and INSERT operation requires $O(\log k)$ time, since there are never more than $2k$ elements in the heap. The loop requires only a constant amount of other work, and is repeated n times, resulting in $O(n \log k)$ running time.

   In order to apply this to our problem, we consider A as a set of sorted lists. In particular, notice that $A[i] < A[i+2k+1]$, for all $i \leq n-2k-1$: the element at slot i can at most move forwards during sorting to slot $i+k$ and the element at slot $i+2k+1$ can at most move backwards during sorting to slot $i+k+1$.

   For the moment, assume that n is divisible by $2k$. We consider that the $t = 2k$ lists defined as follows:
   $A_1 = A[1], A[2k+1], A[4k+1], \ldots, A[n-(2k-1)]$
   $A_2 = A[2], A[2k+2], A[4k+2], \ldots, A[n-(2k-2)]$
   $\vdots$
   $A_t = A[2k], A[4k], A[6k], \ldots, A[n]$

   Each of these lists is sorted, and each is of $size \leq n$. Therefore, we can sort these lists in $O(n \log k)$ time using the procedure above.

We now present the more precise pseudocode:

Algorithm 13 Sort Almost Sorted Algorithm

1: **function** SORT-ALMOST-SORTED(A, n, k)   ▷ Sort A if every element is within k slots of its proper position
2:     $H \leftarrow$ MAKE-HEAP()
3:     **for** $i \leftarrow 1$ **to** 2k **do**
4:         INSERT(H, A[i], i)
5:     **end for**
6:     **for** $i \leftarrow 1$ **to** n **do**
7:         $j \leftarrow$ EXTRACT-MIN(H)
8:         $B[i] \leftarrow A[j]$
9:         **if** $j + 2k \leq n$ **then**
10:             INSERT(H, A[j + 2k], j)
11:         **end if**
12:     **end for**
13:     **return** B
14: **end function**

Recall that a heap is generally used to store a key and its associated value, even though we often ignore the value when describing the heap operations. In this case, the value is an index j, while the key is the element $A[j]$. As a result, the heap returns the index of the next smallest element in the array.

Correctness and performance follow from the argument above.

Notice that there is a second way of solving this problem. Recall that we already know how to merge two sorted lists that (jointly) contain n elements in $O(n)$ time. It is possible, then to merge the lists in a tournament. We give an example for $k = 8$, where $A + B$ means to merge lists A and B:

$$\text{Round 1: } (A_1 + A_2), (A_3 + A_4), (A_5 + A_6), (A_7 + A_8)$$
$$\text{Round 2: } (A_1 + A_2 + A_3 + A_4), (A_5 + A_6 + A_7 + A_8)$$
$$\text{Round 3: } (A_1 + A_2 + A_3 + A_4 + A_5 + A_6 + A_7 + A_8)$$

Notice that there are $\log k$ merge steps, each of which merges n elements (dispersed through up to k lists) and hence has a cost of $O(n)$. This leads to the desired running time of $O(n \log k)$.

1.8 The Longest Upsequence Problem

Problem Description

Consider a sequence of values $(v_0, v_1, \ldots, v_{n-1})$. If one deletes i(not necessarily adjacent) values from the list, one has a subsequence of length $n - i$. This subsequence is called an *upsequence* if its values are in non-decreasing order. For example, the list $(1, 3, 4, 6, 2, 4)$ has a subsequence $(1, 3, 2)$, which is not an upsequence, and another subsequence $(1, 3, 6)$, which is an upsequence.

Write a program that, given a sequence in $b[0..n-1]$, where $n > 0$, calculates the length of the longest upsequence of $b[0..n-1]$.

1.8. The Longest Upsequence Problem

Solution

As an abbreviation, let us use the notation $lup(s)$ to mean:

$lup(s) =$ the length of the longest upsequence of sequence s.

Thus using a variable k to contain the answer, the program has the precondition and postcondition as

$$Q : n > 0$$
$$R : k = lup(b[0..n-1])$$

Note that a change in any one value of a sequence could change its longest upsequence, and this means that possibly every value of a sequence s must be interrogated to determine $lup(s)$. This suggests a loop. Let us begin by writing a possible invariant and an outline of the loop.

The loop will interrogate the values of $b[0..n-1]$ in some order. Since $lup(b[0..0])$ is 1, a possible invariant can be derived by replacing the constant n of R by a variable:

$$P : 1 \leq i \leq n \wedge k = lup(b[0..i-1])$$

The loop itself will have the form

```
1: i ← 1
2: k ← 1
3: while i ≠ n do
4:     increase i, maintaining P
5: end while
```

Increasing i extends the sequence $b[0..i-1]$ for which k is the length of a longest upsequence, and hence may call for an increase in k. Whether k is to be increased depends on whether $b[i]$ is at least as large as a value that ends a longest upsequence of $b[0..i-1]$, there may be more than one longest upsequence. It makes sense to maintain information in other variables so that such a test can be efficiently made. What is the minimum information needed to ascertain whether k should be increased ?

The *smallest* value, say m, that ends an upsequence of length k of $b[0..i-1]$ must be known, for then $b[0..i]$ has an upsequence of length $k+1$ if and only if $b[i] \leq m$. Therefore, we revise invariant P to include m:

$P : 1 \leq i \leq n \wedge k = lup(b[0..i-1]) \wedge m$ is the smallest value in $b[0..i-1]$ that ends an upsequence of length k.

In the case $b[i] \geq m$, k can be increased and m set to $b[i]$, so that the program thus far looks like

1.8. The Longest Upsequence Problem

```
1:  i ← 1
2:  k ← 1
3:  m ← b[0]                                          ▷ P
4:  while i ≠ n do
5:      if b[i] ≥ m then
6:          k ← k + 1
7:          m ← b[i]
8:      else if b[i] < m then
9:          ?
10:     end if
11:     i ← i + 1
12: end while
```

The question now becomes what to do if $b[i] < m$. Variable k should not be changed, but what about m? Under what condition must m be changed?

If $b[0..i-1]$ contains an upsequence of length $k-1$ that ends in a $value \leq b[i]$, then $b[i]$ ends an upsequence of length k of $b[0..i]$. If, in addition, $b[i] < m$, then m must be changed. In order to check this condition, consider maintaining the minimum value m_1 that ends an upsequence of length $k-1$ of $b[0..i-1]$.

This means that two values are needed: the minimum value m that ends an upsequence of length k and the minimum value m_1 that ends an upsequence of length $k-1$.

Maintaining m caused us to introduce m_1; maintaining m_1 will cause us to introduce m_2 to contain the minimum value that ends an upsequence of length $k-2$. And so on. Therefore, an array of values is needed. We modify the invariant once more:

$P: 1 \leq i \leq n \land k = lup(b[0..i-1]) \land (j : 1 \leq j \leq k : m[j]$ is the smallest value that ends an upsequence of length j of $b[0..i-1])$

And the program is changed to

```
1:  i ← 1
2:  k ← 1
3:  m[1] ← b[0]                                       ▷ P
4:  while i ≠ n do
5:      if b[i] ≥ m[k] then
6:          k ← k + 1
7:          m[k] ← b[i]
8:      else if b[i] < m[k] then
9:          ?
10:     end if
11:     i ← i + 1
12: end while
```

Before proceeding further, it makes sense to investigate array m; does it have any properties that might be useful?

Array m is ordered, because the minimum value that ends an upsequence of length, say j, must be at most the minimum value that ends an upsequence of length $j + 1$.

1.8. The Longest Upsequence Problem

We are now faced with determining which values of $m[1..k]$ must be changed in case $b[i] < m[k]$.

The case $b[i] < m[1]$ is the easiest to handle. Since $m[1]$ is the smallest value that ends an upsequence of length 1 of $b[0..i-1]$, if $b[i] < m[1]$, then $b[i]$ is the smallest value in $b[0..i]$ and it should become the new $m[1]$. No other value of m need be changed, since all upsequences of $b[0..i-1]$ end in a value larger than $b[i]$.

Finally, consider the case $m[1] \leq b[i] < m[k]$. Which values of m should be changed? Clearly, only those greater than $b[i]$ can be changed, since they represent minimum values. So suppose we find the j satisfying

$$m[j-1] \leq b[i] < m[j]$$

Then $m[1..j-1]$ should not be changed. Next, since $m[j-1]$ ends an upsequence of length $j-1$ of $b[0..i-1]$, $b[i]$ ends an upsequence of length j of $b[0..i]$. Hence, $m[j]$ should be changed to $b[i]$. Finally, $m[j+1..k]$ should not be changed. Binary search can be used to locate j. The final program is:

Algorithm 14 The Longest Upsequence Program

1:   $i \leftarrow 1$
2:   $k \leftarrow 1$
3:   $m[1] \leftarrow b[0]$ ▷ P
4:   **while** $i \neq n$ **do**
5:     **if** $b[i] \geq m[k]$ **then**
6:       $k \leftarrow k+1$
7:       $m[k] \leftarrow b[i]$
8:     **else if** $b[i] < m[1]$ **then**
9:       $m[1] \leftarrow b[i]$
10:    **else if** $m[1] \leq b[i] < m[k]$ **then**
11:       Establish $m[j-1] \leq b[i] < m[j]$
12:       $h \leftarrow 1$
13:       $j \leftarrow k$
14:       **while** $h \neq j-1$ **do**   ▷
        $invariant : 1 \leq h < j \leq k \wedge m[h] \leq b[i] < m[j], bound : j-h-1$
15:         $e \leftarrow \frac{(h+j)}{2}$
16:         **if** $m[e] \leq b[i]$ **then**
17:          $h \leftarrow e$
18:         **else if** $m[e] > b[i]$ **then**
19:          $j \leftarrow e$
20:         **end if**
21:       **end while**
22:       $m[j] \leftarrow b[i]$
23:    **end if**
24:    $i \leftarrow i+1$
25: **end while**

The execution time of the program is proportional to $n \log n$ in the worst case and to n in the best. It requires space proportional to n in the worst case, for array m. It uses a technique called *dynamic programming*, although it was developed without conscious knowledge of that technique.

1.9 Fixed size generic array in C++

Problem Description

Design and implement a generic array container in C++ which encapsulates constant size arrays with the following interface:

```
template<typename T, std::size_t N> struct array;
```

Please note that this struct should have the same aggregate type semantics as a C-style array. The size and efficiency of array<T, N> for some number of elements s equivalent to size and efficiency of the corresponding C-style array T[N]. The struct should provide the benefits of a standard container, such as knowing its own size, supporting assignment, random access iterators, etc.

Solution

Program 1.14: generic array in C++

```cpp
#include <type_traits>
#include <utility>
#include <iterator>
#include <algorithm>
#include <cassert>

template <class ElementType, size_t N>
struct array
{
    // types:
    typedef array self;
    typedef ElementType value_type;
    typedef value_type& reference;
    typedef const value_type& const_reference;
    typedef value_type* iterator;
    typedef const value_type* const_iterator;
    typedef value_type* pointer;
    typedef const value_type* const_pointer;
    typedef size_t size_type;
    typedef ptrdiff_t difference_type;
    typedef std::reverse_iterator<iterator> reverse_iterator;
    typedef std::reverse_iterator<const_iterator> const_reverse_iterator;

    value_type elements[N > 0 ? N : 1];

    void fill(const value_type& u)
    {
        std::fill_n(elements, N, u);
    }
```

1.9. Fixed size generic array in C++

```
31      void swap(array& a)
32      {
33          std::swap_ranges(elements, elements + N, a.
                elements);
34      }
35
36      // iterators:
37      iterator begin()          {return iterator(elements);}
38      const_iterator begin() const   {return const_iterator(
            elements);}
39      iterator end()    {return iterator(elements + N);}
40      const_iterator end() const   {return const_iterator(
            elements + N);}
41
42      reverse_iterator rbegin()   {return reverse_iterator(
            end());}
43      const_reverse_iterator rbegin() const   {return
            const_reverse_iterator(end());}
44      reverse_iterator rend()   {return reverse_iterator(
            begin());}
45      const_reverse_iterator rend() const   {return
            const_reverse_iterator(begin());}
46
47      const_iterator cbegin() const   {return begin();}
48      const_iterator cend() const   {return end();}
49      const_reverse_iterator crbegin() const  {return rbegin
            ();}
50      const_reverse_iterator crend() const  {return rend();}
51
52      // capacity:
53      constexpr size_type size() const {return N;}
54      constexpr size_type max_size() const {return N;}
55      constexpr bool empty() const {return N == 0;}
56
57      // element access:
58      reference operator[](size_type n)             {return
            elements[n];}
59      const_reference operator[](size_type n) const {return
            elements[n];}
60      reference at(size_type n);
61      const_reference at(size_type n) const;
62
63      reference front()             {return elements[0];}
64      const_reference front() const {return elements[0];}
65      reference back()              {return elements[N > 0
            ? N-1 : 0];}
66      const_reference back() const  {return elements[N > 0
            ? N-1 : 0];}
67
68      value_type* data() {return elements;}
69      const value_type* data() const {return elements;}
70  };
71
72  template <class ElementType, size_t N>
73  typename array<ElementType, N>::reference
74  array<ElementType, N>::at(size_type n)
75  {
76      if (n >= N)
```

1.9. Fixed size generic array in C++

```cpp
        assert(!"array::at out_of_range");
    return elements[n];
}

template <class ElementType, size_t N>
typename array<ElementType, N>::const_reference
array<ElementType, N>::at(size_type n) const
{
    if (n >= N)
        assert(!"array::at out_of_range");
    return elements[n];
}

template <class ElementType, size_t N>
inline bool
operator==(const array<ElementType, N>& x, const array<
    ElementType, N>& y)
{
    return std::equal(x.elements, x.elements + N, y.
        elements);
}

template <class ElementType, size_t N>
inline bool
operator!=(const array<ElementType, N>& x, const array<
    ElementType, N>& y)
{
    return !(x == y);
}

template <class ElementType, size_t N>
inline bool
operator<(const array<ElementType, N>& x, const array<
    ElementType, N>& y)
{
    return std::lexicographical_compare(x.elements, x.
        elements + N, y.elements, y.elements + N);
}

template <class ElementType, size_t N>
inline bool
operator>(const array<ElementType, N>& x, const array<
    ElementType, N>& y)
{
    return y < x;
}

template <class ElementType, size_t N>
inline bool
operator<=(const array<ElementType, N>& x, const array<
    ElementType, N>& y)
{
    return !(y < x);
}

template <class ElementType, size_t N>
inline bool
operator>=(const array<ElementType, N>& x, const array<
    ElementType, N>& y)
```

```cpp
128 {
129     return !(x < y);
130 }
131
132 template <class ElementType, size_t N>
133 swap(const array<ElementType, N>& x, const array<
        ElementType, N>& y)
134 {
135     x.swap(y);
136 }
137
138 template <size_t Index, class ElementType, size_t N>
139 inline ElementType&
140 get(array<ElementType, N>& a)
141 {
142     static_assert(Index < N, "Index out of bounds in std
            ::get<>(std::array)");
143     return a[Index];
144 }
145
146 template <size_t Index, class ElementType, size_t N>
147 inline const ElementType&
148 get(const array<ElementType, N>& a)
149 {
150     static_assert(Index < N, "Index out of bounds in std
            ::get<>(const std::array)");
151     return a[Index];
152 }
153
154 template <size_t Index, class ElementType, size_t N>
155 inline ElementType&&
156 get(array<ElementType, N>&& a)
157 {
158     static_assert(Index < N, "Index out of bounds in std
            ::get<>(std::array &&)");
159     return std::move(a[Index]);
160 }
```

1.10 Seating Problem

Problem Description

GreedSox, a popular major-league baseball team, is interested in one thing: making money. They have hired you as a consultant to help boost their group ticket sales. They have noticed the following problem. When a group wants to see a ballgame, all members of the group need seats (in the bleacher section), or they go away. Since partial groups can't be seated, the bleachers are often not full. There is still space available, but not enough space for the entire group. In this case, the group cannot be seated, losing money for the GreedSox.

The GreedSox want your recommendation on a new seating policy. Instead of seating people first-come/first-serve, the GreedSox decide to seat large groups first, followed by smaller groups, and finally singles (i.e., groups of 1).

You are given a set of groups, $G[1..m] = [g_1, g_2, \ldots, g_m]$, where g_i is a number representing the size of the group. Assume that the bleachers seat n people. Consider the following greedy seating algorithm, where the function ADMIT(i) admits group i, and REJECT(i) sends away group i.

1.10. Seating Problem

Algorithm 15 Seat Algorithm
1: **function** SEAT(G[1..m], n)
2:     $admitted \leftarrow 0$
3:     $G \leftarrow \text{SORT}(G)$ ▷ Sort groups largest to smallest.
4:     **for** $i \leftarrow 1$ to m **do**
5:         **if** $G[i] \leq n$ **then**
6:             ADMIT(i)
7:             $n \leftarrow n - G[i]$
8:             $admitted \leftarrow admitted + G[i]$
9:         **else**
10:            REJECT(i)
11:         **end if**
12:     **end for**
13:     **return** $admitted$
14: **end function**

The SEAT algorithm first sorts the groups by size. It then iterates through the groups from largest to smallest, seating any group that fits in the bleachers. It returns the number of people admitted.

1. The GreedSox owners are right: the greedy seating algorithm works pretty well. Show that if, given G and n, it is possible to admit k people, then the greedy seating algorithm admits at least $\frac{k}{2}$ people.

2. Unfortunately, the SEAT algorithm does not work perfectly. Show that SEAT is not optimal by giving a counterexample in which, asymptotically as n gets large, the ratio between greedy seating and optimal seating approaches $\frac{1}{2}$.

When you present your results to the GreedSox owners, they point out the following problem: unlike numbers in a computer's memory, real people are hard to move around. In particular, people waiting in line do not like to be *sorted*. The GreedSox owners ask you to develop a version of the greedy seating algorithm that does not modify the set G. (You can think of G as being stored in read-only memory.) You suggest the following algorithm:

Algorithm 16 ReSeat Algorithm
1: **function** RESEAT(G[1..m], n)
2:     $admitted \leftarrow 0$
3:     **for** $j \leftarrow 1$ to $\lceil \log n \rceil$ **do**
4:         **for** $i \leftarrow 1$ to m **do**
5:             **if** $G[i] \geq \frac{n}{2^j}$ and $G[i] \leq n$ **then**
6:                 ADMIT(i)
7:                 $n \leftarrow n - G[i]$
8:                 $admitted \leftarrow admitted + G[i]$
9:             **else if** $G[i] > n$ **then**
10:                 REJECT(i)
11:             **end if**
12:         **end for**
13:     **end for**
14:     **return** $admitted$
15: **end function**

1.10. Seating Problem

The RESEAT algorithm iterates through the list of groups several times. In the first iteration, it admits any group of size at least $\frac{n}{2}$. In the second iteration, it admits any group of size at least $\frac{n}{4}$. It continues in the same manner seating smaller and smaller groups until the theater is filled. When RESEAT finishes, it returns the number of people admitted.

3. Assume that, given G and n it is possible to admit at least k people. Show that the RESEAT algorithm still seats at least $\frac{k}{2}$ people.

4. The RESEAT algorithm runs in $O(m \log n)$ time. Devise a new algorithm that runs in $O(m)$ time and still guarantees that if k people can be seated, your algorithm seats at least $\frac{k}{2}$ people.

Solution

1. We begin by proving a lemma about the number of people admitted by the algorithm SEAT.

   Lemma 1

   Algorithm SEAT either admits all groups of $size \leq n$, or it $admits \geq \frac{n}{2}$ people.

   Proof Assume algorithm SEAT does not admit all groups of $size \leq n$. That is, there is some group g_i of $size \leq n$ that SEAT does not admit. There are two cases to consider. First, assume that $g_i \geq \frac{n}{2}$. Then, since the algorithm is greedy, we know that it must have admitted some group larger than g_i ; otherwise, group g_i would have been admitted. Therefore, we can conclude that the algorithm $seats \geq \frac{n}{2}$ people, as required.

   For the second case, assume that $g_i < \frac{n}{2}$. Since g_i is not admitted, we know that at some point $remaining < g_i < \frac{n}{2}$. Since remaining is non-increasing, we thus conclude that at least $\frac{n}{2}$ people are seated.

   We argue that this lemma immediately implies that the SEAT algorithm is 2-competitive. First, if SEAT admits all groups of $size \leq n$, then it admits exactly the same number of people as the optimal seating algorithm. Second, if SEAT admits at least $\frac{n}{2}$ people, we know that the optimal seating algorithm can seat at most n people. Hence $\frac{n}{2} > \frac{k}{2}$, as required.

2. Consider groups $G = \{\frac{(n+2)}{2}, \frac{n}{2}, \frac{n}{2}\}$. Notice that the greedy seating algorithm admits the group of size $\frac{(n+2)}{2}$, and then cannot admit any of the other groups. The optimal algorithm admits the two groups of size $\frac{n}{2}$, filling all n seats. Notice that asymptotically $\frac{\left(\frac{(n+2)}{2}\right)}{n}$ approaches $\frac{1}{2}$ as n gets large.

3. The argument in this case is quite similar to the proof in first part. We begin by reproving the same lemma about the number of people admitted by the algorithm RESEAT.

   Lemma 2

   Algorithm RESEAT either admits all groups of $size \leq n$, or it $admits \geq \frac{n}{2}$ people.

1.10. Seating Problem

Proof Assume algorithm RESEAT does not admit all groups of $size \leq n$. That is, there is some group g_i of $size \leq n$ that RESEAT does not admit.

There are two cases to consider. First, assume that $g_i \geq \frac{n}{2}$. Then, since the algorithm first considers all groups of $size \geq \frac{n}{2}$ (when j = 1), we know that it must have admitted some group of $size \geq \frac{n}{2}$; otherwise, group g_i would have been admitted in the loop when j = 1. Therefore, we can conclude that the algorithm $seats \geq \frac{n}{2}$ people, as required.

For the second case, assume that $g_i < \frac{n}{2}$. Notice that when $j = \lceil \log n \rceil, g_i \geq \frac{n}{2^j}$. Therefore, if g_i is not admitted, we can conclude that $g_i > remaining$. That is, $remaining < g_i < \frac{n}{2}$. Since remaining is non-increasing, we thus conclude that at least $\frac{n}{2}$ people are seated.

As before, this lemma immediately implies that the algorithm RESEAT is 2-competitive, as desired.

Algorithm 17 ReSeat Linear Time Algorithm

4.
1: **function** FAST-RESEAT(G[1..m], n)
2:     $admitted \leftarrow 0$
3:     $remaining \leftarrow 0$
4:     **for** $i \leftarrow 1$ to m **do**
5:         **if** $G[i] \geq \frac{n}{2}$ **and** $G[i] \leq remaining$ **then**
6:             ADMIT(i)
7:             $admitted \leftarrow admitted + G[i]$
8:             $remaining \leftarrow remaining - G[i]$
9:         **end if**
10:     **end for**
11:     **for** $i \leftarrow 1$ to m **do**
12:         **if** $G[i] \leq remaining$ **then**
13:             ADMIT(i)
14:             $admitted \leftarrow admitted + G[i]$
15:             $remaining \leftarrow remaining - G[i]$
16:         **end if**
17:     **end for**
18:     **return** $admitted$
19: **end function**

The argument showing this algorithm is correct is essentially the same as the proof in third part. In particular, we again show the same lemma about the number of people seated.

Lemma 3

Algorithm FAST-RESEAT either admits all groups of $size \leq n$, or it admits $\geq \frac{n}{2}$ people.

Proof Assume algorithm FAST-RESEAT does not admit all groups of $size \geq n$. That is, there is some group g_i of $size \leq n$ that FAST-RESEAT does not admit.

There are two cases to consider. First, assume that $g_i \geq \frac{n}{2}$. Then, since the algorithm first considers all groups of $size \geq \frac{n}{2}$, we know that if g_i was rejected, it must have admitted some group of $size \geq \frac{n}{2}$; otherwise, group g_i would have been admitted.

Therefore, we can conclude that the algorithm $seats \geq \frac{n}{2}$ people, as required.

For the second case, assume that $g_i < \frac{n}{2}$. If g_i is not admitted, we can conclude that $g_i > remaining$. That is, $remaining < g_i < \frac{n}{2}$. Since $remaining$ is non-increasing,

we thus conclude that at least $\frac{n}{2}$ people are seated.

As before, this lemma immediately implies that the algorithm FAST-RESEAT is 2-competitive, as desired.

1.11 Segment Problems

Segment problems involve the computation of a longest or shortest segment that satisfies a certain predicate, usually defined in terms of a given array.

Longest Segments

Let $N \geq 0$ and let $X[0..N]$ be an integer array. We are interested in the length of a longest subsegment $[p..q)$ of $[0..N)$ that satisfies a certain predicate defined in terms of X. Examples of such predicates are:

- all elements are zero : $\forall i : p \leq i < q : X.i = 0$
- the segment is left-minimal : $\forall i : p \leq i < q : X.p \leq X.i$
- the segment contains at most 10 zeros : $(\#i : p \leq i < q : X.i = 0) \leq 10$
- all values are different : $\forall i, j : p \leq i < j < q : X.i \neq X.j$

All Zeros

Let us solve the problem of determining the length of a longest segment of $X[0..N)$ that contains zero only. It is about the simplest longest segment problem one can imagine. This problem can be re-instated as follows:

1: $N : int\{N \geq 0\}$
2: $X : array[0..N)$ of int
3: $r : int$
4: $r = (\mathbf{max}\ p, q : 0 \leq p \leq q \leq N \land (\forall i : p \leq i < q : X.i = 0) : q - p$

Our first step is the introduction of a name for $(\forall i : p \leq i < q : X.i = 0)$. This does not only abbreviate the postcondition, but, more importantly, it enables us to find out which parts of the derivation are independent of the specific form of the predicate.

For $0 \leq p \leq q \leq N$ we define $A.p.q$ by

$$A.p.q \equiv (\forall i : p \leq i < q : X.i = 0)$$

Postcondition R may then be written as

$$R : r = (\mathbf{max}\ p, q : 0 \leq p \leq q \leq N \land A.p.q : q - p)$$

What can be said about predicate A? Its term, $X.i = 0$, does not depend on p or q. It holds for empty segments, i.e.,

$$A.n.n \text{ for } 0 \leq n \leq N$$

1.11. Segment Problems

Furthermore, A is prefix-closed, i.e., if a segment satisfies A then all prefixes of that segment satisfy A as well. More formally,

$$A.p.q \implies (\forall i : p \leq i \leq q : A.p.i) \text{ for } 0 \leq p \leq q \leq N$$

and A is postfix-closed:

$$A.p.q \implies (\forall i : p \leq i \leq q : A.i.q) \text{ for } 0 \leq p \leq q \leq N$$

Since the term, $X.i = 0$, in A neither depends on p nor on q, it does not matter whether we replace in R the constant 0 or the constant N by a variable. We propose as invariants P_0 and P_1 defined by

$$P_0 : r = (\mathbf{max}\ p, q : 0 \leq p \leq q \leq n \land A.p.q : q - p$$

and

$$P_1 : 0 \leq n \leq N$$

For the initialization, we derive

$$\mathbf{max}\ p, q : 0 \leq p \leq q \leq 0 \land A.p.q. : q - p = \mathbf{max}$$
$$p, q : p = 0 \land q = 0 \land A.p.q : q - p = 0$$

from which we infer that $P_0 \land P_1$ is initialized by $n \leftarrow 0$ and $r \leftarrow 0$. For an increase of n by 1 we derive, assuming $P_0 \land P_1 \land n \neq N$,

$$\mathbf{max}\ p, q : 0 \leq p \leq q \leq n + 1 \land A.p.q : q - p = \mathbf{max}$$
$$p, q : 0 \leq p \leq q \leq n \land A.p.q : q - p = \mathbf{max}\ (\mathbf{max}$$
$$p : 0 \leq p \leq n + 1 \land A.p.(n+1) : n + 1 - p) = r\ \mathbf{max}\ (\mathbf{max}$$
$$p : 0 \leq p \leq n + 1 \land A.p.(n+1) : n + 1 - p) = + \text{ distribute over } \mathbf{max} \text{ for a}$$
non-empty range, $A.(n+1).(n+1) = r\ \mathbf{max}\ (\ n + 1 + (\mathbf{max}\ p :$
$$0 \leq p \leq n + 1 \land A.p(n+1) : -p = r\ \mathbf{max}\ (\ n + 1 - (\mathbf{min}\ p :$$
$$0 \leq p \leq n + 1 \land A.p(n+1) : p$$

leading to the introduction of integer variables s and accompanying invariant

$$Q : s = (\ \mathbf{min}\ p : 0 \leq p \leq n \land A.p.n : p)$$

From $(\ \mathbf{min}\ p : 0 \leq p \leq 0 \land A.p.0 : p) = 0$, we infer that s should be initialized at zero and we obtain a program of the following form:

1: $N \geq 0 \land (\forall n : 0 \leq n \leq N : A.n.n)$
2: $n \leftarrow 0$
3: $r \leftarrow 0$
4: $s \leftarrow 0$
5: **Invariant** : $P_0 \land P_1 \land Q$
6: *bound* : $N - n$
7: **while** $n \neq N$ **do**
8:     *establish* $Q(n \leftarrow n + 1)$
9:     $r \leftarrow r\ \mathbf{max}\ (n + 1 - s)$
10:     $n \leftarrow n + 1$
11: **end while**   ▷ $r = (\ \mathbf{max}\ p, q : 0 \leq p \leq q \leq N \land A.p.q : q - p)$

This program leaves "*establish* $Q(n \leftarrow n + 1)$" as a subproblem. Since A holds for empty segments, the range of the quantification in Q is non-empty and Q can be written as the conjunction of Q_0, Q_1, and Q_2, defined as

1.11. Segment Problems

- $Q_0 : 0 \leq s \leq n$
- $Q_1 : A.s.n$
- $Q_2 : (\forall p : 0 \leq p < s : \neg A.p.n)$

Since A is prefix-closed, we have $\neg A.p.n \implies \neg A.p.(n+1)$ for $0 \leq p < n$, and, hence

$$Q_2 \implies Q_2(n \leftarrow n+1)$$

We have $Q_0 \implies Q_0(n \leftarrow n+1)$ as well and we conclude

$$Q_0 \wedge Q_2 \wedge A.s.(n+1) \implies Q(n \leftarrow n+1)$$

The fact that $Q_2(n \leftarrow n+1)$ is implied by Q_2 has another consequence. From

$$Q_2(n \leftarrow n+1) \equiv (\forall p : 0 \leq p < s : \neg A.p.(n+1))$$

we infer

$$Q_2 \implies (\min p : 0 \leq p \leq n+1 \wedge A.p.(n+1) : p) \geq s$$

i.e., only values p for which $s \leq p \leq n+1$ have to be investigated. For $p = n+1$, we know that $A.p.(n+1)$ holds, so we usually start our investigations with the calculation of $A.p.(n+1)$ for $s \leq p \leq n$.

We return to *all zeros*, for which $A.p.q \equiv (\forall i : p \leq i < q : X.i = 0)$, and we compute $A.p.(n+1)$ for $s \leq p \leq n$:

$$A.p.(n+1) \equiv (\forall i : p \leq i < n+1 : X.i = 0) \equiv (\forall i : p \leq i < n : X.n = 0) \wedge X.n = 0 \equiv A.p.n \wedge X.n = 0$$

Hence,

$$Q \wedge X.n = 0 \implies Q(n \leftarrow n+1)$$

and

$$X.n \neq 0 \implies (\forall p : s \leq p \leq n : \neg A.p.(n+1))$$

from which we infer, since $A.(n+1).(n+1)$ holds

$$X.n \neq 0 \implies Q(n \leftarrow n+1)(s \leftarrow n+1)$$

This leads to the following solutions to *all zeros*:

Algorithm 18 All Zeros Program

1: $n, s : int$
2: $n \leftarrow 0$
3: $r \leftarrow 0$
4: $s \leftarrow 0$
5: **while** $n \neq N$ **do**
6:    **if** $X.n == 0$ **then**
7:       $skip$
8:    **else if** $X.n \neq 0$ **then**
9:       $s \leftarrow n+1$
10:    **end if**
11:    $r \leftarrow r \max (n+1-s)$
12:    $n \leftarrow n+1$
13: **end while**

Please note that we did not use the postfix-closedness of A.

1.12 Exponentiation

Problem Description

Write a program that, given two fixed integers $X \geq 0$ and $Y \geq 0$, establishes $z = X^Y$.

Solution

Let us define $0^0 = 1$. The program is to consist of a loop with the following invariant and bound functions:

- $P : 0 \leq y \wedge z \times x^y = X^Y$.
- $t : y$

P is easily established using

$$x \leftarrow X \\ y \leftarrow Y \\ z \leftarrow 1$$

and at least two simple commands can be used to reduce the bound function :

1. $y \leftarrow y - 1$
2. $y \leftarrow \frac{y}{2}$

Finding the weakest preconditions of these commands with respect to the invariant leads directly to the program:

Algorithm 19 Exponentiation

1: $0 \leq X \wedge 0 \leq Y$
2: $x \leftarrow X$
3: $y \leftarrow Y$
4: $z \leftarrow 1$
5: **while** $0 < y \wedge even(y)$ **do**
6: $\quad y \leftarrow \frac{y}{2}$
7: $\quad x \leftarrow x \times x$
8: $\quad$ **if** $0 < y$ **then**
9: $\quad\quad y \leftarrow y - 1$
10: $\quad\quad z \leftarrow z \times x$
11: $\quad$ **end if**
12: **end while** $\qquad\qquad\qquad\qquad\qquad\qquad \triangleright z = X^Y$

Now consider the efficiency of the program. Dividing by 2 generally reduces y more than subtracting 1; hence, division is preferred. However, if $y > 0$ and *even*, then both conditions are true and an implementations is free to choose to execute either command. Please note that we can replace the condition $0 < y$ by

$$0 < y \wedge \neg(0 < y < even(y))$$

1.13. Searching two-dimensional sorted array

and simplify it to the following program :

Algorithm 20 Exponentiation Revisited

1: $0 \leq X \wedge 0 \leq Y$
2: $x \leftarrow X$
3: $y \leftarrow Y$
4: $z \leftarrow 1$
5: **while** $0 < y \wedge even(y)$ **do**
6:      $y \leftarrow \frac{y}{2}$
7:      $x \leftarrow x \times x$
8:      **if** $0 < y \wedge odd(y)$ **then**
9:          $y \leftarrow y - 1$
10:          $z \leftarrow z \times x$
11:      **end if**
12: **end while**   ▷ $z = X^Y$

With the preliminary, nondeterministic version, the loop could iterate up to Y times; in the final, deterministic version, the number of iterations is at most $1 + 2 \times \lceil (\log Y) \rceil$. The algorithm can be rewritten once more as

---
Algorithm 21 Efficient Exponentiation

1: $0 \leq X \wedge 0 \leq Y$
2: $x \leftarrow X$
3: $y \leftarrow Y$
4: $z \leftarrow 1$
5: **while** $0 < y$ **do**
6:      **while** $even(y)$ **do**
7:          $y \leftarrow \frac{y}{2}$
8:          $x \leftarrow x \times x$
9:      **end while**
10:      $y \leftarrow y - 1$
11:      $z \leftarrow z \times x$
12: **end while**   ▷ $z = X^Y$

1.13 Searching two-dimensional sorted array

Problem Description

Let us start analyzing the problem by looking at implied properties related to search space. This array has the following properties:

1. no of rows $m \geq 1$

2. no of columns $n \geq 1$

3. Entries in each row are ordered by $\leq$, i.e., for $0 \leq i < m$ && $0 \leq j < n$
   $\boxed{a[i][j] \leq a[i][j+1]}$

   - $a_{11} \leq a_{12} \leq \ldots \leq a_{1n}$
   - $a_{21} \leq a_{22} \leq \ldots \leq a_{2n}$

   $\vdots$

1.13. Searching two-dimensional sorted array 50

- $a_{m1} \leq a_{m2} \leq \ldots \leq a_{mn}$

4. Entries in each column are ordered by $\leq$, i.e., for $0 \leq i < m$ && for $0 \leq j < n$

   $\boxed{a[i][j] \leq a[i+1][j]}$

   - $a_{11} \leq a_{21} \leq \ldots \leq a_{m1}$
   - $a_{12} \leq a_{22} \leq \ldots \leq a_{m2}$

   $\vdots$

   - $a_{1n} \leq a_{2n} \leq \ldots \leq a_{mn}$

Pictorial representation of two-dimensional sorted array is as follows:

With the properties above, we have to develop an efficient algorithm to find the position of a given integer x in the array a, i.e., the algorithm should find i and j such that $\boxed{x = a[i,j]}$. By efficient we mean to minimize the number of comparisons as much as possible.

Let us treat the input array as some kind of a rectangular region.

The problem demands that the integer x does exist somewhere in this region. Let us label this condition as *Input Assertion* or *Precondition*.

Precondition (aka *Input Assertion*)

$\boxed{x \in a[0..m-1, 0..n-1]}$

i.e., x is present somewhere in this rectangular region a.

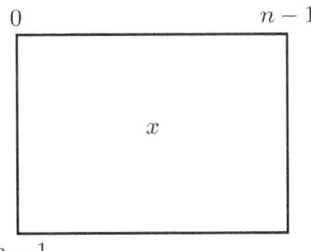

1.13. Searching two-dimensional sorted array

After the program terminates successfully, x has to be found in a rectangular region of a where the rectangular region consists of just one row and column. Let us label this condition as *Output Assertion* or *Result Assertion* or *Postcondition*.

Postcondition (aka *Result Assertion*)

$\boxed{0 \le i \le m-1}$ && $\boxed{0 \le j \le n-1}$ && $\boxed{x = a[i,j]}$

i.e., x is in a rectangular region of a where the rectangular region consists of just one row and column, i.e., x is present at i^{th} row and j^{th} column of a.

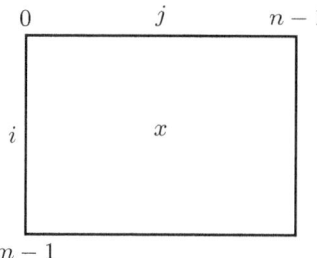

Invariant

Looking at the precondition and postcondition, it is not that difficult to figure out that during the execution of our algorithm, x is guaranteed to be confined within some rectangular region of a, i.e.,

$\boxed{0 \le i \le p \le m-1}$ &&
$\boxed{0 \le q \le j \le n-1}$ &&
$\boxed{x \in a[i..p, q..j]}$.

In simple words, the invariant implies that

- We have exhausted the rows a[0..p-1] and x is not present in these already searched rows.

- We have exhausted the columns a[0..q-1] and x is not present in these already searched columns.

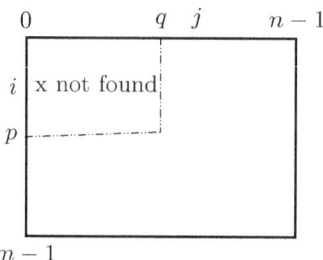

Contract the rectangular region

We have to choose a rectangular region $a[i..p, q..j]$ that contains x followed by making this region smaller till x is found.

Initial bounded searcheable region is represented by :
$i = 0 \quad p = m - 1 \quad q = 0 \quad j = n - 1$

Looking at bounds of the rectangle, there are 4 ways to march towards contracting it:

- if $a[i,j] < x$ then since the row is ordered $\implies i \leftarrow i + 1$, because if $a[i,j] > x$, then all the entries of that row is also greater than x. Please note that its execution will maintain the stated invariant if x is not found in a[i, 0..n-1], i.e., in i^{th} row.

- if $a[p,q] > x \implies p \leftarrow p - 1$

- if $a[p,q] < x \implies q \leftarrow q + 1$

- if $a[i,j] > x \implies j \leftarrow j - 1$

These conditions are also known as *guards*[?].

Saddleback Search Algorithm

Let us put together the complete solution as shown below:

Algorithm 22 Saddleback Search Algorithm

1: **PreCondition** : $x \in a[0..m - 1, 0..n - 1]$
2: **PostCondition** : $0 \leq i \leq m - 1 \ \&\&\ 0 \leq j \leq n - 1 \ \&\&\ x = a[i,j]$
3: **function** SADDLEBACK-SEARCH(a[0..m-1, 0..n-1], x)
4: $\quad i \leftarrow 0$
5: $\quad p \leftarrow m - 1$
6: $\quad q \leftarrow 0$
7: $\quad j \leftarrow n - 1$
8: $\quad$ **Invariant** : $0 \leq i \leq p \leq m - 1 \ \&\&\ 0 \leq q \leq j \leq n - 1 \ \&\&\ x \in a[i..p, q..j]$
9: $\quad$ **while** $x \neq a[i,j]$ **do**
10: $\quad\quad$ **if** a[i, j] < x **then**
11: $\quad\quad\quad i \leftarrow i + 1$
12: $\quad\quad$ **end if**
13: $\quad\quad$ **if** a[p, q] > x **then**
14: $\quad\quad\quad p \leftarrow p - 1$
15: $\quad\quad$ **end if**
16: $\quad\quad$ **if** a[p, q] < x **then**
17: $\quad\quad\quad q \leftarrow q + 1$
18: $\quad\quad$ **end if**
19: $\quad\quad$ **if** a[i, j] > x **then**
20: $\quad\quad\quad j \leftarrow j - 1$
21: $\quad\quad$ **end if**
22: $\quad$ **end while**
23: **end function**

This layout was simple enough to embark on the journey of solving problems using formal programming methodology in somewhat pragmatic manner.

1.13. Searching two-dimensional sorted array

With the above setting in place, now it is time to think towards proving correctness of the result upon termination. As an astute reader, it is not that difficult to surmise that intermediate conditions in form of the points p,q of search space are not really needed to test veracity of the result upon termination. Only the first and last conditions are necessary and sufficient enough to prove it. So let us drop the middle (two) conditions to complete the working program in practice as following:

Algorithm 23 Saddleback Search Algorithm in practice

1: **PreCondition** : $x \in a[0..m-1, 0..n-1]$
2: **PostCondition** : $0 \leq i \leq m-1 \ \&\& \ 0 \leq j \leq n-1 \ \&\& \ x = a[i,j]$
3: **Invariant** : x is in a[i..m-1, 0..j]
4: **function** SADDLEBACK-SEARCH(a[0..m-1, 0..n-1], x)
5:     **while** $x \neq a[i,j]$ **do**
6:         **if** a[i, j] < x **then**
7:             $i \leftarrow i + 1$
8:         **else** $j \leftarrow j - 1$
9:         **end if**
10:     **end while**
11: **end function**

Still, we need to address that why we chose to start from top rightmost corner. We can of course start from bottom leftmost corner as well. We leave this an exercise to the reader to work out and think about the pros n cons of choosing the starting point.

C++11 Implementation

Let us try programming this algorithm in a real language, say C++11 to bring ourselves at workplace-setting environment:

Program 1.15: Saddleback search in C++11

```cpp
#include <algorithm>
#include <array>

using Point = std::pair<int, int>;

template <int m, int n>
using TwoDimArray
    = std::array<std::array<int, n>, m>;

template <int m, int n>
Point saddleback_search(TwoDimArray<m, n> & a,
                        int x)
{
    Point p(-1, -1);

    int i = 0, j = n - 1;

    while(x != a[i][j])
    {
        if(a[i][j] < x) i += 1;
        else j -= 1;
    }
```

1.13. Searching two-dimensional sorted array

```
24      p.first = i;
25      p.second = j;
26
27      return p;
28 }
```

Program 1.16: Using Saddleback Search

```
1 #include "saddleback_search.hpp"
2 #include <iostream>
3
4 int main()
5 {
6     TwoDimArray<4, 4> a = {
7                             2, 2, 3, 5,
8                             3, 4, 5, 6,
9                             3, 5, 6, 8,
10                            3, 6, 7, 9
11                          };
12
13    Point p = saddleback_search<4, 4>(a, 6);
14
15    std::cout << "6 is found at : a["
16              << p.first << "]["
17              << p.second << "]"
18              << std::endl;
19
20 }
```

Output of the program is:

```
6 is found at : a[1][3]
```

Time Complexity

As could be seen that the number of comparisons required in Saddleback search algorithm is at most $n + m$. Hence time complexity is $O(n + m)$.

How to improve it further, is it possible?

Let us take a simple case as a tryst to understand it better. Let us assume that the array is a square one with n x n dimension, i.e., m = n. Please note that the elements lying off-diagonal in the rectangular region form an unordered sequence of integers, i.e., a[0, n-1], a[1, n-2], a[2, n-3], ..., a[n-2, 1] and a[n-1, 0] form an unordered list because this particular sequence is not affected at all by the imposed ordering on row and column respectively. So even if we assume that x could be lying on this off-diagonal set, then at least n comparisons are required in the worst case.

Have we done our bit fully ? Not yet. We request our reader to think about it and be patient for now, thoughts on possible improvement will be taken up soon, whether it is feasible to improve it further or not will reveal itself in due course of time. But for now, we think about a simple variation in the problem statement and try solving it with help of approach discussed so far.

Variation

As mentioned in the problem statement, it was desired to find any one in case of multiple occurrence of the value sought after. How about finding all of these

1.13. Searching two-dimensional sorted array

instead ? This problem is one of the variations of *saddleback search*(discussed in the previous section). Here instead of locating an occurrence, it counts the number of occurrences.

Find First Occurrence

Before we march ahead towards a solution, we need to work on a strategy to spot the very first occurrence of x, because the earlier approach was focused to find any occurrence in case of multiple ones. So if we try to build our logic on the earlier approach, we may miss few occurrences.

Therefore, we have to be a little more judicious in starting point which cannot simply be set to either rightmost top corner or leftmost bottom corner.

To understand it better, let us stick to our earlier solution for now as illustrated ahead and take it from there towards an appropriate solution.

We have to design an efficient algorithm to search for a given integer x in a 2-dimensional **sorted** array a[0..m][0..n]. Please note that it is sorted row-wise and column-wise in ascending order. In case of multiple occurrences, please find the very first occurrence, i.e, the occurrence with the smallest value of the row index and at the same time the occurrence with the smallest value of the column index as well. Please note that row index and column index at topmost left corner is being treated as (0, 0).

1. Find any occurrence using original saddleback search algorithm which finds the entry corresponding to smallest row index and highest column index, i.e., it finds the very first row containing that value but the column index depict the last most occurrence in that particular row.

2. Search backwards to adjust the column index to point to lowest index corresponding to that entry in that row.

Algorithm 24 Saddleback Search Algorithm : Find First Occurrence

1: **function** SADDLEBACK-SEARCH(a[0..m-1, 0..n-1], x)
2:    $i \leftarrow 0$
3:    $j \leftarrow n - 1$
4:    **while** $x \neq a[i, j]$ **do**
5:       **if** a[i, j] < x **then**
6:          $i \leftarrow i + 1$
7:       **else if** a[i, j] > x **thenf**
8:          $j \leftarrow j - 1$
9:       **end if**
10:   **end while**
11:   **while** $x == a[i, j]$ **do**
12:      $j \leftarrow j - 1$
13:   **end while**
14:   $j \leftarrow j + 1$
15: **end function**

Program 1.17: Saddleback Search : First Occurrence

```
#include <algorithm>
#include <array>

```

```cpp
 4 using Point = std::pair<int, int>;
 5
 6 template <int m, int n>
 7 using TwoDimArray
 8     = std::array<std::array<int, n>, m>;
 9
10 template <int m, int n>
11 Point saddleback_search_first (TwoDimArray<m, n>
12                                & a, int x)
13 {
14     Point p(-1, -1);
15
16     int i = 0, j = n - 1;
17
18     while(x != a[i][j])
19     {
20         if(a[i][j] < x) ++i;
21         else --j;
22     }
23
24     while(x == a[i][j]) --j;
25
26     ++j;
27
28     p.first = i;
29     p.second = j;
30
31     return p;
32 }
```

Program 1.18: Using Saddleback Search : First Occurrence

```cpp
 1 #include "saddleback_search_first.hpp"
 2 #include <iostream>
 3
 4 int main()
 5 {
 6     TwoDimArray<4, 4> a = {
 7                            2, 2, 3, 5,
 8                            3, 4, 6, 6,
 9                            3, 5, 6, 6,
10                            3, 6, 6, 9
11                          };
12
13     Point p
14         = saddleback_search_first<4, 4>(a, 6);
15
16     std::cout << "6 is found at : a["
17               << p.first << "]["
18               << p.second << "]"
19               << std::endl;
20
21 }
```

It prints:

```
6 is found at : a[1][2]
```

First part of this algorithm uses original saddleback search whose complexity is $O(n + m)$. Second part involves linear search in backward dimension in the given row $\implies O(n)$. Hence time complexity of *Saddleback Search*

1.13. Searching two-dimensional sorted array

: Find First Occurrence is $O(n + m)$. Please note that second part of this algorithm can be accomplished using binary search. We leave this an exercise to the reader.

Find All Occurrences

Before we undertake solving the problem of finding the count of x, let us turn our attention to a related twister which requires reporting of all the occurrences of a given integer x in the array a[m, n], i.e., it will report all the row-indices (i) and column-indices (j) of the array where $x == a[i,j]$.

So far our termination condition was derived upon the first occurrence of x in the array, but now we need to modify to proceed further till array is completely exhausted and maintain a list of vertices found relevant so far.

Algorithm 25 Saddleback Search Algorithm : Find All Occurrences

1: **function** SADDLEBACK-FINDALL(a[0..m-1, 0..n-1], x)
2:    $i \leftarrow 0$
3:    $j \leftarrow n - 1$
4:    $currrent\_col\_index \leftarrow j$
5:    $List < Pair < rowindex, columnindex >> list\_indices$
6:    **while** $j \leq n - 1$ **do**
7:      **if** a[i, j] < x **then**
8:        $i \leftarrow i + 1$
9:      **else if** a[i, j] > x **then**
10:        $j \leftarrow j - 1$
11:      **else if** a[i, j] == x **then**
12:        $currrent\_col\_index \leftarrow j$
13:        **while** currrent_col_index ≥ 0 **and** a[i][currrent_col_index] == x **do**
14:          list_indices.insert(Pair<rowindex, columnindex>(i, currrent_col_index))
15:          $currrent\_col\_index \leftarrow currrent\_col\_index - 1$
16:        **end while**
17:        $i \leftarrow i + 1$
18:      **end if**
19:    **end while**
20: **end function**

Key thing to notice here is how to start the next search after first occurrence is reported, say a[i, j] ?

If x is equal to a[i, j] for a given row index i and column index j, then it is obvious that these correspond to smallest values of row and column indices. Our algorithm developed for finding the first occurrence ends up traversing the path from the last most to first most in a given row, so all we need to do is to record this path and march towards the next row.

Program 1.19: Saddleback Find All

```
#include <algorithm>
#include <array>
#include <vector>

template <int m, int n>
using TwoDimArray
```

1.13. Searching two-dimensional sorted array

```cpp
7            = std::array<std::array<int, n>, m>;
8
9  typedef std::pair<int, int> PairIndices;
10
11 typedef std::vector<PairIndices> ListIndices;
12
13 template <int m, int n>
14 ListIndices saddleback_findall(
15                 TwoDimArray<m, n> & a, int x)
16 {
17     size_t i = 0, j = n - 1;
18     ListIndices list_indices;
19     int currrent_col_index = j;
20
21     while(j <= n - 1)
22     {
23         if(a[i][j] < x) i += 1;
24         else if(a[i][j] > x) j -= 1;
25         else // a[i][j] == x
26         {
27             currrent_col_index = j;
28             while(currrent_col_index >=0 &&
29                   a[i][currrent_col_index] == x)
30                 list_indices.push_back(
31             PairIndices(i, currrent_col_index--));
32
33             ++i;
34         }
35     }
36
37     return list_indices;
38 }
```

Program 1.20: Using Saddleback Find All

```cpp
1  #include "saddleback_findall.hpp"
2  #include <iostream>
3
4  int main()
5  {
6      TwoDimArray<4, 4> a = {
7                                 2, 2, 3, 5,
8                                 3, 4, 5, 6,
9                                 3, 5, 6, 8,
10                                3, 6, 7, 9
11                          };
12
13     ListIndices indexList
14         = saddleback_findall<4, 4>(a, 6);
15
16     std::cout << "6 is found at : \n";
17     for(PairIndices & p : indexList)
18     std::cout << "a[" << p.first << "]"
19             << "[" << p.second << "]"
20             << std::endl;
21 }
```

It prints :

1.13. Searching two-dimensional sorted array

```
6 is found at :
a[1][3]
a[2][2]
a[3][1]
```

Program 1.21: Another Usage of Saddleback Find All

```cpp
#include "saddleback_findall.hpp"
#include <iostream>

int main()
{
    TwoDimArray<4, 4> a = {
                           2, 2, 3, 5,
                           3, 4, 6, 6,
                           3, 5, 6, 6,
                           3, 6, 6, 9
                          };

    ListIndices indexList
        = saddleback_findall<4, 4>(a, 6);

    std::cout << "6 is found at : \n";
    for(PairIndices & p : indexList)
        std::cout << "a[" << p.first << "]"
                  << "[" << p.second << "]"
                  << std::endl;
}
```

It prints :

```
6 is found at :
a[1][3]
a[1][2]
a[2][3]
a[2][2]
a[3][2]
a[3][1]
```

Program 1.22: Continue Using Saddleback Find All

```cpp
#include "saddleback_findall.hpp"
#include <iostream>

int main()
{
    TwoDimArray<4, 4> a = {
                           6, 6, 6, 6,
                           6, 6, 6, 6,
                           6, 6, 6, 6,
                           6, 6, 6, 6
                          };

    ListIndices indexList
        = saddleback_findall<4, 4>(a, 6);

    std::cout << "6 is found at : \n";
```

```
17      for(PairIndices & p : indexList)
18        std::cout << "a[" << p.first << "]"
19                  << "[" << p.second << "]"
20                  << std::endl;
21  }
```

It prints :

```
6 is found at :
a[0][3]
a[0][2]
a[0][1]
a[0][0]
a[1][3]
a[1][2]
a[1][1]
a[1][0]
a[2][3]
a[2][2]
a[2][1]
a[2][0]
a[3][3]
a[3][2]
a[3][1]
a[3][0]
```

Time Complexity is $O(mn)$.

Saddleback Count

Now our task becomes easier to work out original problem posed earlier, i.e., finding the count of a given integer x in the array a.

Algorithm 26 Saddleback Count Algorithm : Initial Approach

1: **function** SADDLEBACK-COUNT(a[0..m-1, 0..n-1], x)
2:    $i \leftarrow 0$
3:    $j \leftarrow n - 1$
4:    $count \leftarrow 0$
5:    **while** $j \leq n - 1$ **do**
6:      **if** a[i, j] < x **then**
7:        $i \leftarrow i + 1$
8:      **else if** a[i, j] > x **then**
9:        $j \leftarrow j - 1$
10:      **else if** a[i, j] == x **then**
11:        $i \leftarrow i + 1$
12:        $j \leftarrow j - 1$
13:        $count \leftarrow count + 1$
14:      **end if**
15:    **end while**
16: **end function**

1.13. Searching two-dimensional sorted array

C++11 Implementation

Program 1.23: Saddleback Count : Initial Approach

```cpp
#include <algorithm>
#include <array>

template <int m, int n>
using TwoDimArray
    = std::array<std::array<int, n>, m>;

template <int m, int n>
size_t saddleback_count(
    TwoDimArray<m, n> & a, int x)
{
    size_t i = 0, j = n - 1, count = 0;

    while(j <= n - 1)
    {
        if(a[i][j] < x) i += 1;
        else if(a[i][j] > x) j -= 1;
        else // a[i][j] == x
        {
            count += 1;
            i += 1;
            j -= 1;
        }
    }

    return count;
}
```

Program 1.24: Using Saddleback Count

```cpp
#include "saddleback_count.hpp"
#include <iostream>

int main()
{
    TwoDimArray<4, 4> a = {
                            2, 2, 3, 5,
                            3, 4, 5, 6,
                            3, 5, 6, 8,
                            3, 6, 7, 9
                          };

    size_t count
        = saddleback_count<4, 4>(a, 6);

    std::cout << "Count of 6 is: "
              << count << std::endl;
}
```

It prints : Count of 6 is: 3 which is fine so far.

Let us take another example:

Program 1.25: Using Saddleback Count : Count of 6 should be 6

```cpp
#include "saddleback_count.hpp"
#include <iostream>

int main()
```

1.13. Searching two-dimensional sorted array

```
5  {
6      TwoDimArray<4, 4> a = {
7                              2, 2, 3, 5,
8                              3, 4, 6, 6,
9                              3, 5, 6, 6,
10                             3, 6, 6, 9
11                           };
12
13     size_t count
14         = saddleback_count<4, 4>(a, 6);
15
16     std::cout << "Count of 6 is: "
17               << count << std::endl;
18 }
```

This too prints : Count of 6 is: 3 which is wrong because it should print : Count of 6 is: 6.

As an astute reader, you can figure out that ordering of rows and columns plays a key role here. Saddleback search has to locate such an occurrence, more precisely, the occurrence with the smallest value of the row index and at the same time the occurrence with the smallest value of the column index as well. Please note that the earlier logic relied on locating the occurrence with the smallest value of the row index and at the same time the occurrence with the largest value of the column index. So let us use the insight gained in the solution of finding first occurrence followed by finding all the occurrences of saddleback search with necessary modifications.

Algorithm 27 Saddleback Count : Correct Algorithm

1: **function** SADDLEBACK-COUNT(a[0..m-1, 0..n-1], x)
2:   $i \leftarrow 0$
3:   $j \leftarrow n - 1$
4:   $currrent\_col\_index \leftarrow j$
5:   $count \leftarrow 0$
6:   **while** $j \leq n - 1$ **do**
7:     **if** a[i, j] < x **then**
8:       $i \leftarrow i + 1$
9:     **else if** a[i, j] > x **then**
10:       $j \leftarrow j - 1$
11:    **else if** a[i, j] == x **then**
12:       $currrent\_col\_index \leftarrow j$
13:       **while** $currrent\_col\_index \geq 0$ **and** a[i][currrent_col_index] == x **do**
14:         $count \leftarrow count + 1$
15:         $currrent\_col\_index \leftarrow currrent\_col\_index - 1$
16:       **end while**
17:       $i \leftarrow i + 1$
18:     **end if**
19:   **end while**
20:   **return** count
21: **end function**

Program 1.26: Implementing Saddleback Count

```
1 #include <algorithm>
2 #include <array>
```

1.13. Searching two-dimensional sorted array

```cpp
template <int m, int n>
using TwoDimArray
    = std::array<std::array<int, n>, m>;

template <int m, int n>
size_t saddleback_count(
    TwoDimArray<m, n> & a, int x)
{
    size_t i = 0, j = n - 1, count = 0;
    int current_col_index = j;

    while(j <= n - 1)
    {
        if(a[i][j] < x) i += 1;
        else if(a[i][j] > x) j -= 1;
        else // a[i][j] == x
        {
            current_col_index = j;
            while(current_col_index >=0 &&
              a[i][current_col_index] == x)
            {
                ++count;
                current_col_index--;
            }
            ++i;
        }
    }

    return count;
}
```

Program 1.27: Using Saddleback Count

```cpp
#include "saddleback_count_correct.hpp"
#include <iostream>

int main()
{
    TwoDimArray<4, 4> a = {
                          2, 2, 3, 5,
                          3, 4, 6, 6,
                          3, 5, 6, 6,
                          3, 6, 6, 9
                         };

    size_t count
        = saddleback_count<4, 4>(a, 6);

    std::cout << "Count of 6 is: "
              << count << std::endl;
}
```

It prints:

```
Count of 6 is: 6
```

Program 1.28: another Usage of Saddleback Count

```cpp
#include "saddleback_count_correct.hpp"
```

```cpp
#include <iostream>

int main()
{
    TwoDimArray<4, 4> a = {
                            6, 6, 6, 6,
                            6, 6, 6, 6,
                            6, 6, 6, 6,
                            6, 6, 6, 6
                          };

    size_t count
        = saddleback_count<4, 4>(a, 6);

    std::cout << "Count of 6 is: "
              << count << std::endl;
}
```

It prints :

```
Count of 6 is: 16
```

Time complexity is same as that of find all, i.e., $O(mn)$.

Remarks

It is called *Saddleback Search* because the search space is confined by a region with the smallest element at the top-left, largest at bottom-right and two wings gives it a look like a saddle.

1.14 Hamming Problem

Problem Description

Consider the sequence Seq : $q = 1, 2, 3, 4, 5, 6, 8, 9, 10, 12, \ldots$, of all numbers divisible by no primes other than $2, 3$ and 5. Another way to describe Seq is to give axioms that indicate which values are in it:

1. *Axiom 1*: 1 is in Seq.

2. *Axiom 2*: If x is in Seq, so are $2 \times x, 3 \times x$ and $5 \times x$.

3. *Axiom 3*: The only values in Seq are given by *Axioms 1 and 2*.

Write a program that stores the first 1000 values of Seq, in order, in an array $q[0..999]$, i.e., that establishes

$$R : q[0..999] \text{ contains the first 1000 values of } Seq, \text{ in order.}$$

Solution

Since *Axiom 2* specifies that a value is in Seq if a smaller one is, it may make sense to generate the values in order. A possibility, then, is to replace the constant 1000 of R by a variable i, yielding the invariant

$$P = 1 \leq i \leq 1000 \wedge q[0..i-1] \text{ contains the first } i \text{ values of } Seq.$$

1.14. Hamming Problem

With this invariant, the obvious program structure is:

1: $i \leftarrow 1$
2: $q[0] \leftarrow 1$ ▷ P
3: **while** $i \neq 1000$ **do** ▷ $invariant : P; bound : 1000 - i$
4:     Calculate xnext, the ith value in Seq
5:     $i \leftarrow i + 1$
6:     $q[i] \leftarrow xnext$
7: **end while**

It remains to determine how to calculate $xnext$, the next value of Seq to be generated. Since the values of Seq are generated in order, $xnext$ must be $\geq q[i-1]$. Secondly, since 1 is already in $q[0..i-1]$, $xnext$ must satisfy $Axiom\ 2$ above. This means that $xnext$ must have the form $2 \times x$, $3 \times x$ or $5 \times x$ for some value x already in $q[0..i-1]$. Therefore

$$xnext \text{ is the minimum value} > q[i-1] \text{ of the form } 2 \times x, 3 \times x \text{ or } 5 \times x \text{ for } x \text{ in } q[0..i-1].$$

So, we introduce three variables x_2, x_3 and x_5 with meaning as expressed in the following assertion P_1:

- x_2 is the minimum value $> q[i-1]$ with form $2 \times x$ for x in $q[0..i-1]$
- x_3 is the minimum value $> q[i-1]$ with form $3 \times x$ for x in $q[0..i-1]$
- x_5 is the minimum value $> q[i-1]$ with form $5 \times x$ for x in $q[0..i-1]$

Value $xnext$ is the minimum of x_2, x_3 and x_5. We see, then, that variable $xnext$ is not really needed, and we modify the program structure to:

1: $i \leftarrow 1$
2: $q[0] \leftarrow 1$ ▷ P
3: **while** $i \neq 1000$ **do** ▷ $invariant : P; bound : 1000 - i$
4:     Calculate x_2, x_3, x_5 to satisfy P_1
5:     $i \leftarrow i + 1$
6:     $q[i] \leftarrow min(x_2, x_3, x_5)$
7: **end while**

We now illustrate taking an assertion out of a loop. Calculating x_2, x_3 and x_5 to establish P_1 at each iteration can be time consuming. However they change quite slowly as i is increased and P is kept invariant, and it may be possible to speed up the algorithm by taking P_1 out of the loop and making it part of the loop invariant. The fact that $q[0..i-1]$ is ordered gives additional hope. Thus, we investigate the program structure:

1: $i \leftarrow 1$
2: $q[0] \leftarrow 1$ ▷ P
3: Establish P_1 for $i = 1$
4: **while** $i \neq 1000$ **do** ▷ $invariant : P \wedge P_1; bound : 1000 - i$
5:     $i \leftarrow i + 1$
6:     $q[i] \leftarrow min(x_2, x_3, x_5)$
7:     Reestablish P_1
8: **end while**

Now, how is P_1 to be reestablished ? Consider x_2. For some j, $x_2 = 2 \times q[j]$. Further, x_2 can only be increased, and not decreased, to $2 \times q[j+1]$ or $2 \times q[j+2]$, etc. This suggests maintaining the position j. A similar statement holds for x_3 and x_5. We therefore introduce three variables j_2, j_3 and j_5 and modify P_1 as follows : P_1:

- $x_2 = 2 \times q[j_2]$ is the minimum value $> q[i-1]$ with form $2 \times x$ for x in $q[0..i-1]$

- $x_3 = 3 \times q[j_3]$ is the minimum value $> q[i-1]$ with form $3 \times x$ for x in $q[0..i-1]$

- $x_5 = 5 \times q[j_5]$ is the minimum value $> q[i-1]$ with form $5 \times x$ for x in $q[0..i-1]$

We are now able to develop the final program :

Algorithm 28 Hamming Problem

1: $i \leftarrow 1$
2: $q[0] \leftarrow 1$ ▷ P
3: Establish P_1
4: $x_2 \leftarrow 2$
5: $x_3 \leftarrow 3$
6: $x_5 \leftarrow 5$
7: $j_2 \leftarrow 0$
8: $j_3 \leftarrow 0$
9: $j_5 \leftarrow 0$
10: **while** $i \neq 1000$ **do** ▷ $invariant : P \wedge P_1; bound : 1000 - i$
11: $\quad i \leftarrow i + 1$
12: $\quad q[i] \leftarrow min(x_2, x_3, x_5)$ ▷ Reestablish P_1
13: $\quad$ **while** $x_2 \leq q[i-1]$ **do**
14: $\quad\quad j_2 \leftarrow j_2 + 1$
15: $\quad\quad x_2 \leftarrow 2 \times q[j_2]$
16: $\quad$ **end while**
17: $\quad$ **while** $x_3 \leq q[i-1]$ **do**
18: $\quad\quad j_3 \leftarrow j_3 + 1$
19: $\quad\quad x_3 \leftarrow 3 \times q[j_3]$
20: $\quad$ **end while**
21: $\quad$ **while** $x_5 \leq q[i-1]$ **do**
22: $\quad\quad j_5 \leftarrow j_5 + 1$
23: $\quad\quad x_5 \leftarrow 2 \times q[j_5]$
24: $\quad$ **end while**
25: **end while**

1.15 Constant Time Range Query

Problem

Describe an algorithm that, given n integers in the range 0 to k, preprocesses its input and then answers any query about how many of the n integers fall into a range $[a..b]$ in $O(1)$ time. The algorithm should use $\Theta(n+k)$ preprocessing time.

1.15. Constant Time Range Query

Solution

Compute the C array as is done in *counting sort* described below.

Counting sort assumes that each of the n input elements is an integer in the range 0 to k, for some integer k. When $k = O(n)$, the sort runs in $\Theta(n)$ time.

The basic idea of *counting sort* is to determine, for each input element x, the number of elements less than x. This information can be used to place element x directly into its position in the output array.

In the code for counting sort, we assume that the input is an array $A[1..n]$, and thus $length[A] = n$. We require two other arrays:

1. the array $B[1..n]$ holds the sorted output, and

2. the array $C[0..k]$ provides temporary working storage.

Algorithm 29 Counting Sort Algorithm

1: **function** COUNTING-SORT(A, B, k)
2:     **for** $i \leftarrow 0$ **to** k **do**
3:         $C[i] \leftarrow 0$
4:     **end for**
5:     **for** $j \leftarrow 1$ **to** $length[A]$ **do**
6:         $C[A[j]] \leftarrow C[A[j]] + 1$ ▷ $C[i]$ now contains the number of elements $== i$
7:     **end for**
8:     **for** $i \leftarrow 1$ **to** k **do**
9:         $C[i] \leftarrow C[i] + C[i-1]$ ▷ $C[i]$ now contains the number of elements $\leq i$.
10:     **end for**
11:     **for** $j \leftarrow length[A]$ **downto** 1 **do**
12:         $B[C[A[j]]] \leftarrow A[j]$
13:         $C[A[j]] \leftarrow C[A[j]] - 1$
14:     **end for**
15: **end function**

Time Complexity

1. The *for* loop of lines 2-4 takes time $\Theta(k)$,

2. the *for* loop of lines 5-7 takes time $\Theta(n)$,

3. the *for* loop of lines 8-10 takes time $\Theta(k)$, and

4. the for loop of lines 11-14 takes time $\Theta(n)$.

Thus, the overall time is $\Theta(k + n)$.

In practice, we usually use *counting sort* when we have $k = O(n)$, in which case the running time is $\Theta(n)$.

Counting sort beats the lower bound of $\Omega(n \log n)$ because it is not a comparison sort. In fact, no comparisons between input elements occur anywhere in the program. Instead, counting sort uses the actual values of the elements to index into an array. The $\Theta(n \log n)$ lower bound for sorting does not apply when we depart from the comparison-sort model.

An important property of counting sort is that it is *stable*: numbers with the same value appear in the output array in the same order as they do in the input array. That is, ties between two numbers are broken by the rule that whichever number appears first in the input array appears first in the output array.

With counting sort and the array C in place, let us solve our problem posed earlier. The number of integers in the range $[a..b]$ is $C[b] - C[a-1]$, where we interpret $C[-1]$ as 0.

1.16 Linear Time Sorting

Problem

Sort n integers in the range 0 to $n^2 - 1$ in $O(n)$ time.

Solution

Treat the numbers as $2 - digit$ numbers in radix n. Each digit ranges from 0 to $n-1$. Sort these $2 - digit$ numbers with *radix sort* algorithm as given below.

To illustrate radix sort, let us assume that each element in the n-element array A has d digits, where digit 1 is the lowest-order digit and digit d is the highest-order digit.

Algorithm 30 Radix Sort Algorithm

1: **function** RADIX-SORT(A, d)
2:     **for** $i \leftarrow 1$ **to** d **do**
3:         use a stable sort to sort array A on digit i ▷ For example, Counting Sort
4:     **end for**
5: **end function**

In our problem, there are 2 calls to counting sort, each taking $\Theta(n + n)$ time, so that the total time is $\Theta(n)$.

1.17 Writing a Value as the Sum of Squares

Problem Description

Write a program that, given a fixed integer $r \geq 0$, generates all different ways in which r can be written as the sum of two squares, i.e., that generates all pairs (x, y) satisfying

$$x^2 + y^2 = r \wedge 0 \leq y \leq x$$

Solution

Let us assume that two arrays xv and yv will hold the values of the pairs (x, y) satisfying $x^2 + y^2 = r \wedge 0 \leq y \leq x$. Furthermore, the pairs are to be generated in increasing order of their x-values, and a variable x is used to indicate that all pairs with x-value less than x have been generated. Thus, the first approximation to the invariant of the main loop of the program will be

1.17. Writing a Value as the Sum of Squares

$P_1 : 0 \leq i \wedge ordered(xv[0..i-1]) \wedge$ the pairs $(xv[j], yv[j]), 0 \leq j < i$, are all the pairs with x-value $< x$ that satisfy $x^2 + y^2 = r \wedge 0 \leq y \leq x$.

P_1 is easily established using $i \leftarrow 0$ and $x \leftarrow 0$. If $(xv[i], yv[i])$ is a solution to $x^2 + y^2 = r \wedge 0 \leq y \leq x$, then

$$r = (xv[i])^2 + (yv[i])^2 \leq 2 \times (xv[i])^2$$

Hence, all solutions $(xv[i], yv[i])$ to the problem satisfy $r \leq 2 \times (xv[i])^2$. We will write an initial loop to determine the smallest x satisfying $r \leq 2 \times x^2$, and the first approximation to the program is

---

1: $i \leftarrow 0$
2: $x \leftarrow 0$
3: **while** $r > 2 \times x^2$ **do**
4:     $x \leftarrow x + 1$
5: **end while**
6: **while** $x^2 \leq r$ **do**   ▷ $P_1 \wedge r \leq 2 \times x^2$
7:     Increase x, keeping invariant true
8: **end while**

In order to increase x and keep P_1 true, it is necessary to determine if a suitable y exists for x and to insert the pair (x, y) in the arrays if it does. To do this requires first finding the value y satisfying

$$x^2 + y^2 \leq r \wedge x^2 + (y+1)^2 > r$$

Taking the second conjunct,

$$P_2 : x^2 + (y+1)^2 > r$$

as the invariant of an inner loop, rewrite the program as

Algorithm 31 Writing a Value as the Sum of Squares

1: $i \leftarrow 0$
2: $x \leftarrow 0$
3: **while** $r > 2 \times x^2$ **do**
4:     $x \leftarrow x + 1$
5: **end while**
6: **while** $x^2 \leq r$ **do**   ▷ $invariant : P_1 \wedge r \leq 2 \times x^2$
7:     Increase x, keeping invariant true: Determine y to satisfy $x^2 + y^2 \leq r \wedge x^2 + (y+1)^2 > r$:
8:     $y \leftarrow x$
9:     **while** $x^2 + y^2 > r$ **do**
10:        $y \leftarrow y - 1$
11:     **end while**
12:     **if** $x^2 + y^2 == r$ **then**
13:        $xv[v] \leftarrow x$
14:        $yv[v] \leftarrow y$
15:        $i \leftarrow i + 1$
16:        $x \leftarrow x + 1$
17:     **else if** $x^2 + y^2 < r$ **then**
18:        $x \leftarrow x + 1$
19:     **end if**
20: **end while**

Now note that execution of the body of the main loop does not destroy P_2, and therefore P_2 can be taken out of the loop. Rearrangement then leads to the more efficient program

---
Algorithm 32 Writing a Value as the Sum of Squares

1: $i \leftarrow 0$
2: $x \leftarrow 0$
3: **while** $r > 2 \times x^2$ **do**
4:     $x \leftarrow x + 1$
5: **end while**
6: $y \leftarrow x$
7: **while** $x^2 \leq r$ **do**   ▷ $invariant : P_1 \wedge P_2$
8:     Increase x, keeping invariant true: Determine y to satisfy $x^2 + y^2 \leq r \wedge x^2 + (y+1)^2 > r$:
9:     **while** $x^2 + y^2 > r$ **do**
10:         $y \leftarrow y - 1$
11:     **end while**
12:     **if** $x^2 + y^2 == r$ **then**
13:         $xv[v] \leftarrow x$
14:         $yv[v] \leftarrow y$
15:         $i \leftarrow i + 1$
16:         $x \leftarrow x + 1$
17:     **else if** $x^2 + y^2 < r$ **then**
18:         $x \leftarrow x + 1$
19:     **end if**
20: **end while**

1.18 The Celebrity Problem

Problem Description

Among n persons, a *celebrity* is defined as someone who is known by everyone but does not know anyone. The problem is to identity the celebrity, if one exists, by asking questions only of the form, "Excuse me, do you know the person over there?" The assumption is that all the answers are correct, and that even the celebrity will answer. The goal is to minimize the number of questions.

Solution

Since there are $\frac{n(n-1)}{2}$ pairs of persons, there us potentially a need to ask $n(n-1)$ questions, in the worst case, if the questions are asked arbitrarily. It is not clear that we can do better in the worst case.

Graph based approach

We can use a graph-theoretical formulation. We can build a directed graph $G = (V, E)$ (represented by, say, its incident matrix) with the vertices corresponding to the persons and an edge from u to v if person u knows person v. We define a *sink* of a directed graph to be a vertex with indegree $n - 1$ and outdegree 0.

A celebrity corresponds to a sink of the graph.

1.18. The Celebrity Problem

We note that a graph can have at most one sink. The input to the problem corresponds to an $n \times n$ adjacency matrix, whose ij entry is 1 if the ith person knows the jth peson, and 0 otherwise.

With this formulation, the problem can be reworded as:

> Given an $n \times n$ adjacency matrix, determine whether there $\exists$ an i | all the entries in the ith column (except for the $(ii)^{th}$ entry) are 1, and all the entries in the ith row (except for the $(ii)^{th}$ entry) are 0.

Inductive approach The base case of two persons is simple. Let us consider the difference between the problem with $n - 1$ persons and that with n persons. We assume that we can find the celebrity among the first $n - 1$ persons by induction. Since there is at most one celebrity, there are three possibilities :

1. the celebrity is among the first $n - 1$

2. the celebrity is the nth person, or

3. there is no celebrity.

The first case is the easiest to handle. We need only to check that the nth person knows the celebrity, and that the celebrity does not know the nth person. The other two cases are more difficult because, to determine whether the nth person is the celebrity, we may need to ask $2(n - 1)$ questions. If we ask $2(n - 1)$ questions in the nth step, then the total number of questions will be $n(n - 1)$, which is what we are trying to avoid so far ! We definitely need another approach.

The trick here is to consider the problem *backward*. It may be hard to identify a celebrity, but it is probably easier to identify someone as a *non-celebrity*. After all, there are definitely more non-celebrities than celebrities. If we eliminate someone from consideration, then we reduce the size of the problem from n to $n - 1$. Moreover, we do not need to eliminate someone specific; anyone will do. Suppose that we ask Alice whether she knows Bob. If she does, then she cannot be a celebrity; if she does not, then Bob cannot be a celebrity. We can eliminate one of them with one question.

We now consider again the three cases with which we started. We do not just take an arbitrary person as the nth person. We use the idea in the last paragraph to eliminate either Alice or Bob, then solve the problem for the other $n - 1$ persons. We are guaranteed that *case 2* will not occur, since the person eliminated cannot be the celebrity. Furthermore, if *case 3* occurs, namely, there is no celebrity among the $n - 1$ persons, then there is no celebrity among the n persons. Only *case 1* remains, but this case is easy. If there is a celebrity among the $n - 1$ persons, it takes two more questions to verify that this is a celebrity for the whole set. Otherwise there is no celebrity.

Optimal Algorithm

The algorithm proceeds as follows. We ask u whether she knows v, and eliminate either u or v according to the answer. Let us assume that we eliminate u. We then find (by induction) a celebrity among the remaining $n - 1$ persons. If there is no celebrity, the algorithm terminates; otherwise we check that u knows the celebrity and that the celebrity does not know u.

Implementation

It is more efficient to implement the celebrity algorithm iteratively, rather than recursively. The algorithm is divided into *two* phases:

1. *elimination phase* : In the first phase, we eliminate all but one candidate.

2. *verification phase* : In the second phase, we check whether this candidate is indeed the celebrity.

We start with n candidates and for the sake of this discussion, let us assume that they are stored in a stack. For each pair of candidates, we can eliminate one candidate by asking one question : *whether one of them knows the other*. We start by taking the first two candidates from the stack, and eliminating one of them. Then, is each step, we have one remaining candidate, and, as long as the stack is nonempty, we take one additional candidate from the stack, and eliminate one of these two candidates. When the stack becomes empty, one candidate remains. We then check that this candidate is indeed the celebrity.

1.18. The Celebrity Problem

Algorithm 33 Celebrity Algorithm
1: **Input** : an $n \times n$ boolean matrix **M**.
2: **Output** : a celebrity, or *no celebrity* if there is no celebrity.
3: **function** CELEBRITY(M)
4: $\quad i \leftarrow 1$
5: $\quad j \leftarrow 2$
6: $\quad next \leftarrow 3$ $\quad\quad$ ▷ In the first phase we eliminate all but one candidate
7: $\quad$ **while** $next \leq n + 1$ **do**
8: $\quad\quad$ **if** M[i, j] **then**
9: $\quad\quad\quad i \leftarrow next$
10: $\quad\quad$ **else**
11: $\quad\quad\quad j \leftarrow next$
12: $\quad\quad$ **end if**
13: $\quad\quad next \leftarrow next + 1$
14: $\quad$ **end while**
$\quad\quad\quad\quad\quad\quad\quad\quad\quad\quad\quad\quad\quad\quad\quad$ ▷ One of either i or j is eliminated
15: $\quad$ **if** $i \leftarrow n + 1$ **then**
16: $\quad\quad candidate \leftarrow j$
17: $\quad$ **else**
18: $\quad\quad candidate \leftarrow i$
19: $\quad$ **end if**
$\quad\quad\quad\quad\quad\quad\quad\quad\quad$ ▷ Now we check that the candidate is indeed the celebrity
20: $\quad wrong \leftarrow false$
21: $\quad k \leftarrow 1$
22: $\quad M[candidate, candidate] \leftarrow false$ $\quad$ ▷ A dummy variable to pass the test
23: $\quad$ **while** not wrong **and** $k \leq n$ **do**
24: $\quad\quad$ **if** $M[candidate, k]$ **then**
25: $\quad\quad\quad wrong \leftarrow true$
26: $\quad\quad$ **end if**
27: $\quad\quad$ **if** not $M[k, candidate]$ **then**
28: $\quad\quad\quad$ **if** $candidate \neq k$ **then**
29: $\quad\quad\quad\quad wrong \leftarrow true$
30: $\quad\quad\quad$ **end if**
31: $\quad\quad$ **end if**
32: $\quad\quad k \leftarrow k + 1$
33: $\quad\quad$ **if** not wrong **then**
34: $\quad\quad\quad celebrity \leftarrow candidate$
35: $\quad\quad$ **else**
36: $\quad\quad\quad celebrity \leftarrow 0$ $\quad\quad\quad\quad\quad\quad\quad\quad\quad\quad$ ▷ no celebrity
37: $\quad\quad$ **end if**
38: $\quad$ **end while**
39: **end function**

Complexity

At most *3(n - 1)* questions will be asked :

1. *n - 1* questions in the first phase to eliminate *n - 1* persons, and then

2. at most *2(n - 1)* questions to verify that the candidate is indeed a celebrity.

Notice that the size of the input is not *n*, but rather *n(n - 1)*, which is the number of entries of the matrix. This solution shows that it is possible to

1.18. The Celebrity Problem

identify a celebrity by looking at only $O(n)$ entries in the adjacency matrix, even though a priori the solution may be sensitive to each of the $n(n-1)$ entries.

Remarks

The key idea in this elegant solution is to reduce the size of the problem from n to $n-1$ in a clever way. Do not start by simply considering an *arbitrary* input of size $n-1$ and attempting to extend it. Select a *particular* input of size $n-1$.

Uniqueness of Celebrity

In a set S of n people, there can be only one celebrity.

Assume for contradiction that there are two celebrities C_1 and C_2. By definition of celebrity, everyone knows a celebrity. Therefore $\forall \alpha \in S - \{C_1\}$, α knows C_1. Because $C_2 \in S - \{C_1\}$, C_2 knows C_1. But celebrities don't know anyone. Therefore, C_2 is not a celebrity. This contradicts our assumption that C_2 was a celebrity. Therefore the assumption is false. Therefore, we cannot have two celebrities.

The first algorithm is based on a brute-force approach. We essentially look at each pair of people to see if they know each other. If we find a person that knows nobody but is known by all the others, that person is a celebrity:

Algorithm 34 Celebrity Algorithm Brute Force

1: **Input** : set S of n people
2: **Output** : a celebrity, or *no celebrity* if there is no celebrity.
3: **for all** $A \in S$ **do**
4:     **for all** $B \in S - \{A\}$ **do**
5:         **if** A knows B **then**
6:             *Break out of inner loop*
7:         **else**
8:             $C \leftarrow A$
9:         **end if**
10:     **end for**
11: **end for**
12: **for all** $\alpha \in S$ **do**
13:     **if** α does not know C **then**
14:         **return** "No Celebrity"
15:     **end if**
16:     **return** C
17: **end for**

This algorithm runs in $O(n^2)$ time. Can we do better? Yes, we can. The following algorithm is based on the observation that by asking a single question, we can eliminate a person as a possible celebrity. So, if I ask "Does A know B?" and the answer is "no", then B cannot be a celebrity, because a celebrity must be known by everybody else. On the other hand, if the answer is "yes", then A cannot be a celebrity because a celebrity knows nobody. Therefore, with a single question "Does A know B?", we learn something no matter what the answer to the question is. This leads to this algorithm:

1.18. The Celebrity Problem

Algorithm 35 Celebrity Algorithm Optimized

1: **Input** : set S of n people
2: **Output** : a celebrity, or *no celebrity* if there is no celebrity.
3: $Candidates \leftarrow S$
4: **while** $|Candidates| > 0$ **do**
5:     Choose A and B $\mid A \in Candidates$ **and** $B \in Candidates$
6:     **if** A knows B **then**
7:         $Candidates \leftarrow Candidates - \{A\}$
8:     **else**
9:         $Candidates \leftarrow Candidates - \{B\}$
10:     **end if**
11: **end while**
12: Let C be the only remaining element of $Candidates$
13: **for all** $\alpha \in S - \{C\}$ **do**
14:     **if** α does not know C **or** C knows α **then**
15:         **return** "No Celebrity"
16:     **end if**
17:     **return** C
18: **end for**

The first loop here runs $n - 1$ times because every time around the loop we eliminate a possibility (and we stop when there is one possibility left). The second loop runs for $n - 1$ times also because we let α take on $|S| - 1$ different values. Therefore the overall running time is in $O(n)$.

The elimination phase maintains a list of possible celebrities. Initially it contains all n people. In each iteration, we delete one person from the list. We exploit the following key observation: *if person 1 knows person 2, then person 1 is not a celebrity; if person 1 does not know person 2, then person 2 is not a celebrity.* Thus, by asking person 1 if he knows person 2, we can eliminate either person 1 or person 2 from the list of possible celebrities. We can use this idea repeatedly to eliminate all people but one, say person. We now verify by brute force whether is a celebrity: for every other person i, we ask person whether he knows person i, and we ask persons i whether they know person. If person always answers no, and the other people always answer yes, the we declare person as the celebrity. Otherwise, we conclude there is no celebrity in this group.

Correctness

During the elimination phase, we maintain the invariant that is there exists a celebrity, then the celebrity is on the list. We can prove this by induction on the number of iterations. Thus, when elimination phase ends, either person is a celebrity or there is no celebrity. The elimination phase requires exactly $n - 1$ questions, since each question reduces the size on the list by 1. In the verification phase, we ask $n - 1$ questions, and we ask the other $n - 1$ people one question. This phase requires at most $2(n - 1)$ questions, possibly fewer is is not a celebrity. So the total number of questions is $3(n - 1)$. To efficiently implement the elimination phase, we maintain a queue that contains the remaining celebrities. Initially, we insert all n people to the queue. At each iteration we remove the top two elements off the queue, say v and w, and ask v whether he (or she) knows w. Depending on the outcome, we either insert v or w at the end of the queue. Each queue operation rakes $\theta(1)$ time, so the whole process takes $\theta(n)$ time.

1.18. The Celebrity Problem

An even better solution

We note that it is possible to save an additional $\log^2 n$ questions in the verification phase by not repeating any questions we already asked during the elimination phase. By maintaining the elements in a queue, the celebrity is involved (i.e., either asked or asked about) at least $\log^2 n$ questions during the elimination phase. This explains why we chose a queue instead of a stack. Also, it is not hard to see that any algorithm must ask at least $2(n-1)$ questions if there exists a celebrity, since we must verify that the celebrity does not know anyone, and that everyone knows the celebrity.

C++11 Implementation

Program 1.29: Finding Celebrity Program

```
#include <iostream>
#include <stack>
#include <array>

template <int m, int n>
using CelebrityMatrix =
    std::array<std::array<bool, n>, m>;

// Person with 2 is the celebrity
CelebrityMatrix<4, 4> KnowCeleb =
    {
        0, 0, 1, 0,
        0, 0, 1, 0,
        0, 0, 0, 0,
        0, 0, 1, 0
    };

template<int Size>
int FindCelebrity()
{
    // Handle trivial case of size = 2
    std::stack<int> person_stack;

    int i;
    int C; // Celebrity

    i = 0;
    while(i < Size)
    {
        person_stack.push(i);
        i = i + 1;
    }

    int A = person_stack.top();
    person_stack.pop();

    int B = person_stack.top();
    person_stack.pop();

    while(person_stack.size() != 1)
    {
        if( KnowCeleb[A][B] )
        {
            A = person_stack.top();
            person_stack.pop();
```

```cpp
46          }
47          else
48          {
49              B = person_stack.top();
50              person_stack.pop();
51          }
52      }
53
54      // Potential celebrity candidate
55      C = person_stack.top();
56      person_stack.pop();
57
58      // Last candidate was not examined,
59      // it leads one excess comparison (optimize)
60      if(KnowCeleb[C][B])
61          C = B;
62
63      if(KnowCeleb[C][A])
64          C = A;
65
66      i = 0;
67      while(i < Size)
68      {
69          if(C != i)
70          person_stack.push(i);
71          i = i + 1;
72      }
73
74      while(!person_stack.empty())
75      {
76          i = person_stack.top();
77          person_stack.pop();
78
79          // C must not know i
80          if(KnowCeleb[C][i])
81              return -1;
82
83          // i must know C
84          if(!KnowCeleb[i][C])
85              return -1;
86      }
87
88      return C;
89 }
90
91 int main()
92 {
93      int id = FindCelebrity<4>();
94
95      id == -1 ? std::cout << "No celebrity" : std::cout <<
           "Celebrity ID " << id;
96 }
```

1.19 Transport Problem

Problem Description

Let $C_1, C_2, ..., C_n$ be n cities placed along a straight line. Let d_i be the distance between C_i and C_{i+1}, for $1 \leq i < n$. Initially each city C_i possesses some amount $x_i \in \mathbb{R}$ of a certain resource, say water. If $x_i < 0$, what C_i

1.19. Transport Problem

possesses is not real water but deficiency of water, e.g. if C_i has -5.5 units of water and afterwards we transport 6 units of water to it, it is going to have +0.5 units. Each city C_i needs some amount $l_i \in \mathbb{R}^+$ of water. We say C_i is satisfied $\iff l_i \leq x_i$.

Water can be transported between any two adjacent cities but the transportation is lossy: if we start transporting amount z from C_i to C_{i+1} or vice versa, the amount that is going to be delivered is $max\{z-d_i, 0\}$.

Design an algorithm that outputs TRUE, in case there is a way to transport water between the cities so that every city is satisfied, or FALSE, otherwise. Assume that the amount of water in any city is constant unless water is transported to, or from, it. Prove the correctness of your algorithm and analyze its time complexity.

Solution

Define d_n to be zero. Consider the following algorithm:

Algorithm 36 Transport Algorithm

1: **function** TRANSPORT$(x_1, \ldots, x_n, d_1, \ldots, d_n, l_1, \ldots, l_n)$
2:     $s \leftarrow 0$
3:     **for** $i \leftarrow 1$ **to** n **do**
4:        $\Delta \leftarrow x_i - l_i$
5:        **if** $s + \Delta \geq 0$ **then**
6:           $s \leftarrow max(s + \Delta - d_i, 0)$
7:        **else**
8:           $s \leftarrow s + \Delta - d_i$
9:        **end if**
10:    **end for**
11:    **if** $s \geq 0$ **then**
12:        **return** TRUE
13:    **else**
14:        **return** FALSE
15:    **end if**
16: **end function**

For any i such that $1 \leq i \leq n$, let A_i be the subarray of cities $[C_1, C_2, \ldots, C_i]$. A_i is called *good* if there is a way to satisfy its cities by transporting water only between them. Otherwise, A_i is called *wanting*. Suppose q is a positive amount. When we say A_i is q-*redundant* we mean that:

- A_i is good and it remains good even if the amount in C_i is decreased by q units beforehand.

- However, if the amount in A_i is decreased by $q + \epsilon$ units beforehand, for any $\epsilon > 0$, A_i becomes *wanting*.

When we say A_i is isolated we mean that:

- A_i is good.

- However, if the amount in A_i is decreased by $d_i + \epsilon$ units beforehand, for any $\epsilon > 0$, A_i becomes wanting.

When we say A_i is q-*deficient* we mean:

1.19. Transport Problem

- A_i is wanting but it becomes good if the amount in C_i is increased by q units beforehand.
- However, if the amount in A_i is increased by $q-\epsilon$ units beforehand, for any $\epsilon > 0$, A_i remains wanting.

Note the distinction between isolated and redundant: isolatedness is not a special case of redundancy although it may sound like being a special case, namely for $q = d_i$. Now we point out the difference. If A_i is d_i-redundant then it is good and d_i is precisely equal to the largest quantity that can transported out of C_i beforehand (keeping A_i good). So, d_i is a threshold value. On the other hand, if A_i is isolated then it is good and with certainty transporting any amount $\geq d_i$ out of C_i ruins its goodness; the key observation is, it is possible that transporting even the smallest quantity out of C_i may ruin the goodness : the definition of isolatedness allows that. So, in the case with isolatedness, there is no certain threshold quantity that can safely be transported out of C_i.

Please note that

$$\text{Algorithm TRANSPORT returns TRUE} \iff A_n \text{ is good}.$$

Proof

The following is a loop invariant for the **for-loop** (lines 3-10):
Every time the execution of TRANSPORT is at line 3,

- if s > 0 then A_{i-1} is (s + d_{i-1})-redundant.
- if s = 0 then A_{i-1} is isolated.
- if s < 0 then A_{i-1} is | s + d_{i-1} |-deficient.

Basis

The first time the execution is at line 3, i equals 1 and so A_{i-1} is empty. The empty subarray of cities is vacuously isolated because it is vacuously good (no deficiency) and its water : of which there is none : cannot be decreased by any amount. On the other hand, s equals 0 because of the assignment at line 2. So, the invariant holds.

Maintenance

Assume the claim holds at a certain execution of line 3 and the for loop is to be executed at least once more. Δ is set to $x_i - l_i$ at line 4. Let us call the value of s prior to the execution of line 6 or line 8, sold , and the value of s after that execution, s_{new}.

Case I Suppose $s_{old} > 0$. By the assumption, A_{i-1} is ($s_{old} + d_{i-1}$)-redundant. That means we can deliver s_{old} units of water to C_i by transporting $s_{old} + d_i - 1$ out of $C_i - 1$ to C_i (losing d_{i-1} quantity along the way), A_{i-1} remaining good. However, if we transport any more water out of C_{i-1} to C_i , A_{i-1} becomes wanting. So, C_i can get at most s_{old} water more (keeping A_{i-1} good).

1. Suppose $s_{old} + \Delta \geq 0$. Then the assignment at line 6 takes place. The following two facts:

1.19. Transport Problem

a) A_{i-1} is good and C_i can get s_{old} water more, A_{i-1} staying good.

b) $s_{old} + \Delta \geq 0$.

imply A_i is good. Furthermore, $s_{old} + \Delta$ is the surplus in C_i that can be transported out of C_i (towards C_{i+1}), keeping A_i good; that is the threshold value, anything more out of C_i makes A_i wanting. So, A_i is $(s_{old} + \Delta)$-redundant.

- Suppose $s_{old} + \Delta - d_i > 0$. Then $s_{new} = s_{old} + \Delta - d_i$. Now we prove A_i is $(s_{new} + d_i)$-redundant. We know A_i is good and $(s_{old} + \Delta)$-redundant. Observe that $s_{old} + \Delta = s_{old} + \Delta - d_i + d_i = s_{new} + d_i$ and conclude A_i is $(s_{new} + d_i)$-redundant. The next time the execution is at line 3, i gets incremented by one. With respect to the new value of i, it is the case that A_{i-1} is $(s + d_{i-1})$-redundant.

- Suppose $s_{old} + \Delta - d_i = 0$. Then $s_{new} = 0$. Recall that A_i is good. Note that $s_{old} + \Delta - d_i - \epsilon < 0$ for any $\epsilon > 0$. It follows A_i is isolated. As noted before, A_i can be both isolated and redundant. The next time the execution is at line 3, i gets incremented by one. With respect to the new value of i, it is the case that A_{i-1} is isolated.

2. Suppose $s_{old} + \Delta < 0$, which means $\Delta < 0$ since $s_{old} > 0$. But then A_i is wanting because, as we already pointed out, if C_i gets any more water than s_{old}, A_{i-1} becomes wanting. In order to make A_i good, at least $|s_{old} + \Delta|$ has to be transported into C_i. By definition, A_i is $|s_{old} + \Delta|$-deficient. Having in mind that $s_{old} + \Delta = s_{old} + \Delta - d_i + d_i = s_{new} + d_i$, it follows A_i is $|s_{new} + d_i|$-deficient. The next time the execution is at line 3, i gets incremented by one. With respect to the new value of i, it is the case that A_{i-1} is $|s_{new} + d_{i-1}|$-deficient.

Case II Suppose $s_{old} = 0$. By the induction hypothesis, A_{i-1} is closed. That means A_{i-1} is good but we cannot transport $d_{i-1} + \epsilon$ units of water out of C_{i-1} (towards C_i), for any $\epsilon > 0$, and keep A_{i-1} good. So, no amount of water from A_{i-1} can go into C_i if we are to keep A_{i-1} good. It follows the status of A_i depends entirely on Δ and d_i.

1. Suppose $s_{old} + \Delta \geq 0 \iff \Delta \geq 0$. Then the assignment at line 6 takes place.

    a) Suppose $\Delta - d_i > 0$. Then $s_{new} = \Delta - d_i$. A_i is good and it is possible to transport Δ water out of C_i (towards C_{i+1}), keeping A_i good; furthermore, Δ is the threshold value, any more will make A_i wanting. Then A_i is Δ-redundant, i.e. $(s_{new} + d_i)$-redundant. The next time the execution is at line 3, i gets incremented by one. With respect to the new value of i, it is the case that A_{i-1} is $(s + d_{i-1})$-redundant.

    b) Suppose $\Delta - d_i = 0$. Then $s_{new} = 0$. Clearly, A_i is good but no water can be transported out of C_i, if we are to keep A_i good. It follows A_i is isolated. The next time the execution is at line 3, i gets incremented by one. With respect to the new value of i, it is the case that A_{i-1} is isolated.

2. Suppose $s_{old} + \Delta < 0 \iff \Delta < 0$. Then the assignment at line 8 takes place and $s_{new} = \Delta - d_i$, which is a negative amount since $d_i > 0$. Clearly, A_i is wanting. It becomes good if at least $|\Delta|$ water is transported into C_i; any less amount will keep it wanting. By definition, A_i is $|\Delta|$-deficient, i.e. $|s_{new} + d_i|$-deficient. The next time

1.19. Transport Problem

the execution is at line 3, i gets incremented by one. With respect to the new value of i, it is the case that A_{i-1} is $|s_{new} + d_i - 1|$-deficient.

Case III Suppose $s_{old} < 0$. By the induction hypothesis, A_{i-1} is $|s_{old} + d_{i-1}|$-deficient. That means A_{i-1} is wanting and unless we deliver at least $|s_{old} + d_i - 1|$ units of water into C_{i-1}, it stays wanting. To deliver at least $|s_{old} + d_i - 1|$ units of water into C_{i-1} means to transport at least $|s_{old} + d_i - 1| + d_i - 1$ units of water out of C_i (towards C_{i-1}) in order to compensate for the loss of d_{i-1} units along the way.

We claim that $|s_{old}| > d_i - 1$. To see why, note that the negative value sold was assigned to s during the previous execution of the *for*-loop at line 8. Now we discuss the previous iteration, so let us call i_{old} the value of the variable i then. In order to reach line 8, it must have been the case that $s + \Delta$ was negative. But $-d_{i_{old}}$ at line 8 was negative, too. It follows the absolute value of what was assigned to s at line 8 was strictly larger than $d_{i_{old}}$.

In other words, $|s_{old}| > d_{i_{old}}$. Finally, note that i got incremented by one since the previous iteration, so $i_{old} = i - 1$, with respect to the current i.

Having proved that $|s_{old}| > d_i - 1$ and having in mind that $s_{old} < 0$, it is obvious that $|s_{old} + d_{i-1}| + d_{i-1} = |s_{old}|$. So, the threshold amount of water to transport out of C_i (towards C_{i-1}) to make A_{i-1} good is $|s_{old}|$, anything less will keep A_{i-1} wanting.

1. Suppose $s_{old} + \Delta \geq 0$. Then the assignment at line 6 takes place.

   a) Suppose $s_{old} + \Delta - d_i > 0$. then $s_{new} = s_{old} + \Delta - d_i$. Since s_{old} is negative and $-d_i$ is negative, it must be the case that Δ is positive; furthermore, it must be the case that $\Delta > |s_{old}| + d_i$. Now we show A_i is $(s_{old} + \Delta)$-redundant. There are Δ units of water in C_i. Transport $|s_{old}|$ units to C_{i-1}, thus making A_{i-1} good. That amounts to reducing the water in C_i down to $s_{old} + \Delta$ units (recall that s_{old} is negative so $s_{old} + \Delta$ is smaller than Δ, still being a positive quantity). Since $|s_{old}|$ is a threshold quantity, there is no way to have more than $s_{old} + \Delta$ units in C_i and making $A_i - 1$ good.

   Since $s_{old} + \Delta$, the remaining quantity in C_i, is nonnegative, and A_{i-1} is good, A_i is $(s_{old} + \Delta)$-redundant. In other words, A_i is $(s_{new} + d_i)$-redundant. The next time the execution is at line 3, i gets incremented by one. With respect to the new value of i, it is the case that A_{i-1} is $(s + d_{i-1})$-redundant.

   b) Suppose $s_{old} + \Delta - d_t = 0$. Then $s_{new} = 0$. We prove that A_i is closed. Note that the water in C_i is $\Delta = -s_{old} + d_i$, $-s_{old}$ being a positive amount, and A_{i-1} is wanting. We transport $|s_{old}|$ units of water from C_i back to C_{t-1}, making A_{i-1} good. We know that transporting anything less will keep A_{i-1} wanting. After the transportation C_i will be satisfied, too, having d_i water in it. So, A_i is good after the transportation. However, it is not possible to make A_{i-1} good and keep C_i satisfied and deliver ϵ units of water into C_{i+1}, for any $\epsilon > 0$, using the water in C_i. It follows A_i is isolated. The next time the execution is at line 3, i gets incremented by one. With respect to the new value of i, it is the case that A_{i-1} is isolated.

2. Suppose $s_{old} + \Delta < 0$. Then the assignment at line 8 takes place and $s_{new} = s_{old} + \Delta - d_i$, which is a negative amount since $d_i > 0$. We prove

A_i is $\mid s_{old}+\Delta \mid$-deficient. Recall that A_{i-1} is wanting and unless $\mid s_{old} \mid$ units are transported into C_{i-1}, it remains waning. The quantity in C_i, viz. Δ, may be positive, zero, or negative, we do not know that; what matters is that Δ decremented by $\mid s_{old} \mid$, i.e. $s_{old} + \Delta$, is negative : that fact implies A_i is wanting. Furthermore, in order to make A_i good, the amount of water in C_i must be increased by at least $\mid s_{old} + \Delta \mid$, any smaller increase leaves A_i wanting. To see why that is true, note that under the current assumptions, $\Delta- \mid s_{old} \mid + \mid s_{old} + \Delta \mid = 0$. And the latter is true since

$$\forall x, y \in \mathbb{R} \mid x < 0 \text{ and } x+y < 0, y- \mid x \mid + \mid x+y \mid = 0.$$

Since $\mid s_{old} + \Delta \mid$ is the threshold amount to be added to the water in C_i in order to make A_i good, by definition A_i is $\mid s_{old} + \Delta \mid$-deficient. Clearly, that is equivalent to saying that A_i is $\mid s_{new} - d_i \mid$-deficient. The next time the execution is at line 3, i gets incremented by one. With respect to the new value of i, it is the case that A_{i-1} is $\mid s_{new} + d_{i-1} \mid$-deficient.

Termination

Consider the moment when the execution is at line 3 for the last time. Clearly, i equals n+1. If the current s is non-negative then $A_{i-1} = A_n$ is either s-redundant (recall then d_n is defined to be zero) or isolated, therefore it is good. Accordingly, the returned value (line 12) is TRUE. If s is negative then it is wanting. Accordingly, the returned value (line 14) is FALSE.

The time complexity is obviously $\Theta(n)$.

1.20 Find Length of the rope

Problem Description

A rope ran over a pulley. At one end was a monkey. At the other end was a weight. The two remained in equilibrium. The weight of the rope was one-quarter of a pound per foot, and the ages of the monkey and the monkey's mother amounted to four years. The weight of the monkey and the weight of the rope were equal to one-and-a-half of the age of the monkey's mother.

The weight of the weight exceeded the weight of the rope by as many pounds as the monkey was years old when the monkey's mother was twice as old as the monkey's brother was when the monkey's mother was half as old as the monkey's brother will be when the monkey's brother is three times as old as the monkey's mother was when the monkey's mother was three times as old as the monkey was in the previous paragraph.

The monkey's mother was twice as old as the monkey was when the monkey's mother was half as old as the monkey will be when the monkey is three times as old as the monkey's mother was when the monkey's mother was three times as old as the monkey was in the first paragraph.

The age of the monkey's mother exceeded the age of the monkey's brother by the same amount as the age of the monkey's brother exceeded the age of the monkey.

What was the length of the rope?

1.20. Find Length of the rope

Solution

Actually, it's not that difficult to solve the problem once we understand it : when we know how to model it with appropriate equations. The second hardest part here is simply understanding all of the information given in the description of the problem. The hardest part is undoubtedly having the patience to understand the information. Patience is a prerequisite for effective problem solving.

Let's first introduce some variables:

- x: age of monkey,
- y: age of monkey's brother,
- z: age of monkey's mother,
- W: weight of the weight, and
- r: the length of the rope.

Now we can translate each sentence of the puzzle into *equations*. It would be easier if we *read* the puzzle from the *bottom up*, i.e. , if we start interpreting it from the last paragraph. The fourth (last) paragraph of the puzzle says simply that

$$z - y = y - x \qquad (1.4)$$

This is straightforward and doesn't require any further comments.

Now, let's try the sentences of the third paragraph. *The monkey's mother was twice as old as the monkey was* ... can be written as

$$z - A = 2(x - A) \qquad (1.5)$$

where A denotes some (not necessarily integer) number of years, as the sentence refers to the past. Similarly, we can interpret the remaining sentences of this paragraph. The third paragraph says that for some A, B , and C, the following equalities hold:

z-A =2(x - A),
z-A = 0.5(x + B),
x+B = 3(z - C), and
z-C = 3x

This can be simplified into

$$4z = 13x \qquad (1.6)$$

The second paragraph is very much the same as the third and can be interpreted in the same way. (Note that the weight of the rope was $\frac{r}{4}$.) It says that for some A, B, C, and D, the following equations hold:

$W - \frac{r}{4} = x - A$
$z - A = 2(y - B)$
$z - B = 0.5(y + C)$
$y + C = 3(z - D)$, and
$z - D = 3x$

$\Longrightarrow$

$$W - r/4 = 11x - 2z \qquad (1.7)$$

The first paragraph provides more information. First, the ages of the monkey and the monkey's mother amounted to four years:

$$x + z = 4 \qquad (1.8)$$

The weight of the monkey and the weight of the rope were equal to one-and-a-half of the age of monkey's mother:

$$W + r/4 = 3z/2 \tag{1.9}$$

The weight of the monkey is W, and the monkey and the weight remained in equilibrium. From equations 1.4, 1.6 , and 1.8 we obtain

```
x = 16/17,
y = 2, and
z = 52/17.
```

Then equations 1.7 and 1.9 give
$W - \frac{r}{4} = \frac{72}{17}$, and
$W + \frac{r}{4} = \frac{78}{17}$,
$\implies r = \frac{12}{17}$.

Thus the length of the rope was $\frac{12}{17}$ feet .

1.21 Switch Bulb Problem

Problem Description

There are three switches outside a room that control three electrical bulbs inside the room. They each hang on a long wire so you have to be careful not to bump into them when you enter the room! You know that there is a one-to-one connection between the switches and the bulbs. Each switch controls precisely one bulb. You know also that the switches are in the *off* position and the room is dark. Now we shut the door and you can't see anything inside the room.

Your task is to figure out which switch connects to which bulb, but you face a rather imposing constraint: you only get to make *one* trial. You can set the switches any way you like and then you have to enter the room. You can examine the room and based on this examination you have to be able to tell us which switch controls which bulb. Note that you're not allowed to go back out and touch any of the switches again after you've entered the room. You can do anything you like with the switches, but once you open the door to the room, that's it.

Solution

At first you might think that this is an impossible problem! After all, if you don't touch any of the switches, then it would be pointless to enter the room, since you already know it is dark in the room and there will be no way to figure out which switch goes with which bulb. So you have to do something with the switches. But what?

If you flip only one switch to the *on* position and then open the door, certainly one of the bulbs will be lit, but you won't be able to distinguish which of the two remaining switches goes with which of the two remaining bulbs.

Similarly, if you flip some pair of switches to the *on* position, you'll know from the light that remains unlit which switch it corresponds with, but you won't be able to differentiate between the two bulbs that are lit and the two switches that you flipped. What a dilemma.

The crux of the issue here is to *start with the right model*. The preceding thinking relies on a model that captures only one attribute of light bulbs, namely whether they are *on* or *off*. But light bulbs have other attributes. Like what?

How about temperature?

There was nothing in the description above that restricted our attention just to the illumination of the bulb. In fact, that's really only part of your becoming illuminated about the problem.

Once we include the bulbs' temperatures in our model, the problem really is quite easy to solve. All you have to do is

1. set two switches to the *on* position,
2. wait a few minutes, then
3. switch one of these to the *off* position and
4. enter the room.

When you do, one of the bulbs will be *on*, and the other two will be *off*. One of those two unlit bulbs, however, is going to be *hot* and that does make it very easy to give the proper answer. But watch your fingers and don't get burned!

1.22 In, On or Out

Problem Description

We consider a point x and a convex polygon u in the plane. The vertices are assumed to be given clockwise. Furthermore, no three vertices are collinear. Develop an algorithm that determines whether the point x is in the interior, on the boundary, or in the exterior of the polygon u. The algorithm should, moreover, be such that the number of computational steps required is proportional to the logarithm of the number of vertices of the polygon.

Solution

For a simple polygon $\mathbb{Z}$, we use the notations $in.\mathbb{Z}$, $on.\mathbb{Z}$, and $out.\mathbb{Z}$ as shorthands for the conditions

- x is in the interior of $\mathbb{Z}$,
- x is on the boundary of $\mathbb{Z}$,
- x is in the exterior of $\mathbb{Z}$ respectively.

Furthermore, we assume the availability of a three-valued function $p.e$ yielding the clockwise position of the point x with respect to a directed line e:

- $p.e = 1$ if x is on the clockwise side of e,
- $p.e = 0$ if x is on e, and
- $p.e = -1$ if x is on the counterclockwise side of e.

1.22. In, On or Out

To begin with, we give an algorithm that is linear in the number of vertices of u. With e in the domain of the clockwise directed boundary lines of u, we have on account of $u's$ convexity

- $in.u \equiv e : p.e = 1$
- $on.u \equiv e : p.e \geq 0 \land e : p.e = 0$
- $out.u \equiv e : p.e = -1$

The position of x with respect to u is now computed by computing the minimum of the p values : $in.u$, $on.u$, and $out.u$ then correspond to this minimum being equal to 1, 0, and -1 respectively.

For a logarithmic solution we propose to bisect the polygon until a triangle is left. The question then is how to bisect precisely and under control of which invariant.

Let V be a convex polygon (no three vertices collinear, and the vertices being given clockwise, but we will not repeat that all the time), with at least four vertices. For y and z two nonadjacent vertices of V we conclude on account of $V's$ convexity that the interior of the line segment yz is in the interior of V. The line connecting y and z divides V into two convex polygons V_0 and V_1. Now we can state

$in.V \equiv in.V_0 \lor in.V_1 \lor x$ is in the interior of the line segment yz
$on.V \equiv (on.V_0 \lor on.V_1) \land \neg(\text{x is in the interior of the line segment } yz)$
$$out.V \equiv out.V_0 \land out.V_1$$

Please note that $\neg$ stands for *negation*.

From these three relations we conclude that the notion *out* is by far the simplest and is likely to give rise to the fewest case analyses in the bisection procedure. Therefore we choose as an invariant relation $P_0 \land P_1$, given by

- P_0 : V is a convex polygon with at least three vertices, and all vertices are vertices from u.
- P_1 : $out.u \equiv out.V$

The corresponding program becomes :

Algorithm 37 triangle analysis

1: $V \leftarrow u$
2: **while** the number of vertices of $V \neq 3$ **do**
3:    select y and z
4:    **if** B_0 **then**
5:       $V \leftarrow V_0$
6:    **else if** B_1 **then**
7:       $V \leftarrow V_1$
8:    **end if**
9: **end while**

The invariance of P_0 follows from the way in which V_0 and V_1 are constructed from V, y, and z. The invariance of P_1 has to follow from a proper choice of B_0 and B_1. We compute B_0. In order that the assignment $V \leftarrow V_0$ establishes P_1 the precondition should imply

1.22. In, On or Out

$$out.u \equiv out.V_0$$

A precondition is

$$out.u \equiv out.V_0 \wedge out.V_1$$

so that for B_0 the choice

$$out.V_0 \equiv out.V_0 \vee out.V_1$$

or, equivalently,

$$out.V_0 \implies out.V_1$$

will do. With the assumption that the line segment from y to z is a clockwise edge of V_0 this condition is implied by

$$p.(\text{line from } y \text{ to } z) \geq 0$$

By symmetry, we take for B_1

$$p.(\text{line from } z \text{ to } y) \geq 0$$

Next we give the triangle analysis. With the linear algorithm we compute $in.V$, $on.V$, and $out.V$ for the triangle V. If $out.V$ holds, then, on account of P_1, also $out.V$ holds. If $in.V$ holds, then, on account of P_0 and $u's$ convexity, also $in.u$ holds. If $on.V$ holds (i.e. each edge of the triangle has a $p-value \geq 0$, and one or two $p-values = 0$) we distinguish two cases:

1. two edges have a $p-value = 0$; x then coincides with the vertex joining these two edges, hence it coincides with a vertex of u, hence $on.u$ holds.

2. one edge has a $p-value = 0$; x then is in the interior of that edge. If that edge is an edge of u, $on.u$ holds. If that edge is not an edge of u, it is an edge between two nonadjacent vertices of u, so that (u is convex) $in.u$ holds.

Remarks

First we observe that the line from y to z is a clockwise boundary line of V_0, the line from z to y is a clockwise boundary line of V_1, and p.(line from y to z) = -p.(line from z to y).

Secondly we consider two cases for p.(line from y to z) ≥ 0:

1. p.(line from y to z) = 1, hence p.(line from z to y) = -1, hence (because line from z to y is a clockwise boundary line of V_1) $out.V_1$, hence $out.V_0 \implies out.V_1$

2. p.(line from y to z) = 0. Again we distinguish two cases

    a) x on the line segment yz (bounds included), hence $on.V_0$ and $on.V_1$, hence $\neg out.V_0$ and $\neg out.V_1$, hence $out.V_0 \implies out.V_1$

    b) x not on the line segment yz, hence (because line between y and z is a boundary line of V_1) $out.V_1$, hence $out.V_0 \implies out.V_1$

1.23 The problem of the balanced segments

Problem Description

For a sequence $X(i : 0 \leq i < N), N \geq 0$, of 0's and 1's, a balanced segment $X(i : p \leq i < q)$: of length $q - p$ is defined as a segment such that

$$0 \leq p \leq q \leq N \wedge (i : p \leq i < q : X(i) = 0) = (i : p \leq i < q : X(i) = 1)$$

It is requested to construct a program computing the maximum length of a balanced segment of $X(i : 0 \leq i < N)$.

Solution

Using standard strategies, we develop

```
1: n:int
2: n ← 0
3: r ← 0
4: Invariant P₀ : 0 ≤ n ≤ N ∧ r = the maximum length of a balanced
   segment of X(i : 0 ≤ i < n)
5: while n ≠ N do
6:    l:int
7:    S {l = the minimum solution of the equation h : 0 ≤ h ∧ (X(i : h ≤
      i < n + 1) is balanced) }
8:    n ← n + 1
9:    r ← r max(n - l)
10: end while
11: print(r)
```

The equation mentioned in the postcondition of S has at least one solution, viz. $n+1$. For the discovery of its minimum solution we rewrite the equation, using the definiti where on of balancedness and using the abbreviation

$$D(p) : (i : 0 \leq i < p : X(i) = 0) - (i : 0 \leq i < p : X(i) = 1),$$

into

$$h : 0 \leq h \wedge D(h) = D(n+1).$$

Our interest in the minimum solution can, in terms of the sequence D, be phrased as our interest in the *leftmost* occurrence of each D-value. Hence we strengthen P_0 with $P_1 \wedge P_2 \wedge P_3$,

- $P_1 : d = D(n)$
- $P_2 : (h : 0 \leq h < n + 1 : m < D(h) < M)$
- $P_3 : (s : m < s < M : C(s) =$ the minimum solution of $h : 0 \leq h \wedge D(h) = s)$,

so that the required value of l, mentioned in the postcondition of S, is related to C by

$$(P_1 \wedge P_2 \wedge P_3)(n+1/n) \implies l = C(d),$$

1.24. The problem of the most isolated villages

In checking the program text below the reader is suggested to check the invariances of P_1, P_2, and P_3 in succession. One hint is given for the invariance of P_3

```
 1:  n , d, m, M : int
 2:  C(i : −N ≤ i ≤ N): array of int
 3:  n ← 0; d ← 0; m ← −1; M ← 1; C : (0) = 0; r ← 0
 4:  while n ≠ N do
 5:      if X(n) == 0 then
 6:          d ← d + 1
 7:      else if X(n) == 1 then
 8:          d ← d − 1
 9:      end if                                    ▷ P₁(n + 1/n)
10:      if m < d ∧ d < M then
11:          skip
12:      else if m == d then                       ▷ P₁(n + 1/n) ∧ P₂ ∧ P₃ ∧ m = d
13:          C : (m) = n + 1
14:          m ← m − 1                             ▷ P₃(n + 1/n)
15:      else if d == M then
16:          C : (M) = n + 1
17:          M ← M + 1
18:      end if
19:      n ← n + 1
20:      r ← r max (n - C(d))
21: end while
22: print(r)
```

Hint

wp("C:(m) = n + 1; m ← m − 1", $P_3(n + 1/n)$)
= $\{[P_3 \equiv P_3(n + 1/n)]\}$
wp("C:(m) = n + 1; ← m − 1, P_3
= { definition of P_3, and predicate calculus}
$P_3 \wedge m + 1 =$ the minimum solution of $h : 0 \leq h \wedge D(h) = m$
$\implies$ { from $P_2, (h : 0 \leq hn + 1 : D(h) \neq m)$}
$P_2 \wedge P_3 \wedge n + 1 =$ the minimum solution of $h : n + 1 \leq h \wedge D(h) = m$
implies$P_2 \wedge P_3 \wedge m = d \wedge n + 1 =$ the minimum solution of $h : n + 1 \leq h \wedge D(h) = d$
$\implies$ {from $P_1(n + 1/n), d = d(n + 1)$}
$P_1(n + 1/n) \wedge P_2 \wedge P_3 \wedge m = d$

1.24 The problem of the most isolated villages

Problem Description

We consider n villages ($n > 1$), numbered from 0 through $n − 1$; for $0 \leq i < n$ and $0 \leq j < n$, a computable function $f(i, j)$ is given, satisfying for some given positive constant

$$\text{for } i \neq j : 0 < f(i, j) < M$$
$$\text{for } i = j : f(i, j) = M$$

For the ith village, its isolation degree $id(i)$ is given by

1.24. The problem of the most isolated villages

$$id(i) = \text{minimum } f(i,j)$$

Here $f(i,j)$ can be interpreted as the distance from i to j; the rule $f(i,j) = M$ has been added for the purpose of the above simplification.

We are requested to determine the set of maximally isolated villages, i.e. the set of all values of k such that

$$\forall h : 0 \leq h < n : id(h) \leq id(k)$$

The program is expected to deliver this set of values as

$$miv(miv.lob), \ldots, miv(miv.hib)$$

Note that eventually all values $1 \leq miv.dom \leq n$ are possible.

A very simple and straightforward program computes the n isolation degrees in succession and keeps track of their maximum value found thus far. On account of the bounds for $f(i,j)$ we can take as the minimum of an empty set the value M and as the maximum of an empty set 0.

```
 1:  max ← 0
 2:  i ← 0
 3:  miv : integer − array ← (0)
 4:  while i ≠ n do
 5:      min ← M
 6:      j ← 0
 7:      while j ≠ n do
 8:          while f(i,j) < min do
 9:              min ← f(i,j)
10:          end while
11:          j ← j + 1
12:      end while                          ▷ min = id(i)
13:      if max > min then
14:          skip
15:      else if max == min then
16:          miv : hiext(i)
17:      else if max < min then
18:          miv ← (0, i)
19:          max ← min
20:      end if
21:      i ← i + 1
22:  end while
```

The above is a very unsophisticated program: in the innermost loop the value of min is monotonically non-increasing in time, and the following alternative construct will react equivalently to any value of min satisfying $min < max$. Combining these two observations we conclude that there is only a point in continuing the innermost repetition as long as $min \geq max$. We can replace the line **while** $j \neq n$ therefore by

while $j \neq n$ **and** $min \geq max$

and the assertion after the corresponding end of while loop by

$$id(i) \leq min < max$$

or

1.24. The problem of the most isolated villages

$$id(i) = min \geq max$$

Let us call the above modification *Optimization 1*.

A very different optimization is possible if it is given that

$$f(i,j) = f(j,i)$$

and, because the computation of f is assumed to be time-consuming, it is requested never to compute $f(i,j)$ for such values of the argument that $f(j,i)$ has already been computed. Starting from our original program we can achieve that for each unordered argument pair the corresponding *f-value* will only be computed once by initializing j each time with $i+1$ instead of with 0, only scanning the upper triangle of the symmetric distance matrix, so to speak. The program is then only guaranteed to compute min correctly provided that we initialize min instead of with M with

$$0 \leq h < i : \text{minimum } f(i,h)$$

This can be catered for by introducing an array, b say, such that for k satisfying $i \leq k < n$:

$$\textbf{for } i = 0 : b(k) = M$$
$$\textbf{for } i > 0 : b(k) = \text{minimum f(k, h) for } 0 \leq h < i$$

In words: $b(k)$ is the minimum distance connecting village k that has been computed thus far.

The result of Optimization 2 is also fairly straightforward.

1.24. The problem of the most isolated villages

```
 1: max ← 0
 2: i ← 0
 3: miv : integer − array ← (0)
 4: b : integer − array ← (0)
 5: while b.dom ≠ n do
 6:     b : hiext(M)
 7: end while
 8: while i ≠ n do
 9:     j ← i + 1
10:     while j ≠ n do
11:         ff ← f(i, j)
12:         while ff < min do
13:             min ← ff
14:         end while
15:         while ff < b(j) do
16:             b(j) ← ff
17:         end while
18:         j ← j + 1
19:     end while                                 ▷ min = id(i)
20:     if max > min then
21:         skip
22:     else if max == min then
23:         miv : hiext(i)
24:     else if max < min then
25:         miv ← (0, i)
26:         max ← min
27:     end if
28:     i ← i + 1
29: end while
```

To try to combine these two optimizations presents a problem: in *Optimization 1* the scanning of a row of the distance matrix is aborted if *min* has become small enough, in *Optimization 2*, however, the scanning of the row is also the scanning of a column and that is done to keep the values of $b(k)$ up to date. Let us apply *Optimization 1* and replace the line **while** $j \neq n$ by

$$\text{while } j \neq n \text{ and } min \geq max$$

The innermost loop can now terminate with $j < n$; the values $b(k)$ with $j \leq k < n$, for which updating is still of possible interest are now the ones with $b(k) \geq max$, the other ones are already small enough. The following insertion will do the job:

```
 1: while j ≠ n do
 2:     if b(j) < max then
 3:         j ← j + 1
 4:     else if b(j) ≥ max then
 5:         ff ← f(i, j)
 6:         while ff < b(j) do
 7:             b(j) ← ff
 8:         end while
 9:         j ← j + 1
10:     end if
11: end while
```

1.24. The problem of the most isolated villages

The best place for this insertion is immediately preceding $i \leftarrow i+1$, but after the adjustment of max: the higher max, the larger the probability that a $b(k)$ does not need any more adjustments.

The two optimizations that we have combined are of a vastly different nature: *Optimization 2* is just *avoiding redoing work known to have been done*, and its effectiveness is known a priori. *Optimization 1*, however, is a strategy whose effectiveness depends on the unknown values of f: it is just one of the many possible strategies in the same vein.

We are looking for those rows of the distance matrix whose minimum element value S exceeds the minimum elements of the remaining rows and the idea of *Optimization 1* is that for that purpose we do not need to compute for the remaining rows the actual minimum if we can find for each row an upper bound B_i for its minimum, such that $B_i < S$. In an intermediate stage of computation, for some row(s) the minimum S is known because all its/their elements have been captured; for other rows we only know an upper bound B_i. And now the strategic freedom is quite clear: do we first compute the smallest number of additional matrix elements still needed to determine a new minimum, in the hope that it will be larger than the minimum we had and, therefore, may exceed a few more B's.

Chapter 2

Arrays

2.1 The Plateau Problem

Problem Description

The array $b[0..n-1]$ has n elements, may have duplicate elements, and is sorted. A *plateau* of length p is a sequence of p consecutive elements with the same value. Find the length of the *longest plateau* in b.

Solution

The value p is the length of the longest plateau if there is a sequence of p equal values and no sequence of $p + 1$ equal values. i.e.

- $b[0..n-1]$ contains a plateau of length p, and
- $b[0..n-1]$ does not contain a plateau of length $p + 1$

Because the array is sorted, a subsection $b[k..j]$ is a *plateau* if and only if its end elements $b[k]$ and $b[j]$ are equal, i.e.

$$0 \leq k \leq n - p : b[k] = b[k + p - 1]$$
$$\text{and}$$
$$0 \leq k \leq n - p - 1 : b[k] \neq b[k + p]$$

Therefore,

p is the length of the longest plateau of $b[0..i]$ $\iff$ $b[i - p..i]$ is not a plateau
$\implies$ this holds

$$\iff b[i - p] \neq b[i]$$

The length of the *plateau* of an array of length 1 is obviously 1. Using this fact, we can develop an invariant as follows:

$1 \leq i \leq n$ **and** p is the length of the *longest plateau* of $b[0..i - 1]$.

Now, it is easy to see the full program as follows:

2.1. The Plateau Problem

Algorithm 38 The Plateau Problem

1: $i \leftarrow 1$
2: $p \leftarrow 1$
3: **Invariant** : $1 \leq i \leq n$ **and** p is the length of the longest plateau of $b[0..i-1]$
4: **Bound Function** $t = n - i$
5: **function** FIND-PLATEAU(b[0..n-1])
6:     **while** $i \neq n$ **do**
7:         **if** $b[i] \neq b[i-p]$ **then**
8:             $i \leftarrow i + 1$
9:         **else if** $b[i] == b[i-p]$ **then**
10:             $i \leftarrow i + 1$
11:             $p \leftarrow p + 1$
12:         **end if**
13:     **end while**
14: **end function**

Please note that this program finds the length of the longest plateau for any array, even if not sorted, as long as all equal values are adjacent.

Alternative Solution

We can also use the idea that the loop body should investigate one plateau at each iteration. The loop invariant is therefore :

$$0 \leq i \leq n$$
and
$$p = \text{length of longest plateau of } b[0..i-1]$$
and
$$i = 0 \text{ or } i = n \text{ or } b[i-1] \neq b[i]$$

Please note that the length of the longest plateau of an empty array is zero.

Algorithm 39 The Plateau Problem Revisited

1: $i \leftarrow 1$
2: $p \leftarrow 1$
3: **Invariant** :
4: $0 \leq i \leq n$
5: **and**
6: p = length of longest plateau of $b[0..i-1]$
7: **and**
8: $i = 0$ or $i = n$ or $b[i-1] \neq b[i]$
9: **Bound Function** $t = n - i$
10: **function** FIND-PLATEAU(b[0..n-1])
11:     **while** $i \neq n$ **do**
12:         increase i, keeping invariant true
13:         $j \leftarrow i + 1$
14:         **Invariant**: $b[i..j-1]$ are all equal; **Bound Function**: n - j
15:         **while** $j \neq n$ **and** $b[j] == b[i]$ **do**
16:             $j \leftarrow j + 1$
17:         **end while**
18:         $p \leftarrow max(p, j - i)$
19:         $i \leftarrow j$
20:     **end while**
21: **end function**

2.2 Searching in Two Dimensional Sequence

Problem Description

Design and implement an algorithm to search for a given integer x in a 2-dimensional array a[0..m][0..n] where $0 < m$ and $0 < n$. In case of multiple occurrences, it doesn't matter which is found.

Solution

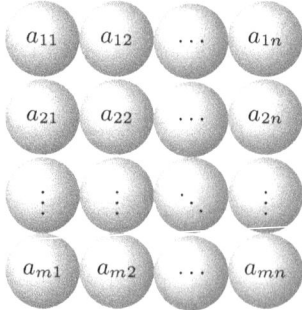

The algorithm should find the position of a given integer x in the array a, i.e., the algorithm should find i and j such that

- $\boxed{x = a[i,j]}$, or

- $i = m$

2.2. Searching in Two Dimensional Sequence

Let us treat the input array as some kind of a rectangular region.

The problem demands that the integer x does exist somewhere in this region. Let us label this condition as *Input Assertion* or *Precondition*.

[Precondition]Precondition (aka *Input Assertion*) $\boxed{x \in a[0..m-1, 0..n-1]}$

i.e., x is present somewhere in this rectangular region a.

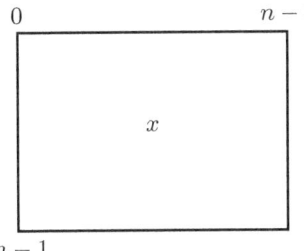

After the program terminates successfully, x has to be found in a rectangular region of a where the rectangular region consists of just one row and column. Let us label this condition as *Output Assertion* or *Result Assertion* or *Postcondition*.

[Postcondition]Postcondition (aka *Result Assertion*) After the program terminates successfully, then x is in a rectangular region of a where the rectangular region consists of just one row and column, i.e., x is present at i^{th} row and j^{th} column of a, or if this is not possible then i = m, i.e., if x is not found in the array, i.e., if $x \neq a[i,j]$, then i = m.

So the Postcondition looks like

$\boxed{(0 \leq i \leq m-1 \wedge 0 \leq j \leq n-1 \wedge x = a[i,j]) \vee (i = m \wedge x \notin a)}$

Is the search space confined to a rectangular region ?

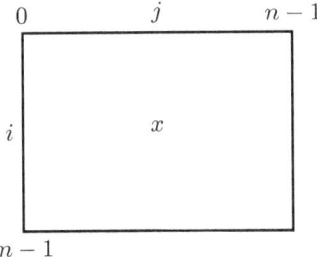

Invariant

Looking at the precondition and postcondition, it is not that difficult to figure out that during the execution of our algorithm, x is guaranteed to be confined

2.2. Searching in Two Dimensional Sequence

within some L-shaped region of a.

Let us revisit this in light of the invariant which bears that x is not in the already-searched rows $a[0..i - 1]$ and not in the already-searched columns $a[i, 0..j - 1]$ of the current row i.

Let us represent this invariant below:

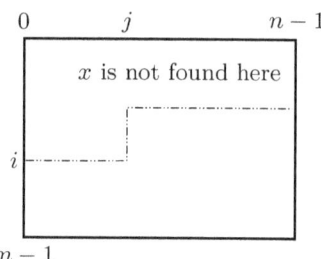

Search space is bounded by L-shaped region Doesn't it look more like a L-shaped region ?

Invariant :

$\boxed{0 \leq m \wedge 0 \leq j < n}\,\wedge$

$\boxed{\text{searcheable-region is bounded by } (m-i) * n - j}$

Initialization

Before we develop body of the program, let us re-think about what should be the starting point of search, i.e., what should be the initial values of the counters i and j ?

Let us say it is set to 0 to start with, i.e., $i = 0$ and $j = 0$. If this is so then the region marked as *x is not found here* is empty to start with. Fair enough. Invariant still holds true.

[

Deducing-Conditional-Statement]Deducing Conditional Statement Let us start with finding complement of the condition, i.e., search still continues. It is not that difficult to see that this complement should maintain the invariant and lead towards the result, i.e.,

$\boxed{Invariant \wedge complement-of-condition \implies Postcondition}$

Revisiting Postcondition

$\boxed{(0 \leq i \leq m-1 \wedge 0 \leq j \leq n-1 \wedge x = a[i,j]) \vee (i = m \wedge x \notin a)}$

As could be seen above, *Postcondition* consists of 2 parts[1]:

1. $\boxed{(0 \leq i \leq m-1 \wedge 0 \leq j \leq n-1 \wedge x = a[i,j])}$

---

[1] i.e. 2 disjunctions

2. $\boxed{(i = m \land x \notin a)}$

Establishing Postcondition

To establish first part of postcondition, the complement of the condition can be $\boxed{i < m \text{ and } x == a[i,j]}$.

And to establish second part of postcondition, it can be $\boxed{i == m}$.

Complement of condition

Putting together, this looks like :

$\boxed{i == m \lor (i < m \text{ and } x == a[i,j])}$

Let us take its complement again to reach to the condition, i.e., complement of the complement of the condition $\implies$ condition.

Condition

$\boxed{i \neq m \land (i \geq m \text{ or } x \neq a[i,j])}$

But this condition has to be evaluated only when the variant is true, i.e., only when $i \leq m$, because as discussed above

$\boxed{Invariant \land complement-of-condition \implies Postcondition}$.

So the condition can be simplified further to look like

$\boxed{i \neq m \land (i == m \text{ or } x \neq a[i,j])}$

Now, we can safely drop the part $i == m$ because it is already covered by $i \neq m$, so the final condition is depicted by

$\boxed{i \neq m \land x \neq a[i,j])}$

Now let us develop corpus of the program.

Internals

Let us recall our stated variant:

Invariant :

$\boxed{0 \leq m \land 0 \leq j < n \land}$ $\land$

$\boxed{\text{searcheable-region is bounded by } (m-i)*n-j}$

Let us try to understand what is meant by the last part of this variant which stands for *searcheable-region is bounded by* $(m-i)*n-j$?

All we were trying to achieve was to contract the search space till the sought after value is found which is nothing but the region depicted by

$\boxed{(m-i)*n-j}$

This contraction takes place as long as both the invariant and the condition hold true which implies that

2.2. Searching in Two Dimensional Sequence

$$i < m \wedge j < n \wedge x \neq a[i,j]$$

This will help move the entry a[i, j] from unexplored search space to already explored search space. Easiest way to achieve this is $j \longleftarrow j+1$, but in order to maintain the invariant it has to satisfy $j < n - 1$.

So we have a beautiful expression as result of this analysis so far :

if $j < n - 1$ then $j \leftarrow j + 1$

In case of $j \geq n - 1$, we can have $j = n - 1$ because the invariant is true.

Let us take the case of a[i, n - 1], which is the rightmost element of ith row. To move this point into the already searched region we can move it to the start of the next row, i.e., $(i \leftarrow i + 1$ and $j = 0)^2$. Simple enough.

Putting together

Algorithm 40 Searching in a 2D Array

1: $i \leftarrow 0$
2: $j \leftarrow 0$
3: **function** 2D-SEARCH(a[0..m-1, 0..n-1], x)
4:     **while** $i \neq m$ **and** $x \neq a[i,j]$ **do**
5:         **if** $j < n - 1$ **then**
6:             $j \leftarrow j + 1$
7:         **else if** $j == n - 1$ **then**
8:             $i \leftarrow i + 1$
9:             $j \leftarrow 0$
10:         **end if**
11:     **end while**
12: **end function**

C++11 Implementation

Let us try programming this algorithm in a real language, say C++11 to bring ourselves at workplace-setting environment:

Program 2.1: searching 2D Array

```cpp
#include <algorithm>
#include <array>

using Point = std::pair<int, int>;

template <int m, int n>
using TwoDimArray =
    std::array<std::array<int, n>, m>;

template <int m, int n>
Point search_2darray(TwoDimArray<m, n> & a,
                     int x)
{
    Point p(-1, -1);

    int i = 0, j = 0;

    while((( i != m) && (x != a[i][j]))
```

---
[2] it was chosen so to take care when j = n

```cpp
19      {
20          if(j < n - 1)
21          {
22              j += 1;
23          }
24          else if(j == n - 1)
25          {
26              i += 1;
27              j = 0;
28          }
29      }
30
31      p.first = i;
32      p.second = j;
33
34      return p;
35  }
```

Please note that point is initialized with (-1, -1) to mark sentinel conditions which in our case stands for unsuccessful search leading to the value being not found in array.

Usage

Program 2.2: Search for 6 : yields a : 2 2

```cpp
1 #include "2darray_search.hpp"
2 #include <iostream>
3
4 int main()
5 {
6     TwoDimArray<4, 4> a = {
7                             12, 2, 83, 5,
8                             30, 14, 15, 16,
9                             13, 5, 6, 81,
10                            23, 6, 7, 19
11                          };
12
13    Point p = search_2darray<4, 4>(a, 6);
14
15    std::cout << "6 is found at : a["
16        << p.first << "][" << p.second << "]"
17        << std::endl;
18 }
```

This prints:

```
6 is found at : a[2][2]
```

Alternative Program

We can simplify it further to look like as follows:

2.2. Searching in Two Dimensional Sequence 103

Algorithm 41 Searching in a 2D Array : Another Program

1: $i \leftarrow 0$
2: $j \leftarrow 0$
3: **function** 2D-SEARCH(a[0..m-1, 0..n-1], x)
4:     **while** $i \neq m$ **and** $x \neq a[i,j]$ **do**
5:         $j \leftarrow j + 1$
6:         **if** $j < n$ **then**
7:             *do nothing*
8:         **else if** $j == n$ **then**
9:             $i \leftarrow i + 1$
10:             $j \leftarrow 0$
11:         **end if**
12:     **end while**
13: **end function**

It could be simplified further to look like

Algorithm 42 Searching in a 2D Array : Another Program(Simplified)

1: $i \leftarrow 0$
2: $j \leftarrow 0$
3: **function** 2D-SEARCH(a[0..m-1, 0..n-1], x)
4:     **while** $i \neq m$ **and** $x \neq a[i,j]$ **do**
5:         $j \leftarrow j + 1$
6:         **if** $j == n$ **then**
7:             $i \leftarrow i + 1$
8:             $j \leftarrow 0$
9:         **end if**
10:     **end while**
11: **end function**

Program 2.3: C++11 Version : Searching 2D Array

```cpp
#include <algorithm>
#include <array>

using Point = std::pair<int, int>;

template <int m, int n>
using TwoDimArray =
    std::array<std::array<int, n>, m>;

template <int m, int n>
Point search_2darray(TwoDimArray<m, n> & a,
                     int x)
{
    Point p(-1, -1);

    int i = 0, j = 0;

    while((i != m) && (x != a[i][j]))
    {
        j += 1;
        if(j == n)
        {
            i += 1;
            j = 0;
```

```
25        }
26      }
27
28      p.first = i;
29      p.second = j;
30
31      return p;
32 }
```

Program 2.4: Usage : C++11 Version : Searching 2D Array

```
1 #include "2darray_search_alt.hpp"
2 #include <iostream>
3
4 int main()
5 {
6     TwoDimArray<4, 4> a = {
7                           12, 2, 83, 5,
8                           30, 14, 15, 16,
9                           13, 5, 6, 81,
10                          23, 6, 7, 19
11                          };
12
13    Point p = search_2darray<4, 4>(a, 6);
14
15    std::cout << "6 is found at : a["
16              << p.first << "][" << p.second << "]"
17              << std::endl;
18 }
```

Time Complexity

It is $O(mn)$ because it ends up traversing the entire region $m \times n$ as far as comparison is concerned.

2.3 The Welfare Crook Problem

Problem Description

The problem of The Welfare Crook is to locate the smallest value to three ascending sequences. Suppose we have three long magnetic tapes, each containing a list of names in alphabetical order. The first list contains the names of people working at IBM Yorktown, the second the names of students at Columbia University and the third the names of people on welfare in New York City. Practically speaking, all three lists are endless, so no upper bounds are given. It is known that at least one person is on all three lists. Write a program to locate the first such person, i.e., the one with the alphabetically smallest name.

Solution

To get at the essence of the problem, consider searching three ordered arrays(with no upper bound) f[0..?], g[0..?] and h[0..?] for the least value that is on all three of them; this least value is known to exist.

Since the lists f, g and h are fixed, we will use the fact that they are alphabetically ordered. Using iv, jv and kv to denote the least values satisfying

2.3. The Welfare Crook Problem

$$f[iv] = g[jv] = h[kv]$$

So the postcondition can be written as

$$i = iv \text{ and } j = jv \text{ and } k = kv$$

and, invariant looks like

$$0 \leq i \leq iv \text{ and } 0 \leq j \leq jv \text{ and } 0 \leq k \leq kv$$

And the bound function is

$$t = iv - i + jv - j + kv - k$$

The initialization is $i \leftarrow 0; j \leftarrow 0; k \leftarrow 0$;
The simplest ways to decrease the bound function are $i \leftarrow i+1, j \leftarrow j+1, k \leftarrow k+1$.

The relation $i + 1 \leq iv$, together with the invariant mentioned above, means that $f(i)$ is not the crook and this is true if $f[i] < g[j]$. Since the crook does not come alphabetically before $g[j]$, if $f[i]$ comes alphabetically before $g[j]$, then $f[i]$ cannot be the crook.

Similarly, $f[i] < h[k]$ is also possible.

So, the program looks like:

Algorithm 43 The Welfare Crook Program

1: **function** WELFARE-CROOK(f, g, h)
2:    $i \leftarrow 0; j \leftarrow 0; k \leftarrow 0$;
3:    **while** $f[i] \neq g[j]$ **and** $g[j] \neq h[k]$ **do**
4:       **if** $f[i] < g[j]$ **or** $f[i] < h[k]$ **then**
5:          $i \leftarrow i + 1$
6:       **else if** $g[j] < h[k]$ **or** $g[j] < f[i]$ **then**
7:          $j \leftarrow j + 1$
8:       **else if** $h[k] < f[i]$ **or** $h[k] < g[j]$ **then**
9:          $k \leftarrow k + 1$
10:      **end if**
11:   **end while**
12: **end function**

The above program can be simplified to:

Algorithm 44 The Welfare Crook Program Simplified

1: **function** WELFARE-CROOK(f, g, h)
2:    $i \leftarrow 0; j \leftarrow 0; k \leftarrow 0$;
3:    **while** $f[i] \neq g[j]$ **and** $g[j] \neq h[k]$ **do**
4:       **if** $f[i] < g[j]$ **then**
5:          $i \leftarrow i + 1$
6:       **else if** $g[j] < h[k]$ **then**
7:          $j \leftarrow j + 1$
8:       **else if** $h[k] < f[i]$ **then**
9:          $k \leftarrow k + 1$
10:      **end if**
11:   **end while**
12: **end function**

Upon termination: $f[i] = g[j] = h[k]$ and the following hold: $i = iv$ **and** $j = jv$ **and** $k = kv$.

2.4 2D Array Rotation

Problem

Design and implement an algorithm for rotating a $n \times n$ two dimensional array by 90 degrees clockwise. It can be safely assumed that $n = 2^k$ for some positive integer k.

Solution

After rotation by 90 degrees clockwise, the above array will look like:

We can decompose the 2D array, say A, into four equal sized sub-arrays as following:

1. $A[0 : \frac{n}{2} - 1][0 : \frac{n}{2} - 1]$
2. $A[0 : \frac{n}{2} - 1][\frac{n}{2} : n - 1]$
3. $A[\frac{n}{2} : n - 1][0 : \frac{n}{2} - 1]$
4. $A[\frac{n}{2} : n - 1][\frac{n}{2} : n - 1]$

We can recursively rotate each of these sub-arrays. Time complexity $T(n) = 4T(\frac{n}{4}) + O(n) = O(n \log n)$ for $n = 2^k$.

C++11 Implementation

Program 2.5: rotate 2D array

```
#include <iostream>
#include <algorithm>
#include <cassert>
#include <vector>
#include <iterator>

template <typename T>
void print_2darray(const std::vector<std::vector<T>> & A)
{
    for (auto e : A)
```

2.4. 2D Array Rotation

```cpp
11    {
12        copy(e.begin(), e.end(), std::ostream_iterator<
              int>(std::cout, " "));
13        std::cout << std::endl;
14    }
15 }
16
17 template <typename T>
18 void validate(const std::vector<std::vector<T>> &A)
19 {
20     int k = 1;
21     size_t len = A.size();
22
23     for (int j = len - 1; j >= 0; --j)
24     {
25         for (int i = 0; i < len; ++i)
26         {
27             assert(k++ == A[i][j]);
28         }
29     }
30 }
31
32 template <typename T>
33 void copy_2darray(std::vector<std::vector<T>> &A,
34                   const int &A_x_s,
35                   const int &A_x_e,
36                   const int &A_y_s,
37                   const int &A_y_e,
38                   const std::vector<std::vector<T>> &S,
39                   const int &S_x, const int &S_y)
40 {
41     for (int i = 0; i < A_x_e - A_x_s; ++i)
42     {
43         copy(S[S_x + i].cbegin() + S_y,
44              S[S_x + i].cbegin() + S_y + A_y_e - A_y_s,
45              A[A_x_s + i].begin() + A_y_s);
46     }
47 }
48
49 template <typename T>
50 void rotate_2darray_helper(std::vector<std::vector<T>> &A
       , const int &x_s,
51                            const int &x_e, const int &y_s,
                              const int &y_e)
52 {
53     if (x_e > x_s + 1)
54     {
55         int mid_x = x_s + ((x_e - x_s) >> 1),
56             mid_y = y_s + ((y_e - y_s) >> 1);
57
58         // Move submatrices
59         std::vector<std::vector<T>> C(mid_x - x_s, std::
             vector<T>(mid_y - y_s));
60
61         copy_2darray(C, 0, C.size(), 0, C.size(), A, x_s,
             y_s);
62
```

```cpp
            copy_2darray(A, x_s, mid_x, y_s, mid_y, A, mid_x,
                y_s);
            copy_2darray(A, mid_x, x_e, y_s, mid_y, A, mid_x,
                mid_y);
            copy_2darray(A, mid_x, x_e, mid_y, y_e, A, x_s,
                mid_y);
            copy_2darray(A, x_s, mid_x, mid_y, y_e, C, 0, 0);

            // Recursively rotate submatrices
            rotate_2darray_helper(A, x_s, mid_x, y_s, mid_y);
            rotate_2darray_helper(A, x_s, mid_x, mid_y, y_e);
            rotate_2darray_helper(A, mid_x, x_e, mid_y, y_e);
            rotate_2darray_helper(A, mid_x, x_e, y_s, mid_y);
        }
}

template <typename T>
void rotate_2darray(std::vector<std::vector<T>> &A)
{
    rotate_2darray_helper(A, 0, A.size(), 0, A.size());
}
```

This is a recursive approach. Alternatively, the rotation can be done using $O(1)$ additional space with time complexity as $O(n)$ by iterating through any of the four sub-arrays and rotating elements in sets of four.

2.5 A Queuing Problem in A Post Office

Problem Description

Given an integer t_0 and two integer arrays $a[0..n-1], b[0..n-1]$, such that

- $n \geq 1$
- $a[0] < a[1] < \ldots < a[n-1]$
- $0 \leq i < n : b[i] > 0$

A post office, equipped with four mutually equivalent service desks, is used by n customers numbered from 0 through $n-1$.

The post office opens at t_0.

Customer i arrives at moment $a[i]$ and requests a service of $b[i]$ time units. Customers are served in the order of their arrival.

The desk officers are never idle when a customer is waiting for service, the post office closes as soon as all n customers have been served.

Write a program to compute the total amount of time during which at least one customer is waiting for service.

Solution

It is requested to compute r, where r is the total amount of time during which at least one customer is waiting for service.

One of the few openings to the solution of this problem seems to be to study how r functionally depends on the waits of the individual customers. Thus we are led to define, $\forall i : 0 \leq i < n$ s_i as the moment at which the service of customer i begins, in terms of which we can grasp the wait imposed on customer i by the length of the interval $(a[i], s_i)$.

2.5. A Queuing Problem in A Post Office

If the n intervals defined like this are colored *black* on a time axis which is *white* to begin with, then we agree, assuming that black plus black gives black, that the value of r to be computed is the total length of whatever looks black.

i.e., r is the length of the superposition of the intervals $(a[i], s_i) : 0 \leq i < n$.
We observe two properties of the numbers s_i :

$$0 \leq i < n : a[i] \leq s_i$$
and
$$s_0 \leq s_1 \leq \ldots \leq s_{n-1}$$

the first one stems from the thought that a customer's service cannot start before its arrival, and the second one from the rule that customers are served in the order of their arrival.

Now let us think towards the computation of the $s - sequence$.

We imagine that, upon its arrival, a customer i finds the residues of what could have happened in the past : a chaotic variety of possibilities, like a not yet opened post office or zero, more or even four desks occupied or a perhaps empty queue or combinations of these.

What matters about the earlier customers $j : 0 \leq j < i$ is their departure times: these entirely describe the changing occupancy of the four desks. More specifically even, as inspired from $s_0 \leq s_1 \leq \ldots \leq s_{n-1}$, the only aspect determinative of the moment s_i is the fourth largest departure time among those of the earlier customers: this describes the earliest instant at which a desk is available to customer i.

Thus we are led to define, $\forall i : 4 \leq in$,

$$d4_i = \text{the fourth largest departure time among those of customers}$$
$$j : 0 \leq j < i.$$

and similarly, for reasons that become apparent soon, $d3_i$, $d2_i$, $d1_i$ for the third, second and first largest departure time among those of the earlier customers.

In terms of these numbers we then grasp s_i by :

$$4 \leq i < n : s_i = max(a[i], d4_i)$$
$$0 \leq i < 4 : s_i = max(a[i], t_0$$

in obedience to the rule that desk officers are never idle when a customer is waiting for service.

Herewith we have an effective way of computing the $s - sequence$, provided we have an effective way to compute $d4 - sequence$.

The $d4 - sequence$ is computed very effectively if we realize that, in terms of s_i, customer i's departure time is conveniently expressed as $s_i + b[i]$. Since $b[i] > 0$, we have $s_i + b[i] > d4_i$ on account of $4 \leq i < n : s_i = max(a[i], d4_i)$, so that it is not difficult to see that

$$4 \leq i < n-1 : d4_{i+1} = min(s_i + b[i], d3_i, d2_i, d1_i)$$

or, to accommodate the other three sequences as well, the more general

$$4 \leq i < n-1 : (d4_{i+1}, d3_{i+1}, d2_{i+1}, d1_{i+1}) = \text{nondecreasing arrangement of}$$
$$(s_i + b[i], d3_i, d2_i, d1_i).$$

2.5. A Queuing Problem in A Post Office

Let the invariant be $r =$ the length of the superposition of the intervals $(a[i], s_i) : 0 \leq i < j$ and $0 \leq j \leq n$,
and investigate an increase of j by 1.

We have to examine which part of the interval $(a[j], s_j)$ is not covered by any of the intervals $(a[i], s_i) : 0 \leq i < j$.

We infer that for $a[j] \geq s_{j-1}$ the interval $(a[j], s_j)$ is disjoint with the other ones. For $a[j] < s_{j-1}$, we conclude that above and the monotonicity of the $a - sequence$ that the part $(a[j], s_{j-1})$ is contained in $(a[j-1], s_{j-1})$ and that the part (s_{j-1}, s_j) is disjoint with all intervals $(a[i], s_i) : 0 \leq i < j$.

Hence, the part $(max(a[j], s_{j-1}), s_j)$ is not covered by any of the other intervals, and we conclude:

$r =$ the length of the superposition of the intervals $(a[i], s_i) : 0 \leq i < j$ and $0 \leq j \leq n$ and $1 \leq j < n \implies r \leftarrow r + s_j - max(a[j], s_{j-1}); n \leftarrow n + 1$

Or, if we are willing to define: $s_{-1} \leq a[0]$,

$r =$ the length of the superposition of the intervals $(a[i], s_i) : 0 \leq i < j$ and $0 \leq j \leq n$ and $0 \leq j < n \implies r \leftarrow r + s_j - max(a[j], s_{j-1}); n \leftarrow n + 1$

The corresponding program then is

1: $r \leftarrow 0$
2: $j \leftarrow 0$
3: **while** $j \neq n$ **do**
4:    $r \leftarrow r + s_j - max(a[j], s_{j-1})$
5:    $n \leftarrow n + 1$
6: **end while**

Or,

1: $q \leftarrow s_{j-1}$
2: $r \leftarrow 0$
3: $j \leftarrow 0$
4: $q : q \leq a[0]$
5: **while** $j \neq n$ **do**
6:    $p \leftarrow s_j$
7:    $r \leftarrow r + p - max(a[j], q)$
8:    $n \leftarrow n + 1$
9:    $q \leftarrow p$
10: **end while**

Let us define

$$0 \leq i < 4 : d4_i = t_0$$

then we have

$$0 \leq i < N : s_i = max(a[i], d4_i))$$

and the definition of the $d - sequences$ becomes

$$(d4_0, d3_0, d2_0, d1_0) = (t_0, t_0, t_0, t_0)$$
$$0 \leq i < n - 1 : (d4_{i+1}, d3_{i+1}, d2_{i+1}, d1_{i+1}) =$$
$$\text{nondecreasing arrangement of } (s_i + b[i], d3_i, d2_i, d1_i).$$

Strengthening the invariant further with the relation
$$h_4, h_3, h_2, h_1 = d4_j, d3_j, d2_j, d1_j$$
results in what we consider as our ultimate program:

1: $r \leftarrow 0$
2: $j \leftarrow 0$
3: $q \leftarrow a[0]$
4: $h_4, h_3, h_2, h_1 = t_0, t_0, t_0, t_0$
5: **while** $j \neq n$ **do**
6:     $p \leftarrow max(a[j], h_4)$
7:     $r \leftarrow r + p - max(a[j], q)$
8:     $q \leftarrow p$
9:     $h_4 \leftarrow p + b[j]$
10:    **loop**
11:        **if** $h_4 > h_3$ **then**
12:            $h_4 \leftarrow h_3$
13:            $h_3 \leftarrow h_4$
14:        **else if** $h_3 > h_2$ **then**
15:            $h_3 \leftarrow h_2$
16:            $h_2 \leftarrow h_3$
17:        **else if** $h_2 > h_1$ **then**
18:            $h_2 \leftarrow h_1$
19:            $h_1 \leftarrow h_2$
20:        **end if**
21:    **end loop**
22:    $j \leftarrow j + 1$
23: **end while**

2.6 Interpolation Search

In binary search, the search space is always cut in half, which guarantees the logarithmic performance. However, if during the search we find a value that is very close to the number we are searching for, say, x, it seems more reasonable to continue the search in that *neighborhood* instead of blindly going to the next half point. In particular, if x is very small, we should start the search somewhere in the beginning of the sequence instead of at the halfway point.

Interpolation search is a method of retrieving a desired record by key in an ordered sequence by using the value of the key and the statistical distribution of the keys.

Consider the way we open a book when we are searching for a certain page number, say 200, and the book consists of 800 pages. Page 200 is thus around the one-fourth mark, and we use this knowledge as an indication of where to open the book. We will probably not hit page 200 on the first try; suppose that we get page 250 instead. We now cut the search to a range of 250 pages, and the desired page is at about the 80 percent mark between page 1 and 250. We now try to go back about $\left(\frac{1}{5}\right)^{th}$ of the way. We can continue this process until we get close enough to page 200, that we can flip one page at a time. This is exactly the idea behind interpolation search. Instead of cutting the search space by a fixed half, we cut it by an amount that seems the most likely to succeed. This amount is determined by interpolation.

2.6. Interpolation Search

Given a file of 1000 records with keys $X_1 < X_2 < \ldots < X_{1000}$ uniformly distributed between 0 and 1, our task is to find an index $i \mid X_i = 0.7$. It is reasonable to expect that about $0.7 \times 1000 = 700$ keys are lesaa than or equal to 0.7 and the required record should be near the 700th record.

However, looking into the file may reveal that $X_{700} = 0.68 < 0.7$. Although we have not retrieved the record, we can deduce that the desired index lies between 700 and 1000. The corresponding keys are uniformly distributed between 0.68 and 1. The new file contains 300 records. $P_2 = \frac{(0.7-0.68)}{(1-0.68)} = 0.0675$ is the probability that these records have smaller or equal keys; therefore we should now look at the $300 \times 0.675 \approx 20^{th}$ record of the new file.

This process is continued by using the same method; at each iteration either the record is found or the length of the files is decreased.

Interpolation search was first suggested by Peterson as a method for searching in sorted sequences stored in contiguous storage locations.

Algorithm

Algorithm 45 Interpolation Search Algorithm

1: **Input** : A (a sorted array) and x (the search key).
2: **Output** : $position$ (an index $i \mid A[i] = x$, or 0 if no such index exist).
3: **function** INTERPOLATION-SEARCH(A[0..n - 1], x)
4:    **if** $x < A[0]$ **or** $x > A[n-1]$ **then**
5:       $position \leftarrow 0$ ▷ unsuccessful search
6:    **else**
7:       $position =$ INTERPOLATION-SEARCH-HELPER$(x, 0, n-1)$
8:    **end if**
9:    **return** $position$
10: **end function**
11: **function** INTERPOLATION-SEARCH-HELPER(x, l, r)
12:    $found \leftarrow 0$
13:    **if** $A[l] == x$ **then**
14:       $found = l$
15:    **else if** $l == r$ **or** $A[l] == A[r]$ **then**
16:       $found = 0$
17:    **else**
18:       $next = \left\lceil l + \frac{(x-A[l])(r-l)}{A[r]-A[l]} \right\rceil$
19:       **if** x < A[next] **then**
20:          $found =$ INTERPOLATION-SEARCH-HELPER$(x, l, next-1)$
21:       **else**
22:          $found =$ INTERPOLATION-SEARCH-HELPER$(x, next, r)$
23:       **end if**
24:    **end if**
25:    **return** $found$
26: **end function**

Complexity

The performance of interpolation search depends not only on the size of the sequence, but also on the input itself. There are inputs for which interpolation search checks every number in the sequence. However, interpolation search is very efficient for inputs consisting of relatively uniformly distributed

2.6. Interpolation Search

elements, for example, the pages of a book are uniformly distributed without any doubt. It can be shown that the average number of comparisons performed by interpolation search, where the average is taken over all possible sequences, is $O(\log \log n)$. Although this seems to be an order of magnitude improvement over the performance of binary search, interpolation search is not much better than binary search in practice because

1. unless n is very large, the value of $\log_2 n$ is small enough that the logarithm of it is not much smaller.

2. interpolation search requires more elaborate arithmetic.

C++ Implementation

Program 2.6: Interpolation Search

```cpp
#include <vector>
#include <cassert>

template<typename T>
T interpolation_search_helper(T A[], std::size_t l, std::size_t r, T value)
{
    std::size_t found = 0, next;

    if(A[l] == value)
    {
        found = 1;
    }
    else if((l == r) || (A[l] == A[r]))
    {
        found = 0;
    }
    else
    {
        next = l + (value - A[l])*(r - l) / (A[r] - A[l]);

        if(value < A[next])
        {
            found = interpolation_search_helper(A, l, next - 1, value);
        }
        else
        {
            found = interpolation_search_helper(A, next, r, value);
        }
    }

    return found;
}


template<typename T>
T interpolation_search(T sorted_array[], std::size_t l, std::size_t r, T value)
{
    std::size_t position = 0;
```

```
39
40      if(value < sorted_array[l] || value > sorted_array[r
            ])
41      {
42          position = 0;
43      }
44      else
45      {
46          position = interpolation_search_helper(
                sorted_array, l, r, value);
47      }
48      return position;
49  }
50
51
52  int main()
53  {
54      int sorted_array[] = {1, 2, 3, 4, 5, 6, 7, 8, 9};
55
56      assert(interpolation_search(sorted_array, 0, 8, 5) ==
            4);
57  }
```

Remarks

For external search (the file resides on an external device), interpolation search is superior to binary search since the search time is determined by the number of accesses. However, in internal search the computation time of each iteration should also be considered. Computer experiments showed that interpolation search and binary search take approximately the same time. Interpolation search is slightly faster only for files larger than 5000 records. However, using shift operations instead of division in binary search or the use of Fibonaccian search results in faster internal search methods. After a few iterations of interpolation search, we are quite close to the required record. When the difference between the indices of two successive iterations is small, it may be advantageous to switch to sequential search and save computation time.

2.7 Robot Walk

Problem Description

Given are two integer arrays $x[0..46]$ and $y[0..46]$. The pair $(x[i], y[i])$ represents the Cartesian coordinates of a point P_i in a plane ($0 \leq i < 47$). The arrays are such that all 47 points are different.

A robot walks from P_0 to P_1, from P_1 to P_2, ..., from P_{45} to P_{46}, and finally from P_{46} to P_0. It does so in obedience to the following rules:

- it shall start from P_0, while looking towards P_1
- it shall always walk into the direction in which it is looking
- it shall only alter its direction of looking in the points P_i, namely by performing a clockwise rotation of $\alpha : 0 \leq \alpha < 2\pi$
- it shall end in P_0, while looking towards P_1.

As a consequence of this walk the robot has made a clockwise rotation which is a multiple of 2π.

2.7. Robot Walk

Write a program to compute this multiple, under the additional requiement that all expressions and variables occurring in the program have to be of integer or of boolean type.

Solution

A first inspection of the problem tells us that the requested answer does not change whenever the set of points is translated through the plane. Only the relative position of each pair of successive points plays a role in the determination of the answer.

Therefore we introduce the vectors $\vec{u}_i$, to be defined as $\vec{u}_i = (P_i \to P_{i+1})$ for $0 \leq i < 47$, where $P_{47} = P_0$ and $P_{48} = P_1$.

The direction of looking during the walk from P_i to P_{i+1} then equals $\vec{u}_i$. Hence the successive directions of looking during the robot's walk are $\vec{u}_0, \vec{u}_1, \vec{u}_2, \ldots, \vec{u}_{46}, \vec{u}_{47}(=\vec{u}_0)$.

The clockwise rotation in the point P_i towards P_{i+1} now corresponds to a clockwise rotation from $\vec{u}_{i-1}$ to $\vec{u}_i$.

Since in the initial state, the robot looks into the same direction as in the final state, it is suggested to take this direction as *reference direction*. And then the final answer will approximately be equal to total number of times that during rotation the robot's eye *passes* this *reference direction*.

A more precise, and a more manageable formulation of the problem is at hand as soon as we realize that the answer does not change either if the set of points is rotated inside the plane. This has as a consequence that any direction $\vec{r}$ can be taken as a *reference direction*.

If we define $\theta(\vec{u}_i) : 0 \leq \theta(\vec{u}_i) < 2\pi$ to be the angle of the clockwise rotation from $\vec{r}$ to $\vec{u}_i$, then the final answer p will have to satisfy the following

$$0 \leq i < 47 : \theta(\vec{u}_{i+1}) < \theta(\vec{u}_i)$$

i.e.

$$0 \leq i < 47 : \theta(\vec{u}_{i+1}) < \theta(\vec{u}_i)$$

Based on the above, our program is :

```
1:  j ← 0
2:  p ← 0
3:  while j ≠ 47 do
4:      if θ(u_{j+1}) < θ(u_j) then
5:          p ← p + 1
6:      else if θ(u_{j+1}) ≥ θ(u_j) then
7:          skip
8:      end if
9:      j ← j + 1
10: end while
```

If the computation of θ is felt to be expensive, we can introduce $\alpha = \theta(\vec{u}_j)$, then the program is

2.7. Robot Walk

```
1: j ← 0
2: p ← 0
3: α = θ(u⃗₀)
4: while j ≠ 47 do
5:     j ← j + 1
6:     β = θ(u⃗ⱼ)
7:     if β < α then
8:         p ← p + 1
9:     else if β ≥ α then
10:        skip
11:    end if
12:    α ← β
13: end while
```

A next remark is that, in fact, we do not want to compute the angles α and β, but just to compare them.

Comparing two angles α and β is fairly easy in the case that $0 \geq \alpha < \frac{\pi}{2}$ and $0 \geq \beta < \frac{\pi}{2}$, because then $\beta < \alpha$ is equivalent to $\tan(\beta) < \tan(\alpha)$, tangents being compared at the expense of two simple multiplications, when points are given in a Cartesian coordinate system.

Comparing two angles α and β is not so difficult either in general case, if we are willing to represent α and β in the angle system with base $\frac{\pi}{2}$:

$$\alpha \leftarrow a \times \frac{\pi}{2} + \alpha' \qquad \qquad \triangleright\ 0 \leq \alpha' < \frac{\pi}{2}$$
$$\beta \leftarrow b \times \frac{\pi}{2} + \beta' \qquad \qquad \triangleright\ 0 \leq \beta' < \frac{\pi}{2}$$

Then, the inequality $\beta < \alpha$ is equivalent to

$$b < a \text{ or } (b = a \text{ and } \beta' < \alpha')$$

which in turn is equivalent to

$$b < a \text{ or } (b = a \text{ and } \tan(\beta') < \tan(\alpha'))$$

Now, the program is:

```
1: j ← 0
2: p ← 0
3: a : a × π/2 + α' = θ(u⃗₀)
4: α' : 0 ≤ α' < π/2
5: while j ≠ 47 do
6:     j ← j + 1
7:     b : b × π/2 + β' = θ(u⃗ⱼ)
8:     β' : 0 ≤ β' < π/2
9:     if b < a or (b == a and tan(β') < tan(α')) then
10:        p ← p + 1
11:    else if b > a or (b == a and tan(β') ≥ tan(α')) then
12:        skip
13:    end if
14:    a ← b
15:    α' ← β'
16: end while
```

2.7. Robot Walk

Looking for a simple initialization of a and α', it seems attractive to choose $\vec{r} = \vec{u_0}$ as a reference direction, but in that case the computations of b, β' and of $\tan(\beta') < \tan(\alpha')$ becomes rather cumbersome. With respect to these later computations, there is hardly another possibility than taking one of the four coordinate directions as reference direction $\vec{r}$. The choice being immaterial (on account of symmetry), we shall select the negative y-axis.

Now we switch back in our representation from angles to vectors, because in order to compute $\tan(\alpha')$ and $\tan(\beta')$, it is convenient to have two vectors (ux, uy) and (vx, vy) respectively, such that

$$\theta(ux, uy) = \alpha'$$
$$\text{and}$$
$$\theta(vx, vy) = \beta'$$

Then $\tan(\beta') < \tan(\alpha')$ is coded as

$$\frac{-vx}{-vy} < \frac{-ux}{-uy}$$

or, preferably as $vx \times uy < ux \times vy$.

In order to achieve that $0 \leq \beta' < \frac{\pi}{2}$, we have to achieve that $vx \leq 0$ and $vy < 0$. In order to compute b we have to investigate counterclockwise turns of $\frac{\pi}{2}$ of the vector $\vec{u_j}$.

Now we obtain for
$b, \beta' : (b \times \frac{\pi}{2} + \beta' = \theta(\vec{u_j})$ and $0 \leq \beta' < \frac{\pi}{2})$
the following piece of code

1: $vx \leftarrow x[j+1] - x[j]$
2: $vy \leftarrow y[j+1] - y[j]$
3: $b \leftarrow 0$
4: **while** $vx > 0$ **or** $vy \geq 0$ **do**
5: $\quad vx \leftarrow -vy$
6: $\quad vy \leftarrow vx$
7: $\quad b \leftarrow b + 1$
8: **end while**

---

where, in view of the original data, $x[j+1] - x[j]$ and $y[j+1] - y[j]$ are the components of the vector $\vec{u_j}$.

The initialization of a and α' can become quite simple if we succeed in finding some vector $\vec{u_1}$ such that $\theta(\vec{u_0}) \geq \theta(\vec{u_1})$, because then our final result can be written as

$$-1 \leq i < 47 : \theta(\vec{u_{i+1}}) < \theta(\vec{u_i})$$

and invariant as

$$-1 \leq i < j : \theta(\vec{u_{i+1}}) < \theta(\vec{u_i}) \text{ and } -1 \leq j \leq 47$$

We hardly have any choice, because $\vec{u_1}$ must be defined such that $\theta(\vec{u_1}) = 0$, ($\vec{u_0}$ could coincide with the negative y-axis), for instance $\vec{u_1} = (0, -1)$. Then the initialization of a and α' results into:

$$ux \leftarrow 0$$
$$uy \leftarrow -1$$
$$a \leftarrow 0$$

2.8. Linear Time Sorting

To implement the extra points P_{47} and P_{48}, we introduce an auxiliary variable $h \leftarrow (j+1) \mod 47$, by means of which we can round the arrays.

So, the final program becomes:

Algorithm 46 Robot Walk Algorithm

1: $j \leftarrow -1$
2: $h \leftarrow 0$
3: $p \leftarrow 0$
4: $ux \leftarrow 0$
5: $uy \leftarrow -1$
6: $a \leftarrow 0$
7: **while** $j \neq 47$ **do**
8:     $j \leftarrow j + 1$
9:     $h0 \leftarrow h$
10:     $h \leftarrow (j+1) \mod 47$
11:     $vx \leftarrow x[h] - x[h0]$
12:     $vy \leftarrow y[h] - y[h0]$
13:     $b \leftarrow 0$
14:     **while** $vx > 0$ **or** $vy \geq 0$ **do**
15:         $vx \leftarrow -vy$
16:         $vy \leftarrow vx$
17:         $b \leftarrow b + 1$
18:     **end while**
19:     **if** $b < a$ **or** $(b == a$ **and** $vx \times uy < ux \times vy)$ **then**
20:         $p \leftarrow p + 1$
21:     **else if** $b > a$ **or** $(b == a$ **and** $vx \times uy \geq ux \times vy)$ **then**
22:         skip
23:     **end if**
24:     $ux \leftarrow vx$
25:     $uy \leftarrow vy$
26:     $a \leftarrow b$
27: **end while**

2.8 Linear Time Sorting

Problem

Given an array of integers, where different integers may have different numbers of digits, but the total number of digits over all the integers in the array is n. Show how to sort the array in $O(n)$ time.

Solution

The usual, unadorned *radix sort* algorithm will not solve this problem in the required time bound. The number of passes, d, would have to be the number of digits in the largest integer.

Suppose that there are m integers; we always have $m \leq n$. In the worst case, we would have one integer with $\frac{n}{2}$ digits and $\frac{n}{2}$ integers with one digit each. We assume that the range of a single digit is constant. Therefore, we would have $d = \frac{n}{2}$ and $m = \frac{n}{2} + 1$, and so the running time would be $(dm) = \Theta(n^2)$.

Let us assume without loss of generality that all the integers are positive and have no leading zeros. (If there are negative integers or 0, deal with the positive numbers, negative numbers, and 0 separately.)

Under this assumption, we can observe that integers with more digits are always greater than integers with fewer digits. Thus, we can first sort the integers by number of digits (using *counting sort*), and then use *radix sort* to sort each group of integers with the same length. Noting that each integer has between 1 and n digits, let m_i be the number of integers with i digits, for $i = 1, 2, \ldots, n$. Since there are n digits altogether, we have $\sum_{i=1}^{n} i \times m_i = n$.

It takes $O(n)$ time to compute how many digits all the integers have and, once the numbers of digits have been computed, it takes $O(m + n) = O(n)$ time to group the integers by number of digits. To sort the group with m_i digits by *radix sort* takes $\Theta(i \times m_i)$ time. The time to sort all groups, therefore, is

$$\sum_{i=1}^{n} \Theta(i \times m_i) = \Theta\left(\sum_{i=1}^{n} i \times m_i\right) = \Theta(n)$$

2.9 Write as sum of consecutive positive numbers

Problem Description

Given a positive integer N, write a program to determine the number of ways in which N can be written as then sum of consecutive positive integers.

Solution

We observe that for each positive k, the number of ways in which N can be written as the sum of exactly k consecutive positive integers is at most *one*. Is it amazing therefore that we start analyzing when this is possible ?

The simplest sequence of k consecutive positive integers we can think of is the sequence

$$(1, 2, \ldots, k)$$

which sums to

$$\frac{k(k+1)}{2}$$

The simplest sequence but one of length k definitely is

$$(1+1, 2+1, \ldots, k+1)$$

which therefore has a sum equal to

$$\frac{k(k+1)}{2} + 1 \times k$$

And thus we observe that N can be written as the sum of k consecutive positive integers if and only if

$$N - \frac{k(k+1)}{2}$$

is a non-negative multiple of k.

So, here is the program:

2.10. Print 2D Array in Spiral Order

Algorithm 47 Write as sum of consecutive positive numbers
1: $k \leftarrow 1$
2: $e \leftarrow N - 1$ $\qquad \triangleright e = N - \frac{k(k+1)}{2}$
3: $c \leftarrow 0$
4: **while** $e \geq 0$ **do**
5:   **if** $e \mod k == 0$ **then**
6:     $C \leftarrow C + 1$
7:   **else if** $e \mod k > 0$ **then**
8:     $skip$
9:   **end if**
10:   $k \leftarrow k + 1$
11:   $e \leftarrow e - (k + 1)$
12: **end while**
13: $print(C)$

2.10 Print 2D Array in Spiral Order

Problem

Design and implement an algorithm to print a given two dimensional array in spiral order.

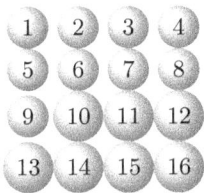

Printing this array in spiral form would give

1 2 3 4 8 12 16 15 14 13 9 5 6 7 11 10

Solution

Program 2.7: Print 2D Array in Spiral Order

```
#include <array>
#include <iostream>

template <int m, int n>
using TwoDimArray =
    std::array<std::array<int, n>, m>;

template<int m, int n>
void spiral_print(TwoDimArray<m, n> & a)
{
    int end_row_index = m;
    int end_col_index = n;

    int cur_index, start_row_index = 0, start_col_index =
        0;

    while (start_row_index < end_row_index &&
        start_col_index < end_col_index)
```

2.10. Print 2D Array in Spiral Order

```cpp
    {
        // Print the first row from the remaining rows
        for (cur_index = start_col_index; cur_index <
            end_col_index; ++cur_index)
        {
            std::cout << a[start_row_index][cur_index] <<
                " ";
        }
        start_row_index++;

        // Print the last column from the remaining
            columns
        for (cur_index = start_row_index; cur_index <
            end_row_index; ++cur_index)
        {
            std::cout << a[cur_index][end_col_index-1] <<
                " ";
        }
        end_col_index--;

        // Print the last row from the remaining rows
        if ( start_row_index < end_row_index)
        {
            for (cur_index = end_col_index-1; cur_index
                >= start_col_index; --cur_index)
            {
                std::cout << a[end_row_index-1][cur_index
                    ] << " ";
            }
            end_row_index--;
        }

        // Print the first column from the remaining
            columns
        if (start_col_index < end_col_index)
        {
            for (cur_index = end_row_index-1; cur_index
                >= start_row_index; --cur_index)
            {
                std::cout << a[cur_index][start_col_index
                    ] << " ";
            }
            start_col_index++;
        }
    }
    std::cout << std::endl;
}


int main()
{
    TwoDimArray<3, 6> matrix = {
                                 1,  2,  3,  4,  5,  6,
                                 7,  8,  9, 10, 11,
                                12,
                                13, 14, 15, 16, 17, 18
                              };
```

```
65      spiral_print <3, 6>(matrix);
66
67      TwoDimArray<4, 4> m = {
68                              1,  2,  3,  4,
69                              5,  6,  7,  8,
70                              9, 10, 11, 12,
71                             13, 14, 15, 16
72                          };
73
74      spiral_print <4, 4>(m);
75 }
```

Output of this program is:

```
1 2 3 4 5 6 12 18 17 16 15 14 13 7 8 9 10 11
1 2 3 4 8 12 16 15 14 13 9 5 6 7 11 10
```

2.11 The Problem of the Circular Racecourse

Problem Description

Given two integer arrays $p[0..N-1]$ and $q[0..N-1]$, $N \geq 1$, such that

$$\forall i : 0 \leq i < N : p[i] \geq 0 \land q[i] > 0),$$

and

$$\sum_{i=0}^{N-1} p[i] = \sum_{i=0}^{N-1} q[i]$$

Along a circular racecourse are N pits, clockwise numbered from 0 through $N-1$. The amount of petrol available at pit i equals $p[i]$, whereas the amount of petrol needed to travel from pit i to the clockwise next pit equals $q[i]$.

Write a program to determine all pits from which a car, with an initially empty and sufficiently large tank, can start and complete the whole course in clockwise direction.

Solution

A necessary and sufficient condition for the car to round the circuit, when starting at pit k is

$$(p[k] - q[k]) \geq 0,$$

so that pit $k+1$ can be reached, and

$$(p[k] - q[k]) + (p[k+1] - q[k+1]) \geq 0$$

so that pit $k+2$ can also be reached and

$\vdots$

$$(p[k] - q[k]) + (p[k+1] - q[k+1]) + \ldots + (p[k+N-1] - q[k+N-1]) \geq 0$$

so that pit $k+N$, which is pit k, can be reached as well.

We can formulate this condition a little bit more precisely by writing

$$C(k, N) : (\forall h : 0 \geq h < N : \sum_{i=k}^{k+h} (p[i] - q[i]) \geq 0)$$

2.11. The Problem of the Circular Racecourse

Now we could proceed by checking for each pit k whether or not $C(k, N)$ is fulfilled. Such a progression, however, would be too much wasteful, because up to N^2 partial sums which are in the game, are mutually strongly dependent. In order to do better, we might observe that, for instance,

$$\sum_{i=k}^{k+h}(p[i] - q[i]) = \left(\sum_{i=0}^{k+h} - \sum_{i=0}^{k-1}\right)(p[i] - q[i])$$

which has the virtue that it reduces arbitrary partial sums to special ones, namely, those from 0 onwards.

If we introduce as an abbreviation

$$x_k = \sum_{i=0}^{k-1}(p[i] - q[i]), k \geq 0$$

then

$$C(k, N) = (\forall h : 0 \leq h < N : x_{k+h+1} \geq x_k)$$

Thanks to the fact that

$$x_N = \sum_{i=0}^{N-1}(p[i] - q[i]) = 0,$$

the condition $C(k, N)$ can be simplified drastically.

$$C(k, N) : (\forall h : 0 \leq h < N : x_h \geq x_k),$$

expressing that $x_k = min\,(x_0, x_1, \ldots, x_{N-1})$.

We can capture the desired net effect of the program to be constructed as the computation of the set $\mathbb{Z}$ of pit numbers such that the relation

$$\mathbb{Z} = \{k \mid 0 \leq k < N \land C(k, N)\}$$

is satisfied.

We propose to develop the program by sticking to the invariant

$$0 \leq n \leq N \land \mathbb{Z} = \{k \mid 0 \leq k < n \land C(k, n)\},$$

strengthened, for rather obvious reasons, with

$$xx = min\,(x_0, x_1, \ldots, x_{n-1})$$
$$\text{and}$$
$$x = x_{n-1} = \left(\sum_{i=0}^{n-2}(p[i] - q[i])\right)$$

respectively.

If, furthermore, the set $\mathbb{Z}$ is represented as

$$\mathbb{Z} = \{\Gamma[0], \Gamma[1], \ldots, \Gamma[l-1]\},$$

in which Γ refers to an integer array and l is an integer, the program is readily constructed. The detailed derivation of it is, by now, left as an exercise.

The final program is:

2.12. Sparse Array Trick

Algorithm 48 Circular Racecourse Program
1: $n \leftarrow 1$
2: $F[0] \leftarrow 0$
3: $l \leftarrow 1$
4: $xx \leftarrow 0$
5: $x \leftarrow 0$
6: **while** $n \neq N$ **do**
7: $\quad x \leftarrow x + p[n-1] - q[n-1]$
8: $\quad$ **if** $x > xx$ **then**
9: $\quad\quad skip$
10: $\quad$ **else if** $x == xx$ **then**
11: $\quad\quad F[l] \leftarrow n$
12: $\quad\quad l \leftarrow l + 1$
13: $\quad$ **else if** $x < xx$ **then**
14: $\quad\quad xx \leftarrow x$
15: $\quad\quad F[0] \leftarrow n$
16: $\quad\quad l \leftarrow 1$
17: $\quad$ **end if**
18: $\quad n \leftarrow n + 1$
19: **end while**

Remarks

The above program is such that, when under execution, the elements $p[N-1]$ and $q[N-1]$ of the arrays p and q are never inspected.

One of the outcomes of the above analysis is that the condition $\sum_{i=0}^{N-1} p[i] = \sum_{i=0}^{N-1} q[i]$ is a sufficient condition for the existence of at least one pit from which a car can round the circuit.

2.12 Sparse Array Trick

Problem

Suppose you want to use a large array A for random access, although you won't actually be referring to very many of its entries. You want $A[k]$ to be zero the first time you access it, yet you don't want to spend the time to set every location to zero. Explain how it is possible to read and write any desired elements $A[k]$ reliably, given k, without assuming anything about the actual initial memory contents, by doing only a small fixed number of additional operations per array access.

Solution

We have to develop a technique to initialize an entry of a matrix to zero the first time it is accessed, thereby eliminating the $O(|V|^2)$ time to initialize an adjacency matrix. It is a neat trick that lets you avoid initializing large array.

To illustrate the idea, suppose we are trying to solve the element distinctness problem on a restricted universe. In this problem we are given a list of integers and we want to determine if there are any repeated elements. The input is an

2.12. Sparse Array Trick

array A[1..n] of integers, where each integer is between (say) 1 and M, where M is not so large compared to n, maybe M is about 10n or something like that.

The usual way to do this is to create an array B[1..M] such that B[j] = 1 if j is an element of A, and 0 otherwise. We start by initializing all the entries of B to 0. Then we loop through the elements of A. For each i, $1 \le i \le n$, we first check B[A[i]]. If it equals 1, then the value A[i] already occurred in A. Otherwise, we set B[A[i]] = 1, to signify that we've seen A[i].

If $M = O(n)$, this gives a linear-time algorithm for element distinctness. It even lets us list the repeated elements, if there are any.

Now here's the deal. Suppose we are solving element distinctness many times in a program, as a subroutine. Then it is conceivable that initializing all the entries of B to 0 could actually be a significant time drain. Although we have to allocate the memory for B once at the start, could there be a way to avoid the time-consuming $\Theta(M)$ initialization for B each time we call the subroutine again? We have to handle the problem that the entries of B could be arbitrary junk that we have no control over.

The answer is yes, using the following trick: instead of containing 1 or 0, we will set it up so that B[j] contains the position p in A where j is found. The key point is that we always actually verify this by looking at A[p], so we can never go wrong, even if B[j] is junk. More precisely, we want to ensure that if B[j] = p, then A[p] = j.

Now for each i we are going to check to see if A[i] = d has already been seen. To do this, we look in B[d]; say it equals c. If c is not between 1 and i-1, then we know that c represents uninitialized junk, so we can confidently ignore it and set B[d] = i.

If c is between 1 and i-1, then it either represents a true pointer back to the place in A where d was found earlier, or it just happens to be junk that is in the right range. In either case, we look at A[c]. Either it equals d, in which case we have found d earlier in the array at the entry A[c], or it equals something else. In the latter case we also set B[d] = i. This works whether B[d] is a true pointer or not!

Here's the code:

```
1 for i := 1 to n do
2     d := A[i]
3     c := B[d]
4     if (c < 1) or (c   i) then
5             B[d] := i
6     else if A[c] = d then
7             print(d, " occurred at positions ", c ," 
                    and ", i)
8     else B[d] := i;
```

And that's it! This code fragment prints out the duplications. Of course, if you'd rather terminate as soon as a repeated element is found, you can do that instead. Or if you'd rather save the repeated elements in a linked list, you can do that, too. And of course, this trick can be used in other settings, such as large sparse matrices, where you want to avoid initialization costs.

Algorithm

Maintain a pointer in each initialized entry to a back pointer on a stack. Each time an entry is accessed, verify that the contents are not random by making sure the pointer in that entry points to the active region on the stack and that the back pointer points to the entry.

Remarks

Besides the array A, maintain also a verification array V of the same size, and a list L of the locations used. Let n be the number of items in L; initially $n = 0$ and the contents of L, A and V are arbitrary. Whenever you want to access $A[k]$ for a value of k that you might not have used before, first check whether $0 \leq V[k] < n$ and $L[V[k]] = k$. If not, set $V[k] \leftarrow n$, $L[n] \leftarrow k$, $A[k] \leftarrow 0$, and $n \leftarrow n + 1$. Otherwise you can be sure that $A[k]$ already contents legitimate data. By a slight extension of this method, it is possible to save and eventually restore the contents of all entries of A and V that change during the computation.

2.13 Bulterman's Reshuffling Problem

Problem Description

Consider an array $X[0..N-1]$, such that

- $N = R \times M, R \geq 1$ and $M \geq 1$
- R of its elements are *red*
- the remaining $N - R$ elements are *blue*.

It is requested to permute the array elements such that

1. the relative order of the blue elements remains unaltered, and
2. the red elements are moved to the positions $r \times M, 0 \leq r < R$.

Solution

The standard trick to trivialize the proof that the final value of X is a permutation of its original value is to stick to array alternations of the form $X : swap(i, j), 0 \leq i \leq j < N$. So, let us adopt the trick.

Of the two remaining requirements (1) and (2), the first one seems to be the hardest: incautiously swapping of blue elements is likely to create irrevocable chaos. So, let us try to swap the blue elements with care:

- swapping two distinct blue elements is so harmful to (1) that we simply disallow it;
- swapping a red and a blue element is at least suspect, unless all elements *in between* are red, in which case we allow it.

Thus having covered all cases, we arrive at a regime in which swapping two elements is constrained to the two outer elements of a non-empty *train of elements*, all elements of which are red with the possible exception of one element at an end, which may be blue.

More specifically, if we see to it that $X : swap(i, j)$ takes place subject to the condition

$$Tr(i,j) : (i \leq h < j : X[h] \text{ is red}),$$

2.13. Bulterman's Reshuffling Problem

then (1) is *automatically* satisfied.

When obeying this rule for swapping elements our remaining obligation consists of fulfilling (2), i.e. of establishing

$$0 \leq k < R : X[k \times M] \, is \, red,$$

which mentions red elements only.

We can view $\{Tr(i,j)\}\ X : swap(i,j)$ as a movement of the red train $(X[i], \ldots, X[j-1])$ over one position *to the right*.

So, comes the idea that the problem of satisfying Z is readily solved if we succeed in forming a red train comprising all red elements at the left end of the array X and then let it travel to the right, each time uncoupling its leftmost wagon at the appropriate positions.

If we can move a red train to the right we can move it to the left as well, and if we can uncouple a wagon we can also couple one, simply by inverting the operations, So, the problem of allocating a red train comprising all red elements at the left end of the array X can be solved by letting a red train travel from right to left picking up all red wagons its encounters. More precisely, we propose

1. $\{Tr(i,j)\}\ X : swap(i,j); i \leftarrow i+1, j \leftarrow j+1\ \{Tr(i,j)\}$ as the mechanism to move the train to the right, and hence

2. $\{Tr(i,j)\}\ i \leftarrow i-1, j \leftarrow j-1; X : swap(i,j)\ \{Tr(i,j)\}$ as the mechanism to move it to the left;

3. $\{Tr(i,j)\ and\ i < j\}\ i \leftarrow i+1\ \{(X[i-1]\ is\ red)\ and\ Tr(i,j)\}$ as the procedure to uncouple a wagon at the left end of the train, and hence

4. $\{Tr(i,j)\ and\ (X[i-1]\ is\ red)\}\ i \leftarrow i-1\ \{\ i < j\ and\ Tr(i,j)\}$ as the procedure to couple a wagon at the left end.

With the abbreviations

$$P(r) : 0 \leq r \leq R\ and\ (0 \leq k < r : X[k \times M]\ is\ red)$$
$$Q(j) : j \leq h < N : X[h]\ is\ blue),$$

the program, which is somewhat lavishly annotated is as follows:

2.14. Finding the majority

Algorithm 49 Bulterman's Reshuffling Problem
1: $i, j, r : int$
2: $i \leftarrow N$
3: $j \leftarrow N$
4: $\{Tr(i,j)\} \{Q(j)\} \{0 \leq i \leq j \leq N\}$
5: **while** $i \neq 0$ **do** ▷ $i > 0$
6:    **if** X[i - 1] is red **then**
7:       $i \leftarrow i - 1$ ▷ See (4)
8:    **else if** X[i - 1] is blue **then**
9:       $i \leftarrow i - 1$
10:      $j \leftarrow j - 1$
11:      $X : swap(i, j)$ ▷ See (2)
12:    **end if**
13:    $\{Tr(i, j)\} \{Q(j)\} \{0 \leq i \leq j \leq N\}$
14: **end while** ▷ Tr(i, j) and Q(j) and i = 0, hence j = R
15: $r \leftarrow 0$ ▷ $\{Tr(i,j)\} \{Pr(r)\} \{j = R - r + i\} \{i \leq r \times M\}$
16: **while** $r \neq R$ **do** ▷ $r < R$ ▷ Tr(i, j), j = R - r + i, $i \leq r \times M$
17:    **while** $i \neq r \times M$ **do** ▷ $i < r \times M$, hence $j < N$
18:       $X : swap(i, j)$
19:       $i \leftarrow i + 1$
20:       $j \leftarrow j + 1$ ▷ Tr(i, j), see (1), j = R - r + i, $i \leq r \times M$
21:    **end while** ▷ Tr(i, j) and j = R - r + i and $r < R$, hence Tr(i, j) and $i < j$, hence X[i] is red, $i = r \times M$, P(r)
22:    $i \leftarrow i + 1$
23:    $r \leftarrow r + 1$ ▷ Tr(i, j), see (3), P(r), j = R - r + i, $i \leq r \times M$
24: **end while** ▷ P(r) and r = R, hence Z

2.14 Finding the majority

The majority problem

We are given a set S of n objects ($n \geq 1$), each of which has a color. Furthermore, we are told that there is a majority color in S, i.e., a color that occurs strictly more than $\frac{n}{2}$ times. We denote this majority color by $mc(S)$. Our task is to find an element of S whose color is equal to $mc(S)$. We are only allowed to use the operation *same_color*. This operation takes two arbitrary elements, say x and y, of S, and returns the value

$$same\_color(x, y) = \begin{cases} true, & \text{if } x \text{ and } y \text{ have the same color.} \\ false, & \text{otherwise.} \end{cases} \quad (2.1)$$

In particular, we cannot determine the color of any element of S.

The basic algorithm

Our algorithm will be based on the following observation.

Observation 1

Let x and y be two elements of S that have different colors. Then there is a majority color in the set $S \setminus \{x, y\}$, and

$$mc(S) = mc(S \setminus \{x, y\})$$

Proof

Assume that $mc(S) = red$. Let k be the number of red elements in S. Then we know that $k > \frac{n}{2}$. We have to show that the set $S \setminus \{x, y\}$ contains more than $\frac{(n-2)}{2}$ red elements.

Case 1 Neither x nor y is red. In this case, the number of red elements in $S \setminus \{x, y\}$ is equal to $k > \frac{n}{2} > \frac{(n-2)}{2}$.

Case 2 Exactly one x and y is red. In this case, the number of red elements in $S \setminus \{x, y\}$ is equal to $k-1 > \frac{n}{2} - 1 = \frac{(n-2)}{2}$. ∎

Invariant

We maintain the following *invariant*:

1. S is the disjoint union of three sets N, I, and D.
2. All elements of I have the same color.
3. There is a majority color in the set $N \cup I$.
4. $mc(S) = mc(N \cup I)$.

Notation

- $N \equiv$ *Not seen yet*
- $I \equiv$ *Identical colors*
- $D \equiv$ *Discarded*

Here is the basic version of our algorithm:

Algorithm 50 Find Majority Simple Algorithm

1: $N \leftarrow S$
2: $I \leftarrow \emptyset$
3: $D \leftarrow \emptyset$
4: **while** $N \neq \emptyset$ **do**
5:    **if** $I == \emptyset$ **then**
6:       *move one element from N to I*
7:    **else**
8:       $x \in N$
9:       $y \in I$
10:      **if** *same_color(x, y)* **then**
11:         *move x from N to I*
12:      **else**
13:         *move y from I to D*
14:         *move x from N to D*
15:      **end if**
16:    **end if**
17: **end while**
18: **return** *an arbitrary element of I*

2.14. Finding the majority

A simple representation of the algorithm

Until now, we did not specify how the sets N, I, and D are represented. There turns out to be a very simple way to do this: Let the elements of S be stored in an array $A[1...n]$. We will use two indices i and j to represent the sets N, I, and D:

1. $0 \leq i \leq j - 1 \leq n$
2. $D = A[1..i]$
3. $I = A[i+1..j-1]$
4. $N = A[j..n]$

If we *translate* our basic algorithm, then we get the following algorithm:

Algorithm 51 Find Majority Algorithm Revisited

1:   $i \leftarrow 0$
2:   $j \leftarrow 1$
3:   **while** $j \leq n$ **do**
4:     **if** $j \leq i+1$ **then**
5:       $j \leftarrow j+1$
6:     **else if** $same\_color(A[j], A[i+1])$ **then**
7:       $j \leftarrow j+1$
8:     **else**
9:       $i \leftarrow i+1$
10:       $swap(A[j], A[i+1])$
11:       $i \leftarrow i+1$
12:       $j \leftarrow j+1$
13:     **end if**
14:   **end while**
15:   **return** $A[i+1]$

If we change the order of the operations, then we get the following algorithm:

Algorithm 52 Find Majority Algorithm Simplified

1:   $i \leftarrow 0$
2:   $j \leftarrow 1$
3:   **while** $j \leq n$ **do**
4:     **if** $j \geq i+2$ **and** $same\_color(A[j], A[i+1]) == false$ **then**
5:       $i \leftarrow i+2$
6:       $swap(A[j], A[i])$
7:     **end if**
8:     $j \leftarrow j+1$
9:   **end while**
10:   **return** $A[i+1]$

Observation 2

In the pseudocode above, the condition

$$j \geq i+2 \text{ and } same\_color(A[j], A[i+1]) == false$$

is equivalent to the condition

$$same\_color(A[j], A[i+1]) == false$$

Proof Assume that $same\_color(A[j], A[i+1]) = false$. We have to show that $j \geq i+2$. We know from the invariant that $j \geq i+1$. If $j = i+1$, then $same\_color(A[j], A[i+1]) = true$. Therefore, $j \neq i+1$. It follows that $j \geq i+2$. ∎

Using this observation, we can further simplify the algorithm, and obtain the final algorithm:

Algorithm 53 Find Majority Algorithm Final

1: $i \leftarrow 0$
2: $j \leftarrow 1$
3: **while** $j \leq n$ **do**
4:    **if** $same\_color(A[j], A[i+1]) == false$ **then**
5:       $i \leftarrow i + 2$
6:       $swap(A[j], A[i])$
7:    **end if**
8:    $j \leftarrow j + 1$
9: **end while**
10: **return** $A[i+1]$

2.15 Mode of a Multiset

Problem

Let $S = (x_1, x_2, \ldots, x_n)$ be a multiset of (not necessarily distinct) elements from a totally ordered set. A *mode* of a multiset is defined as an element that occurs most frequently in the multiset (there may be more than one mode). The number of times an element occurs is called its *multiplicity*. The mode is thus the element with the highest multiplicity.

Find a mode of a given multiset S.

Solution

Our goal is to minimize the number of comparisons. One possible way to find the mode is to use sorting. Once the elements are sorted, we can scan the sorted sequence and count the multiplicities (equal elements will be consecutive in the sorted sequence). We will see that sorting is not always necessary. The reason for thinking that sorting may not be required is that finding the majority can be done in linear time, whereas sorting requires $O(n \log n)$ time. This leads us to suspect that, if the multiplicity of the mode is high, then there may be a fast way of finding it without sorting.

Inductive Approach

Let's try the straightforward induction approach. We assume that we know the mode of a multiset with $n-1$ elements, and try to find the mode of an n element multiset. This is not easy since there may be several elements with the highest multiplicity; the nth element may break the tie. Suppose that the induction hypothesis states that we know *all* the elements with the highest

2.16. Circular Array

multiplicity. Then, we can determine whether the nth element breaks the tie, but it may also increase the multiplicity of another number, which

2.16 Circular Array

A circular array $A[1, \ldots, n]$ is an array such that $n \geq 3$ and $A[1]$ and $A[n]$ are considered to be adjacent elements just like $A[1]$ and $A[2]$, $A[2]$ and $A[3]$, etc., are adjacent. We are given a circular array $A[1, \ldots, n]$ of non-negative integers.

Problem

For any $i, j \in \{1, 2, ..., n\}$ such that $i = j, dist(i,j) = max\{|i-j|, n-|i-j|\}$. Design a linear time algorithm that computes a maximum number t such that for some $i, j \in \{1, 2, ..., n\}, i = j, t = A[i] + A[j] + dist(i,j)$.

Solution

Algorithm 54 Circular Array Algorithm

1: let $B[0 \ldots n]$ and $C[1 \ldots n]$ be linear arrays of nonnegative integers
2: $B[0] \leftarrow 0$
3: **for** $i \leftarrow 1$ **to** n **do**
4: $\quad B[i] \leftarrow max\{B[i-1], A[i] - (i-1)\}$
5: $\quad C[i] \leftarrow B[i-1] + A[i] + (i-1)$
6: **end for**
7: $x \leftarrow max\{C[i] \mid 1 \leq i \leq n\}$
8: **for** $i \leftarrow 1$ **to** n **do**
9: $\quad B[i] \leftarrow max\{B[i-1], A[i] + (i-1)\}$
10: **end for**
11: $C[n] \leftarrow A[n] + 1$
12: **for** $i \leftarrow n - 1$ **downto** 2 **do**
13: $\quad C[i] \leftarrow max\{C[i+1], A[i] + n - (i-1)\}$
14: **end for**
15: $y \leftarrow max\{B[i] + C[i+1] \mid 1 \leq i \leq n-1\}$
16: **return** $max\{x, y\}$

It is obvious that the time complexity is $\Theta(n)$.

Whenever the execution of the first for loop (lines 3-6) of Circular Array is at line 5 and $i \geq 2$, $C[i]$ is assigned $max\{A[k] + A[i] + i-k \mid 1 \leq k < i\}$. It is fairly obvious that at line 5 the value $B[i-1]$ is such that

$$B[i-1] = \begin{cases} 0, & \text{if } A[k] - (k-1) \leq 0 \; \forall k \mid 1 \leq k < i. \\ max A[k] - (k-1) \mid 1 <= k < i, & \text{otherwise.} \end{cases}$$
(2.2)

However, $A[1] - (1-1)$ cannot be negative, therefore there is at least one non-negative value in the sequence $A[k] - (k-1), 1 \leq k < i$, so we can say simply that B[i - 1] at line 5 is $B[i-1] = max\{A[k] - k + 1 \mid 1 \leq k < i\}$. It follows that $C[i]$ is assigned the value $max\{A[k]k+1 \mid 1 \leq k < i\} + A[i] + i - 1 = max\{A[k] + A[i] + i - k \mid 1 \leq k < i\}$.

It follows that x is assigned the value $max\{A[i] + A[j] + j - i \mid 1 \leq i < j \leq n\}$

at line 7 of CIRCULAR ARRAY.

y is assigned the value $max\{A[i] + A[j] + n - (j1i) \mid 1 \leq i < j \leq n\}$ at line 13 of CIRCULAR ARRAY.

Consider the second for loop (lines 8-10). Since $A[1] + (1-1) \geq 0$, it is the case that $\forall i, 1 \leq i \leq n, B[i] = max\{A[k] + (k-1) \mid 1 \leq k \leq i\}$ after the second for loop terminates.

Now consider the third for loop at lines 12-14. Think of the assignment at line 11 as $C[n] = A[n] + n - (n-1)$. Having that in mind, it is fairly obvious that after that **for** loop terminates, it is the case that $C[i] = max\{A[k] + n - (k-1) \mid i \leq k \leq n\}, \forall i, 2 \leq i \leq n$.

From these two considerations it follows immediately that at line 15, y is assigned the value

$$max\{A[i] + (i-1) + A[j] + n - (j-1) \mid 1 \leq i < j \leq n\} =$$
$$max\{A[i] + A[j] + n - (j-i) \mid 1 \leq i < j \leq n\}$$

It follows immediately that CIRCULAR ARRAY indeed returns the maximum number t such that for some $i, j \in \{1, 2, ..., n\}, i = j, t = A[i] + A[j] + dist(i, j)$.

2.17 Find Median of two sorted arrays

Problem

Let $X[1, \ldots, n]$ and $Y[1, \ldots, n]$ be two arrays, each containing n numbers already in sorted order. Give an $O(\log n)$-time algorithm to find the median of all 2n elements in arrays X and Y.

Solution

Assume that when n is even the median of X is $X[\frac{n}{2} + 1]$. If the arrays are of equal size, and that is the current case, we can solve the problem by a divide and conquer algorithm that compares the medians of the two arrays and then discards the lower half of the array with the smaller median and the upper half of the array with the bigger median. The algorithm proceeds likewise until both arrays are reduced to 2 elements each. Then we solve the reduced problem in constant time. In case the size is odd, by upper and lower half we mean, the subarray from one end until and excluding the median. It is easy to show this dichotomy brings the size of the array down to 2 regardless of what the initial n is, because the iterator $n \leftarrow \frac{n}{2}$ reaches 2 regardless of the starting value of n.

Now consider a more general version of this problem where the arrays are $X[1, \ldots, p]$ and $Y[1, \ldots, q]$ for possibly unequal values of p and q. Let us call Z the array that would be obtained if we merged X and Y. Let $m = p + q$. The essence is the fact that we can check in $\Theta(1)$ time whether $X[i]$ is the median of Z, for any i such that $1 \leq i \leq p$. According to our definition of median, the median is greater than or equal to $\lfloor m \rfloor$ elements of an m-element array. Having that in mind, clearly if $X[i]$ is the median then:

- $X[i]$ is greater than or equal to i - 1 elements of X.
- $X[i]$ is greater than or equal to $j = \lfloor m \rfloor - i + 1$ elements of Y.

It takes only constant time to check if $Y[j] \leq X[i] \leq Y[j+1]$. To avoid excessive boundary checks, pad X and Y at the left side with $-\infty$ and with $+\infty$ at the right side. If that is fulfilled we have found the median and it is

X[i]. Otherwise, we binary search in X to see if the median is in X. If that fails, the median must be from Y, and we can repeat the analogous process with X and Y swapped.

Algorithm 55 Find Median of two sorted array

1: **function** COMMON-MEDIAN(X[1,..., p], Y[1,..., q])   ▷ sorted arrays
2:     $m \leftarrow p + q$
3:     $k \leftarrow$ MEDIAN-BIN-SEARCH$(X, Y, 1, p)$
4:     **if** k > 0 **then**
5:         **return** X, k
6:     **end if**
7:     $k \leftarrow$ MEDIAN-BIN-SEARCH$(Y, X, 1, q)$
8:     **return** Y, k
9: **end function**

Algorithm 56 Median Search

1: **function** MEDIAN-BIN-SEARCH(A, B: sorted arrays, l, r:integers)
2:     **if** l > r **then**
3:         **return** -1
4:     **end if**
5:     $i \leftarrow \lfloor \frac{l+r}{2} \rfloor$
6:     $j \leftarrow \lfloor \frac{m}{2} \rfloor - i + 1$
7:     **if** $B[j] \leq A[i] \leq B[j+1]$ **then**
8:         **return** i
9:     **end if**
10:    **if** $A[i] < B[j]$ **then**
11:        MEDIAN-BIN-SEARCH(A, B, l, i)
12:    **end if**
13:    **if** $A[i] > B[j+1]$ **then**
14:        MEDIAN-BIN-SEARCH(A, B, i + 1, r)
15:    **end if**
16: **end function**

A not too formal proof of correctness of COMMON-MEDIAN is simply pointing out the preceding discussion and knowing that the binary search idea is correct. The time complexity is obviously $\Theta(\log m)$. Alternatively, we can say the complexity is $\Theta(max\{\log p, \log q\})$.

2.18 Finding the missing integer

Problem Description

An array $A[1, \ldots, n]$ contains all the integers from 0 to n except one. It would be easy to determine the missing integer in $O(n)$ time by using an auxiliary array $B[0, \ldots, n]$ to record which numbers appear in A. In this problem, however, we cannot access an entire integer in A with a single operation. The elements of A are represented in binary, and the only operation we can use to access them is *fetch the jth bit of A[i]*, which takes constant time. Show that if we use only this operation, we can still determine the missing integer in $O(n)$ time.

2.18. Finding the missing integer

Solution

Analysis

Let m be the number of bits required to represent n in binary. It is well known that $m = \lfloor \log_2 n \rfloor + 1$. In this problem we think of A as an $m \times n$, 0-1 matrix. Row number m of A consists of the least significant bits of the numbers in A, row number $m - 1$ consists of the second least significant bits, etc., row number 1 consists of the most significant bits.

For instance, if $n = 10$ and the missing number is $6 = 0110_b$, A may look like:

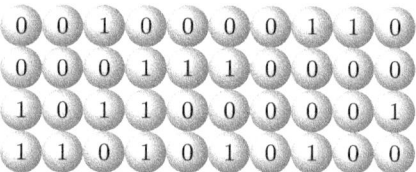

Printing this array in spiral form would give

1 2 3 4 8 12 16 15 14 13 9 5 6 7 11 10

The only constant time access to it is of the form A[j][i], which can be labeled as *fetch the jth bit of A[i]*, assuming the first bit is the most significant, etc.

C++ Implementation

Consider the following program:

```
int m = floor(logb(n)) + 1;
int A[m][n];

int main()
{
    int i, j, t, numrow, n0, n1, ntemp = n;
    int B[n], res[m];

    for(i = 0; i < n; i++)
    {
        B[i] = i;
    }

    for(i = m - 1; i >= 0; i--)
    {
        n0 = n1 = 0;

        for(j = 0; j < ntemp; j++)
        {
            if (A[i][B[j]] == 0) n0++;
            else n1++;
        }

        if(n0 - n1 == 2 || n0 - n1 == 1) res[i] = 1;
        if(n0 - n1 == 0 || n0 - n1 == -1) res[i] = 0;

        for(j = 0, t = 0; j < ntemp; j++)
        {
```

2.18. Finding the missing integer

```
                if((res[i] == A[i][B[j]]))
                {
                    B[t] = B[j];
                    t++;
                }
            }

            if(ntemp \% 2 == 0) ntemp = (ntemp / 2);
            else if(res[i] == 0) ntemp = floor(ntemp / 2);
            else ntemp = ceil(ntemp / 2);
        }

        for(i = 0; i < n; i++)
            std::cout << res[i]);
    }
```

We claim the algorithm implemented by this program solves correctly the problem of determining the missing bit. First we prove it is correct.

Proving the Correctness of the program

Define that a complete array of size n is a two dimensional bit array similar to the above A but without any missing column from it. Clearly, such an array has n + 1 columns. For instance, a complete array of size 10 would be the following:

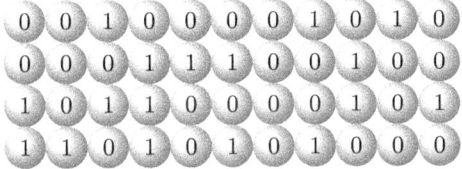

Define that an almost complete array of size n is a two dimensional bit array with precisely one missing column from it. It follows the array A in the current problem is an almost complete array of size n. Now consider any complete array $\tilde{A}$ of size n. Call $\tilde{L}$ the bottom row of $\tilde{A}$. That $\tilde{L}$ consists of the least significant bits of the numbers from $\tilde{A}$. Let $\tilde{n}_0$ be the number of zeros and $\tilde{n}_1$, the number of ones, in $\tilde{L}$. Let $\tilde{\Delta} = \tilde{n}_0 - \tilde{n}_1$. We claim that :

$$\tilde{\Delta} = \begin{cases} 0, & \text{if } n \text{ is odd.} \\ 1, & \text{if } n \text{ is even..} \end{cases} \quad (2.3)$$

Indeed, it is trivial to prove by induction that if the number n + 1 of columns in $\tilde{A}$ is even then $\tilde{\Delta} = 0$ and if it is odd, $\tilde{A} = 1$.

Now consider A: any almost complete array of size n, obtained from $\tilde{A}$ by deleting a column, i.e., the missing number. Let L be the bottom row of A. Let n_0 be the number of zeros and n_1, the number of ones, in L. Let $\Delta = n_0 - n_1$. We claim that:

$$\Delta = \begin{cases} \tilde{\Delta} + 1, & \text{if the missing number is odd.} \\ \tilde{\Delta} - 1, & \text{if the missing number is even.} \end{cases} \quad (2.4)$$

Indeed, if the missing number is even there is a 0 less in L in comparison with $\tilde{L}$, while the number of ones is the same; that is, $n_0 = \tilde{n}_0 - 1$ and $n_1 = \tilde{n}_1$.

2.18. Finding the missing integer

Likewise, if the missing number is odd there is a 1 less in L in comparison with $\tilde{L}$, while the number of zeros is the same; that is, $n_0 = \tilde{n}_0$ and $n_1 = \tilde{n}_1 - 1$. Having in mind the above considerations, it is clear that:

$$\Delta = \begin{cases} 2, & \text{if } n \text{ is even and the missing number is odd.} \\ 1, & \text{if } n \text{ is odd and the missing number is odd.} \\ 0, & \text{if } n \text{ is even and the missing number is even.} \\ -1, & \text{if } n \text{ is odd and the missing number is even.} \end{cases} \quad (2.5)$$

We conclude that :

$\Delta \in \{1, 2\} \implies$ the least significant bit of the missing number is 1.
$\Delta \in \{-1, 0\} \implies$ the least significant bit of the missing number is 0.

So, with one linear scan along the bottom row of A we can compute Δ and then in constant time we can compute the least significant bit of the missing number. However, if we attempt a similar approach for the other bits of the missing number, we will end up with $\Omega(n \log n)$ computation because the number of rows is logarithmic in n. The key observation is that in order to determine the second least significant bit of the missing number, we need to scan approximately half the columns of A. Namely, if the least significant bit was determined to be 1, for the computation of the second least significant bit we need to scan only the columns having 1 at the bottom row. Likewise, if the least significant bit was determined to be 0, for the computation of the second least significant bit we need to scan only the columns having 0 at the bottom row. Next we explain why this is true.

The number of rows of A is $m = \lfloor \log_2 n \rfloor + 1$. Define that $A_0^{(m-1)}$ is the two dimensional array obtained from A by deleting the columns that have 0 in row m - 1, and then deleting row m - 1. Define that $A_1^{(m-1)}$ is the two dimensional array obtained from A by deleting the columns that have 1 in row m - 1, and then deleting row m - 1. Call the process of deriving $A_0^{(m-1)}$ and $A_1^{(m-1)}$, the *reduction* of A, and the two obtained arrays, the *reduced arrays*. Let b be the least significant bit of the missing number and $\bar{b}$ be its complement.

Lemma

Under the current naming conventions, $A_b^{(m-1)}$ is complete, and $A_{\bar{b}}^{(m-1)}$ is almost complete. Furthermore, the missing number in $A_{\bar{b}}^{(m-1)}$ is obtained from the missing number in A by removing the least significant bit (i.e., shift right).

Proof

First we will see an example and then make a formal proof. To use the previously given example with n = 10, m = 4, missing number 6 = 0110_b, and A as

```
0 0 1 0 0 0 0 1 1 0
0 0 0 1 1 1 0 0 0 0
1 0 1 1 0 0 0 0 0 1
1 1 0 1 0 1 0 1 0 0
```

2.18. Finding the missing integer

the two derived subarrays : $A_0^{(3)}$ and $A_1^{(3)}$ are respectively:

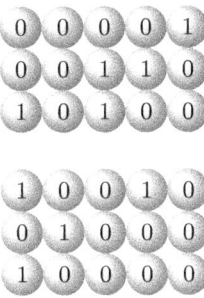

Obviously, $A_0^{(3)}$ is complete and $A_1^{(3)}$ is almost complete: column {0 1 1} is missing from it. The least significant bit of the missing number in A is 0; if we did not know which is the missing number, we could deduce that its least significant bit is 0 by computing the aforementioned $\Delta = 5 - 5 = 0$. Indeed $A_0^{(3)} = \tilde{A}_1^{(3)}$ is the array that is almost complete. And indeed the missing number in it 011 is obtained from 0110 by shift right.

Let us prove it. It is clear that if $\tilde{A}$ is a complete array of size n, both $A_0^{(m-1)}$ and $A_1^{(m-1)}$ are complete. If n is odd then they contain the same columns (possibly in different order left to right), otherwise $A_1^{(m-1)}$ contains one column more and the other columns are the same. Now imagine A; the array obtained from $\tilde{A}$ by the deletion of precisely one column. If the bit at the bottom row of the deleted column is 0 then $A_0^{(m-1)}$ is the same as $\tilde{A}_0^{(m-1)}$, so $A_0(m-1)$ is complete. However, $A_1^{(m-1)}$ is not the same as $\tilde{A}_1^{(m-1)}$: $\tilde{A}_1^{(m-1)}$ contains one more column that corresponds to the missing number. It follows that $A_1^{(m-1)}$ is almost complete. Alternatively, if the bit at the bottom row of the deleted column is 1 then $A_1^{(m-1)}$ is the same as $\tilde{A}_1^{(m-1)}$, so $A_1^{(m-1)}$ is complete, but $A_0^{(m-1)}$ is almost complete. ∎

Verification of the algorithm

Having all that in mind, the verification of the algorithm is straightforward. m is the number of bits, i.e. the number of rows of A. The array res is the output: at each iteration of the main for loop, one bit of res is computed, the direction being from the least significant bit *upwards*. B is an auxilliary array of integers. The definition of the problem requires bitwise access only to the elements of A; the array B can be accessed *normally*. B keeps the indices of the columns whose i^{th} row we scan at every iteration of the main for loop.

Initially, of course, B contains the indices 0, 1, . . . , n-1, in that order, so when i is m-1 we simply scan the bottom row of A. At every iteration of the main for loop, ntemp is the number of columns in the almost complete array whose last row we scan. Initially, ntemp is n, which reflects the fact that at the first iteration we scan the bottom row of A. We will verify the assignment of new value to ntemp later on.

Within the main for loop, the first nested for loop simply counts the zeros and ones and stores the results in n0 and n1, respectively.

The difference n0 - n1 determines the ith least significant bit res[i] according to the following

$\Delta \in \{1, 2\} \implies$ the least significant bit of the missing number is 1.
$\Delta \in \{-1, 0\} \implies$ the least significant bit of the missing number is 0.

The second nested for loop discovers the indices of the columns that correspond to the columns of the next reduced array that is almost complete. To see why we consider only values (of the last row of A) equal to res[i], check the above Lemma.

Finally, the assignment of new value to ntemp is done in accordance to the following considerations. If ntemp is even then both derived arrays have the same length $\frac{ntemp}{2}$. Otherwise, note that we are interested in that derived subarray that is almost complete. If res[i] is one then that subarray is the one obtained by deleting the columns with zeros at the bottom; it has one more column than the complete derived subarray, so res[i] should be $ceil(\frac{ntemp}{2})$. Analogously, if res[i] is zero then res[i] should be $floor(\frac{ntemp}{2})$. That concludes the verification of the algorithm. The reader is invited to make an even more rigorous proof of correctness using *loop invariant*.

The number of accesses to A at each iteration of the main for loop is proportional to the current value of ntemp. Clearly, the total number of accesses is proportional to

$$n + \frac{n}{2} + \frac{n}{4} + \ldots + 1 \leq 2n = \Theta(n)$$

2.19 Finding the missing number with sorted columns

Problem Description

Consider the previous problem under the additional assumption that the numbers in A, that is, the columns, appear in sorted order. Find the missing number with $O(\log n)$ bit accesses to A.

Solution

If the numbers in A are sorted the problem can be solved by first determining the most significant bit, then the second most significant bit, etc., the least significant bit, of the missing number, with precisely one access to A for each bit.

Suppose $\tilde{A}$ is the the complete array of size n (see the definition of *complete array* in the solution to the previous problem), i.e. there is no missing number. For instance, if n = 10 then $\tilde{A}$ is:

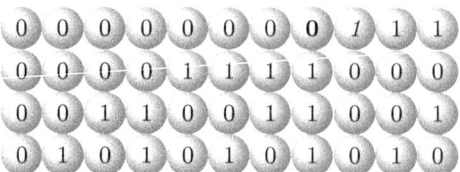

Consider the boundary on the top row between the zeros and the ones. The **rightmost zero** is in column 7 ($7 = 2^{\lfloor \log_2 10 \rfloor} - 1$) and the *leftmost one* is in the column 8 ($8 = 2^{\lfloor \log_2 10 \rfloor}$). It is easy to generalize that the boundary is between columns $2^{\lfloor \log_2 n \rfloor} - 1$ and $2^{\lfloor \log_2 n \rfloor}$, provided the leftmost column is number 0.

Now consider the boundary on the top row between the zeros and the ones in

2.19. Finding the missing number with sorted columns

an almost complete array A of size n. For instance, if n = 10 and the missing number is $6 = 0110_b$ then A is :

0	0	0	0	0	0	0	1	1	1
0	0	0	0	1	1	1	0	0	0
0	0	1	1	0	0	1	0	0	1
0	1	0	1	0	1	1	0	1	0

Consider positions $7 = 2^{\lfloor \log_2 10 \rfloor} - 1$ and $8 = 2^{\lfloor \log_2 10 \rfloor}$ on the top row. Now the boundary is not between them because the missing number has most significant bit 0, so the boundary is *shifted* one position to the left in comparison with $\tilde{A}$. However, if we do not know what the missing number's most significant bit is, we can deduce it is 0 from the fact that there are two 1's at positions 7 and 8 on the top row.

Clearly, if there were 0 and 1 at positions 7 and 8, respectively, on the top row, that would mean the missing number's most significant bit is 1, as in the following example where the array is called B, n = 10 and the missing number is $9 = 1001_b$:

0	0	0	0	0	0	0	0	1	1
0	0	0	0	1	1	1	1	0	0
0	0	1	1	0	0	1	1	0	1
0	1	0	1	0	1	0	1	0	0

So, by inspecting only position $2^{\lfloor \log_2 n \rfloor} - 1$ on the top row, we can deduce the most significant bit of the missing number as follows:

$$themissingnumber'smostsignificantbit = \begin{cases} 0, & if \ A[0][2^{\lfloor \log_2 n \rfloor} - 1] == 1. \\ 1, & if \ A[0][2^{\lfloor \log_2 n \rfloor} - 1] == 0. \end{cases} \quad (2.6)$$

Having computed the most significant bit of the missing number in $\Theta(1)$ time, we compute the second most significant bit in $\Theta(1)$ time, etc., until we compute all bits of the missing number with $\Theta(\log n)$ attempts, each taking $\Theta(1)$ time.

Case I

If the most significant bit is 0, to compute the second most significant bit we consider only the subarray of columns $0, 1, \ldots, 2^{\lfloor \log_2 n \rfloor} - 2$ and rows 1, 2, $\ldots, \lfloor \log_2 n \rfloor$. Using the above A as an example, that subarray is, say, A':

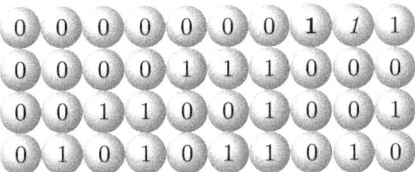

⟹ A':

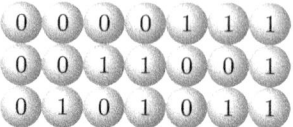

We proceed recursively with A' exactly as with A because A' is an almost complete array. Let us compute the size of A'. The initial A can be of any size but the size of A' is uniquely determined by n. Let $m = \lfloor \log_2 n \rfloor + 1$, , that is, the number of bits necessary to represent n in binary (thus m is the number of rows in A). Let $m' = m - 1$. The derived A' is of size $2^{m'} - 1$. The -1 comes from the fact that A' has a missing number.

Case II

If the most significant bit is 1, to compute the second most significant bit we consider only the subarray whose columns have 1's in the top row. Using the above B as an example, that subarray is, say, B' :

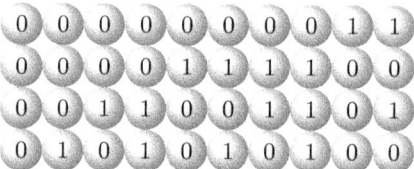

⟹ A' :

$$\begin{matrix} 0 & 0 \\ 0 & 1 \\ 0 & 0 \end{matrix}$$

The number of columns, call it c', in B' is easy to compute: it is $c' = n - 2^{m'}$, where $m = \lfloor \log_2 n \rfloor$. In the concrete example, n = 10, $m' = 3$, thus $c' = n - 2^{m'} = 10 - 8 = 2$.

However, B' is not necessarily an almost complete array: in order to be an almost complete array it has to have at least one 1 at its top row. In fact, B' is an almost complete array only when $c' > \frac{1}{2}\left(2^{m'}\right) = 2^{m'-1}$. In this example, B' is not an almost complete array, it has one row too many. We can conclude the second most significant bit of the missing number is 0 (the missing number is $9 = 1001_b$) just by knowing the dimensions of B' ; we do not have to scan, or even examine bits of, the top row to make that conclusion. The rule is, while $c' \leq 2^{m'-1}$, write 0's to into the missing number's bit positions and perform $m' \leftarrow m' - 1$. This process is equivalent to removing the necessary number of top rows from B'. Once the process is over and B' is reduced as necessary, it can be dealt with recursively.

Consider the following program:

2.20. Re-arranging an array

```
1 int m = floor(logb(n)) + 1;
2 int A[m][n], res[m];
3
4 void find(int low, int high, int row)
5 {
6     int j, c, n1, n2, numel = high - low + 1;
7     if(row == m-1)
8     {
9         res[row] = !(A[i][0]);
10        PrintResult();
11        return;
12    }
13
14    n1 = floor(logb(numel));
15    n2 = 1 << n1;
16
17    if(A[row][low+n2-1] == 1)
18    {
19        res[row] = 0;
20        find(low, n2-2, row+1);
21    }
22    else
23    {
24        j = 1;
25        res[row] = 1;
26        c = numel - n2;
27
28        while((n1 >= 0) && c <= (1<<(--n1)))
29        {
30            j++;
31            res[row+j] = 0;
32        }
33
34        if(row+j == m-1)
35        {
36            PrintResult();
37            return;
38        }
39
40        find(n2, high, row+j);
41    }
42 }
43
44 int main()
45 {
46     find(0, n-1, 0);
47 }
```

The correctness of the fragment follows from the previous discussion. The time complexity is obviously $\Theta(\log n)$. ∎

2.20 Re-arranging an array

Problem

An array $a[1..n]$ and a threshold b are given. Rearrange the elements of the array in such a way that all elements on the left of some boundary do not exceed b whereas all elements on the right of the boundary are greater than or equal to b. The number of operations should be proportional to n.

2.20. Re-arranging an array

Solution

Algorithm 57 Re-arranging an array

1: **function** REARRANGE-ARRAY(a[1..n], b)
2:     $l \leftarrow 0$
3:     $r \leftarrow n$
4:     **Invariant** : $l \leq r;\ a[1..l] \leq b;\ a[r+1..n] \geq b$
5:     **while** $l \neq r$ **do**
6:         **if** $a[l+1] \leq b$ **then**
7:             $l \leftarrow l + 1$
8:         **else if** $a[r] \geq b$ **then**
9:             $r \leftarrow r - 1$
10:        **else**   ▷ $a[l+1] > b;\ a[r] < b;\ l+1 < r;$
11:             $swap(a[l+1], a[r])$
12:             $l \leftarrow l + 1$
13:             $r \leftarrow r - 1$
14:         **end if**
15:     **end while**
16: **end function**

Problem

Repeat the previous problem with the additional restriction that the elements smaller than b should precede elements equal to b which themselves should precede elements greater than b.

Solution

We need three boundaries to divide our segment into four parts.

1. The first part contains elements smaller than b
2. the second part contains only elements equal to b
3. the third part may contain anything, and
4. the fourth part contains only elements greater than b.

Please note that we can get a more symmetric solution using a *fourth* boundary.

At each step we consider the left element of the third part (just to the right of the second boundary).

Algorithm 58 Re-arranging an array revisited
```
 1: function REARRANGE-ARRAY(a[1..n], b)
 2:     l ← 0
 3:     m ← 0
 4:     r ← n
 5:     Invariant : a[1..l] < b; a[l + 1..m] = b; a[r + 1..n] > b
 6:     while m ≠ r do
 7:         if a[m + 1] == b then
 8:             m ← m + 1
 9:         else if a[m + 1] > b then
10:             swap(a[m + 1], a[r])
11:             r ← r − 1
12:         else                                    ▷ a[m + 1] < b
13:             swap(a[m + 1], a[l + 1])
14:             l ← l + 1
15:             m ← m + 1
16:         end if
17:     end while
18: end function
```

2.21 Switch and Bulb Problem

Problem Description

Imagine two rooms with no visibility between them. In one room there n numbered light switches $s_1, s_2, \ldots, s_n$. In the other room there are n numbered light bulbs $l_1, l_2, \ldots, l_n$. It is known that each switch turns on and off to exactly one bulb but we do not know anything about the wiring between the switches and the bulbs. Initially we are in the room with the switches. Our job is to tell the exact wiring, i.e. which switch operates which bulb. We are allowed to press any switches and then go to the room with the bulbs and perform an observation. We are not allowed to touch the bulbs : our only source of information is the observation of the bulbs.

The switches are such that their physical appearance does not change when toggled so we have no way of knowing beforehand whether pressing a certain switch leads to turning on or turning off of a bulb. Every switch has, of course, two states only, as any normal light switch.

Describe an algorithm that discovers the wiring with minimum number of observations, i.e. with minimum visits to the room with the bulbs. The algorithm should work iteratively, at each iteration simulating toggling some switches and then simulating an observation by calling some function OBSERVE. The toggling is simulated by writing into a 0-1 array P[1, . . . , n]. Say, P[i] = 1 means s_i is toggled, and P[i] = 0 means s_i is not toggled. The result of the *observation* is written in some 0-1 array L[1, . . . , n]. Say, L[i] = 1 means l_i is on, and L[i] = 0 means l_i is off. After every call to OBSERVE, the algorithm temporarily halts, the execution is supposed to be transferred to an outside agent and the algorithm resumes after the outside agent finishes writing into L.

Prove an asymptotic lower bound for the number of observations. Is your algorithm optimal in the asymptotic sense?

2.21. Switch and Bulb Problem

Solution

Our algorithm maintains the following data structures:

- a 0-1 array $A[1, \ldots, n]$ to keep the result of the previous observation,

- an array $S[1, \ldots, n]$ that refers to the switches. Every element of S is a pointer. Namely, $S[i]$ points to a (doubly) linked list that represents the set of the bulbs, each of which can possibly be connected to s_i according to currently available information. We call this set of bulbs, *the candidate set* for s_i.

- an array B of positive integers of size 2n. During iteration i, B contains 2i elements that determine a partitioning of S into subarrays. $B[2j]$ and $B[2j+1]$ are numbers such that $B[2j]$ $B[2j+1]$ and the pair $B[2j]$, $B[2j+1]$ represents the subarray $S[\,B[2j], \ldots, B[2j+1]\,]$.

- a multitide of doubly linked lists with n elements altogether. They represent a partition of the set of the bulbs. Each element contains an integer that corresponds to the ID of precisely one bulb, and each list represents precisely one candidate set. Initially, there is only one list in this multitude, call this list C. That reflects the fact that at the beginning we have no restrictions on the possible connections between bulbs and switches. At the end, there are n non-empty lists in this multitude. That reflects the fact that at the end we know precisely the wiring between the switches and the bulbs.

Here is the pseudocode. Initially $P[\,]$ is arbitrary.

2.21. Switch and Bulb Problem

Algorithm 59 Switches and Bulbs

```
 1: function SWITCHES-AND-BULBS
 2:     create doubly linked list C of n elements, one for each bulb
 3:     create S and set every pointer in it to C
 4:     B ← [1, n]
 5:     OBSERVE()
 6:     copy L into A
 7:     while t do ▷ here are less than 2n entities in B
 8:         for all pair B[2j], B[2j + 1] such that B[2j] < B[2j + 1]
 9:             mid ← ½(B[2j] + B[2j + 1])
10:             set P[B[2j], ..., mid] to ones
11:             set P[mid + 1, ..., B[2j + 1]] to zeros
12:         end for
13:         update B so that for each applicable pair B[2j], B[2j + 1], it is substituted by two pairs <B[2j], mid> and <mid + 1, B[2j + 1]>
14:         OBSERVE()
15:         for i ← 1 to n do
16:             if A[i] ≠ L[i] then
17:                 mark bulb i as changed
18:             end if
19:             for all list of bulbs do
20:                 split the list, if necessary, into two lists: changed and unchanged bulbs
21:             end for
22:             for all element of S do
23:                 update the pointer to the relevant list of bulbs
24:             end for
25:         end for
26:         copy L into A
27:     end while
28:     for i ← 1 to n do
29:         print the sole element of the list pointed to by S[i]
30:     end for
31: end function
```

The query complexity of the algorithm, i.e. the number of calls of OBSERVE, is the number of executions of the while loop plus one. The number of executions of the while loop is logarithmic in n because we split each subarray, delineated by a couple from B, roughly in half, with each execution. So, the number of queries is $\Theta(\log n)$.

Now we prove an $\Omega(\log n)$ lower bound of the number of such queries. We use the decision tree model. The decision tree model is used, for instance, for proving an $\Omega(n \log n)$ lower bound for comparison based sorting. However, the decision trees for comparison based sorting are binary because there are precisely two possible outcomes of each comparison of the kind $a_i < a_j$. In contrast to that, any decision tree that corresponds to the current problem of switches and bulbs has branching factor of 2^n. To why this is true, note that there are precisely 2^n possible outcomes from each observation of the n bulbs.

The current problem is, essentially, computing a permutation, because the mapping from switches to bulbs is a *bijection*. It follows that any decision tree for that problem has to distinguish all possible n! permutations of n elements: if the decision tree has a leaf labeled by at least two permutations then the corresponding algorithm is not correct. It follows that the leaves must be at least n!.

The height of the tree is approximately logarithm to base the branching factor of the number of leaves:

$$\log_{2^n} n! = \frac{\log_2 n!}{\log_2 2^n} = \frac{\Theta(n \log n)}{n} = \Theta(\log n)$$

The height of the tree is a lower bound for the query complexity of any observation-based algorithm for the problem of switches and bulbs. It follows that $\Theta(\log n)$ observations are required if the only testing allowed is direct observation. It follows that algorithm SWITCHES-AND-BULBS is asymptotically optimal with respect to the number of performed observations. ∎

2.22 Compute sum of sub-array

Problem Description

A square matrix a[1..n][1..n] and a number $m \leq n$ are given. For any $m \times m$ subsquare, compute the sum of its elements. The total number of operations should be of order n^2.

Solution

The algorithm is a straightforward two step process:

1. First compute the sum for all horizontal rectangles of size $m \times 1$. When such a rectangle is shifted to the right, one element is added and one is subtracted.

2. After computing all these sums, we compute the sums for squares. When a square is shifted down, one rectangle is added and another rectangle is subtracted.

2.23 Find a number not sum of subsets of array

Problem Description

A non-decreasing integer array a[1..n] contains positive numbers only. Find the minimal positive integer that cannot be represented as a sum of several elements of this array (no element may be used more than once). The number of operations should be of order n.

Solution

Assume all numbers that can be represented as sums of subsets of $\{a[1], \ldots, a[k]\}$ form the set $\{1, 2, \ldots, N\}$ for some N. If $a[k+1]$ is greater than $N+1$, then $N+1$ is the smallest number that cannot be represented as the sum of some subset of $\{a[1], \ldots, a[n]\}$. If $a[k+1] \leq N+1$, then all numbers that can be represented as sums of subsets of $\{a[1] \ldots a[k+1]\}$ form the set $\{1, 2, \ldots, N + a[k+1]\}$.

Algorithm 60 Find a number not sum of subsets of array
1: $k \leftarrow 0$
2: $N \leftarrow 0$
3: **Invariant** : all the numbers that can be represented as sums of subsets of $\{a[1], \ldots, a[k]\}$, form the set $\{1, 2, \ldots, N\}$
4: **while** $k \neq n$ **and** $a[k+1] \leq N+1$ **do**
5: $\quad N \leftarrow N + a[k+1]$
6: $\quad k \leftarrow k+1$
7: **end while** $\triangleright$ $(k = n)$ or $(a[k+1] > N+1)$; the answer is $N+1$ in both cases
8: **print**(N + 1)

2.24 K^{th} Smallest Element in Two Sorted Arrays

Problem Description

Given two sorted arrays a[1..n] and b[1..m], find the kth smallest element in the union of the two arrays. Time Complexity should be $\Theta(\log n + \log m)$.

Solution

We are searching the kth smallest element s_k in the union of the arrays $a[1, ..., n]$ and $b[1, ..., m]$.

Because we are looking at the kth smallest element, we can restrict our attention to the arrays a[1, . . . , k] and b[1, . . . , k]. If $k > m$ or $k > n$, we can take all the elements with index larger than the array boundary to have infinite value.

Algorithm

Our algorithm start off by comparing $a[\lfloor \frac{k}{2} \rfloor]$ and $a[\lceil \frac{k}{2} \rceil]$:

1. If $a[\lfloor \frac{k}{2} \rfloor] > b[\lceil \frac{k}{2} \rceil]$, then s_k will be the $\lfloor \frac{k}{2} \rfloor$-th smallest element of the union of the subarrays $a[1, \ldots, \lfloor \frac{k}{2} \rfloor]$ and $b[\lceil \frac{k}{2} \rceil + 1, \ldots, k]$.

2. If $a[\lfloor \frac{k}{2} \rfloor] < b[\lceil \frac{k}{2} \rceil]$, then s_k will be the $\lceil \frac{k}{2} \rceil$-th smallest element of the union of the subarrays $a[\lfloor \frac{k}{2} \rfloor + 1, \ldots, k]$ and $b[1, \ldots, \lceil \frac{k}{2} \rceil]$.

3. The base case of the recursion is $a[\lfloor \frac{k}{2} \rfloor] = b[\lceil \frac{k}{2} \rceil]$ and we return $s_k = a[\lfloor \frac{k}{2} \rfloor] = b[\lceil \frac{k}{2} \rceil]$

2.24. K^{th} Smallest Element in Two Sorted Arrays

Algorithm 61 K^{th} Smallest Element in Two Sorted Arrays

1: **function** KTHSMALLESTUNION(a, b, k)
2:    $a \leftarrow$ RESTRICT(a, k)
3:    $b \leftarrow$ RESTRICT(b, k)
4:    $fl \leftarrow floor(\frac{k}{2})$
5:    $cl \leftarrow ceil(\frac{k}{2})$
6:    **if** $a[fl-1] > b[cl-1]$ **then**
7:       **return** KTHSMALLESTUNION(a[0..fl - 1], b[cl..k - 1], fl)
8:    **else if** $a[fl-1] < b[cl-1]$ **then**
9:       **return** KTHSMALLESTUNION(a[fl..k - 1], b[0..cl - 1], cl)
10:   **else**
11:       **return** $a[cl-1]$
12:   **end if**
13: **end function**
14: **function** RESTRICT(a, k)
15:    $n \leftarrow size(a)$
16:    **if** $k \leq n-1$ **then**
17:       $a \leftarrow a[0..n-1]$
18:    **else**
19:       $a \leftarrow a + [INFINITY] \times (k-n)$
20:    **end if**
21:    **return** a
22: **end function**

Time Complexity

Our algorithm is characterized by the recurrence:

$$T(k) = T(\tfrac{k}{2}) + O(1)$$

Using the Master Theorem with a = 1, b = 2 and d = 0, as $\log_b a = 0 = d$, we get

$$T(k) = O(\log k) = O(\log n + \log m)$$

Proof of correctness

Our algorithm start off by comparing $a[\lfloor\frac{k}{2}\rfloor]$ and $b[\lceil\frac{k}{2}\rceil]$:

- Suppose $a[\lfloor\frac{k}{2}\rfloor] > b[\lceil\frac{k}{2}\rceil]$. Then:
  - In the union of a and b there can be at most $k-2$ elements smaller than $b[\lceil\frac{k}{2}\rceil]$, i.e., $a[1, \ldots, \lfloor\frac{k}{2}\rfloor - 1]$ and $b[1, \ldots, \lceil\frac{k}{2}\rceil - 1]$ and we must necessarily have $s_k > b[\lceil\frac{k}{2}\rceil]$.
  - Similarly, all elements $a[1, \ldots, \lfloor\frac{k}{2}\rfloor]$ and $b[1, \ldots, \lceil\frac{k}{2}\rceil]$ will be smaller than $a[\lfloor\frac{k}{2}\rfloor + 1]$. But these are k elements, so we must have $s_k < a[\lfloor\frac{k}{2}\rfloor + 1]$.

  This shows that s_k must be contained in the union of the subarrays $a[1, \ldots, \lfloor\frac{k}{2}\rfloor]$ and $b[\lceil\frac{k}{2}\rceil] + 1, \ldots, k]$.

  In particular, as we discarded $\lceil\frac{k}{2}\rceil$ elements smaller than s_k, then s_k will be the $\lfloor\frac{k}{2}\rfloor$-th smallest element in this union.

  We can then find s_k by recursing on this smallest problem.

- The case $a[\lfloor \frac{k}{2} \rfloor] < b[\lceil \frac{k}{2} \rceil]$ is symmetric.

- The last case, which is also the base case of the recursion, is $a[\lfloor \frac{k}{2} \rfloor] = b[\lceil \frac{k}{2} \rceil]$, for which we have $s_k = a[\lfloor \frac{k}{2} \rfloor] = b[\lceil \frac{k}{2} \rceil]$

2.25 Sort a sequence of sub-sequences

Problem Description

There is a sequence of n elements, say S, which needs to be sorted. The input sequence consists of $\frac{n}{k}$ sub-sequences, each containing k elements. The elements in a given sub-sequence are all smaller than the elements in the succeeding sub-sequence and larger than the elements in the preceding sub-sequence. Time Complexity should be $\Omega(n \log k)$.

Solution

All that is needed to sort the whole sequence of length n is to sort the k elements in each of the $\frac{n}{k}$ sub-sequences. Please note that simply combining the lower bounds for the individual sub-sequences would not meet this lower bound on the number of comparisons needed to solve this variant of the sorting problem. That would only prove that there is no faster algorithm *that sorts the sub-sequences independently.*

Now, consider the decision tree of height h for any comparison sort for S. Since the elements of each sub-sequence can be in any order, any of the $k!$ permutations correspond to the final sorted order of a sub-sequence. And, since there are $\frac{n}{k}$ such sub-sequences, each of which can be in any order, there are $(k!)^{\frac{n}{k}}$ permutations of S that could correspond to the sorting of some input order.

Thus, any decision tree for sorting S must have at least $(k!)^{\frac{n}{k}}$ leaves. Since a binary tree of height h has no more than 2^h leaves, we must have

$$2^h \geq (k!)^{\frac{n}{k}}$$

$\implies$

$$h \geq \log((k!)^{\frac{n}{k}})$$

$\implies$

$$h \geq \log((k!)^{\frac{n}{k}})$$
$$= \frac{n}{k} \log(k!)$$
$$\geq \frac{n}{k} \log((\frac{k}{2})^{\frac{k}{2}})$$
$$= \frac{n}{k} \log(\frac{k}{2})$$

Since there exists at least one path in any decision tree for sorting S that has length at least $\frac{n}{2} \log(\frac{k}{2})$, the worst-case running time of any comparison-based sorting algorithm for S is $(n \log k)$.

2.26 Find missing integer

Problem

An array $a[0..n-1]$ contains all integers in $[0..n]$ except one. Find this omitted integer with fixed additional memory. Number of operations should be proportional to n.

Solution

1. Get the sum of numbers: $total = \frac{n(n+1)}{2}$

2. Subtract all the numbers from sum and we will get the missing number.

Program 2.8: Find the missing integer

```cpp
#include <vector>
#include <iostream>

int find_missing_number(std::vector<int> & v, int n)
{
    int total = n*(n + 1)/2;

    for(auto e : v)
        total -= e;

    return total;
}

int main()
{
    std::vector<int> v {1, 2, 3, 5, 6};

    std::cout << find_missing_number(v, 6) << std::endl;
}
```

It prints:

```
4
```

2.27 Inplace Reversing

Problem Description

Given an array a[1..n], put its elements in reverse order without using any other arrays.

Solution

$swap(a[i], a[n+1-i])\ \forall i < n+1-i$, i.e., $2i < n+1 \iff 2i \leq n \iff i \leq \frac{n}{2}$
:

Algorithm 62 Reversing an array inplace

1: **function** REVERSE-INPLACE(a[1..n])
2:     **for** $i \leftarrow 1$ **to** $\frac{n}{2}$ **do**
3:         $swap(a[i], a[n+1-i])$
4:     **end for**
5: **end function**

2.28 Find the number not occurring twice in an array

Problem Description

An array $a[0..n-1]$ contains some integers, and every element appears *twice* except for one element that appears *only once*. Find this element with fixed additional memory. Number of operations should be proportional to n.

Solution

Using *xor* operation, we can find out the number that occurred odd number of times.

- *xor* is commutative and associative (so the order in which it's done is irrelevant).
- a number *xor*ed with itself will always be zero.
- zero *xor*ed with a number will be that number.

So, if we simply *xor* all the values together, all of the ones that occur *twice* will cancel each other out (giving 0) and the one remaining number (*value*) will *xor* with that result (0) to give *value*.

Program 2.9: Find the number not occurring twice in an array

```cpp
#include <vector>
#include <iostream>

size_t get_orphan(std::vector<int> & v)
{
    int value = 0;

    for (auto e : v)
        value ^= e;

    std::cout << "number : " << value << std::endl;
    // value now contains the number that occurred odd
        number of times.
    // Retrieve its index in the array.

    size_t len = v.size();

    size_t index_orphan = -1;

    for (size_t index = 0; index < len; ++index)
    {
        if (v[index] == value)
        {
            index_orphan = index;
            std::cout << "index : " << index_orphan <<
                std::endl;
```

2.28. Find the number not occurring twice in an array

```
25            return index_orphan;
26        }
27    }
28    return index_orphan;
29 }
30
31 int main()
32 {
33     std::vector<int> v {12, 8, 14, 13, 3, 12, 13, 8, 14};
34
35     get_orphan(v);
36 }
```

It prints:

```
number : 3
index : 4
```

Chapter 3

Trees

3.1 Lowest Common Ancestor(LCA) Problem

Problem

Find the lowest common ancestor(aka lca), i.e., ancestor with maximal depth, of a pair of nodes in a rooted tree.

Solution

Basic Analysis

In a rooted tree T, a node u is an *ancestor* of a node v if u is on the unique path from the root to v. It can be easily inferred from this definition that a node is an ancestor of itself. A *proper ancestor* of v refers to an ancestor that is not v.

In a rooted tree T, the *lowest common ancestor(aka lca)* of two nodes x and y is the deepest node in T that is an ancestor of both x and y.

LCA problem is one of the most fundamental algorithmic problems on trees and it has been intensively studied mainly due to:

- It is inherently algorithmically beautiful.
- Fast algorithms for the LCA problem can be used to solve other algorithmic problems.

The set of ancestors $a(u)$ of a node $u \in V$ is defined as:

$$a(u) = \begin{cases} \{x\} \cup a(parent(x)), & x \neq root \\ \{x\} & \text{otherwise} \end{cases}$$

where parent(x) is the parent of a node x in the tree.

3.1. Lowest Common Ancestor(LCA) Problem

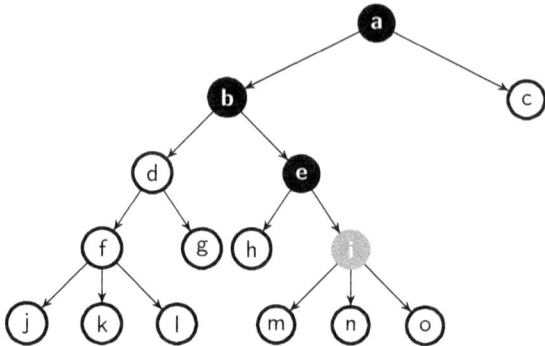

In the tree drawn above, $a(i) = \{i, e, b, a\}$

The set of common ancestors $ca(u, v)$ of nodes u and v is defined as

$$ca(u, v) = a(u) \cap a(v)$$

The lowest common ancestors $lca(u, v)$ is a common ancestor of u and v with maximal depth, i.e. order common ancestors $ca(u, v) = \{x_1, \ldots, x_k\}$ according to their level:

$$l(x_1) < l(x_2) < l(x_3) \ldots < l(x_k)$$

where $l(u)$ is the level of a node, x_1 is the root vertex r and x_k is the *least common ancestor*.

Properties of the lowest common ancestor can be summarized as:

- $lca(\{u\}) = u$
- *Identity* : $\forall u \in V : lca(u, u) = u$
- *Commutativity* : $\forall \{u, v\} \subseteq V \times V : lca(u, v) = lca(v, u)$
- Number of different lca pairs

$$\binom{n}{2} = \frac{n(n-1)}{2}$$

- If neither u nor v is an ancestor of the other, than u and v lie in different immediate subtrees of $lca(u, v)$, i.e., the child of the lca of which u is a descendant is not the same as the child of the lca of which v is a descendant.). Please note that the lca is the only node in the tree for which this is true.

- The entire set of common ancestors of $S = \{v_1, v_2, \ldots, v_n\}$ is given by $lca(S)$ and all of its ancestors (all the way up to the root of the tree). In particular, every common ancestor of S is an ancestor of $lca(S)$.

- $lca(S)$ precedes all nodes in S in the tree's preordering, and follows all nodes in S in the tree's postordering.

- If $S = A \cup B$ with A and B both nonempty, then $lca(S) = lca(lca(A), lca(B))$. For example, $lca(u,v,w) = lca(u,lca(v,w))$. (The lca shares this property with the similar-sounding *lowest common multiple* and *greatest common divisor*; and this property can be used to compute the emphlca of arbitrarily large sets using only binary lca computations.)

- $d(u, v) = h(u) + h(v) - 2h(lca(u, v))$, where d represents the distance between two nodes and h represents the height of a node.

3.1. Lowest Common Ancestor(LCA) Problem

Simple Solution

Given P as parent of a node and r as the root of the tree, we can easily find lca of the nodes u and v by computing these two sequences:

1. $u, P(u), P(P(u)), \ldots, r$
2. $v, P(v), P(P(v)), \ldots, r$

The first element of the *longest common suffix* of these two sequences is then trivially the lca.

Time complexity of this algorithm is $O(h)$ where h is the height of the tree. For a quite balanced tree, h is $O(\log |V|)$ else it is $O(|V|)$ for a degenerate tree.

C++ Implementation

Tree Structure

Program 3.1: Simple n-ary tree

```cpp
#ifndef TREE_HPP
#define TREE_HPP

#include <memory>
#include <iterator>
#include <iostream>

template<typename T>
struct node
{
    node()
    : parent(0), first_child(0), last_child(0),
      prev_sibling(0), next_sibling(0) {}
    node(const T& val)
    : parent(0), first_child(0), last_child(0),
      prev_sibling(0), next_sibling(0), data(val)
    {}

    node<T> *parent;
    node<T> *first_child, *last_child;
    node<T> *prev_sibling, *next_sibling;
    T data;
};

template <typename T, typename Allocator
            = std::allocator<node<T>>>
struct tree
{
    typedef node<T> tree_node;
    typedef T value_type;

    tree()
    {
        head = alloc_.allocate(1,0);
        feet = alloc_.allocate(1,0);
        alloc_.construct(head, node<T>());
        alloc_.construct(feet, node<T>());
        head->parent, head->first_child = 0;
        head->last_child, head->prev_sibling=0;
```

3.1. Lowest Common Ancestor(LCA) Problem

```cpp
            head->next_sibling=feet;
            feet->parent, feet->first_child = 0;
            feet->last_child, feet->next_sibling=0;
            feet->prev_sibling=head;
        }

        struct iterator
        {
            typedef T   value_type;
            typedef T*  pointer;
            typedef T&  reference;
            typedef size_t size_type;
            typedef std::ptrdiff_t difference_type;
            typedef std::bidirectional_iterator_tag
                    iterator_category;

            iterator() : node(0) {}
            iterator(tree_node * tn) : node(tn) {}

            T& operator*() const
            { return node->data; }

            T* operator->() const
            { return &(node->data); }

            bool operator==(const iterator& o) const
            {
                if(o.node==this->node) return true;
                else return false;
            }
            bool operator!=(const iterator& o) const
            {
                if(o.node!=this->node) return true;
                else return false;
            }
            tree_node *node;
        };

        iterator begin() const
        {
            return iterator(head->next_sibling);
        }

        iterator end() const
        { return iterator(feet); }

        template<typename iter>
        static iter parent(iter p)
        {
            return iter(p.node->parent);
        }

        template<typename iter>
        iter append(iter p, const T& x)
        {
            tree_node* tmp = alloc_.allocate(1,0);
            alloc_.construct(tmp, x);
            tmp->first_child, tmp->last_child=0;
            tmp->parent=p.node;
            if(p.node->last_child!=0)
```

```
            {
                p.node->last_child->next_sibling=tmp;
            }
            else
            {
                p.node->first_child=tmp;
            }
            tmp->prev_sibling=p.node->last_child;
            p.node->last_child=tmp;
            tmp->next_sibling=0;
            return tmp;
        }

        static int level(const iterator& it)
        {
            tree_node* pos=it.node;
            int l = 0;
            while(pos->parent!=0)
            {
                    pos=pos->parent;
                    ++l;
            }
            return l;
        }

        template<typename iter>
        iter insert(iter p, const T& x)
        {
            if(p.node==0)
            {
                p.node=feet;
            }
            tree_node* tmp = alloc_.allocate(1,0);
            alloc_.construct(tmp, x);
            tmp->first_child, tmp->last_child = 0;
            tmp->parent=p.node->parent;
            tmp->next_sibling=p.node;
            tmp->prev_sibling=p.node->prev_sibling;
            p.node->prev_sibling=tmp;

            if(tmp->prev_sibling==0)
            {
                if(tmp->parent)
                    tmp->parent->first_child=tmp;
            }
            else
            {
                tmp->prev_sibling->next_sibling=tmp;
            }
            return tmp;

        }
        tree_node *head, *feet;
private:
        Allocator alloc_;
};

#endif
```

3.1. Lowest Common Ancestor(LCA) Problem

Compute LCA : C++ : Stack Based

Program 3.2: Compute LCA : C++ : Stack Based

```cpp
#include <iostream>
#include <stack>
#include "tree.hpp"

template<typename T>
typename tree<T>::iterator
lca(const tree<T> & tree,
    typename tree<T>::iterator u,
    typename tree<T>::iterator v)
{
    std::stack<typename tree<T>::iterator>
        s1, s2;

    typename tree<T>::iterator lca;

    do
    {
        s1.push(u);
        if (u!= tree.begin())
            u = tree.parent(u);
    } while (u != tree.begin());

    s1.push(tree.begin());

    do
    {
        s2.push(v);
        if (v!= tree.begin())
            v = tree.parent(v);
    } while(v != tree.begin());

    s2.push(tree.begin());

    while(!s1.empty() && !s2.empty()
        && (s1.top() == s2.top()))
    {
        lca = s1.top();

        s1.pop();
        s2.pop();
    }

    return lca;
}

int main()
{
    tree<std::string> st;
    tree<std::string>::iterator itra =
        st.insert(st.begin(), "a");
    tree<std::string>::iterator itrb =
        st.append(itra, "b");
    tree<std::string>::iterator itrc =
        st.append(itra, "c");

    tree<std::string>::iterator itrd, itre;
    itrd = st.append(itrb, "d");
```

3.1. Lowest Common Ancestor(LCA) Problem

```
58      itre = st.append(itrb, "e");
59      st.append(itre, "h");
60
61      tree<std::string>::iterator itri =
62          st.append(itre, "i");
63      tree<std::string>::iterator itrm =
64          st.append(itri, "m");
65      tree<std::string>::iterator itrn =
66          st.append(itri, "n");
67      tree<std::string>::iterator itro =
68          st.append(itri, "o");
69
70      tree<std::string>::iterator itrf =
71          st.append(itrd, "f");
72      tree<std::string>::iterator itrg =
73          st.append(itrd, "g");
74      tree<std::string>::iterator itrj =
75          st.append(itrf, "j");
76      tree<std::string>::iterator itrk =
77          st.append(itrf, "k");
78      tree<std::string>::iterator itrl =
79          st.append(itrf, "l");
80
81
82      tree<std::string>::iterator pi, pe, pb;
83      pi = tree<std::string>::parent(itri);
84      pe = tree<std::string>::parent(pi);
85      pb = tree<std::string>::parent(pe);
86
87      std::cout << "Parent of nodes : "
88          << "\ni :" << *pi
89          << "\ne :" << *pe
90          << "\nb :" << *pb << "\n" << std::endl;
91
92      std::cout << "lca of b and c : "
93          << *lca(st, itrb, itrc) << std::endl;
94      std::cout << "lca of d and e : "
95          << *lca(st, itrd, itre) << std::endl;
96      std::cout << "lca of f and e : "
97          << *lca(st, itrf, itre) << std::endl;
98      std::cout << "lca of f and i : "
99          << *lca(st, itrf, itri) << std::endl;
100     std::cout << "lca of f and g : "
101         << *lca(st, itrf, itrg) << std::endl;
102     std::cout << "lca of j and l : "
103         << *lca(st, itrj, itrl) << std::endl;
104     std::cout << "lca of l and o : "
105         << *lca(st, itrl, itro) << std::endl;
106     std::cout << "lca of b and o : "
107         << *lca(st, itrb, itro) << std::endl;
108     std::cout << "lca of a and a : "
109         << *lca(st, itra, itra) << std::endl;
110     std::cout << "lca of j and c : "
111         << *lca(st, itrj, itrc) << std::endl;
112 }
```

This prints:

```
Parent of nodes :
```

3.1. Lowest Common Ancestor(LCA) Problem

```
i :e
e :b
b :a

lca of b and c  : a
lca of d and e  : b
lca of f and e  : b
lca of f and i  : b
lca of f and g  : d
lca of j and l  : f
lca of l and o: b
lca of b and o  : b
lca of a and a  : a
lca of j and c  : a
```

Let us draw the tree again for quick reference:

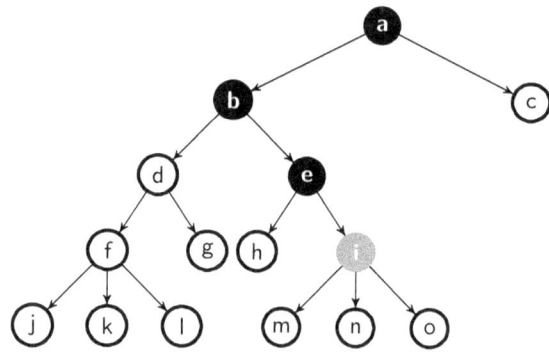

Compute LCA : C++ : Level Based

Program 3.3: Compute LCA : C++ : Level Based

```cpp
#include <iostream>
#include <stack>
#include "tree.hpp"

template<typename T>
typename tree<T>::iterator
lca(const tree<T>& tree,
    typename tree<T>::iterator u,
    typename tree<T>::iterator v)
{
    while(tree.level(u) > tree.level(v))
    {
        u = tree.parent(u);
    }

    while(tree.level(v) > tree.level(u))
    {
        v = tree.parent(v);
    }

```

3.1. Lowest Common Ancestor(LCA) Problem

```
21      while(u != v)
22      {
23          u = tree.parent(u);
24          v = tree.parent(v);
25      }
26
27      return u;
28  }
29
30  int main()
31  {
32      tree<std::string> st;
33      tree<std::string>::iterator itra
34          = st.insert(st.begin(), "a");
35      tree<std::string>::iterator itrb
36          = st.append(itra, "b");
37      tree<std::string>::iterator itrc
38          = st.append(itra, "c");
39
40      tree<std::string>::iterator itrd, itre;
41      itrd = st.append(itrb, "d");
42      itre = st.append(itrb, "e");
43      st.append(itre, "h");
44
45      tree<std::string>::iterator itri
46          = st.append(itre, "i");
47      tree<std::string>::iterator itrm
48          = st.append(itri, "m");
49      tree<std::string>::iterator itrn
50          = st.append(itri, "n");
51      tree<std::string>::iterator itro
52          = st.append(itri, "o");
53
54      tree<std::string>::iterator itrf
55          = st.append(itrd, "f");
56      tree<std::string>::iterator itrg
57          = st.append(itrd, "g");
58      tree<std::string>::iterator itrj
59          = st.append(itrf, "j");
60      tree<std::string>::iterator itrk
61          = st.append(itrf, "k");
62      tree<std::string>::iterator itrl
63          = st.append(itrf, "l");
64
65
66      std::cout << "levels of nodes \n:"
67          << "\na: " << st.level(itra)
68          << "\nb: " << st.level(itrb)
69          << "\nd: " << st.level(itrd)
70          << "\ne: " << st.level(itre)
71          << "\ni: " << st.level(itri)
72          << "\nf: " << st.level(itrf)
73          << "\n" << std::endl;
74
75      tree<std::string>::iterator pi, pe, pb;
76      pi = tree<std::string>::parent(itri);
77      pe = tree<std::string>::parent(pi);
78      pb = tree<std::string>::parent(pe);
79
80      std::cout << "lca of b and c: "
```

3.1. Lowest Common Ancestor(LCA) Problem

```cpp
81          << *lca(st, itrb, itrc) << std::endl;
82     std::cout << "lca of d and e : "
83          << *lca(st, itrd, itre) << std::endl;
84     std::cout << "lca of f and e : "
85          << *lca(st, itrf, itre) << std::endl;
86     std::cout << "lca of f and i : "
87          << *lca(st, itrf, itri) << std::endl;
88     std::cout << "lca of f and g : "
89          << *lca(st, itrf, itrg) << std::endl;
90     std::cout << "lca of j and l : "
91          << *lca(st, itrj, itrl) << std::endl;
92     std::cout << "lca of l and o: "
93          << *lca(st, itrl, itro) << std::endl;
94     std::cout << "lca of b and o : "
95          << *lca(st, itrb, itro) << std::endl;
96     std::cout << "lca of a and a : "
97          << *lca(st, itra, itra) << std::endl;
98     std::cout << "lca of j and c : "
99          << *lca(st, itrj, itrc) << std::endl;
100    std::cout << "lca of d and c : "
101         << *lca(st, itrd, itrc) << std::endl;
102 }
```

This prints:

```
levels of nodes
:
a: 0
b: 1
d: 2
e: 2
i: 3
f: 3

lca of b and c : a
lca of d and e : b
lca of f and e : b
lca of f and i : b
lca of f and g : d
lca of j and l : f
lca of l and o: b
lca of b and o : b
lca of a and a : a
lca of j and c : a
lca of d and c : a
```

Constant Time LCA

The LCA problem is then, given a rooted tree T for preprocessing, preprocess it in a way so that the LCA of any two given nodes in T can be retrieved in constant time. Let us present a preprocessing algorithm that requires no more than linear time and space complexity.

We make the following two assumptions on our computational machine model. Let n denote the size of our input in unary representation:

3.1. Lowest Common Ancestor(LCA) Problem

1. All arithmetic, comparative and logical operations on numbers whose binary representation is of size no more then $\log n$ bits can be done in *constant* time.

2. We assume that finding the left-most bit or the right-most bit of a $\log n$ sized number can be done in *constant* time.

Complete Binary Tree

Our discussion begins with a particularly simple instance of the LCA problem, LCA queries on complete binary trees. We will use our knowledge of solving the LCA problem on complete binary trees and expand it later on, to solve the LCA problem on any arbitrary rooted tree T.

Let B denote a complete binary tree with n nodes. The key thing here is to encode the unique path from the root to a node in the node itself. We assign each node a *path number*, a $\log n$ bit number that encodes the unique path from the root to the node.

Path Number For each node v in B we encode a *path number* in the following way:

- Counting from the left most bit, the i'th bit of the path number for v corresponds to the i'th edge on the path from the root to v.

- A **0** for the i'th bit from the left indicates that the i'th edge on the path goes to a left child, and a **1** indicates that it goes to a right child.

- Let k denote then number of edges on the path from the root to v, then we mark the $k+1$ bit (the height bit) of the path number **1**, and the rest of the $\log n - k - 1$ bits **0**.

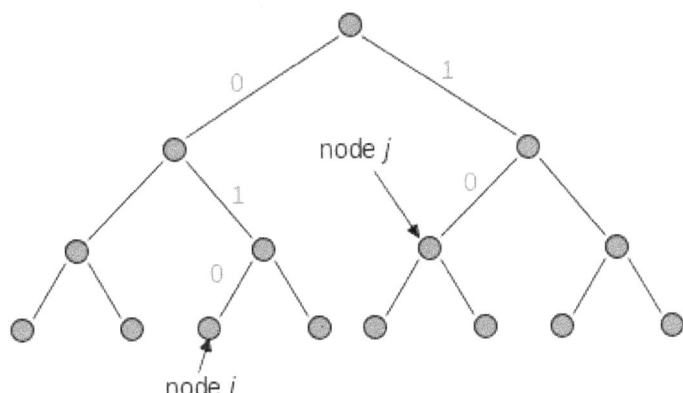

- Node i's path number is

$$0\ 1\ 0\ 1$$

- Node j's path number is

$$1\ 0\ 1\ 0$$

3.1. Lowest Common Ancestor(LCA) Problem

Please note that the height bit is marked in **bold** and padded bits are marked in *italics*.

Path numbers can easily be assigned in a simple $O(n)$ *in-order* traversal on B.

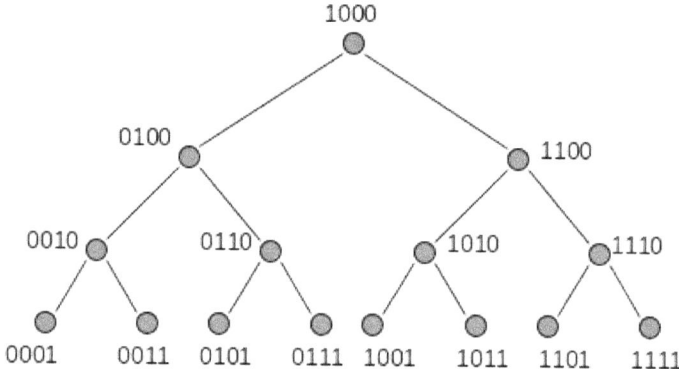

LCA Queries in Complete Binary Tree

Suppose now that u and v are two nodes in B, and that $path(u)$ and $path(v)$ are their appropriate path numbers.

We denote the lowest common ancestor of u and v as $lca(u,v)$.

We denote the prefix bits in the path number, those that correspond to edges on the path from the root, as the *path bits* of the path number.

1. First we calculate $path(u)\ XOR\ path(v)$ and find the left most bit which equals **1**.

2. If there is no such bit then $path(u) = path(v)$ and so $u = v$, so assume that the k'th bit of the result is **1**.

3. If both the k'th bit in $path(u)$ and the k'th bit in $path(v)$ are *path bits*, then this means that u and v agree on k-1 edges of their path from the root, meaning that the *k-1* prefix of each node's path number encodes within it the path from the root to $lca(u,v)$.

3.1. Lowest Common Ancestor(LCA) Problem

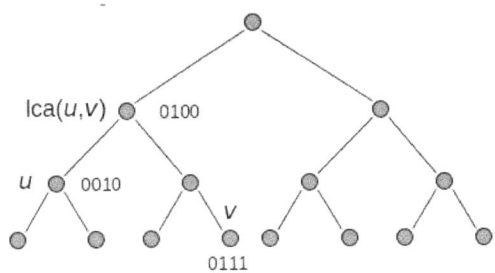

path(u) **XOR** path(v) =

$$\begin{array}{r} 0\,0\,1\,0 \\ \text{XOR} \\ 0\,1\,1\,1 \\ \hline 0\,1\,0\,1 \end{array}$$

path(lca(u,v) =

0 1 0 0
  ↑   ↑
height bit padded bits

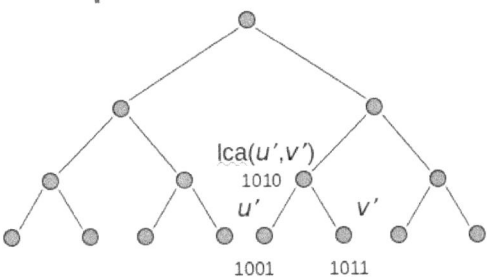

path(u') **XOR** path(v') =

$$\begin{array}{r} 1\,0\,0\,1 \\ \text{XOR} \\ 1\,0\,1\,1 \\ \hline 0\,0\,1\,0 \end{array}$$

path(lca(u,v) =

1 0 1 0
    ↑ ↑
height bit padded bit

This concludes that if we take the prefix $k-1$ bits of the result of $path(u)$ XOR $path(v)$, add **1** as the k'th bit, and pad $\log n - k$ **0** suffix bits, we get $path(lca(u,v))$.

If either the k'th bit in $path(u)$ or the k'th bit in $path(v)$ (or both) is not a path bit then one node is ancestor to the other, and $lca(u,v)$ can easily be retrieved by comparing $path(u)$ and $path(v)$'s height bit.

The general LCA algorithm

The following are the two stages of the general LCA algorithm for any arbitrary tree T:

1. First, we reduce the *LCA* problem to the *Restricted Range Minima* problem. The *Restricted Range Minima* problem is the problem of finding the smallest number in an interval of a fixed list of numbers, where the difference between two successive numbers in the list is exactly one.

2. Second, we solve the *Restricted Range Minima* problem and thus solve the *LCA* problem.

For more details, please refer [?].

3.2 Spying Campaign

Problem Description

Bitter about his defeat in the presidential election, Rob Roll decides to hire a seedy photographer to trail Will Clintwood. (The names have been changed to protect the guilty.) The photographer stealthily takes pictures of Clintwood, and he marks each picture with the time t it was taken. Roll tells the photographer to mark especially scandalous pictures with a big, red X, because these pictures will be used in future negative advertisements. Roll requires a data structure that contains the Clintwood pictures and supports the following operations:

- INSERT(x) : Inserts picture x into the data structure. Picture x has an integer field $time[x]$ and a boolean field $scandalous[x]$.

- DELETE(x) : Deletes picture x from the data structure.

- NEXT-PICTURE(x) : Returns the picture that was taken immediately after picture x.

- SCANDAL!(t) : Returns the first scandalous picture that was taken after time t.

Describe an efficient implementation of this data structure. Show how to perform these operations, and analyze their running times. Be succinct.

Solution

To allow us to implement these operations efficiently, we'll use a *red-black tree* representation keying photographs by time, and augmenting each node x with these additional fields:

- $scandalous?[x]$
- $max - scand - time[x]$

The field $max - scand - time[x]$ stores the time when the latest scandalous picture in the subtree rooted at x was taken. It contains either an integer time, or NIL if there are no scandalous pictures in the subtree. We implement the operations (all in $O(\log n)$ running time) on this data structure as follows:

- INSERT(x) : Place x in the tree, keyed by $time[x]$, just like in a regular red-black tree. Update $max - scand - time$ fields if necessary after rotations. This can be done in $O(1)$ time.

3.2. Spying Campaign

- DELETE(x) : Just like INSERT(x); do what's normally done in a red-black tree, taking care to fix $max - scand - time$ fields after deleting node x. When node n is encountered where $max - scand - time[n] = time[x]$ and $scandalous?[x] = \text{TRUE}$, look at the node's children and set $max - scand - time[n] \leftarrow max(max - scand - time[right[n]], max - scand - time[left[n]])$.

- NEXT-PICTURE(x) : Just like SUCCESSOR(x) in a red-black tree.

- SCANDAL!(t) : We use the $max - scand - time$ field to search for this element.

    - If there is no such element in the tree, i.e. $max - scand - time[root] < t$, then return NIL.
    - Otherwise we recursively descent the tree as follows: at each node n check whether $max - scand - time[left[n]] > t$. If so recursively descent to the left subtree. Otherwise, check whether $time[n] > t$ and $scandalous?[n] = \text{TRUE}$. If so return n. Otherwise, recursively descent the right subtree.

Chapter 4

Dynamic Programming

Dynamic programming is a method that in general solves optimization problems that involve making a sequence of decisions by determining, for each decision, subproblems that can be solved in like fashion, such that an optimal solution of the original problem can be found from optimal solutions of sub-problems. This method is based on *Bellman's Principle of Optimality*:

> *An optimal policy has the property that whatever the initial state and initial decision are, the remaining decisions must constitute an optimal policy with regard to the state resulting from the first decision.*

More succinctly, this principle asserts that

> *Optimal policies have optimal subpolicies.*

That the principle is valid follows from the observation that, if a policy has a subpolicy that is not optimal, then replacement of the subpolicy by an optimal subpolicy would improve the original policy. The principle of optimality is also known as the **Optimal Substructure** property in the literature.

For DP to be computationally efficient (especially relative to evaluating all possible sequences of decisions), there should be common subproblems such that subproblems of one are subproblems of another. In this event, a solution to a subproblem need only be found once and reused as often as necessary.

Simple serial DP formulations can be modeled by a state transition system or directed graph, where a state S corresponds to a node (or vertex) and a decision d that leads from state S to next-state S' is represented by a branch (or arc or edge) with label $C(d_i \mid S)$. D(S) is the set of possible decisions when in state S, hence is associated with the successors of node S. More complex DP formulations require a more general graph model.

Dynamic programming works on the principle of finding an overall solution by operating on an intermediate point that lie between where you are now and where you want to go. The term dynamic was used to identify the approach as being useful for problems in which times plays a significant role, and in which the order of operations may be crucial. The procedure is recursive, in that each next intermediate point is a function of the points already visited.

4.1. Stage Coach Problem

A prototypical problem that is suitable for dynamic programming has the following properties:

- The problem can be decomposed into a sequence <;>f decisions made at various stages.
- Each stage has a number of possible states.
- A decision takes you from a state at one stage to some state at the next stage.
- The best sequence of decisions (also known as a policy) at any stage is independent of the decisions made at prior stages.
- There is a well-defined cost for traversing from state to state across stages . Moreover, there is a recursive relationship for choosing the best decisions to make.

The method can be applied by starting at the goal and working backward to the current state. That is, we can first determine the best decision to make at the last stage. From there, we determine the best decision at the next to last stage, presuming we will make the best decision at the last stage, and so forth.

4.1 Stage Coach Problem

The problem has a lot of window dressing involving a salesman taking his stagecoach through territory with hostile Native American Indians, but we'll dispense with that to cut straight to the core of the issue.

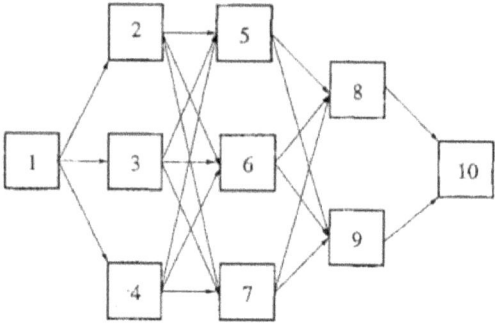

Figure 4.1: The flow diagram indicating the choices for the salesman as he takes his stagecoach through hostile territory

The salesman must start from his current position and arrive at a fixed destination. He effectively has three stages at which he can make alternative choises about how to proceed as shown in Figure 4.1. At the first stage, he has three alternative paths. Likewise, at the second stage, there are three alternatives. Finally, at the third stage there are two alternatives. The fourth stage does not offer a choice. The costs for traversing from each state at each stage to each next possible state are shown in Figure ??. The problem is to find the least-cost path from the first state (1) to the last state (10).

4.1. Stage Coach Problem

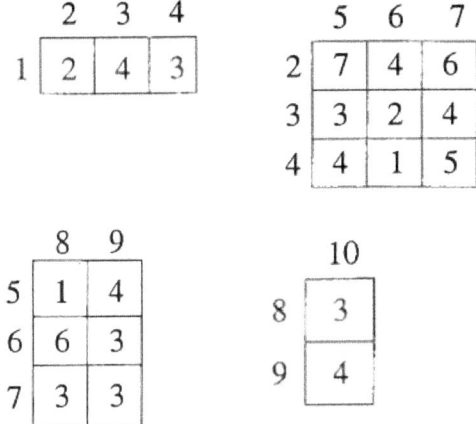

Figure 4.2: The cost for making each possible choice at each decision stage

The row indicates the current state and the column indicates the next state. The four matrices correspond to the four stages. Note that only the first three stages offer a choice of which state to choose.

We need to introduce some notation here before proceeding to work out the answer:

- There are n stages and the decision of which state to choose at the nth stage is x_n. Here, n = 4.

- $f_n(s, x_n)$ is the cost of the best sequence of decisions (policy) for all of the remaining stages, given that the salesman is in state s, stage n, and chooses x_n as the immediate next state.

- $x_n^*(s)$ is the value of x_n that minimizes $f_n(s, x_n)$ and $f_n^*(s)$ is the corresponding minimum value.

- The goal is to find $f_1^*(1)$ because the salesman is starting in state 1. This is accomplished by finding $f_4^*(s)$, $f_3^*(s)$, $f_2^*(s)$ and then finally $f_1^*(1)$.

What then is $f_4^*(s)$? For which x_4 is $f_4(s, x_4)$ minimized? This is almost a trick question because there's only one state to choose while in the fourth stage: $x_4 = 10$. Thus we easily compute the values shown ahead, and we have completed the first phase of the dynamic programming procedure.

s	$f_4^*(s)$	$x_4^*(s)$
8	3	10
9	4	10

The above matrix displays the cost of going from states 8 or 9 to a state at the final stage (in this case, there is only one such state).

The next phase asks for the value of $f_3^*(s)$. Recall that since the decisions are independent, $f_3(s, x_3) = c_{sx_3} + f_4^*(x_3)$, where c_{sx_3} is the cost of travelling from s to x_3. The matrix shown below indicates the relevant values of $f_3(s, x_3)$ for every possible choice of destination presuming s is 5, 6, or 7.

s	$f_3(s,8)$	$f_3(s,9)$	$f_3^*(s)$	$x_3^*(s)$

4.1. Stage Coach Problem

5	4	8	4	8
6	9	7	7	9
7	6	7	6	8

We can see, for example, that if we're in state 5, then state 8 minimizes the total remaining cost. State 9 minimizes the cost if s = 6, and state 8 minimizes the cost if s = 7.

Working backward again, we must find the value of $f_2^*(s)$. In an analogous manner to what appears directly above, the matrix shown below provides the relevant values of $f_2(s, x_2)$. Note that $f_2(s, x_2) = c_{sx_2} + f_3^*(x_2)$.

s	$f_2(s,5)$	$f_2(s,6)$	$f_2(s,7)$	$f_2^*(s)$	$x_2^*(s)$
2	11	11	12	11	5 or 6
3	7	9	10	7	5
4	8	8	11	8	5 or 6

Finally, with regard to $f_1^*(s)$, the last matrix offers the costs of proceeding to states 2, 3, or 4:

s	$f_1(s,2)$	$f_1(s,3)$	$f_1(s,4)$	$f_1^*(s)$	$x_1^*(s)$
1	13	11	11	11	3 or 4

This is the final table for the stagecoach problem. Now the dynamic programming method has been applied all the way back to the first stage. The values in the above matrix indicate the cost of travelling from state 1 to 2, 3 , or 4.

At this point we can identify the best answer to the overall problem. In fact , here there are three best answers (policies), each with an equal cost of 11 units :

- $1 \to 3 \to 5 \to 8 \to 10$
- $1 \to 4 \to 5 \to 8 \to 10$
- $1 \to 4 \to 6 \to 9 \to 10$

Note that the obverse procedure of choosing the least-cost path moving forward through the stages does not give the optimum solution. That greedy solution has a cost of 13 units (can be verified easily). Thus, here is a case where the greedy approach fails, but dynamic programming generates the right answer. One drawback of the approach, however, is that it can be computationally intensive. If N is both the number of stages and states per stage, then the required number of operations scales as N^3. The method can, however, be extended to handle a variety of optimization problems including the order of multiplying matrices and finding the best organization for a tree to minimize the cost of searching.

Dynamic programming algorithms tend to be somewhat complicated to understand. This is because, in practice, the construction of a dynamic program depends on the problem. It is a sort of *artistic intellectual activity depending in part on the specific structure of the sequential decision problem*. This is why we'll illustrate this technique by two additional examples: matrix multiplication and the TSP.

4.2 Matrix Multiplication

Suppose that the dimensions of the matrices A_1, A_2, A_3 and A_4 are $20 \times 2, 2 \times 15, 15 \times 40$ and 40×4, respectively, and that we want to know the optimum way to compute $A_1 \times A_2 \times A_3 \times A_4$, i.e. , we would like to compute this product with a minimum number of multiplications . Here we assume that to multiply two matrices, P, which is $n \times k$, by Q, which is $k \times m$, it takes nkm multiplications. The resulting matrix R is $n \times m$ and

$$r_{ij} = \sum_{v=1}^{k} p_{iv} q_{vj}$$

$\forall 1 \leq i \leq n$ and $1 \leq j \leq m$.

Note that different orders of multiplications have different costs. For example,

- ☞ A(B(C D)) requires $15 \cdot 40 \cdot 4 + 2 \cdot 15 \cdot 4 + 20 \cdot 2 \cdot 4 = 2680$ multiplications,
- ☞ (AB) (C D) requires $20 \cdot 2 \cdot 15 + 15 \cdot 40 \cdot 4 + 20 \cdot 15 \cdot 4 = 4200$ multiplications, whereas
- ☞ ((AB)C)D requires $20 \cdot 2 \cdot 15 + 20 \cdot 15 \cdot 40 + 20 \cdot 40 \cdot 4 = 15800$ multiplications!

In a dynamic programming approach we create a structure M(i , j) where we maintain a record of the minimum number of multiplications required to multiply matrices from A_i to $A_j (i \leq j)$. Clearly, M(1, 1) = M (2, 2) = M(3, 3) = M(4, 4) = 0 , as no multiplications are required in these cases. Note that the problem involves finding M(1, 4).

The connection between solutions of the smaller problems and a bigger one is

$$M(i,j) = min_{i \leq k < j} M(i,k) + M(k+1,j) + cost_{ij}^{k}$$

where $cost_{ij}^{k}$ is the number of multiplications required for multiplying the product $A_i \ldots A_k$ by $A_{k+1} \ldots A_j$. The point is that to multiply a sequence from A_i to A_j in the optimal way, we must find the optimal breaking point k such that the total number of multiplications required for calculating the product $A_i \ldots A_k$, which is M(i, k), the product $A_{k+1} \ldots A_j$, which is M(k + 1, j), and these two products together (which is $cost_{ij}^{k}$) is minimal.

Keeping this in mind, we can proceed as follows. It's a basic exercise to get :

M(1 , 2) = 600,
M(2, 3) = 1200,
M (3 , 4) = 2400,

because there's no room for a breaking point in multiplying two matrices. Then,

M(1, 3) = 2800 M(2, 4) = 1520.

Note that M(1, 3) is the smaller of two possibilities

M(1, 1) + M(2, 3) + $cost_{13}^{1}$ = 0 + 1200 + 1600 = 2800 , and
M(1 , 2) + M(3, 3) + $cost_{13}^{2}$ = 600 + 0 + 12000 = 12600.

Similarly, M(2, 4) is the smaller of two possibilities

M(2, 2) + M(3, 4) + $cost_{24}^{2}$ = 0 + 2400 + 120 = 2520, and M(2, 3) + M(4, 4) + $cost_{24}^{3}$ = 1200 + 0 + 320 = 1520.

Finally, we find

M(1, 4) = 1680,

as the smallest value from three possibilities:

1. $M(1,1) + M(2,4) + cost_{14}^1 = 0 + 1520 + 160 = 1680$,
2. $M(1,2) + M(3,4) + cost_{14}^2 = 600 + 2400 + 1200 = 4200$, and
3. $M(1,3) + M(4,4) + cost_{14}3 = 2800 + 0 + 3200 = 6000$.

Thus, the minimal cost in terms of the number of multiplications is 1680, but we still need to find the corresponding order of matrix multiplications. To find this best order we need an additional data structure, O(i, j), where we keep the index of the best breaking point. In other words, O(i, j) = k if and only if M(i, j) attains the minimum value for $M(i,k) + M(k+1,j) + cost_{ij}^k$. The indices kept in the matrix O reveal the order we were searching for: $A_1((A_2A_3)A_4)$.

4.3 TSP Problem

Let's tackle a five-city TSP. The matrix L of distances between cities is given below:

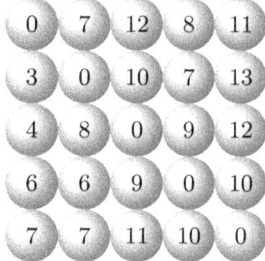

4.4 A Simple Path Problem

Suppose for the moment that you live in a city whose streets are laid out as shown in Figure 4.4.

4.5. String Edit Distance

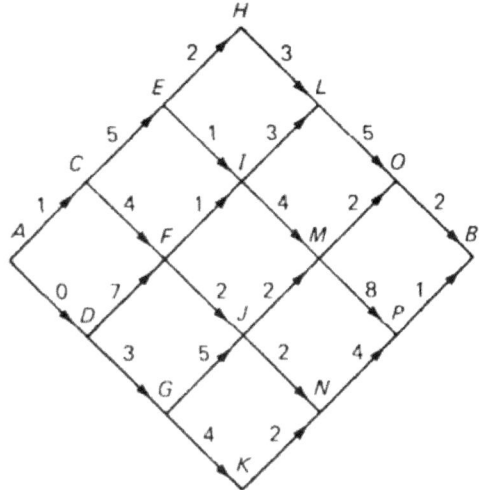

All streets are one-way, and that the numbers shown on the map represent the effort (usually time but some- times cost or distance) required to traverse each individual block. You live at A and wish to get to B with minimum total effort. You could, of course, solve this problem by enumerating all possible paths from A to B; adding up the efforts, block by block, of each; and then choosing the smallest such sum. There are 20 distinct paths from A to B and five additions yield the sum of the six numbers along a particular path, so 100 additions would yield the 20 path sums to be compared. Since one comparison yields the smaller of two numbers, one additional comparison (of that number with a third) yields the smallest of three, etc., 19 comparisons complete this enumerative solution of the problem. As you might suspect, one can solve this problem more efficiently than by brute-force enumeration. This more efficient method is called *dynamic programming*.

4.5 String Edit Distance

Problem

Given two strings and a set of edit operations, design and implement an algorithm to minimize the number of edit operations needed to transform the first string into the second. Please note that matches are not counted.

Solution

Introduction

Finding the occurrences of a given query string (pattern) from a possibly very large text is an old and fundamental problem in computer science. It emerges in applications ranging from text processing and music retrieval to bioinformatics. This task, collectively known as *string matching*, has several different variations. The most natural and simple of these is *exact string matching*, in which, like the name suggests, one wishes to find only occurrences that are exactly identical to the pattern string. This type of search, however,

4.5. String Edit Distance

may not be adequate in all applications if for example the pattern string or the text may contain typographical errors. Perhaps the most important applications of this kind arise in the field of bioinformatics, as small variations are fairly common in DNA or protein sequences.

Other related areas of applications include(but not limited to)

- stochastic transduction
- syntactic pattern recognition
- spelling correction
- string correction
- string similarity
- string classification
- pronunciation modeling
- Switchboard corpus
- string permutations

The field of approximate string matching, which has been a research subject since the 1960's, answers the problem of small variation by permitting some error between the pattern and its occurrences. Given an error threshold and a metric to measure the distance between two strings, the task of approximate string matching is to find all substrings of the text that are within (a distance of) the error threshold from the pattern.

Edit Distance

In this solution we concentrate on approximate string matching that uses so called *unit-cost edit distance* as the metric to measure the distance between two strings. *Edit Distance* between the string S_1 and S_2 is defined in general as the minimal cost of any sequence of edit operations that transforms S_1 into S_2 or vice verse.

There are various types of edit distance metrics available:

- *Levenshtein edit distance* : The allowed edit operations are

    1. insertion,
    2. deletion or
    3. substitution

    of a single character, and each operation has the cost 1. This type of edit distance is sometimes called *unit-cost edit distance*. *Levenshtein edit distance* is perhaps the most common form of edit distance, and often the term edit distance is assimilated to it.

- *Damerau edit distance* : Otherwise identical to the *Levenshtein edit distance*, but allows also the fourth operation of transposing two adjacent characters. A further condition is that the transposed characters must be adjacent before and after the edit operations are applied.

- *Weighted/generalized edit distance* : Allows the same operations as the Levenshtein/Damerau edit distance, respectively, but each operation may have an arbitrary cost.

4.5. String Edit Distance

- *Hamming distance* : Allows only the operation of substituting a character, and each substitution has the unit cost.
- *Longest common subsequence* : Measures the similarity between S_1 and S_2 by the length of their longest common subsequence. This is in effect equivalent to allowing the edit operations of deleting or inserting a single character with the unit cost.

For the sake of simplicity, we will consider two different kinds of edit distances:

1. *Levenshtein edit distance* and
2. *Damerau edit distance*.

These two, and especially the *Levenshtein edit distance*, are the most commonly used forms of unit-cost edit distance.

Levenshtein edit distance

The unit-cost *Levenshtein edit distance* between the strings S_1 and S_2 can be defined as the minimum number of single-character insertions, deletions and substitutions needed in transforming S_1 into S_2 or vice versa.

For example, if $S_1 =$ "cat" and $S_2 =$ "act", then there are two ways to transform S_1 into S_2 with exactly two operations:

1. either
   a) delete $S_1[1] =$ 'c', i.e., "cat" $\Longrightarrow$ "at"
   b) insert a 'c' between the present $S_1[1] =$ 'a' and $S_1[2] =$ 't', i.e., "at" $\Longrightarrow$ "act"
2. or,
   a) substitute $S_1[1] =$ 'c' with an 'a', i.e., "cat" $\Longrightarrow$ "aat"
   b) and substitute the present $S_1[2] =$ 'a' with a 'c', i.e., "aat" $\Longrightarrow$ "act"

So, in either case, *Levenshtein edit distance*(S_1, S_2) is 2.

Damerau edit distance

In similar fashion, the unit-cost *Damerau edit distance* can be defined as the minimum number of single-character insertions, deletions or substitutions or transpositions between two permanently adjacent characters that are needed in transforming S_1 into S_2 or vice versa.

Continuing with the same example of strings $S_1 =$ "cat" and $S_2 =$ "act", we have that *Damerau edit distance*$(S_1, S_2) = 1$ as now a single transposition of the characters $S_1[0] =$ 'c' and $S_1[1] =$ 'a' is enough to convert S_1 into S_2, i.e.

transpose "ca" : "cat" $\Longrightarrow$ "act"

Both the *Levenshtein* and the *Damerau edit distance* suit well the technique of dynamic programming. We begin by discussing the dynamic programming algorithm for the *Levenshtein edit distance*.

Let $D(i,j)$ be the edit distance of the strings $S_1[1..i]$ and $S_2[1..j]$, i.e., $D(i,j)$ denotes the minimum number of edit operations needed to transform the first i characters of S_1 into the first j characters of S_2.

If S_1 has m characters and S_2 has n characters, then the edit distance is $D(m,n)$.

4.5. String Edit Distance

Recurrence : Computing the Levenshtein edit distance

We will compute $D(m, n)$ by solving the more general problem of computing $D(i, j)$ for all combinations of i and j, where i ranges from *0* to m and j ranges from *0* to n.

The base conditions are :

- $D(i, 0) = i$, i.e., the only way to transform the first i characters of S_1 to *0* characters of S_2 is to *delete* all the i characters of S_1.
- $D(0, j) = j$, i.e., the only way to transform the *0* characters of S_1 to the first j characters of S_2 is to *insert* the j characters of S_2 into S_1.

Then $D(i, j)$ is the minimum of the following three possibilities:

1. $D(i-1, j-1) + \delta(i, j)$, where $\delta(i, j)$ is the cost associated with either substitution(unit cost) or matching(zero cost), i.e.,

    a) $\delta(i, j) = 1$ if $S_1[i] \neq S_2[j]$
    b) $\delta(i, j) = 0$ if $S_1[i] == S_2[j]$

2. $D(i, j-1) + 1$, i.e., *deletion* cost of the character $S_2[j]$

3. $D(i-1, j) + 1$, i.e., *deletion* cost of the character $S_1[i]$

C++ Implementation

Program 4.1: Simple Implementation : Levenshtein edit distance

```cpp
#include <vector>
#include <algorithm>
#include <cassert>

size_t edit_distance(const std::string & s1,
                     const std::string & s2)
{
    const size_t len1 = s1.size(),
                 len2 = s2.size();

    std::vector<std::vector<size_t> >
        d(len1 + 1,
          std::vector<size_t>(len2 + 1));

    d[0][0] = 0;

    for(size_t i = 1; i <= len1; ++i)
    {
        d[i][0] = i;
    }

    for(size_t j = 1; j <= len2; ++j)
    {
        d[0][j] = j;
    }

    for(size_t i = 1; i <= len1; ++i)
        for(size_t j = 1; j <= len2; ++j)
        {
            d[i][j] =
                std::min(
```

```cpp
                        std::min(
                          d[i - 1][j] + 1,
                          d[i][j - 1] + 1
                        ),
                        d[i - 1][j - 1] +
                        (s1[i - 1] == s2[j - 1]
                         ? 0 : 1)
                    );
        }
        return d[len1][len2];
}

int main()
{
    assert(edit_distance("cat", "act") == 2);
    assert(edit_distance("combo", "coin")
                                    == 3);
}
```

Program 4.2: Improved Implementation : Levenshtein edit distance

```cpp
#include <vector>
#include <algorithm>
#include <cassert>

size_t levenshtein_distance(
            const std::string &s1,
            const std::string & s2)
{
    const size_t len1 = s1.size(),
                 len2 = s2.size();

    std::vector<size_t> col(len2 + 1),
                        prevCol(len2 + 1);

    for(size_t i = 0; i < prevCol.size(); i++)
            prevCol[i] = i;

    for (size_t i = 0; i < len1; i++)
    {
        col[0] = i+1;

        for (size_t j = 0; j < len2; j++)
        {
            col[j+1] =
              std::min(
                std::min(
                  1 + col[j],
                  1 + prevCol[1 + j]
                ),
                prevCol[j] + (s1[i]==s2[j]
                    ? 0 : 1)
              );
        }
        col.swap(prevCol);
    }
    return prevCol[len2];
}
```

4.5. String Edit Distance

```
38
39 int main()
40 {
41     assert(levenshtein_distance(
42         "cat", "act") == 2);
43
44     assert(levenshtein_distance(
45         "COMBO", "COIN") == 3);
46 }
```

Program 4.3: Boost Implementation : Levenshtein edit distance

```
1 #include <boost/numeric/ublas/matrix.hpp>
2
3 int levenshtein_distance(
4         const std::string & s1,
5         const std::string & s2)
6 {
7     const size_t len1 = s1.length(),
8                  len2 = s2.length();
9
10    boost::numeric::ublas::matrix<size_t> m(
11        len1 + 1, len2 + 1);
12
13    for(size_t i = 0; i< len1 + 1; ++i)
14    {
15        m(i, 0) = i;
16    }
17
18    for(size_t j = 0; j < len2 + 1; ++j)
19    {
20        m(0, j) = j;
21    }
22
23    size_t cost, cell_cost, min_cost = 0;
24
25    for(size_t i = 0; i < len1; ++i)
26    {
27        cost = 0;
28
29        for(size_t j = 0; j < len2; ++j)
30        {
31            cell_cost = 1;
32
33            if(s2[j] == s1[i])
34            {
35                cell_cost = 0;
36            }
37
38            min_cost = m(i, j);
39
40            if(min_cost > m(i, j + 1))
41                min_cost = m(i, j + 1);
42
43            if(min_cost > m(i + 1, j))
44                min_cost = m(i + 1, j);
45
46            cell_cost += min_cost;
47
48            m(i + 1, j + 1) = cell_cost;
49
50            if(j == 0)
```

4.5. String Edit Distance

```
51                    cost = cell_cost;
52                else
53                {
54                    if(cell_cost < cost)
55                        cost = cell_cost;
56                }
57            }
58        }
59        return m(len1, len2);
60 }
61
62 int main()
63 {
64     assert(levenshtein_distance(
65                     "cat", "act") == 2);
66
67     assert(levenshtein_distance(
68                     "combo", "coin") == 3);
69 }
```

Time Complexity

For the computation of $D(i, j)$, we examine only the cells $D(i-1, j-1)$, $D(i, j-1)$ and $D(i-1, j)$, along with the 2 characters $S_1[i]$ and $S_2[j]$. Hence, to fill in one cell takes a constant number of cell examinations, arithmetic operations and comparisons. Because there are $m \times n$ cells in the table computed above, so total time complexity of $D(m, n)$ is $O(mn)$.

Recurrence : Computing the Damerau edit distance

- $D(i, 0) = i$
- $D(0, j) = j$

Then $D(i, j)$ is one of the following three possibilities:

1. $D(i-1, j-1)$ if $S_1[i] == S_2[j]$
2. $1 + min(D(i-2, j-2), D(i-1, j), D(i, j-1))$ if $S_1[i-1..i] == reverse(S_2[j-1..j])$
3. $1 + min(D(i-1, j-1), D(i-1, j), D(i, j-1))$ otherwise.

We leave the implementation of this algorithm as an exercise to the reader.

Space Optimization

These basic dynamic programming algorithms clearly have a run time and space consumption of $O(mn)$, as they fill $O(mn)$ cells and filling a single cell takes a constant number of operations and space. It is simple to diminish the needed space into $O(m)$ when column-wise filling order of D is used: When column j is filled, only the cell values in one or two previous columns are needed, depending on whether the *Levenshtein* or the *Damerau distance* is used. This means that it is enough to have only column $(j-1)$ or also column $(j-2)$ in memory when computing column j, and so the needed space is $O(m)$.

Properties

It is straightforward to verify that the following properties hold for both the edit distance computation and approximate string matching versions of D under both the *Levenshtein* and the *Damerau* edit distance:

- Diagonal Property : $D(i,j)-D(i-1,j-1) = 0$ or 1
- Adjacency Property :
    - $D(i,j)-D(i,j-1) = -1, 0,$ or 1 and
    - $D(i,j)-D(i-1,j) = -1, 0,$ or 1

Reduction to Single Source Shortest Path Problem

The solution given by dynamic programming approach involves constructing a table of size $m \times n$, where each entry correspond to a *partial edit* and the goal is to compute the *rightmost bottom* entry, i.e., $D(m,n)$, of the table.

Another way to look at the problem is to consider each entry of the table as a vertex of a directed graph. Thus a vertex corresponds to a *partial* edit. There is an edge (i, j) if the partial edit corresponding to j involves one more edit operation than the partial edit corresponding to i. A simplified directed graph may depict insertions as horizontal edges, deletions as vertical edges and substitutions(or replacements) as diagonal edges.

Hence the string edit distance problem is reduced to a single source shortest path problem as finding a shortest path from the vertex $(0,0)$ to the vertex (m, n). We leave the implementation details as an exercise to the reader.

4.6 Music recognition

A **recorder** is a simple blown musical instrument that sounds much like a flute. Prof. Lin Quan has recently programmed his computer to listen to a stream of music from a recorder and convert it into a set $T = \{T_1, T_2, \ldots, T_n\}$ of (possibly overlapping) time intervals, where each interval corresponds to the duration of a note transcribed by the system. Moreover, the professor has developed a heuristic that gives for each interval $T_i \in T$, a metric m_i indicating how likely it is that note i was played by the recorder. The larger m_i the greater the confidence that note i was played by the recorder.

Problem Description

The professor would like to determine which notes are played by the recorder. Since the recorder can produce only one note at a time (when properly played), if two intervals have a common intersection, one of the notes must be spurious (produced by background noise). Give an efficient algorithm to determine a set $S \subseteq T$ of overlapping intervals (ostensibly corresponding to the notes played by the recorder) that maximizes

$$\sum_{T_i \in S} m_i$$

4.6. Music recognition

Solution

We will solve this using dynamic programming. Let $start(T_j)$ and $end(T_j)$ denote the start and end time, respectively, of interval T_j. First, sort the intervals in increasing order of start time. This takes $O(n \log n)$ time. Of course, we can avoid this step if the intervals are already sorted in this order. This seems reasonable since the recorder encounters the time intervals in increasing order of their start times.

Our subproblems have the following form: find a non-overlapping set of intervals $S \subseteq \{T_j, T_{j+1}, \ldots, T_n\}$ such that the quantity (henceforth called the objective function)

$$\sum_{T_i \in S} m_i$$

is maximized. Thus, there are n subproblems, one for each $1 \leq j \leq n$. Let n_j be the smallest value of j' such that $start(T_{j'}) > end(T_j)$. That is, if the instrument is played during interval T_j, then the earliest interval that the instrument can be played next is T_{n_j}. Let ϕ_j be the maximum value of the objective function for the subproblem $\{T_j, T_{j+1}, \ldots, T_n\}$. The answer to the original problem is ϕ_1.

In any optimal subset of non-overlapping intervals for the subproblem $\{T_j, T_{j+1}, \ldots, T_n\}$, there are two possible cases for time interval T_j. It is easy to observe the optimal substructure in both these cases.

Case 1: The instrument is not played during interval T_j. Then, the value of the objective function for the optimal subset is equal to ϕ_{j+1}.

Case 2: The instrument is played during interval T_j. Then, the earliest interval during which it can be played next is T_{n_j}. In this case, the value of the objective function for the optimal subset is $m_j + \phi_{n_j}$.

Combining the above two cases, we have

$$\phi_j = max(\phi_{j+1}, m_j + \phi_{n_j})$$

The boundary condition for this dynamic program is given by $\phi_n = m_n$. The table can be filled up in a bottom-up fashion in order of decreasing value of j. Computation of each table entry takes $O(1)$ time if the n_j's are precomputed. Hence, the time to fill up the table is $O(n)$. Precomputing the n_j's for all takes $O(n \log n)$ time (try to figure out how to do this using binary search !), so that the overall running time is $O(n \log n)$.

Another Problem

The professor now wishes to extend his algorithm to recorder quartets, which consist of soprano, alto, tenor, and bass instruments. He upgrades his heuristic to give for each interval $T_i \in T$, a metric m_{ik} indicating how likely it is that note i was played by the recorder k for $k = 1, 2, 3, 4$. Give an efficient algorithm to determine four disjoint sets $S_1, S_2, S_3, S_4 \subseteq T$, where each S_k contains nonoverlapping intervals (ostensibly corresponding to the notes played by the four respective recorders), that maximizes

$$\sum_{k=1}^{4} \sum_{T_i \in S_k} m_{ik}.$$

4.7. Max Sub-Array Problem

Solution

Observe that if we allow two or more instruments to play during the same time interval T_j, then the optimal solution is obtained by solving separately for each instrument, using the algorithm for the previous problem.

The problem is more complicated when two instruments cannot play during the same time interval. However, note that this allows two instruments to play during the same *time instant*, e.g., when two instruments play during two overlapping time intervals. We will solve this by generalizing the dynamic program from the previous problem.

Let $\phi_{j1,j2,j3,j4,j}$ be the maximum value of the objective function for the subproblem $\{T_j, T_{j+1}, \ldots, T_n\}$ under the restriction that the earliest interval during which instrument k *can play* is j_k for $1 \leq k \leq 4$. Note that j_k is at least j for each $1 \leq k \leq 4$ and the answer to the original problem is $\phi_{1,1,1,1}$. We will divide the number of table entries into $2_4 = 16$ categories depending on whether j_k is equal to or strictly greater than j for $1 \leq k \leq 4$. We give the dynamic programming equations for the case when $j_1 = j_2 = j$ and $j_3, j_4 > j$. You are encouraged to work out the equations for the other cases.

In the case when $j_1 = j_2 = j$ and $j_3, j_4 > j$, there are three possible cases for time interval t_j. It is easy to observe the optimal substructure in each of these three cases.

1. No instrument is played during interval T_j. Then, the value of the objective function in this case is equal to $\phi_{j1+1,j2+1,j3,j4,j+1}$.

2. Instrument 1 is played during interval T_j. Then, the earliest interval during which it can be played next is $T_{n_{j1}}$. In this case, the value of the objective function is equal to $\phi_{n_{j1},j2+1,j3,j4,j+1}$.

3. Instrument 2 is played during interval T_j. Then, the earliest interval during which it can be played next is $T_{n_{j2}}$. In this case, the value of the objective function is equal to $\phi_{j1+1,n_{j2},j3,j4,j+1}$.

As before, $\phi_{j1,j2,j3,j4,j}$ will be the maximum of the objective function values in each of the above cases. The boundary condition is given by $\phi_{n,n,n,n,n} = max_{1 \leq k \leq 4} m_{nk}$.

Note that there can be at most $4+1 = 5$ cases for each table entry (the largest number of cases occurs when $j_1 = j_2 = j_3 = j_4 = j$. Thus computation of each table entry takes $O(1)$ time. The number of table entries is at most n^5, so that the table filling time is $O(n^5)$ (try to figure out the order in which you need to fill up the table in a bottom-up approach !). Note that this dominates the $O(n \log n)$ time for sorting of the intervals and precomputation of the n_j's. Thus, the overall running time is $O(n^5)$.

Please note that the coordinate j in the above dynamic program can be removed without changing the essential structure of the dynamic programming equations. Then, the running time becomes $O(n^4)$.

4.7 Max Sub-Array Problem

Problem

Design and implement an efficient program to find a contiguous subarray within a one-dimensional array of integers which has the largest sum. Please note that there is at least one positive integer in the input array.

4.7. Max Sub-Array Problem

Kadane's Algorithm

There is scanning algorithm known as *Kadane's algorithm* which keeps track of the maximum sum subarray by starting at the leftmost element and scanning through to the rightmost element. It works in a dynamic programming set-up because it has an optimal substructure, i.e., the maximum sum subarray upto the $(i-1)^{th}$ element is used to find maximum sum subarray upto i^{th} element.

The algorithm accumulates a partial sum in max_ending_here and updates the current solution max_so_far appropriately. It is increased by the value contained in i^{th} index as far as it keeps it positive, it is reset to zero otherwise. If all elements of an array are non-negative, this problem is trivial, as the entire array represents the solution. Similarly, if all elements are non-positive, the solution is empty with value 0. So we consider a data set containing both positive and negative values.

Algorithm 63 Kadane's 1D Algorithm

1: **function** KADANE1D(start, end)
2:     $max\_so\_far \leftarrow 0$
3:     $max\_ending\_here \leftarrow 0$
4:     **while** $start \neq end$ **do**
5:         max_ending_here $\leftarrow$ max(max_ending_here + *start, 0)
6:         max_so_far $\leftarrow$ max(max_so_far, max_ending_here)
7:         start $\leftarrow$ start + 1
8:     **end while**
9:     **return** max_so_far
10: **end function**

C++11 Implementation

Program 4.4: Implementing Kadane's Algorithm

```cpp
#include <algorithm>

template <typename ForwardIterator>
typename std::iterator_traits<
    ForwardIterator >::value_type
kadane1d(ForwardIterator start,
         ForwardIterator end)
{
    typedef typename std::iterator_traits<
            ForwardIterator
            >::value_type value_type;

    value_type max_so_far = 0,
               max_ending_here = 0;

    while(start != end)
    {
        max_ending_here =
            std::max(max_ending_here + *start++,
                0);
        max_so_far =
            std::max(max_so_far, max_ending_here);
    }
    return max_so_far;
```

4.7. Max Sub-Array Problem

```
25 }
```

Usage

Program 4.5: Implementing Kadane's Algorithm

```cpp
#include <iostream>
#include <array>
#include <vector>
#include <forward_list>
#include "kadane1d.hpp"

int main()
{
    std::array<int, 8> a
    {-2, -3, 4, -1, -2, 1, 5, -3};
    std::cout << kadane1d(a.cbegin(), a.cend())
              << std::endl;

    std::vector<int> v
    {-1, 4, -2, 5, -5, 2, -20, 6};
    std::cout << kadane1d(v.cbegin(), v.cend())
              << std::endl;

    std::forward_list<int> l
    {-2, 1, -3, 4, -1, 2, 1, -5, 4};
    std::cout << kadane1d(l.cbegin(), l.cend())
              << std::endl;
}
```

It prints

```
7
7
6
```

Find indices of max subarray

Problem

Design and implement an efficient program to find a contiguous subarray within a one-dimensional array of integers which has the largest sum. The result should include sum and (start, end) of the subarray.

It is easy to see that

- the maximum subarray starts and ends in positive elements
- if we start from the first positive element, i.e., a[l], and sum over the subsequent elements until the sum drops negative at a[r], then the optimal subarray is either
  - in a[l..r] and starts from a[l], or
  - in a[r + 1..n].

4.7. Max Sub-Array Problem

Algorithm 64 Kadane's 1D Algorithm : Find Indices

1: **function** KADANE1D(start, end)
2:    $max\_so\_far \leftarrow 0$
3:    $max\_ending\_here \leftarrow 0$
4:    $l \leftarrow 0$
5:    $r \leftarrow 0$
6:    $li \leftarrow 0$
7:    **while** $start \neq end$ **do**
8:       max_ending_here $\leftarrow$ (max_ending_here + *start)
9:       **if** max_ending_here < 0 **then**
10:          max_ending_here $\leftarrow$ 0
11:          li $\leftarrow$ start + 1
12:       **end if**
13:       **if** max_so_far < max_ending_here **then**
14:          max_so_far $\leftarrow$ max_ending_here
15:          l $\leftarrow$ li
16:          r $\leftarrow$ start
17:       **end if**
18:       start $\leftarrow$ start + 1
19:    **end while**
20:    **return** <max_so_far, l, r>
21: **end function**

C++11 Implementation

Program 4.6: Implementing Kadane's Algorithm : Finding Indices

```cpp
#include <algorithm>
#include <tuple>

template <typename ForwardIterator>
std::tuple<typename std::iterator_traits<
                    ForwardIterator
                    >::value_type,
           ForwardIterator, ForwardIterator>
kadane1d(ForwardIterator start,
         ForwardIterator end)
{
    typedef typename std::iterator_traits<
                    ForwardIterator
                    >::value_type value_type;

    int max_so_far = 0, max_ending_here = 0;

    ForwardIterator starti,
                    sum_start, sum_end = start;

    while(start != end)
    {
        max_ending_here += *start;

        if(max_ending_here < 0)
        {
            max_ending_here = 0;
            starti = start;
            ++starti;
        }
```

4.7. Max Sub-Array Problem

```
32          if(max_so_far < max_ending_here)
33          {
34              max_so_far = max_ending_here;
35              sum_start = starti;
36              sum_end = start;
37          }
38          ++start;
39      }
40
41      return std::make_tuple(max_so_far,
42                             sum_start,
43                             sum_end);
44  }
```

Usage

In practice, a bitmap image has all non-negative pixel values. When the average is subtracted from each pixel, we can apply the maximum subarray algorithm to find the brightest area within the image.

Program 4.7: Using Kadane's Algorithm : Finding Indices

```
1 #include <iostream>
2 #include <forward_list>
3 #include "kadane1d_indices.hpp"
4
5 template<typename ForwardIterator>
6 void printcontents(ForwardIterator start,
7                    ForwardIterator end)
8 {
9       std::cout << "{";
10      while(start != end)
11      {
12          std::cout << *start++ << " ";
13      }
14      std::cout << *start << "}" << std::endl;
15  }
16
17  int main()
18  {
19      std::tuple<int, int*, int*> sum_start_end;
20
21      std::array<int, 8> a
22      {-2, -3, 4, -1, -2, 1, 5, -3};
23
24      sum_start_end =
25          kadane1d(a.begin(), a.end());
26
27      auto max_sum = std::get<0>(sum_start_end);
28
29      auto start_index =
30          std::distance(std::begin(a),
31              std::get<1>(sum_start_end));
32
33      auto end_index =
34          std::distance(std::begin(a),
35              std::get<2>(sum_start_end));
36
37      std::cout << "<sum : " << max_sum << ","
38          << " start_index : " << start_index << ","
39          << " end_index : " << end_index << ">"
40          << "\nMax subarray is : ";
```

```cpp
        printcontents(std::get<1>(sum_start_end),
                      std::get<2>(sum_start_end));

    std::vector<int> v
    {-1, 4, -2, 5, -5, 2, -20, 6};

    typedef std::vector<int>::iterator vitr;
    std::tuple<int, vitr, vitr>
        sum_start_end_v;

    sum_start_end_v =
        kadane1d(v.begin(), v.end());

    max_sum = std::get<0>(sum_start_end_v);

    start_index =
        std::distance(v.begin(),
            std::get<1>(sum_start_end_v));

    end_index = std::distance(v.begin(),
                    std::get<2>(sum_start_end_v));

    std::cout << "<sum : " << max_sum << ","
        << " start index : " << start_index << ","
        << " end index : " << end_index << ">"
        << " \nMax subarray is : ";

    printcontents(std::get<1>(sum_start_end_v),
                  std::get<2>(sum_start_end_v));


    std::forward_list<int> l
    {-2, 1, -3, 4, -1, 2, 1, -5, 4};

    typedef std::forward_list<int>::iterator
        litr;
    std::tuple<int, litr, litr> sum_start_end_l;

    sum_start_end_l =
        kadane1d(l.begin(), l.end());

    max_sum = std::get<0>(sum_start_end_l);

    start_index = std::distance(l.begin(),
                    std::get<1>(sum_start_end_l));

    end_index = std::distance(l.begin(),
                    std::get<2>(sum_start_end_l));

    std::cout << "<sum : " << max_sum << ","
        << " start index : " << start_index << ","
        << " end index : " << end_index << ">"
        << " \nMax subarray is : ";
    printcontents(std::get<1>(sum_start_end_l),
                  std::get<2>(sum_start_end_l));
}
```

It prints

```
<sum : 7, start index : 2, end index : 6>
Max subarray is : {4 -1 -2 1 5}
```

```
<sum : 7, start index : 1, end index : 3>
Max subarray is : {4 -2 5}
<sum : 6, start index : 3, end index : 6>
Max subarray is : {4 -1 2 1}
```

Time Complexity

This algorithm consists of n additions and at most 2n comparisons, so the complexity is around 3n.

Hence complexity is linear, i.e., $O(n)$.

Find subarray with sum closest to zero

Problem

Find a sub-array whose sum is closest to zero rather than that with maximum sum. Please note that closest to zero doesn't mean minimum sum.

Assuming input array is a, let us have a notion of *prefix array prefixa* such that
$prefixa[i] = a[0] + a[1] + a[2] + \ldots + a[i-1] + a[i]$
$\implies$
$prefixa[i] = prefixa[i-1] + a[i]$
$\implies$
$a[i] = prefixa[i] - prefixa[i-1]$

Suppose a[l..k] be such a sub-array with sum closest to zero. Then we have the sum of this sub-array as :
$a[l] + a[l+1] + \ldots + a[k-1] + a[k]$
$=$
$prefixa[l] - prefixa[l-1] +$
$prefixa[l+1] - prefixa[l] +$
$\vdots$
$prefixa[k-1] - prefixa[k-2] +$
$prefixa[k] - prefixa[k-1]$
$=$
$prefixa[k] - prefixa[l-1]$

Hence for the sum of a[l..k] to be equal to zero, we should have
$prefixa[k] = prefixa[l-1]$

Hence the sum closest to zero can be found by locating the two closest elements in *prefixa*.

Let us formalize the above algorithm as follows:

1. Compute prefix array with index of original array as well, so it is a collection of pair(value, index). $O(n)$

2. Sort the above prefix array by value. $O(nlogn)$

3. Compute pair-wise diff by value. Prepare absolute values to get a measure of how far/close these are to zero. $O(n)$

4. The closest pair is that with minimum value found above. $O(n)$

5. Report the indices found above in the original array. This is the subarray with sum being closest to zero. (2 comparisons needed).

4.7. Max Sub-Array Problem

Please note that the first and last entries of the suffix array are sentinel points(hence special cases) because these cannot be represented effectively by any other two sub prefix sum. Suppose the closest pair indices reported above is (l, k), then the subarray with sum closest to zero will be decided by the minimum of (closest pair-wise diff val, first entry of prefix, last entry of prefix), i.e. the desired subarray would be

- a[l..k] if closest pair-wise diff val is minimum
- a[0] if first entry of prefix is minimum
- a[0..n - 1] is last entry of prefix is minimum

Hence overall time complexity is $O(n+nlogn)$ Let us start walking through an implementation approach in C++ to understand it better.

Program 4.8: Finding sum closest to zero

```cpp
#include <utility>
#include <algorithm>
#include <tuple>
#include <iostream>

typedef std::pair<int, size_t> ValueIndexPair;

std::vector<int> i
findSubArraySumZero(std::vector<int> & a)
{
    typedef std::tuple<int, size_t, size_t>
        ValStartEndIndices;

    size_t len = a.size();
    std::vector<ValueIndexPair> prefixa(len);

    prefixa[0] = ValueIndexPair(a[0], 0);

    for(size_t i = 1; i < len; ++i)
    prefixa[i] =
    ValueIndexPair(
      prefixa[i - 1].first + a[i], i);

    std::cout <<
    "Printing Prefix Array with Value and"
    " Original Index"
    << std::endl;

    for(ValueIndexPair vip : prefixa)
    std::cout << vip.first << ":"
              << vip.second << " ";
    std::cout << std::endl;

    int start_prefix = prefixa[0].first;
    int end_prefix = prefixa[len - 1].first;

    std::sort(prefixa.begin(), prefixa.end(),
      [](ValueIndexPair f, ValueIndexPair s)
      {
          return f.first < s.first;
      }
    );

    std::cout
        << "Printing Value Sorted Prefix Array"
```

4.7. Max Sub-Array Problem

```cpp
         << std::endl;

      for(ValueIndexPair vip : prefixa)
      std::cout << vip.first << ":"
                << vip.second << " ";
      std::cout << std::endl;

      std::vector<ValStartEndIndices>
          pairwisediff_vec(len - 1);
      for(size_t i = 0; i < len - 1; ++i)
      {
          pairwisediff_vec[i] =
          std::make_tuple(
          prefixa[i + 1].first - prefixa[i].first,
          prefixa[i].second,
          prefixa[i + 1].second);
      }

      std::cout <<
      "Printing Pairwise Value Differences with"
      " original indices"
      << std::endl;

      for(ValStartEndIndices vsei :
          pairwisediff_vec)
      std::cout << "("
                << std::get<0>(vsei) << ":"
                << std::get<1>(vsei) << ":"
                << std::get<2>(vsei) << ") ";
      std::cout << std::endl;

      std::vector<ValStartEndIndices>::iterator
      itr =
      std::min_element(
          pairwisediff_vec.begin(),
          pairwisediff_vec.end(),
        [](ValStartEndIndices f,
           ValStartEndIndices s)
        {
           return std::abs(std::get<0>(f))
                < std::abs(std::get<0>(s));
        }
      );

      ValStartEndIndices closest_indices = *itr;

      std::vector<int> vcandidates(3);

      vcandidates[0] =
       std::abs(std::get<0>(closest_indices));
      vcandidates[1] =
       std::abs(start_prefix); // a[0]
      vcandidates[2] =
       std::abs(end_prefix); // a[0..n - 1]

      int close_zero = *std::min_element(
       vcandidates.begin(), vcandidates.end());

      std::vector<int> vsumzero;
```

4.7. Max Sub-Array Problem

```cpp
        size_t start_index, end_index = 0;

        if(close_zero == vcandidates[1])
        {
            vsumzero.push_back(a[0]);
        }
        else if(close_zero == vcandidates[2])
        {
            vsumzero = a;
        }
        else // close_zero == vcandidates[0])
        {
            std::pair<size_t, size_t> se =
            std::minmax(std::get<1>(
                closest_indices),
                std::get<2>(closest_indices));

            vsumzero.assign(a.begin() +
                            se.first + 1,
                    a.begin() + se.second + 1);
        }

        return vsumzero;
}

int main()
{
    std::vector<int> v
    { 8, -3, 2, 1, -4, 10, -5 };

    std::vector<int> vclosest_sum_zero =
        findSubArraySumZero(v);

    std::cout << "Subarray with sum closest"
        "to zero is" << std::endl;
    for(int e : vclosest_sum_zero)
        std::cout << e << " ";
    std::cout << std::endl;
    std::cout << std::endl;

    v = {-3,2,4,-6,-8,10,11};
    vclosest_sum_zero = findSubArraySumZero(v);

    std::cout << "Subarray with sum closest to"
        " zero is" << std::endl;
    for(int e : vclosest_sum_zero)
        std::cout << e << " ";
    std::cout << std::endl;
    std::cout << std::endl;

    v = {10, -2, -7};
    vclosest_sum_zero = findSubArraySumZero(v);

    std::cout << "Subarray with sum closest to"
        " zero is" << std::endl;
    for(int e : vclosest_sum_zero)
        std::cout << e << " ";
    std::cout << std::endl;
    std::cout << std::endl;
}
```

It prints

4.7. Max Sub-Array Problem

```
Printing Prefix Array with Value and Original Index
8:0 5:1 7:2 8:3 4:4 14:5 9:6
Printing Value Sorted Prefix Array
4:4 5:1 7:2 8:0 8:3 9:6 14:5
Printing Pairwise Value Differences with
original indices
(1:4:1) (2:1:2) (1:2:0) (0:0:3) (1:3:6) (5:6:5)
Subarray with sum closest to zero is
-3 2 1

Printing Prefix Array with Value and Original Index
-3:0 -1:1 3:2 -3:3 -11:4 -1:5 10:6
Printing Value Sorted Prefix Array
-11:4 -3:0 -3:3 -1:1 -1:5 3:2 10:6
Printing Pairwise Value Differences with
original indices
(8:4:0) (0:0:3) (2:3:1) (0:1:5) (4:5:2) (7:2:6)
Subarray with sum closest to zero is
2 4 -6

Printing Prefix Array with Value and Original Index
10:0 8:1 1:2
Printing Value Sorted Prefix Array
1:2 8:1 10:0
Printing Pairwise Value Differences with
original indices
(7:2:1) (2:1:0)
Subarray with sum closest to zero is
10 -2 -7
```

Find subarray with sum closest to k

Problem

Find a sub-array whose sum is closest to a integer s.

As can be seen from the previous problem that the sum of $a[l..k] = prefixa[k] - prefixa[l-1] = s$

Hence in order to find the sub-array with sum closest to zero, all we need to find is to locate 2 elements in the prefix array which are closest with respect to k-distance.

Rest of the exercise is left for the reader to work out.

Maximum 2D subarray problem

Problem

Design and implement an efficient program to find a contiguous 2D subarray within a two-dimensional array of integers which has the largest sum.

Bentley has given a nice algorithm based on Kadane's one dimensional algorithm to solve this problem in two-dimensional array thus making it look like Kadane's 2D algorithm.

It applies Kadane's algorithm to every possible row interval, summing over

4.7. Max Sub-Array Problem

the rows in each interval to produce one dimensional array for Kadane's algorithm to find the optimal column interval. One of the central idea of Bentley's algorithm is the *prefix sum*, which aims to avoid repeating summations when processing subsequent row intervals. The 1D Kadane'e algorithm is run on the elements of each row of the array ($row_1, row_2 \ldots row_m$) considered as a 1D stream, then, on the sum of each pair of rows ($row_1 + row_2, row_1 + row_3 \ldots row_1 + row_m$). The solution is given by the maximal sum produced by the 1D Kadane's algorithm on these cases. If x_1 and x_2 are the pointers to the beginning and the end of the maximal sub-stream, and Row_i and Row_j are the two added rows for which the sum is maximal, then the solution is delimited by the rectangle given by the **upper-left** (Row_i, x_1) and the **lower-right** corners (Row_j, x_2). This algorithm can be summarized as below:

1. Compute the *prefix array* in the dimension of length m. This requires $O(mn)$ computations.

2. If the maximum sum sub-array is between Row_i and Row_j, inclusive, then there are $\frac{m(m+1)}{2}$ such pairs.

3. The sum of elements in the array between Row_i and Row_j for a given column is already computed as a part of our prefix sum. So each column sum looks like a single element of a one dimensional array across all columns, i.e., it looks like a one dimensional array with one row and n columns.

4. Apply Kadane's 1D algorithm on such pairs to get the maximum sub-array as described above. Thus total time complexity is $O(m^2n)$.

Let us formalize the algorithm as follows:

1. Let us denote the input array as $a[0..m, 0..n]$, i.e., it has m rows and n columns. Let a_i denote the ith row of this array.

2. Let us denote i^{th} rowa of the prefix array as $prefixa_i$ which stands for $a_1 + a_2 \ldots a_i$.

3. Please note that $prefixa_i = prefixa_{i-1} + a_i$, where $i \in 1..m$. As described earlier, the computation of prefix array requires mn additions. Hence
$a_i = prefixa_i - prefixa_{i-1}$

4. It is easy to see that the sum over the rows l and k, i.e. $a[l..k]$ can be computed as $a_l + a_{l+1} \ldots a_{k-1} + a_k =$
$prefixa_l - prefixa_{l-1} +$
$prefixa_{l+1} - prefixa_l +$
$\vdots$
$prefixa_{k-1} - prefixa_{k-2} +$
$prefixa_k - prefixa_{k-1} =$
$prefixa_k - prefixa_{l-1}$
These consists of $\frac{m(m+1)}{2}$ pairs.

5. Kadane's 1D algorithm is applied on $prefixa_k - prefixa_{l-1}$ for each interval [l,k] to find the maximum sum. Thus overall time complexity is $O(m^2n)$.

We leave the coding exercise in C++ to the reader.

K-Maximum Sub-array problem

Problem

Design and implement an efficient program to find the K subarrays with largest sums. Please note that the maximum subarray problem for a one- or two-dimensional array is to find the array portion that maiximizes the sum of array elements in it.

Let us revisit our prefix array concept as $a[l..k] = prefixa[k] - prefix[l-1]$. To find the maximum sub-array a[l..k], we have to find the indices l and k which maximizes sum of the entries a[l..k]. Let us denote minprefixa[i] as a minimum prefix array for the sub-array $a[0..i-1]$.
max(a[l..k]) = max(prefixa[k] - prefix[l - 1]) = max(prefixa[k] - min(prefix[l - 1])) = max(prefixa[k] - minprefixa[k]). So to compute the maximum sub-array all we need to do is to accumulate the prefix sums along with maintaining minimum of the preceding prefix sums which could be subtracted from the accumulated prefix sums to get the maximum sum so far.

Algorithm 65 Maximum sub-array sum using prefix array

1: **function** MAXSUBARRAY(a[0..n - 1])
2:    $minprefixsum \leftarrow 0$
3:    $curmaxsum \leftarrow 0$
4:    $prefixa[0] \leftarrow 0$
5:    **for** $i \leftarrow 0, n-1$ **do**
6:       $prefixa[i] \leftarrow prefixa[i-1] + a[i]$
7:       $cand \leftarrow prefixa[i] - minprefixsum$
8:       $curmaxsum \leftarrow max(curmaxsum, cand)$
9:       $minprefixsum \leftarrow min(minprefixsum, prefixa[i])$
10:   **end for**
11:   **return** max_so_far
12: **end function**

Based on the above algorithm, we can easily extend it to find K-maximum subarray in one dimensional case. Instead of having a single variable that safeguards the minimum prefix sum, we maintain a list of K minimum prefix sums, sorted in non-decreasing order. The merged list of two sorted sequences x and y are denoted by merge(x, y).

4.7. Max Sub-Array Problem

Algorithm 66 K-Maximum sub-array sum using prefix array

1: **function** KMAXSUMARRAY(a[0..n - 1])
2:     **for** k ← 1, K **do**
3:         $min[k] \leftarrow \infty$
4:         $M[k] \leftarrow \infty$
5:     **end for**
6:     $sum[0] \leftarrow 0$
7:     $min[1] \leftarrow 0$
8:     $M[1] \leftarrow 0$
9:     **for** i ← 1, n **do**
10:        $sum[i] \leftarrow sum[i-1] + a[i]$
11:        **for** k ← 1, K **do**
12:            $cand[k] \leftarrow sum[i] - min[k]$
13:        **end for**
14:        $M \leftarrow Klargestelementsofmerge(M, cand)$
15:        insert sum[i] into min
16:     **end for**
17: **end function**

As we need to perform n iterations, the total time complexity is $O(Kn)$. When K = 1, this result is comparable to O(n) time of Kadane's algorithm and prefix array.

Chapter 5

Graphs

5.1 Reliable distribution

Problem

A communication network consists of a set V of nodes and a set $E \subset V \times V$ of directed edges (communication links). Each edge $e \in E$ has a *weight* $w(e) \geq 0$ representing the cost of using e. A *distribution* from a given source $s \in V$ is a set of directed $|V|-1$ paths from s to each of the other $|V|-1$ vertices in $V-\{s\}$. The *cost* of a distribution is the sum of the weights of its constituent paths. (Thus, some edges may be counted more than once in the cost of the distribution.)

1. Give an efficient algorithm to determine the cheapest distribution from a given source $s \in V$. You may assume all nodes V in are reachable from s.

2. One of the edges in the communication network may fail, but we don't know which one. Give an efficient algorithm to determine the maximum amount by which the cost of the cheapest distribution from s might increase if an adversary removes an edge from E. (The cost is infinite if the adversary can make a vertex unreachable from s.)

Solution

1. This problem can be modeled as a single-source shortest paths problem. A distribution is a tree of paths from s to every other vertex in the graph. Since the cost of a distribution is the sum of the lengths of its paths, a minimum cost distribution is a set of shortest paths. Since the edge weights are non-negative, we can use Dijkstra's algorithm. The running time of Dijkstra's algorithm can be improved from $O((|V|)^2)$ to $O((|V|+|E|)\log|V|)$ using a binary heap. Since we assumed that the graph is connected, the running time is $O(|E|\log|V|)$. If we use a Fibonacci heap, the running time is $O(|V|\log|V|+|E|)$.

    In addition, we need to return the minimum cost distribution. Dijkstra's algorithm computes backpointers $\pi[v]$ to represent the shortest paths. We can use these to represent the distribution; when asked for the shortest path from s to v, we trace the backpointers from v to s and return the traversed edges (in reverse order).

2. If an edge is removed from the graph, it is possible that the cost of the minimum cost distribution on the resulting graph may be more than the cost of original cheapest distribution. That is, let D be the minimum cost distribution found in the first part, and let $C(D)$ be its cost. If we remove edge e from the graph, let $C(e)$ denote the cost of the minimum cost distribution for the new graph (with edge set $E - \{e\}$). We need to compute

$$max_{e \in E} C(e) - C(D)$$

First recall that cost of a distribution is $\sum_{v \in V} d[v]$, where the $d[v]$ are the distance values returned by Dijkstra.

The straightforward brute-force approach to solve this problem is compute $C(e)$ by deleting e from the graph and rerunning the algorithm from the first part. However, note that if the deleted edge $e \notin D$ then $C(e) = C(D)$, since the removal of e does not affect the distribution D. So we only need to find

$$max_{e \in E} C(e) - C(D)$$

Since the edges in D are a set of shortest paths, they form a tree, and a tree has $|V|-1$ edges. To compute $C(e)$ for an edge $e \in D$, we can delete and then rerun Dijkstra's algorithm on the resulting graph. It is important to note that removing e may make some vertices unreachable from s. To check this, we remove e, rerun Dijkstra, and then check if any of the $d.$ distances are ∞. If so, then $C(e) = \infty$ and we should halt the algorithm and return ∞ as the maximum possible increase. If so, then $C(e) = \sum_v d.[v]$.

The running time of this solution is the cost of $|V|-1$ calls to Dijkstra's algorithm. Using Fibonacci heaps, this is $O((|V|)^2 \log |V| + |V||E|)$.

5.2 Independent Set

Problem

Given a graph G, we have to compute the size of a maximum independent set of G.

Please note that

For any graph $G = (V, E)$, for any $U \subseteq V$, U is an independent set iff $V \setminus U$ is a vertex cover.

Solution

First assume U is an independent set. Assume $V \setminus U$ is not a vertex cover. It follows there is an edge (u, v) such that $u \in V \setminus U$ and $v \in V \setminus U$. But that is equivalent to saying there is an edge (u, v) such that $u \in U$ and $v \in U$. By definition, U is not an independent set, contrary to the initial assumption.

Now assume $V \setminus U$ is a vertex cover. Assume U is not an independent set. Negating the definition of independent set, we derive $\exists u \in U \exists v \in U : (u, v) \in E$. The definition of vertex cover says that for every edge, at least one of its vertices is in the cover. Since $V \setminus U$ is a vertex cover and (u, v) is an edge, $u \in V \setminus U$ or $v \in V \setminus U$. It follows $u \in U$ or $v \in U$, contrary to the previous conclusion that $u \in U$ and $v \in U$. ∎

5.2. Independent Set

For any graph $G = (V, E)$ with n vertices, if m is the size of a minimum vertex cover and t is the size of a maximum independent set, then $m + t = n$. Furthermore, every minimum vertex cover U trivially gives us a maximum independent set, namely $V \setminus U$, and vice versa.

Problem

Construct a linear time algorithm for INDEPENDENT SET *on trees.*

Solution

The arrays A[ ] and B[ ] keep the following information with respect to the *rooted* tree T. Let T_u denote the subtree rooted at u, for every u. For every vertex u,

- A[u] is the size of a maximum independent set in T_u that contains u, and
- B[u] is the size of a maximum independent set in T_u that does not contain u.

The verification of the algorithm is based on the trivial fact that an optimum independent set either contains a certain vertex, or does not contain that vertex. The assignments

$$A[u] \leftarrow 1 \quad B[u] \leftarrow 0$$

are obviously correct. If we imagine a recursive implementation of the algorithm, those lines correspond to the bottom of the recursion. The assignment

$$A[u] \leftarrow 1 + \sum_{i=1}^{k} B[v_i]$$

is because the if u is necessarily contained in any independent set, then $v_1, \ldots, v_k$ are necessarily not in that set; therefore, we choose max independent sets in $T_{v_1}, \ldots, T_{v_k}$ that do not contain the respective roots $v_1, \ldots, v_k$. Consider the assignment

$$B[u] \leftarrow \sum_{i=1}^{k} max A[v_i], B[v_i]$$

If u is not in the independent set, for any child v_i we can pick the maximum independent set in T_{v_1} regardless of whether it contains v_i or not. The key observation, unmentioned so far, with respect to the correctness, is that the optimum set at any internal vertex is obtained from the optimum sets of its children, independently of one another. That allows the divide and conquer approach.

The time complexity can be made as low as linear if we run a modified DFS. The recursive function does not have to return any value because the relevant information can be kept in global arrays A[ ] and B[ ].

Algorithm 67 Independent Set on trees

1: IS on trees, v1(T = (V, E): tree)
2: the algorithm uses arrays A[1, ... , n] and B[1, ... , n]
3: let r be an arbitrary vertex from V
4: make T rooted tree with root r
5: work from the leaves upwards in the following way
6: **for all** leaf vertex u **do**
7: $\quad A[u] \leftarrow 1$
8: $\quad B[u] \leftarrow 0$
9: **end for**
10: **for all** internal vertex u **do**
11: $\quad$ let $v_1, v_2, ..., v_k$ be the children of u
12: $\quad A[u] \leftarrow 1 + \sum_{i=1}^{k} B[v_i]$
13: $\quad B[u] \leftarrow \sum_{i=1}^{k} max A[v_i], B[v_i]$
14: $\quad$ **return** $max\{A[r], B[r]\}$
15: **end for**

5.3 Party Problem

Problem Description

Students at the Monotonic Institute of Technology are reluctant to go to a party if they don't know many people there. Moreover, cycles of indecision lead to situations where Alice will go to a party if Bob goes and Bob will go if Alice goes, but neither ends up going, since neither knows the other's conditions for attending.

To encourage more social behavior, the Student Invitational Party Board (SIPB) is developing a web service to help organize party going. For a given party, each student registers if he definitely wishes to attend or if he conditionally wishes to attend depending on whether a sufficient quorum of friends also attends. Specifically, the student indicates his condition on a SIPB web form by giving a threshold $t \geq 0$ and a list L of t or more other students such that he agrees to attend if at least t of the students on L also attend. Some of the students on L may not register, in which case we assume that they will not attend. At some designated time before the party, the SIPB service emails a message to each registered student whether the student should attend. The service guarantees that if all students who are emailed positive responses attend, then all the attendees' conditions are satisfied. We assume that a student is honor-bound to attend if his condition is satisfied, and that he doesn't register for conflicting parties.

The SIPB party service wishes to process the database of conditions so that as many people go to a given party as possible. Thus, in the Alice and Bob example, both should be sent a positive response. Model the problem formally, and give an efficient algorithm to select as many party- goers as possible subject to the students' conditions. For bonus points, devise a more general set of conditions that can be efficiently processed by a similar algorithm.

5.3. Party Problem

Solution

Model

Let L_i and t_i be the list and threshold submitted by student i.

Algorithm PARTY accepts as input a directed graph, $G(V, E)$. G is represented as an array of adjacency lists. That is $Adj[i]$ lists neighbors of i. In addition to a name, each vertex has attributes *Slack* and *Attend*. There is an edge $e_{ij} \in E$ (from v_i to v_j) if and only if student i appears in list L_j. That is student j's attendance may depend on student i's attendance. We define $Slack[i] = |L_i| - t_i$. We initialize, $Attend[i] = true$. We use one key additional data structure. Queue, Q, lists indices *recently* discovered not to be attending the party. Initially Q is empty.

party(G)

1. For each vertex $v \in V$, if $Slack[v] < 0$, then assign $Attend[v] = false$ and enqueue v on Q.

2. While Q is not empty do the following. Dequeue the head index i. For each student j listed in $Adj[i]$, decrement $Slack[j]$. If $Attend[j] = true$ and $Slack[j] < 0$ enqueue j on Q.

3. For each vertex $v \in V$, if $Attend[v] = true$, add v to the solution set of students to be informed to attend.

Analysis

The loop in step 1 does constant work for each vertex in V. Step 1 running time : $\Theta(|V|)$.

In step 2, each vertex is added to Q at most once. To see this, note that an index i is added to Q only if $Attend[i] = true$, $Attend[i]$ is assigned $false$ before enqueing, and $Attend[i]$ never transitions from $false$ to $true$. Thus, each adjacency list is traversed at most once. Therefore, the while loop does constant work for each edge in E. Step 2 running time: $\Theta(|E|)$. Tallying the solution set takes takes time proportional to the number of students.

Step 3 running time: $\Theta(|V|)$.

Thus, the running time for PARTY : $\Theta(|V| + |E|)$. (Not the same as $\Theta()((|V|)^2)$

Correctness

To show correctness, we show that every solution is *feasible* and *optimal*.

At any point a student i is *viable* if there exist members, j, of L_i such that $Attend[j] = true$. A solution is feasible if every student in the solution set is viable. To show feasibility it is sufficient to prove the following loop invariant I.

$$I : \forall v \in V, (Attend[v] = true) \implies (v\ is\ viable)$$

This can be shown by induction on the iteration of step 2. Step 1 sets up the base case by enqueuing every non-viable i. Each iteration of the while loop explicitly sets $Attend[j] = false$ if viability is violated.

A solution is optimal if the solution set is as large as any other feasible solution set. To show optimality, it is sufficient to show that a node i is enqueued only if is not viable. Again we show this by induction on the iterations of step 2.

5.3. Party Problem

Step 1 sets up the base case by enqueuing every non-viable i. Similarly, step 2 only enqueues i if viability is violated.

Building the graph

Many people worry about transforming lists of student names into a graph. Using a hash function, this operation takes time proportional to the total size of the lists submitted.

First, assume every student is uniquely named (by e-mail address, for example). For each student mentioned in a list, hash the name. If the student is in the table, replace the name on the list with the index found in the hash table. If not, insert the student with a new index and slack -1. For each student that registers, hash the name. If the student is in the table, update the slack. If not, insert the student with a new index and the correctly calculated slack. Insert the list of indices of friends in the appropriate slot in the array of adjacency lists.

Now, we have a graph with edges from students to their friends. To get our input graph, transpose this graph. Transposing a graph takes time $\Theta(|V| + |E|)$.

Chapter 6

Miscellaneous

6.1 Compute Next Higher Number

Problem

Compute the next higher number of a given integer using the same digits. It is also know as *next higher permutation* of a given number.

Solution

Let us assume that such a permutation exists and n be the number of digits for the array a. Let us take an example to understand this problem closely. Let the input integer sequence be :

```
{1, 2, 3, 5, 4, 2}
```

Here $n = 6$. We observe the following property for index i = 2:

- a[2] = 3 < 5 = a[3], i.e., a[i] < a[i + 1]
- 5, 4, 2 is a non-increasing sequence, i.e., a[i + 1.. n - 1] is non-increasing
- 4 is the smallest value of the sequence 5, 4, 2 which is greater than 3 such that the immediate next values(2) is less than 3. Let us denote this index as j(4), i.e., a[j] = 4 and $a[j+1..n-1] \leq a[i]$.
- Hence the next permutation can be achieved by swapping a[i] with a[j]. $\implies$ 1, 2, 4, 5, 3, 2 is a higher permutation than the original sequence.
- Please note that 5, 3, 2 is a non-increasing sequence. Hence the next higher permutation can be achieved by reversing this part to look like 2, 3, 5.
- Hence the next higher permutation is

```
{1, 2, 4, 2, 3, 5}
```

6.1. Compute Next Higher Number

Algorithm

So, the process to achieve the next higher permutation can be summarized as below:

1. Compute an index i, $0 \leq i < n$ such that $a[i+1..n-1]$ is a non-increasing sequence and $a[i] < a[i+1]$.

2. Compute an index j, $i < j < n$ such that $a[j] > a[i]$ and $a[j+1..n-1] \leq a[i]$.

3. swap $a[i]$ and $a[j]$. Now a[i + 1, n - 1] is a non-increasing sequence.

4. reverse $a[j+1..n-1]$ to make it an increasing sequence hence as small as possible.

C++ Implementation

Program 6.1: C++ Implementation : Find the next higher permutation

```cpp
#include <algorithm>
#include <cassert>
#include <vector>

template <typename BidirectionalIterator>
void next_higher_permutation(
          BidirectionalIterator first,
          BidirectionalIterator last)
{
    BidirectionalIterator i = last;
    if (first == last || first == --i) return;
    while (true)
    {
        BidirectionalIterator i1 = i;
        if (*--i < *i1)
        {
            BidirectionalIterator j = last;
            while (!(*i < *--j)) ;
            std::iter_swap(i, j);
            std::reverse(i1, last);
            return;
        }
    }
}

int main()
{
    int a[] = {1, 2, 3, 5, 4, 2};
    int aref[] = {1, 2, 4, 2, 3, 5};

    next_higher_permutation(
        std::begin(a), std::end(a));

    assert(std::equal(a, a + 6, aref));

    int b[] = {1, 3, 5, 7, 9, 8, 6, 4, 2};
    int bref[] = {1, 3, 5, 8, 2, 4, 6, 7, 9};

    next_higher_permutation(
        std::begin(b), std::end(b));
```

6.1. Compute Next Higher Number

```cpp
    assert(std::equal(std::begin(b),
                      std::end(b), bref));

    int c[] = {3, 8, 2, 7, 6};
    int cref[] = {3, 8, 6, 2, 7};

    next_higher_permutation(c, c + 5);
    assert(std::equal(c, c + 5, cref));

    int d[] =
        {8, 3, 4, 2, 6, 6, 6, 4, 1, 1};
    int dref[] =
        {8, 3, 4, 4, 1, 1, 2, 6, 6, 6};

    next_higher_permutation(
        std::begin(d), std::end(d));

    assert(std::equal(std::begin(d),
                      std::end(d), dref));

    std::vector<int> v
    {1,2,3,4,5,6,7,8,4,9,8,7,6,5,4,3,2,1};
    std::vector<int> vref
    {1,2,3,4,5,6,7,8,5,1,2,3,4,4,6,7,8,9};

    next_higher_permutation(
        v.begin(), v.end());

    assert(std::equal(v.begin(), v.end(),
                      vref.begin()));
}
```

std::next_permutation

The following version(STL) takes a sequence defined by the range $[first, last)$ and transforms it into the next permutation which is found by assuming that the set of all permutations is lexicographically sorted with respect to *comp*. If such a permutation exists, it returns true. Otherwise, it transforms the sequence into the smallest permutation, that is, the ascendingly sorted one, and returns false.

Program 6.2: next_permutation

```cpp
template <typename BidirectionalIterator>
bool next_permutation(
        BidirectionalIterator first,
        BidirectionalIterator last)
{
    BidirectionalIterator i = last;
    if (first == last || first == --i)
        return false;

    while (true)
    {
        BidirectionalIterator i1 = i;
        if (*--i < *i1)
        {
            BidirectionalIterator j = last;
            while (!(*i < *--j)) ;
            std::iter_swap(i, j);
```

6.1. Compute Next Higher Number

```
18              std::reverse(i1, last);
19              return true;
20          }
21          if (i == first)
22          {
23              std::reverse(first, last);
24              return false;
25          }
26      }
27  }
```

Program 6.3: reversing a sequence

```
 1  template <typename BidirectionalIterator>
 2  inline void
 3  reverse(BidirectionalIterator first,
 4          BidirectionalIterator last,
 5          bidirectional_iterator_tag)
 6  {
 7      while (first != last)
 8      {
 9          if (first == --last)
10              break;
11          swap(*first, *last);
12          ++first;
13      }
14  }
15
16  template <typename RandomAccessIterator>
17  inline void
18  reverse(RandomAccessIterator first,
19          RandomAccessIterator last,
20          random_access_iterator_tag)
21  {
22      if (first != last)
23          for (; first < --last; ++first)
24              swap(*first, *last);
25  }
26
27  template <typename BidirectionalIterator,
28            typename OutputIterator>
29  inline OutputIterator
30  reverse_copy(BidirectionalIterator first,
31               BidirectionalIterator last,
32               OutputIterator result)
33  {
34      for (; first != last; ++result)
35          *result = *--last;
36      return result;
37  }
38
39  template <typename T>
40  typename enable_if<
41      std::is_move_constructible<T>::value &&
42      std::is_move_assignable<T>::value
43  >::type
44  swap(T & x, T & y)
45  {
46      T t(std::move(x));
```

6.1. Compute Next Higher Number

```
47      x = std::move(y);
48      y = std::move(t);
49  }
50
51  template <typename ForwardIterator1,
52            typename ForwardIterator2>
53  inline void iter_swap(ForwardIterator1 a,
54                        ForwardIterator2 b)
55  {
56      swap(*a, *b);
57  }
```

Time Complexity is at most (last - first)/2 swaps.

Compute previous lower number

The previous lower permutation of a given number is defined as the previous lower number comprising of the same digits.

Compute the previous lower number of a given integer using the same digits.

Let the input integer sequence be :

{1, 2, 4, 2, 3, 5}

Here $n = 6$. We observe the following property for index i = 2:

1. a[2] = 4 < 2 = a[3], i.e., a[i] < a[i + 1]

2. 2, 3, 5 is a non-decreasing sequence, i.e., a[i + 1.. n - 1] is non-decreasing

3. 3 is the value of the sequence 2, 3, 5 which is immediately smaller than 4 such that the next values(5) is greater than(or equal to) 4. Let us denote this index as j(4), i.e., a[j] = 3 and $a[j+1..n-1] \geq a[i]$.

4. Hence the next permutation can be achieved by swapping a[i] with a[j] $\implies$ 1, 2, 3, 2, 4, 5 is a lower permutation than the original sequence.

5. Please note that 2, 4, 5 is a non-decreasing sequence. Hence the previous lower permutation can be achieved by reversing this part to look like 5, 4, 2.

6. Hence the previous lower permutation is

{1, 2, 3, 5, 4, 2}

So, the process to achieve the previous lower permutation can be summarized as below:

1. Compute an index i, $0 \leq i < n$ such that $a[i+1..n-1]$ is a non-decreasing sequence and $a[i] < a[i+1]$.

2. Compute an index j, $i < j < n$ such that $a[j] < a[i]$ and $a[j+1..n-1] \geq a[i]$.

6.1. Compute Next Higher Number

3. swap $a[i]$ and $a[j]$. Now $a[i + 1, n - 1]$ is a non-decreasing sequence.

4. reverse $a[j + 1..n - 1]$ to make it a decreasing sequence hence to bring to the just previous higher one.

Program 6.4: C++ Implementation of prev_permutation

```
template <typename BidirectionalIterator>
bool prev_permutation(
          BidirectionalIterator first,
          BidirectionalIterator last)
{
    BidirectionalIterator i = last;
    if (first == last || first == --i)
        return false;
    while (true)
    {
        BidirectionalIterator i1 = i;
        if (*i1 < *--i)
        {
            BidirectionalIterator j = last;
            while (!(*--j < *i)) ;
            std::iter_swap(i, j);
            std::reverse(i1, last);
            return true;
        }
        if (i == first)
        {
            std::reverse(first, last);
            return false;
        }
    }
}
```

Program 6.5: Usage of previous permutation

```
#include <algorithm>
#include <cassert>
#include <vector>

int main()
{
    int aref[] = {1, 2, 3, 5, 4, 2};
    int a[] = {1, 2, 4, 2, 3, 5};

    std::prev_permutation(std::begin(a),
                          std::end(a));
    assert(std::equal(a, a + 6, aref));

    int bref[] = {1, 3, 5, 7, 9, 8, 6, 4, 2};
    int b[] = {1, 3, 5, 8, 2, 4, 6, 7, 9};

    std::prev_permutation(std::begin(b),
                          std::end(b));
    assert(std::equal(std::begin(b), std::end(b),
                      bref));
```

```
23
24      int cref[] = {3, 8, 2, 7, 6};
25      int c[] = {3, 8, 6, 2, 7};
26
27      std::prev_permutation(c, c + 5);
28      assert(std::equal(c, c + 5, cref));
29
30      int dref[] = {8, 3, 4, 2, 6, 6, 6, 4, 1, 1};
31      int d[] = {8, 3, 4, 4, 1, 1, 2, 6, 6, 6};
32
33      std::prev_permutation(std::begin(d),
34                            std::end(d));
35
36      assert(std::equal(std::begin(d), std::end(d),
37                        dref));
38
39      std::vector<int> vref
40      {1,2,3,4,5,6,7,8,4,9,8,7,6,5,4,3,2,1};
41      std::vector<int> v
42      {1,2,3,4,5,6,7,8,5,1,2,3,4,4,6,7,8,9};
43
44      std::prev_permutation(v.begin(), v.end());
45
46      assert(std::equal(v.begin(), v.end(),
47                        vref.begin()));
48 }
```

Time Complexity is at most (last - first)/2 swaps.

6.2 Searching in Possibly Empty Two Dimensional Sequence

Problem

Design a algorithm to search for a given integer x in a 2-dimensional array a[0..m][0..n] where $0 < m$ and $0 < n$. In case of multiple occurrences, it doesn't matter which is found. This is similar to the problem discussed earlier except that here the array may be empty, i.e., it may have 0 rows or 0 columns.

Solution

The algorithm should find the position of a given integer x in the array a, i.e., the algorithm should find i and j such that

- $\boxed{x = a[i,j]}$, or

- i = m.

Let us treat the input array as some kind of a rectangular region.

6.2. Searching in Possibly Empty Two Dimensional Sequence

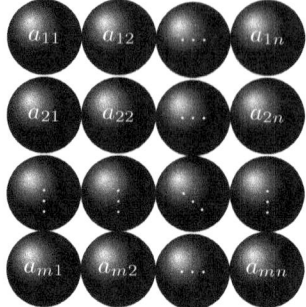

The problem demands that the integer x does exist somewhere in this region. Let us label this condition as *Input Assertion* or *Precondition*.

[

Input Assertion]Precondition (aka *Input Assertion*)

$$\boxed{x \in a[0..m-1, 0..n-1]}$$

i.e., x is present somewhere in this rectangular region a.

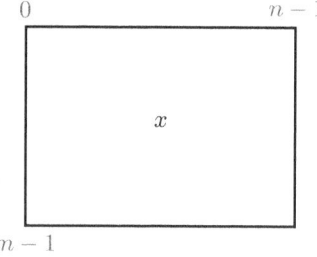

After the program terminates successfully, x has to be found in a rectangular region of a where the rectangular region consists of just one row and column. Let us label this condition as *Output Assertion* or *Result Assertion* or *Postcondition*.

[

Output Assertion]Postcondition (aka *Result Assertion*)
After the program terminates successfully, then x is in a rectangular region of a where the rectangular region consists of just one row and column, i.e., x is present at i^{th} row and j^{th} column of a, or if this is not possible then i = m, i.e., if x is not found in the array, i.e., if $x \neq a[i,j]$, then i = m.

$$\boxed{(0 \leq i \leq m-1 \land 0 \leq j \leq n-1}$$
$$\boxed{\land x = a[i,j]) \lor (i = m \land x \notin a)}$$

6.2. Searching in Possibly Empty Two Dimensional Sequence

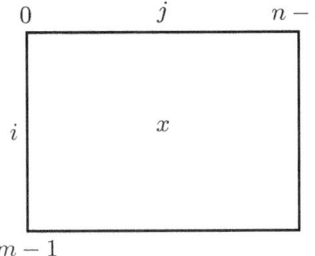

Invariant

The invariant states that x is not in the already-searched rows a[0..i - 1] and not in the already-searched columns a[i, 0..j - 1] of the current row i.

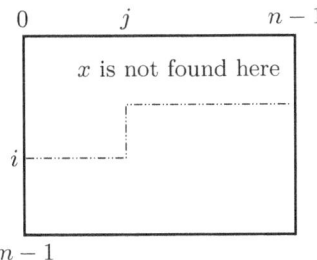

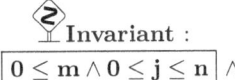 **Invariant :**

$\boxed{0 \leq m \wedge 0 \leq j \leq n}$ $\wedge$

$\boxed{\text{searcheable-region is bounded by } (m-i)*n - j + m - i}$, i.e., the bound function is the sum of number of values in the untested section and the number of rows in the untested section represented by $(m-i)*n - j + m - i$. The extra value $m - i$ is required here because j can take up the boundary value n, i.e., $j = n$. As an astute reader, you must have noticed that now the variant includes $j \leq n$, instead of $j < n$. This is required here because the number of columns, n, could be 0 here.

Initialization step is same as discussed earlier.

Condition

Similar to the problem discussed earlier, we can think about $j \leftarrow j+1$ and/or $i \leftarrow i+1$ to maintain the invariance.

$\boxed{\text{if } i \neq m \wedge (j \geq n \text{ and } x \neq a[i,j]) \text{ then } j \leftarrow j+1}$

Taking this as a condition, the program can terminate when $i < m \wedge j == n$. If x is not found in the very first row, then this will terminate. So we need to some suitable condition for handling increase of i as well. We can try $i \leftarrow i+1$ but this is only possible till $i < m$ and it can maintain the invariant only if the $x \notin a[i, 0..n]$, so we can think of additional condition being $j == n \implies j = 0$ to maintain the condition on the ith row.

6.2. Searching in Possibly Empty Two Dimensional Sequence 215

Algorithm 68 Searching in a possibly empty 2D Array

1: $i \leftarrow 0$
2: $j \leftarrow 0$
3: **function** 2D-SEARCH(a[0..m-1, 0..n-1], x)
4:     **while** $i \neq m$ **and** $j \neq n$ **and** $x \neq a[i,j]$ **do**
5:         $j \leftarrow j + 1$
6:         **if** $i \neq m$ **and** $j == n$ **then**
7:             $i \leftarrow i + 1$
8:             $j \leftarrow 0$
9:         **end if**
10:     **end while**
11: **end function**

C++11 Implementation

Program 6.6: Searching 2D Array

```cpp
#include <algorithm>
#include <array>

using Point = std::pair<int, int>;

template <int m, int n>
using TwoDimArray =
    std::array<std::array<int, n>, m>;

template <int m, int n>
Point search_2darray(TwoDimArray<m, n> & a,
                     int x)
{
    Point p(-1, -1);

    int i = 0, j = 0;

    while((i != m) && (j != n) && (x != a[i][j]))
    {
        j += 1;
        if((i != m) && (j == n))
        {
            i += 1;
            j = 0;
        }
    }

    p.first = i;
    p.second = j;

    return p;
}
```

Usage

Program 6.7: Search for 6 : yields a 2 2

```cpp
#include "2darray_search_contd.hpp"
#include <iostream>

int main()
{
    TwoDimArray<4, 4> a = {
```

```
 7                        12, 2, 83, 5,
 8                        30, 14, 15, 16,
 9                        13, 5, 6, 81,
10                        23, 6, 7, 19
11              };
12
13       Point p = search_2darray<4, 4>(a, 6);
14
15       std::cout << "6 is found at : a["
16           << p.first << "][" << p.second << "]"
17           << std::endl;
18
19 }
```

Time Complexity

It is $O(mn)$ because it ends up traversing the entire region $m \times n$ as far as comparison is concerned.

Correctness

As discussed in the problem discussed earlier, let us try proving correctness of the program developed by proving the veracity of *Postcondition* upon termination, i.e.,

$$\boxed{Invariant \wedge Condition - Complement \implies Postcondition}$$

Please note that the algorithm has 2 conditions namely

1. $i \neq m \wedge j \neq n$. If this is false $\implies i == m$ may be true. In this case, the invariant implies that $x \notin a$, i.e., x is not present in a$[0..m-1, j]$.

2. $i \neq m \wedge j == n$. (If this is false and $i \neq m$) $\implies j \neq n$.

Therefore the first condition being false $\implies x = a[i, j]$.

Hence if both conditions stated above are false then the following condition holds true:

$$\boxed{(i == m) \vee (i \neq m \wedge j \neq n \wedge x == a[i,j])}$$

Complement of this condition in conjunction with invariant $\implies$ the result assertion, which proves correctness of our program developed above.

6.3 Matching Nuts and Bolts Optimally

Problem Description

There is a bag full of n nuts and n bolts, each of distinct sizes, such that there is one-to-one correspondence between the nuts and the bolts, i.e., for every nut, there is a bolt and vice verse. Nuts cannot be compared to nuts and bolts cannot be compared to bolts directly, but nuts can be compared to bolts by trying to fit one into the other. Design and implement an optimal algorithm for fitting all nuts to bolts. By optimal we mean to minimize the number of comparisons involved in the algorithm.

6.3. Matching Nuts and Bolts Optimally

Solution

The same problem can be posed to a computer scientist as follows:

Given two sets $B : \{b_1, \ldots, b_n\}$ and $N : \{n_1, \ldots, n_n\}$, where B is a set of n distinct real numbers (representing the sizes of the bolts) and N is a permutation of B, we wish to find efficiently the unique permutation $\sigma \in N_n$ so that $b_i = n_{\sigma(i)} \forall i$, based on queries of the form *compare b_i and n_j*. The answer to each such query is either

1. $b_i > n_j$ or
2. $b_i = n_j$ or
3. $b_i < n_j$

Since there are n! possibilities for σ, the obvious information theoretic lower bound shows that any bounded degree decision tree that solves the problem has depth at least $\log_3(n!)$.

Using Sterling's approximation :

$\log_3(n!) \approx \theta(n \log_3 n)$

Similar to comparison-based sorting, it can be analyzed using decision tree. Please note that we can model any algorithm for matching nuts and bolts as a decision tree.

The tree will be a *ternary tree*, since every comparison has *three* possible outcomes:

1. *less than,*
2. *equal,* or
3. *greater than*

The height of such a tree corresponds to the worst-case number of comparisons made by the algorithm it represents, which in turn is a lower bound on the running time of that algorithm. We therefore want a lower bound of $\Omega(n \log n)$ on the height, H, of any decision tree that solves nuts n bolts problem mentioned in earlier section.

To begin with, note that the number of leaves L in any ternary tree must satisfy $L \leq 3^H$. Next, consider the following class of inputs.

Let the input array of nuts N be fixed and consist of n nuts in increasing sorted order, and consider one potential input for every permutation of the bolts. In order to match the nuts and bolts, our algorithm must in this case essentially sort the array of bolts.

In our decision tree, if two different inputs of this type were mapped to the same leaf node, our algorithm would attempt to apply to both of these the same permutation of bolts with respect to nuts, and it follows that the algorithm could not compute a matching correctly for both of these inputs.

Therefore, we must map every one of these n! different inputs to a distinct leaf node, i.e.

$L \geq n!$

$\implies 3^H \geq n!$

$\implies H \geq \log_3 n$

$\implies H = \Omega(n \log n)$

Please note that base of logarithm doesn't matter in complexity, it is a kind

6.3. Matching Nuts and Bolts Optimally

of constant, so we will ignore this too.

In particular, at least $\Omega(n \log n)$ comparisons are needed. This is a lower bound for the expected number of comparisons in any randomized algorithm for the problem as well.

A simple modification of *Randomized Quicksort* shows that there are simple randomized algorithms whose expected number of comparisons (and running time) are $O(n \log n)$:

- pick a random bolt
- compare it to all the nuts
- find its matching nut, thus splitting the nuts into three parts:
    1. nuts smaller for the bolt
    2. nuts exactly fit with the bolt
    3. nuts bigger for the bolt
- compare the matching nut found above to rest of the remaining $n-1$ bolts, thus splitting the bolts into three parts:
    1. bolts looser for the nut
    2. bolt exactly fit to the nut
    3. bolts tighter for the nut
- thus splitting the problem into two problems, one consisting of the nuts and bolts smaller than the matched pair and one consisting of the larger ones.

This pair of partitioning operations can easily implemented in $\Theta(n)$ time, and it leaves the nuts and bolts nicely partitioned so that the *pivot* nut and bolt are aligned with each-other and all other nuts and bolts are on the correct side of these pivots :

- smaller nuts and bolts precede the pivots, and
- larger nuts and bolts follow the pivots.

This algorithm then finishes by recursively applying itself to the subarrays to the left and right of the pivot position to match these remaining nuts and bolts. We can assume by induction on n that these recursive calls will properly match the remaining bolts.

To analyze the running time of this algorithm, we can use the same analysis as that of *randomized quicksort*. We are performing a partition operation in $\Theta(n)$ time that splits our problem into two subproblems whose sizes are randomly distributed exactly as would be the subproblems resulting from a partition in randomized quicksort. Therefore, applying the analysis from quicksort, the expected running time of our algorithm is $\Theta(n \log n)$.

This problem provides a striking example of how randomization can help simplify the task of algorithm design.

Rawlins[?] posed this problem as :

> We wish to sort a bag of n nuts and n bolts by size in the dark. We can compare the sizes of a nut and a bolt by attempting to screw one into the other. This operation tells us that either the nut is bigger than the bolt; the bolt is bigger than the nut; or

6.3. Matching Nuts and Bolts Optimally

they are the same size (and so fit together). Because it is dark we are not allowed to compare nuts directly or bolts directly. How many fitting operations do we need to sort the nuts and bolts in the worst case?

Let us try understanding two kinds of algorithms:

- *deterministic* and
- *randomized*

A *deterministic algorithm* is one that always behaves the same way given the same input; the input completely determines the sequence of computations performed by the algorithm.

Normally, when we talk about the running time of an algorithm, we mean the worst-case running time. This is the maximum, over all problems of a certain size, of the running time of that algorithm on that input:

$T_{worst-case}(n) = max_{|X|=n} T(X)$

On extremely rare occasions, we will also be interested in the best-case running time:

$T_{best-case}(n) = min_{|X|=n} T(X)$

So let us try understanding the meaning of *average case*. The average-case running time is best defined by the expected value, over all inputs X of a certain size, of the algorithm's running time for X:

$T_{average-case}(n) = \mathbb{E}_{|X|=n}[T(X)] = \sum_{|X|=n} T(X).Pr[X]$.

Randomized algorithms, on the other hand, base their behavior not only on the input but also on several random choices.

The same randomized algorithm, given the same input multiple times, may perform different computations in each invocation. This means, among other things, that the running time of a randomized algorithm on a given input is no longer fixed, but is itself a random variable.

When we analyze randomized algorithms, we are typically interested in the worst-case expected running time. That is, we look at the average running time for each input, and then choose the maximum over all inputs of a certain size:

$T_{worst-caseexpected}(n) = max_{|X|=n} \mathbb{E}[T(X)]$.

It's important to note here that we are making no assumptions about the probability distribution of possible inputs. All the randomness is inside the algorithm, where we can control it.

Suppose we want to find the nut that matches a particular bolt. The obvious algorithm can be: test every nut until we find a match. This requires exactly n - 1 tests in the worst case. We might have to check every bolt except one; if we get down the the last bolt without finding a match, we know that the last nut is the one we are looking for.

As far as time complexity of this algorithm is concerned, this algorithm will look at approximately n/2 nuts *on average*.

6.3. Matching Nuts and Bolts Optimally

Partitioning

It is very much clear by now that the key part in this algorithm is *partition* step as it is in *quicksort*. So before we jump to *randomized* part, let us go through *deterministic* version.

Algorithm 69 Partitioning a sequence

1: **function** PARTITION(a, l, r)
2:     $p \leftarrow a[r]$
3:     $i \leftarrow l - 1$
4:     **for** $j \leftarrow l, r - 1$ **do**
5:        **if** $a[j] \leq p$ **then**
6:           $i \leftarrow i + 1$
7:           $swap(a[i], a[j])$
8:        **end if**
9:     **end for**
10:    **return** $i + 1$
11: **end function**

---

partition always selects the last element a[r] in the sequence a[l..r] as the *pivot*: partitioning element. It partitions the sequence into four regions, some of which may be empty.

Loop Invariant:

- $\forall x \in a[l..i] : x \leq pivot$
- $\forall x \in a[i+1..j-1] : x \geq pivot$
- $a[r] = pivot$.

The fourth region is $a[j..r-1]$ which is yet to be evaluated.
Time complexity of *partition* is $\Theta(n)$ where $n = r - l + 1$

Program 6.8: Partitioning in C++

```cpp
#include <algorithm>
#include <cassert>

void swap(int *a, int *b)
{
    int t;
    t = *a;
    *a = *b;
    *b = t;
}

int partition(int a[], int l, int r)
{
    int p = a[r];
    int i = l - 1;

    for(int j = l; j <= r - 1; j++)
    {
        if(a[j] <= p)
        {
            i = i + 1;
            swap(&a[i], &a[j]);
        }
```

6.3. Matching Nuts and Bolts Optimally

```
24      }
25
26      swap(&a[i + 1], &a[r]);
27
28      return i + 1;
29 }
30
31 int main()
32 {
33      int a[]    = {8, 1, 6, 4, 0, 3, 9, 5};
34      int aref[] = {1, 4, 0, 3, 5, 8, 9, 6};
35
36      int p = partition(a, 0, 7);
37
38      assert(std::equal(std::begin(a),
39                        std::end(a),
40                        std::begin(aref)));
41      assert(p == 4);
42      assert(a[p] == 5);
43 }
```

STL style partitioning

Program 6.9: STL style implementation of partition

```
1 #include <iostream>
2 #include <algorithm>
3
4 template <typename RandomIter>
5 RandomIter partition(RandomIter l,
6                      RandomIter r)
7 {
8      for(RandomIter j = l; j < r; j++)
9      {
10         if(*j <= *r)
11         {
12             std::iter_swap(l++, j);
13         }
14     }
15     std::iter_swap(l, r);
16
17     return l;
18 }
19
20 int main()
21 {
22     int a[] = {8, 1, 6, 4, 0, 3, 9, 5};
23
24     int *p = partition(a, a + 7);
25
26     std::cout << "Array after partition"
27               << std::endl;
28
29     for(auto e : a)
30         std::cout << e << " ";
31
32     std::cout << std::endl;
33
34     std::cout << "partition index : "
35               << std::distance(std::begin(a), p) << ", ";
```

6.3. Matching Nuts and Bolts Optimally

```
36          << "partitioning element : " << *p
37          << std::endl;
38  }
```

This prints :

```
Array after partition
1 4 0 3 5 8 9 6
partition index : 4, partitioning element : 5
```

std::partition

STL also provides a version of partition algorithm which looks like:

Program 6.10: std::partition
```
1  template <typename BidirectionalIterator ,
2             typename Predicate>
3  BidirectionalIterator
4  partition( BidirectionalIterator first ,
5             BidirectionalIterator last ,
6             Predicate pred)
7  {
8      while (true)
9      {
10         while (true)
11         {
12             if (first == last)
13                 return first;
14             if (!pred(*first))
15                 break;
16             ++first;
17         }
18         do
19         {
20             if (first == --last)
21                 return first;
22         } while (!pred(*__last));
23         std::iter_swap(first , last);
24         ++first;
25      }
26  }
```

It places all the elements in the range [first,last) that satisfy predicate before all the elements that do not satisfy it and returns an iterator i such that for any iterator j in the range [first,i) pred(*j) != false, and for any iterator k in the range [i,last), pred(*k) == false. Time complexity is at most (last - first) / 2 swaps.

Quicksort

Quicksort is a two step divide and conquer based algorithm for sorting a sequence.

1. **Divide** : Partition the sequence $a[l..r]$ into two subsequences $a[l..p-1]$ and $a[p+1,r]$ such that each element of $a[l..p-1] \leq a[p]$ and each element of $a[p+1,r] \geq a[p]$, i.e.
$\forall x \in a[l..p-1]$ and $\forall y \in a[p+1,r] : x \leq a[p] \leq y$.

6.3. Matching Nuts and Bolts Optimally

2. recursively call quicksort to sort the resulting two sub-sequences in place, namely, $a[l..p-1]$ and $a[p+1,r]$.

Algorithm 70 Quicksort to sort a sequence

1: **function** QUICKSORT(a, l, r)
2:     $p \leftarrow$ PARTITION(a, l, r)
3:     QUICKSORT$(a, l, p-1)$
4:     QUICKSORT$(a, p+1, r)$
5: **end function**

As can be seen easily that running time of quicksort depends on the partitioning of sequence.

Worst case partition(for example in case of sorted sequence as input) will result into two subsequences of lengths n - 1 and 0 respectively.
$T(n) = T(n-1) + T(0) + \Theta(n) = T(n-1) + \Theta(n) = \Theta(n^2)$

Best case partition will result into almost equal size subsequences every time.
$T(n) = 2T(n/2) + \Theta(n) = \Theta(n \log n)$

QUICKSORT's average case is closer to the best case than to the worst case.

To understand it better, let us assume that partitioning always results into subsequences of 9:1 ratio:
$T(n) = T(9n/10) + T(n/10) + \Theta(n) = \Theta(n \log n)$

Program 6.11: quicksort in C++

```cpp
#include <iostream>

void swap(int *a, int *b)
{
    int t;
    t = *a;
    *a = *b;
    *b = t;
}

int partition(int a[], int l, int r)
{
    int p = a[r];
    int i = l - 1;

    for(int j = l; j <= r - 1; j++)
    {
        if(a[j] <= p)
        {
            i = i + 1;
            swap(&a[i], &a[j]);
        }
    }
    swap(&a[i + 1], &a[r]);
    return i + 1;
}


void quicksort(int a[], int l, int r)
{
```

```
33      int p;
34      if( l < r )
35      {
36          p = partition(a, l, r);
37          quicksort(a, l, p - 1);
38          quicksort(a, p + 1, r);
39      }
40  }
41
42
43  int main()
44  {
45      int a[] = {8, 1, 6, 4, 0, 3, 9, 5};
46
47      quicksort(a, 0, 7);
48
49      std::cout << "Array after sorting"
50                << std::endl;
51
52      for(auto e : a)
53          std::cout << e << " ";
54
55      std::cout << std::endl;
56  }
```

This prints :

```
Array after sorting
0 1 3 4 5 6 8 9
```

STL style Quicksort

Program 6.12: STL style implementation of quicksort

```
1  #include <iostream>
2  #include <algorithm>
3
4  template <typename RandomIter>
5  void quicksort(RandomIter first,
6                 RandomIter last)
7  {
8      RandomIter left = first, right = last,
9                 pivot = left++;
10
11     if( first != last )
12     {
13         while(left != right)
14         {
15             if(*left < *pivot)
16             {
17                 ++left;
18             }
19             else
20             {
21                 while((left != right)
22                     && (*pivot < *right))
23                     --right;
24
25                 std::iter_swap(left, right);
```

6.3. Matching Nuts and Bolts Optimally

```
26              }
27          }
28
29          --left;
30          std::iter_swap(pivot, left);
31
32          quicksort(first, left);
33          quicksort(right, last);
34      }
35 }
36
37 int main()
38 {
39      int a[] = {8, 1, 6, 4, 0, 3, 9, 5};
40
41      quicksort(a, a + 7);
42
43      std::cout << "Array after sorting"
44                << std::endl;
45
46      for(auto e : a)
47          std::cout << e << " ";
48
49      std::cout << std::endl;
50 }
```

Quicksort using std::partition

Program 6.13: Implementing quicksort

```
1 #include <algorithm>
2 #include <iterator>
3 #include <functional>
4
5 template <typename RandomaccessIterator>
6 void quicksort(RandomaccessIterator begin,
7                RandomaccessIterator end)
8 {
9      if (begin != end)
10     {
11         RandomaccessIterator pivot =
12             std::partition(begin, end, bind2nd(
13                 std::less<typename iterator_traits<
14                     T>::value_type>(), *begin));
15
16         quicksort(begin, pivot);
17         RandomaccessIterator new_pivot = begin;
18         quicksort(++new_pivot, end);
19     }
20 }
```

Randomized Quicksort

So far we have assumed that all input permutations are equally likely which is true always, hence we add randomization to quicksort. We could randomly shuffle input sequence, but randomized quicksort employs *random sampling*, i.e. chosing element at random, to achieve this. So instead of picking the last element $a[r]$ as pivot, it is picked up randomly from the sequence.

6.3. Matching Nuts and Bolts Optimally 226

Algorithm 71 Randomized Partition Algorithm

1: **function** RANDOMIZED-PARTITION(a, l, r)
2:     $i \leftarrow random(l, r)$
3:     $swap(a[r], a[i])$
4:     **return** PARTITION(a, l, r)
5: **end function**

Program 6.14: randomized partition in C++

```
#include <iostream>

void swap(int *a, int *b)
{
    int t;
    t = *a;
    *a = *b;
    *b = t;
}

int partition(int a[], int l, int r)
{
    int p = a[r];
    int i = l - 1;

    for(int j = l; j <= r - 1; j++)
    {
        if(a[j] <= p)
        {
            i = i + 1;
            swap(&a[i], &a[j]);
        }
    }

    swap(&a[i + 1], &a[r]);

    return i + 1;
}


int randomized_partition(int a[], int l, int r)
{
    int i = l + std::rand() % (r - l + 1);
    swap(&a[r], &a[i]);
    return partition(a, l, r);
}


int main()
{
    int a[] = {8, 1, 6, 4, 0, 3, 9, 5};

    int p = randomized_partition(a, 0, 7);

    std::cout <<
    "Array after randomized partition"
    << std::endl;

    for(auto e : a)
    std::cout << e << " ";
```

```cpp
52        std :: cout << std :: endl;
53
54        std :: cout
55           << "partition index : " << p << ", "
56           << "partitioning element : "
57           << a[p] << std :: endl;
58  }
```

Output of this program is:

```
Array after randomized partition
1 4 0 3 5 8 9 6
partition index : 4, partitioning element : 5
```

Randomly selecting the pivot element will result into reasonably well balanced partitioned subsequences on average.

Algorithm 72 Randomized Quicksort Algorithm

1: **function** RANDOMIZED-QUICKSORT(a, l, r)
2:   $p \leftarrow$ RANDOMIZED-PARTITION(a, l, r)
3:   RANDOMIZED-QUICKSORT$(a, l, p - 1)$
4:   RANDOMIZED-QUICKSORT$(a, p + 1, r)$
5: **end function**

Randomization of quicksort stops any specific type of sequence from causing worst- case behavior. For example, an already-sorted array causes worst-case behavior in non randomized quicksort, but not in randomized-quicksort.

In each level of recursion, the partition obtained by RANDOMIZED-PARTITION puts any constant fraction of the elements on one side of the partition, then the recursion tree has depth $\theta(\log n)$, and $O(n)$ work is performed at each level. Even if we add new levels with the most unbalanced partition possible between these levels, the total time remains $O(n \log n)$.

We can analyze the expected running time of
RANDOMIZED-QUICKSORT precisely by first understanding how the partitioning procedure operates and then using this understanding to derive an $O(n \log n)$ bound on the expected running time. This upper bound on the expected running time, combined with the $\theta(n \log n)$ best-case bound we saw earlier, yields a $O(n \log n)$ expected running time.

Thus time complexity of randomized-quicksort $O(n \log n)$.

Program 6.15: randomized quicksort in C++

```cpp
#include <iostream>

void swap(int *a, int *b)
{
    int t;
    t = *a;
    *a = *b;
    *b = t;
}

int partition(int a[], int l, int r)
```

```cpp
{
    int p = a[r];
    int i = l - 1;

    for(int j = l; j <= r - 1; j++)
    {
        if(a[j] <= p)
        {
            i = i + 1;
            swap(&a[i], &a[j]);
        }
    }

    swap(&a[i + 1], &a[r]);

    return i + 1;
}


int randomized_partition(int a[], int l,
                                  int r)
{
    int i = l + std::rand() % (r - l + 1);
    swap(&a[r], &a[i]);
    return partition(a, l, r);
}


void randomized_quicksort(int a[], int l,
                                   int r)
{
    int p;
    if(l < r)
    {
        p = randomized_partition(a, l, r);
        randomized_quicksort(a, l, p - 1);
        randomized_quicksort(a, p + 1, r);
    }
}


int main()
{
    int a[] = {8, 1, 6, 4, 0, 3, 9, 5};

    randomized_quicksort(a, 0, 7);

    std::cout << "Array after sorting"
              << std::endl;

    for(auto e : a)
        std::cout << e << " ";

    std::cout << std::endl;
}
```

Output of this program is:

```
Array after sorting
0 1 3 4 5 6 8 9
```

6.3. Matching Nuts and Bolts Optimally

Deterministic Algorithm for nuts n bolts

Unfortunately, it seems much harder to find an efficient deterministic algorithm for nuts and bolts problem. The first $O(n \log^{O(1)} n)$-time deterministic algorithm was by Alon et al. [?] which is also based on Quicksort and takes $\Theta(n \log^4 n)$ time. To find a good pivot element which splits the problem into two subproblems of nearly the same size, they run $\log n$ iterations of a procedure which eliminates half of the nuts in each iteration while maintaining at least one good pivot; since there is only one nut left in the end, this one must be a good pivot. This procedure uses the edges of an efficient expander of degree $\Theta(\log^2 n)$ to define its comparisons. Therefore, finding a good pivot takes $\Theta(n \log^3 n)$ time, and the entire Quicksort takes $\Theta(n \log^4 n)$ time. Alon et al. [?] mention two potential applications of the nuts and bolts problem:

1. local sorting of nodes in a given graph

2. selection of read only memory with a little read/write memory

Phillip G. Bradford has a given a simple deterministic algorithm [?] for solving the nuts and bolts problem that makes $O(n \log n)$ nut-and-bolt comparisons. This algorithm is based on certain expander based comparator networks and it demonstrates the existence of a decision tree with depth $O(n \log n)$ that solves this problem. They do this by showing that comparator networks that are $\epsilon - halvers$ exist for nuts and bolts. An $\epsilon - halvers$ approximately splits a set of n elements with $O(n)$ complexity. This approximate splitting is enough to allow this algorithm to select good pivots while iterating $\epsilon - halvers$ on geometrically smaller sets of nuts and bolts. The hard part in building these $\epsilon - halvers$ is to ensure that nuts are never compared to nuts and bolts are never compared to bolts while maintaining the $\epsilon - halving$ property. Let $S = s_1, \ldots, s_n$ be a set of nuts of different sizes and $B = b_1, \ldots, b_n$ be a set of corresponding bolts.

For a nut $s \in S$ define rank(s) as $|t \in B | s \geq t|$. The rank of a bolt is defined similarly.

For a constant $c < \frac{1}{2}$, s is called a *c-approximate median* if $cn \leq rank)s) \leq (1-c)n$.

Similarly, define the *relative rank* of s with respect to a subset $T \in B$ as $rank_T(s) := \frac{|t \in T | s \geq t|}{|T|}$.

The algorithm for matching nuts and bolts works as follows:

☛ Find a c-approximate median s of the n given nuts (constant c will be determined later). This requires $O(n)$ nut-and-bolt comparisons.

☛ Find the bolt b corresponding to s.

☛ Compare all nuts to b and all bolts to s. This gives two piles of nuts (and bolts as well), one with the nuts (bolts) smaller than s and one with the nuts (bolts) bigger than s.

☛ Run the algorithm recursively on the two piles of the smaller nuts and bolts and the two piles of the bigger nuts and bolts.

Please note that this algorithm can match n nuts with their corresponding bolts in $O(n \log n)$ nut-and-bolt comparisons because each subproblem has size at most $(1-c)n$, hence the depth of the recursion is only $O(n \log n)$, and in each level of the recursion the total number of nut-and-bolt comparisons to get all of the c-approximate medians in $O(n)$.

6.3. Matching Nuts and Bolts Optimally

Let us summarize the components of this algorithm as follows.

Algorithm 73 Selecting a c-approximate median of X with O(n) complexity

1: **function** GET-C-APPROXIMATE-MEDIAN(X)
2:    $n \leftarrow \frac{|X_0|}{2}$
3:    $l \leftarrow 1$
4:    $r \leftarrow 2n$
5:    $i \leftarrow 0$
6:    **while** $|X_i| \geq C$ **do**
7:       $Y_i \leftarrow$ nut-and-bolt-ϵ-halve(X_i)
8:       $B \leftarrow$ BACK-TRACK(Y_i, i, Z)
9:       $Z \leftarrow$ FIND-MISPLACED-ELEMENTS $\left(Y_i, i, \frac{n}{2^i}\right)$
10:      **if** i is odd **then**
11:         $r \leftarrow \frac{(l+r)}{2}$
12:      **else**
13:         $l \leftarrow \frac{(l+r)}{2}$
14:      **end if**
15:      $i \leftarrow i + 1$
16:      $X_i \leftarrow Y_{i-1}[l, r] \cup Z \cup B$
17:    **end while**
18:    **return** X_i
19: **end function**

Algorithm 74 Back-Tracking

1: **function** BACK-TRACKING(Y, i, Z)
2:    **if** $i \leq 2$ **then**
3:       **return** $\emptyset$
4:    **end if**
5:    **if** i is even **then**
6:

       for any members of Z that are in the right half of Y find all members of all of the left fringes that are supported exclusively by these members of Z or other active elements. Put these candidate illicitly supported elements in B.

7:    **else**
8:

       for any members of Z that are in the left half of Y find all members of all of the right fringes that are supported exclusively by these members of Z or other active elements. Put these candidate illicitly supported elements in B.

9:    **end if**
10:    **return** B
11: **end function**

6.4 Random-number generation

Algorithm 75 Finding Misplaced Nuts and Bolts

```
1: function FIND-MISPLACED-ELEMENTS(X, i, m)
2:     r ← |X|
3:     l ← 1
4:     if i is odd then
5:         Z₁ ← X [(l+r)/2, r]
6:     else
7:         Z₁ ← X [l, (l+r)/2]
8:     end if
9:     j ← 1
10:    while |Zⱼ| ≥ Kεm do
11:        Zⱼ ← nut-and-bolt-ε-halve(Zⱼ [l, r])
12:        if i is odd then
13:            r ← r − (l+r)/2
14:        else l ← l + (l+r)/2
15:        end if
16:        Zⱼ ← (Zⱼ [l, r])
17:        j ← j + 1
18:    end while
19:    return Zⱼ
20: end function
```

Remarks

In this chapter, we discussed the design and implementation of a randomized version of QUICKSORT algorithm for solving the nuts and bolts problem in $O(n \log n)$ nut-and-bolt matching operations. There are huge constants hidden in the asymptotic notation here, though those are not discussed explicitly in this chapter. Reducing these constants (perhaps by removing the expanders) would be an interesting endeavor in itself. This is left an exercise to the interested reader.

6.4 Random-number generation

Problem Description

The array $A[1..n]$ contains a probability distribution over the set $\{1, 2, \ldots, n\}$; that is, we have $A[i] \geq 0$ and $\sum_{i=1}^{n} A[i] = 1$. We wish to generate a random integer X in the range $1 \leq X \leq n$ such that

$$Pr\{X = i\} = A[i].$$

A uniform random-number generator UNIFORM() is available which generates in constant time a real number y uniformly in the range $0 \leq y < 1$. Using UNIFORM() as a subroutine, devise an efficient algorithm to generate a random integer according to the distribution specified by A.

Your algorithm may include an initialization phase to preprocess the array A. After the preprocessing phase, the user can make any number of calls to your random-number generator, each of which should return a random integer according to the distribution A. The highest priority in your design is to make your random-number generator run as fast as possible, but your preprocessing phase should be efficient as well. Analyze both the time for preprocessing and the time for actual random-numb.er generation.

6.4. Random-number generation

Solution

First, we present an algorithm based on generating random variates from a given probability distribution by inverting the cumulative distribution function. This algorithm uses $\Theta(n)$ preprocessing time and then takes $\Theta(\log n)$ time for actual generation of a random number according to the distribution A.

Algorithm 76 Random number generation using binary search

1: **function** RAND-BINARY(A)
2:     $C[1] \leftarrow A[1]$
3:     **for** $i \leftarrow 2$ **to** n **do**
4:         $C[i] \leftarrow C[i-1] + A[i]$
5:     **end for**
6:     $u \leftarrow$ UNIFORM()
7:     **return** BINARYSEARCH(C, 1, n, u)
8: **end function**

BINARYSEARCH in line 7 returns $r \mid C[r-1] \leq u < C[r]$.

This implies $Pr\{X = r\} = Pr\{C[r-1] \leq u < C[r]\} = C[r] - C[r-1] = A[r]$, which established correctness. RAND-BINARY takes $\Theta(n)$ preprocessing time (lines 2-5), while lines 6-7 take $\Theta(\log n)$ time.

Our next algorithm is based on expressing a given probability distribution as a weighted sum of some other probability mass functions that are easy to generate from (using the inversion technique mentioned above), and then selecting one of these probability functions according to the weights followed by generating (easily) from it. We give an algorithm that performs the preprocessing in time $\Theta(n^2)$, but generates random numbers from the distribution A in time $\Theta(1)$. The idea is that if we write a probability mass function as an equally weighted mixture of $n-1$ probability mass functions Q_k, e.g. $A = \frac{1}{n-1} \sum_{k=1}^{n-1} Q_k$, with the special property that each Q_k assigns positive probabilities to at most two components, then in order to sample from A, all we need to do is to generate a uniform random variate to select a distribution Q_j, and then to generate another uniform to select the correct positive component of Q_j. In fact we will use the fact that for a uniformly generated random variate $u, (n-1)u - \lfloor (n-1)u \rfloor$ is independent of u and thus we only need to generate one uniform random variable to sample from distribution A.

One way to implement this idea is to first create $n-1$ buckets such that each bucket contains exactly two elements from $\{1, 2, \ldots, n\}$ and the total mass according to the distribution A in each bucket is $\frac{1}{n-1}$.

6.4. Random-number generation

Algorithm 77 Random number generation : Preprocess

1: **function** PREPROCESS(A)
2:     $A^{'} \leftarrow [(\sigma(1), A[\sigma(1)]), (\sigma(2), A[\sigma(2)]), \ldots, (\sigma(n), A[\sigma(n)])]$, where $A[\sigma(1)] \leq \ldots \leq A[\sigma(n)]$ and σ is a permutation of $\{1, 2, \ldots, n\}$.
3:     **for** $i \leftarrow 1$ **to** $n-1$ **do**
4:       $B[i][1].element \leftarrow FIRST(A^{'}).element$
5:       $B[i][1].mass \leftarrow FIRST(A^{'}).mass$
6:       $slack \leftarrow \frac{1}{n-1} - FIRST(A^{'}).mass$
7:       $B[i][2].element \leftarrow LAST(A^{'}).element$
8:       $B[i][2].mass \leftarrow slack$
9:       $massLast \leftarrow LAST(A^{'}).mass - slack$
10:      REMOVE($A^{'}, FIRST(A^{'})$)
11:      REMOVE($A^{'}, LAST(A^{'})$)
12:      ADDINORDER($A^{'}, (B[i][2].element, massLast)$)
13:     **end for**
14: **end function**

Line 1 creates a list $A^{'}$ of tuples (element, mass) from the elements of the array A, where $element \in \{1, 2, \ldots, n\}$, $mass = A[element]$, and the tuples in $A^{'}$ are sorted on mass. This operation takes time $\Theta(n \log n)$. FIRST takes a list as argument and returns the element at the head of the list in time $\Theta(1)$. LAST likewise returns the last element in the list in time $\Theta(1)$. REMOVE takes as argument a list and an element in the list and removes the element from the list. This takes time $\Theta(n)$ if done using a linear scan. ADDINORDER inserts the given element in the given list such that the new list is still sorted on mass. This also takes time $\Theta(n)$. Hence, in all, the preprocessing stage takes $\Theta(n^2)$ time.

Algorithm 78 Random number generation

1: **function** RAND-CONSTANT(A)
2:     PREPROCESS(A)
3:     $u \leftarrow$ UNIFORM()
4:     $bucket \leftarrow 1 + \lfloor (n-1)u \rfloor$
5:     $index \leftarrow u - \frac{bucket-1}{n-1}$
6:     **if** $B[bucket][1].mass > index$ **then**
7:       **return** $B[bucket][1].element$
8:     **else**
9:       **return** $B[bucket][2].element$
10:     **end if**
11: **end function**

The preprocessing time in the above algorithm can be improved to $\Theta(n \log n)$ using a min-heap and a max-heap, though a slight modification is needed to the data structures.

Correctness follows by observing that the sum of masses associated with element $i \in \{1, 2, \ldots, n\}$ over all the buckets is $A[i]$ and $Pr\{\cup (u \in I_m)\}$, if no two distinct intervals I_n, I_p overlap.

6.5 Weighted Median

Problem

For n distinct elements $x_1, x_2, \ldots, x_n$ with positive weights $w_1, w_2, \ldots, w_n$ such that $\sum_{i=1}^{n} w_i = 1$, the weighted (lower) median is the element x_k satisfying

$$\sum_{x_i < x_k} w_i < \frac{1}{2}$$

$$\sum_{x_i > x_k} w_i \leq \frac{1}{2}$$

1. Argue that the median of $x_1, x_2, \ldots, x_n$ is the weighted median of $x_1, x_2, \ldots, x_n$ with weights $w_i = \frac{1}{n}$ for $i = 1, 2, \ldots, n$.

2. Show how to compute the weighted median of n elements in $O(n \log n)$ worst-case time using sorting.

3. Show how to compute the weighted median in $\Theta(n)$ worst-case time using a linear-time median algorithm.

4. The **post-office location problem** is defined as follows. We are given n points $p_1, p_2, \ldots, p_n$ with associated weights $w_1, w_2, \ldots, w_n$. We wish to find a point p (not necessarily one of the input points) that minimizes the sum $\sum_{i=1}^{n} w_i d(p, p_i)$, where $d(a, b)$ is the distance between points a and b.

    Argue that the weighted median is a best solution for the one-dimensional post-office location problem, in which points are simply real numbers and the distance between points a and b is $d(a,b) =| a-b |$.

5. Find the best solution for the two-dimensional post-office location problem, in which the points are (x, y) coordinate pairs and the distance between points $a = (x_1, y_1)$ and $b = (x_2, y_2)$ is the Manhattan distance given by $d(a, b) =| x_1 - x_2 | + | y_1 - y_2 |$.

Solution

1. Let x_k be median of $x_1, x_2, \ldots, x_n$. By the definition of median, x_k is larger than exactly $\lfloor \frac{n+1}{2} \rfloor - 1$ other elements x_i. Then the sum of the weights of elements less than x_k is

$$\sum_{x_i < x_k} w_i = \frac{1}{n} \times \left(\lfloor \tfrac{n+1}{2} \rfloor - 1 \right)$$
$$= \frac{1}{n} \times \lfloor \tfrac{n-1}{2} \rfloor$$
$$\leq \frac{n-1}{2n}$$
$$< \frac{n}{2n}$$
$$< \frac{1}{2}$$

Since all the elements are distinct, x_k is also smaller than exactly $n - \lfloor \frac{n+1}{2} \rfloor$ other elements. Therefore

$$\sum_{x_i > x_k} w_i = \frac{1}{n} \times \left(n - \lfloor \tfrac{n+1}{2} \rfloor \right)$$
$$= 1 - \frac{1}{n} \times \lfloor \tfrac{n+1}{2} \rfloor$$
$$\leq 1 - \left(\tfrac{1}{n} \right) \left(\tfrac{n}{2} \right)$$

6.5. Weighted Median

$\le \frac{1}{2}$

Therefore by the definition of weighted median, x_k is also the weighted median.

2. To compute the weighted median of n elements, we sort the elements and then sum up the weights of the elements until we have found the median.

Algorithm 79 Weighted Median

1: **function** WEIGHTED-MEDIAN(A)
2: $\quad k \leftarrow 1$
3: $\quad s \leftarrow 0$
4: $\quad$ **while** $s + w_k < \frac{1}{2}$ **do**
5: $\quad\quad s \leftarrow s + w_k$
6: $\quad\quad k \leftarrow k + 1$
7: $\quad$ **end while**
8: $\quad$ **return** x_k
9: **end function**

The loop invariant of this algorithm is that s is the sum of the weights of all elements less than x_k:

$$s = \sum_{x_i < x_k} w_i$$

We prove this is true by induction. The base case is true because in the first iteration $s = 0$. Since the list is sorted, for all $i < k$, $x_i < x_k$. By induction, s is correct because in every iteration through the loop s increases by the weight of the next element.

The loop is guaranteed to terminate because the sum of the weights of all elements is 1. We prove that when the loop terminates x_k is the weighted median using the definition of weighted median.

Let s' be the value of s at the start of the next to last iteration of the loop: $s = s' + w_{k-1}$. Since the next to last iteration did not meet the termination condition, we know

$$s' + w_{k-1} < \frac{1}{2}$$
$$\sum_{x_i < x_k} w_i = s < \frac{1}{2}$$

Note that if the loop has zero iterations this is still true since $s = 0 < \frac{1}{2}$. This proves the first condition for being a weighted median. Next we prove the second condition. The sum of the weights of elements greater than x_k is

$$\sum_{x_i > x_k} w_i = 1 - \left(\sum_{x_i < x_k} w_i\right) - w_k = 1 - s - w_k$$

By the loop termination condition,

$$\sum_{x_i < x_k} w_i = s \le \frac{1}{2} - w_k$$
$$-s \ge -\frac{1}{2} + w_k$$

6.5. Weighted Median

$$1 - s - w_i \leq \tfrac{1}{2}$$
$$\sum_{x_i > x_k} w_i \leq \tfrac{1}{2}$$

Thus x_k also satisfies the second condition for being the weighted median. Therefore x_k is the median and the algorithm is correct.

The running time of the algorithm is the time required to sort the array plus the time required to find the median. We can sort the array in $O(n \log n)$ time. The loop in WEIGHTED-MEDIAN has $O(n)$ iterations requiring $O(1)$ time per iteration, so the overall running time is $O(n \log n)$.

3. The weighted median can be computed in $\Theta(n)$ worst case time given a $\Theta(n)$ time median algorithm. The basic strategy is similar to a binary search: the algorithm computes the median and recurses on the half of the input that contains the weighted median.

Algorithm 80 Linear Time Weighted Median

```
 1: function LINEAR-TIME-WEIGHTED-MEDIAN(A, l)
 2:     n ← length[A]
 3:     m ← MEDIAN(A)
 4:     B ← ∅                                    ▷ B = {A[i] < m}
 5:     C ← ∅                                    ▷ C = {A[i] ≥ m}
 6:     w_B ← 0                                  ▷ w_B = total weight of B
 7:     if length[A] == 1 then
 8:         return A[1]
 9:     end if
10:     for i ← 1 to n do
11:         if A[i] < m then
12:             w_B ← w_B + w_i
13:             Append A[i] to array B
14:         else
15:             Append A[i] to array C
16:         end if
17:     end for
18:     if l + w_B > ½ then                      ▷ Weighted median ∈ B
19:         LINEAR-TIME-WEIGHTED-MEDIAN(B, l)
20:     else
21:         LINEAR-TIME-WEIGHTED-MEDIAN(C, w_B)
22:     end if
23: end function
```

The initial call to this algorithm is LINEAR-TIME-WEIGHTED-MEDIAN(A, 0). In this algorithm, A is an array that contains the median of the initial input and l is the total weight of the elements of the initial input that are less than all the elements of A.

B contains all elements less than the median, C contains all elements greater or equal to the median, and w_B is the total weight of the elements in B.

To prove this algorithm is correct, we show that the following precondition holds for every recursive call: the weighted median y of the initial A is always present in the recursive calls of A, and l is the total weight of all elements x_i less than all the elements of A. This precondition is trivially true for the initial call. We prove that the precondition is also

6.5. Weighted Median

true in every recursive call by induction. Assume for induction that the precondition is true. First let us consider the case in which $l + w_B > \frac{1}{2}$. Since y must be in A, at line 18 y must be either in B or C. Since the total weight of all elements less than any element in C is greater than $\frac{1}{2}$, then by definition the weighted median cannot be in C, so it must be in B. Furthermore, we have not discarded any elements less than any element in B, so l is correct and the precondition is satisfied.

If $l + w_B \le 1$ on line 18, then y must be in C. All elements of C are greater than all elements of B, so the total weight of the elements less than the elements of C is $l + w_B$ and the precondition of the recursive call is also satisfied. Therefore by induction the precondition is always true.

This algorithm always terminates because the size of A decreases for every recursive call. When the algorithm terminates, the result is correct. Since the weighted median is always in A, then when only one element remains it must be the weighted median.

The algorithm runs in $\Theta(n)$ time. Computing the median and splitting A into B and C takes $\Theta(n)$ time. Each recursive call reduces the size of the array from n to $\lceil \frac{n}{2} \rceil$.

Therefore the recurrence is $T(n) = T\left(\frac{n}{2}\right) + \Theta(n) = \Theta(n)$.

4. We argue that the solution to the one-dimensional post-office location problem is the weighted median of the points. The objective of the post-office location problem is to choose p to minimize the cost

$$c(p) = \sum_{i=1}^{n} w_i d(p, p_i)$$

We can rewrite $c(p)$ as the sum of the cost contributed by points less than p and points greater than p:

$$c(p) = \left(\sum_{p_i < p} w_i(p - p_i)\right) + \left(\sum_{p_i > p} w_i(p_i - p)\right)$$

Note that if $p = p_k$ for some k, then that point does not contribute to the cost. This cost function is continuous because $\lim_{p \to x} c(p) = c(x)$ for all x. To find the minima of this function, we take the derivative with respect to p:

$$\frac{dc}{dp} = \left(\sum_{p_i < p} w_i\right) - \left(\sum_{p_i > p} w_i\right)$$

Note that this derivative is undefined where $p = p_i$ for some i because the left- and right-hand limits of $c(p)$ differ. Note also that $\frac{dc}{dp}$ is a non-decreasing function because as p increases, the number of points $p_i < p$ cannot decrease. Note that $\frac{dc}{dp} < 0$ for $p < min(p_1, p_2, \ldots, p_n)$ and $\frac{dc}{dp} > 0$ for $p > max(p_1, p_2, \ldots, p_n)$. Therefore there is some point $p*$ such that $\frac{dc}{dp} \le 0$ for points $p < p*$ and $\frac{dc}{dp} \ge 0$ for points $p > p*$, and this point is a global minimum. We show that the weighted median y is such a point.

For all points $p < y$ where p is not the weighted median and $p \ne p_i$ for some i,

$$\sum_{p_i<p} w_i < \sum_{p_i>p} w_i$$

This implies that $\frac{dc}{dp} > 0$. For the cases where $p = p_i$ for some i and $p \neq y$, both the left- and right-hand limits of $\frac{dc}{dp}$ always have the same sign so the same argument applies. Therefore $c(p) > c(y)$ for all p that are not the weighted median, so the weighted median y is a global minimum.

5. Solving the 2-dimensional post-office location problem using Manhattan distance is equivalent to solving the one-dimensional post-office location problem separately for each dimension. Let the solution be $p = (p_x, p_y)$. Notice that using Manhattan distance we can write the cost function as the sum of two one-dimensional post-office location cost functions as follows:

$$g(p) = \left(\sum_{i=1}^{n} w_i \mid x_i - p_x \mid\right) + \left(\sum_{i=1}^{n} w_i \mid y_i - p_y \mid\right)$$

Notice also that $\frac{\partial g}{\partial p_x}$ does not depend on the y coordinates of the input points and has exactly the same form as $\frac{dc}{dp}$ from the previous part using only the x coordinates as input. Similarly, $\frac{\partial g}{\partial p_y}$ depends only on the y coordinate. Therefore to minimize $g(p)$, we can minimize the cost for the two dimensions independently. The optimal solution to the two dimensional problem is to let p_x be the solution to the one-dimensional post-office location problem for inputs $x_1, x_2, \ldots, x_n$, and p_y be the solution to the one-dimensional post-office location problem for inputs $y_1, y_2, \ldots, y_n$.

6.6 Compute a^n

Problem Description

Let a be an integer and n be a nonnegative integer. Compute a^n. In other words, we ask for a program that does not change the values of a and n and assigns the value a^n to another variable (say, b). (The program may use other variables as well.)

Solution

Consider an integer variable k, whose range is $0..n$. (We maintain the property: $b = a^k$.)

Algorithm 81 Compute a^n program

1: $k \leftarrow 0$
2: $b \leftarrow 1$
3: **while** $k \neq n$ **do** $\triangleright b = a^k$
4: $\quad k \leftarrow k + 1$
5: $\quad b \leftarrow b \times a$
6: **end while**

6.7. Compute a^n revisited

Alternative Solution

Algorithm 82 Compute a^n alternative program

1: $k \leftarrow n$
2: $b \leftarrow 1$
3: **while** $k \neq 0$ **do** $\triangleright$ $a^n = b \times a^k$
4: $\quad k \leftarrow k - 1$
5: $\quad b \leftarrow b \times a$
6: **end while**

6.7 Compute a^n revisited

Problem Description

Solve the preceding problem with the additional requirement that the number of execution steps should be of order $\log n$ (i.e., it should not exceed $C \log n$ for some constant C).

Solution

Let us make some changes in the second solution of the preceding problem:

Algorithm 83 Compute a^n program revisited

1: $k \leftarrow n$
2: $b \leftarrow 1$
3: $c \leftarrow a$
4: **while** $k \neq 0$ **do**
5: $\quad$ **if** $k \mod 2 == 0$ **then**
6: $\quad\quad k \leftarrow k \div 2$
7: $\quad\quad c \leftarrow c \times c$
8: $\quad$ **else**
9: $\quad\quad k \leftarrow k - 1$
10: $\quad\quad b \leftarrow b \times c$
11: $\quad$ **end if**
12: **end while**

In both cases (even k and odd k) the value of k decreases; if k is even, it is divided by 2; if k is odd, after $k \leftarrow k - 1$ it becomes even and is divided by 2 during the next iteration. Therefore, after any two iterations k becomes twice smaller (or even less), so the number of steps is *logarithmic*.

6.8 Compute the product $a \times b$

Problem Description

Two nonnegative integers a and b are given. Compute the product $a \times b$ (only +, -, =, $\neq$ are allowed).

Solution

Algorithm 84 Compute the product $a \times b$
1: $k \leftarrow 0$
2: $c \leftarrow 0$
3: **while** $k \neq b$ **do** $\triangleright$ invariant : $c = a \times k$
4: $\quad k \leftarrow k + 1$
5: $\quad c \leftarrow c + a$
6: **end while** $\triangleright c = a \times k$ and $k = b$, therefore $c = a \times b$

6.9 Compute the quotient and remainder

Problem Description

A nonnegative integer a and positive integer d are given. Compute the quotient q and the remainder r when a is divided by d. Do not use the operations *div* or *mod*.

Solution

By definition, $a = q \times d + r$ and $0 \leq r < d$.

Algorithm 85 Compute the quotient and remainder
1: $r \leftarrow a$ $\triangleright a \geq 0; d > 0$
2: $q \leftarrow 0$ $\triangleright$ invariant : $a = q \times d + r, 0 \leq r$
3: **while** $!(r < d)$ **do** $\triangleright r \geq d$
4: $\quad r \leftarrow r - d$ $\triangleright r \geq 0$
5: $\quad q \leftarrow q + 1$
6: **end while**

6.10 Compute GCD

Problem Description

Two nonnegative integers a and b are not both zero. Compute $GCD(a, b)$, the greatest common divisor of a and b.

6.11. Computed Constrained GCD

Solution

Version 1

Algorithm 86 Compute GCD

1: **if** $a < b$ **then**
2:     $k \leftarrow a$
3: **else**
4:     $k \leftarrow b$
5: **end if** $\triangleright$ k = min(a, b)
6: *Invariant : no numbers greater than k (and therefore than a or b) are common divisors*
7: **while** !((a mod $k == 0$)&&(b mod $k == 0$)) **do**
8:     $k \leftarrow k - 1$
9: **end while** $\triangleright$ k is a common divior, all larger k are not
---

Version 2 : Euclid's algorithm

We assume that $GCD(0,0) = 0$. Then $GCD(a,b) = GCD(a-b,b) = GCD(a, b-a)$ with $GCD(a,0) = GCD(0,a) = a \forall a, b \geq 0$. This property allows us to decrease a and b without changing $GCD(a,b)$.

Algorithm 87 Compute GCD : Euclid's Algorithm

1: $m \leftarrow a$
2: $n \leftarrow b$ $\triangleright$ invariant relation: $GCD(a,b) = GCD(m,n); m, n \geq 0$
3: **while** !(($m == 0$)||($n == 0$)) **do**
4:     **if** $m \geq n$ **then**
5:        $m \leftarrow m - n$
6:     **else**
7:        $n \leftarrow n - m$
8:     **end if**
9: **end while** $\triangleright$ $m = 0 || n = 0$
10: **if** $m == 0$ **then**
11:     $k \leftarrow n$
12: **else** $\triangleright$ $n = 0$
13:     $k \leftarrow m$
14: **end if**

6.11 Computed Constrained GCD

Problem Description

Nonnegative integers a and b are given, at least one of which is not zero. Find $d = GCD(a,b)$ and integers x and y such that $d = a \times x + b \times y$.

Solution

Add the auxiliary variables p, q, r, s to Euclid's algorithm and add the requirements $m = p \times a + q \times b$ and $n = r \times a + s \times b$ to the invariant relation:

Algorithm 88 Computed Constrained GCD

1: $m \leftarrow a$
2: $n \leftarrow b$
3: $p \leftarrow 1$
4: $q \leftarrow 0$
5: $r \leftarrow 0$
6: $s \leftarrow 1$
7: **Invariant:** $GCD(a,b) = GCD(m,n); m, n \geq 0; m = p \times a + q \times b; n = r \times a + s \times b$
8: **while** $!((m == 0) || (n == 0))$ **do**
9:    **if** $m \geq n$ **then**
10:       $m \leftarrow m - n$
11:       $p \leftarrow p - r$
12:       $q \leftarrow q - s$
13:    **else**
14:       $n \leftarrow n - m$
15:       $r \leftarrow r - p$
16:       $s \leftarrow s - q$
17:    **end if**
18: **end while**
19: **if** $m == 0$ **then**
20:    $k \leftarrow n$
21:    $x \leftarrow r$
22:    $y \leftarrow s$
23: **else**
24:    $k \leftarrow m$
25:    $x \leftarrow p$
26:    $y \leftarrow q$
27: **end if**

6.12 Alternative Euclid' Algorithm

Problem

Write a version of Euclid's algorithm using the identities

$$GCD(2a, 2b) = 2 \times GCD(a, b);$$
$$GCD(2a, b) = GCD(a, b)$$

for odd b.

The algorithm should avoid division (*div* and *mod* operations); only division by 2 and the test *to be even* are allowed. (The number of operations should be of order $\log k$ if both numbers do not exceed k.)

Solution

Algorithm 89 Alternative Euclid' Algorithm

1: $m \leftarrow a$
2: $n \leftarrow b$
3: $d \leftarrow 1$ ▷ $GCD(a,b) = d \times GCD(m,n)$
4: **while** $!((m == 0) || (n == 0))$ **do**
5:     **if** $m \bmod 2 == 0 \&\& n \bmod 2$ **then**
6:        $d \leftarrow d \times 2$
7:        $m \leftarrow m \div 2$
8:        $n \leftarrow n \div 2$
9:     **else if** $(m \bmod 2 == 0) \&\& (n \bmod 2 == 1)$ **then**
10:        $m \leftarrow m \div 2$
11:     **else if** $(m \bmod 2 == 1) \&\& (n \bmod 2 == 0)$ **then**
12:        $n \leftarrow n \div 2$
13:     **else if** $(m \bmod 2 == 1) \&\& (n \bmod 2 == 1)$ **then**
14:        **if** $m \geq n$ **then**
15:           $m \leftarrow m - n$
16:        **else** ▷ $m < n$
17:           $n \leftarrow n - m$
18:        **end if**
19:     **end if**
20: **end while** ▷ $m = 0 \implies answer = d \times n; n = 0 \implies answer = d \times m$

If both numbers m and n do not exceed k, the number of operations does not exceed $C \log k$; indeed, each other operation makes at least one of the numbers m and n twice smaller.

6.13 Revisit Constrained GCD

Problem

Modify the solution of the preceding problem to find x and y such that $ax + by = \text{GCD(a, b)}$.

Solution

Assume that both a and b are even. In this case we divide both of them by 2; the values of x and y we are looking for remain unchanged. Therefore, without loss of generality, we may assume that at least one of the numbers a and b is odd. (This property will remain true.)

As before, we wish to maintain the numbers p, q, r, s such that

$$m = a \times p + b \times q$$
$$n = a \times r + b \times s$$

The problem, however, is that if we divide m by 2 (say), then we should at the same time divide p and q by 2. In this case p and q are no longer integers but become finite binary fractions; that is, numbers of the type $\frac{r}{2^s}$. Such a number can be represented by a pair $<r, s>$. As a result, we get d as a linear combination of a and b with coefficients being finite binary fractions. In other words, we have

$$2^i \times d = a \times x + b \times y$$

for some integers x, y and nonnegative integer i. What should we do if $i > 0$? If both x and y are even, we may divide them by 2 (and decrease i by 1). If not, we apply the transformations:

$$x \leftarrow x + b$$
$$y \leftarrow y - a$$

(this transformation leaves $a \times x + b \times y$ unchanged). Let us see why this works. Recall that one of the numbers a and b is odd (according to our assumption). Let a be odd. If y is even, then x is even as well (otherwise $a \times x + b \times y$ is odd); this case is considered above. If a and y are odd, then y becomes even after executing the statement $y \leftarrow y - a$.

6.14 Compute Square using only addition and subtraction

Problem Description

Write a program that prints the squares of the natural numbers $0, \ldots, n$ for a given $n \geq 0$, but only addition and subtraction are allowed. The number of steps should be of order n.

Solution

We use the variable $ksquare$, and maintain the invariant relation $ksquare = k^2$:

Algorithm 90 Compute Square using only addition and subtraction
1: $k \leftarrow 0$
2: $ksquare \leftarrow 0$
3: $print(ksquare)$
4: **while** $!(k == n)$ **do**
5:     $k \leftarrow k + 1$ ▷ $ksquare = (k-1) \times (k-1) = k \times k - 2 \times k + 1$
6:     $ksquare \leftarrow ksquare + k + k - 1$
7:     $print(ksquare)$
8: **end while**

We can avoid subtraction by the following trick:

1: **while** $!(k == n)$ **do**
2:     $ksquare \leftarrow ksquare + k$ ▷ $ksquare = k \times k + k$
3:     $k \leftarrow k + 1$ ▷ $ksquare = (k-1) \times (k-1) + (k-1) = k \times k - k$
4:     $ksquare \leftarrow ksquare + k$
5: **end while**

6.15 Factorization

Problem Description

Write a program that prints the factorization of a given integer $n > 0$. (In other words, it should print prime numbers whose product is equal to n; if $n == 1$, nothing should be printed.)

Solution

Version 1

Algorithm 91 Factorization Program

1: $k \leftarrow n$
2: **while** $!(k == 1)$ **do**   ▷ invariant relation: the product of k and all numbers printed is equal to n; only prime numbers are printed
3:    $t \leftarrow 2$
4:    **while** $k \mod t \neq 0$ **do** ▷ invariant relation: k has no divisors in $(1, t)$
5:       $t \leftarrow t + 1$
6:    **end while**
7:    $print(t)$
8:    $k \leftarrow k \div t$
9: **end while**

Version 2

Algorithm 92 Factorization Alternative Program

1: $k \leftarrow n$
2: $t \leftarrow 2$
3: **while** $!(k == 1)$ **do**▷ the product of k and all number printed is equal to n; only prime numbers are printed; k has no divisors in $(1, t)$
4:    **if** $k \mod t == 0$ **then**   ▷ k is a multiple of t and has no divisors less than t; therefore, t is prime
5:       $k \leftarrow k \div t$
6:       $print(t)$
7:    **else**   ▷ k is not a multiple of t
8:       $t \leftarrow t + 1$
9:    **end if**
10: **end while**

6.16 Factorization Revisited

Problem Description

Solve the preceding problem taking into account the following fact: any composite number N has a factor not exceeding $\sqrt{N}$.

Solution

In *version 2* of the above solution, replace $t \leftarrow t + 1$ by

---
Algorithm 93 Factorization Program Revisited

1: **if** $t \times t > k$ **then**
2:    $t \leftarrow k$
3: **else**
4:    $t \leftarrow t + 1$
5: **end if**

6.17 Decimal Representation

Problem Description

Assume the command $write(i)$ is allowed for $i = 0, 1, 2, \ldots, 9$. Write a program that prints the decimal representation of a given positive integer n.

Solution

Algorithm 94 Decimal Representation

1: $base \leftarrow 1$
2: **while** $10 \times base \leq n$ **do** ▷ base is an integer power of 10 not exceeding n
3: $\quad base \leftarrow base \times 10$
4: **end while**
5: $k \leftarrow n$ ▷ base is a maximal power of 10 not exceeding n
6: **while** $base \neq 1$ **do** ▷ invariant relation: it remains to print k with the same number of digits as in base; $base = 100..00$
7: $\quad print(k \div base)$
8: $\quad k \leftarrow k \bmod base$
9: $\quad base \leftarrow base \div 10$
10: **end while**
11: $write(k)$ ▷ $base = 1$; it remains to write one digit k

Please note that this program assumes that $n > 0$. A typical mistake while solving this problem is that the numbers with zeros in the middle are printed incorrectly. The invariant relation mentioned above allows the case $k < base$; in this case, the decimal representation of k begins with zero.

6.18 Reverse Decimal Representation

Problem Description

Write a program that prints the decimal representation of a positive integer n in reverse. (For $n = 173$, the program should print 371.)

Solution

Algorithm 95 Reverse Decimal Representation

1: $k \leftarrow n$
2: **while** $k \neq 0$ **do** ▷ invariant relation: it remains to print k reversed
3: $\quad print(k \bmod 10)$
4: $\quad k \leftarrow k \div 10$
5: **end while**

6.19 Solve Inequality

Problem Description

A nonnegative integer n is given. Count all the solutions of the inequality $x^2 + y^2 < n$ where x and y are nonnegative integers. The program should not use operations with real numbers (square roots, etc.).

Solution

Algorithm 96 Solve Inequality Program
1: $a \leftarrow 0$
2: $s \leftarrow 0$
3: **while** $a \times a < n$ **do**   ▷ invariant relation: s = the number of all pairs $<x,y>$ such that $(x \times x + y \times y < n$ and $x < a)$
4:      ...   ▷ t = the number of nonnegative integers y such that $a \times a + y \times y < n$ (for fixed a)
5:      $a \leftarrow a + 1$
6:      $s \leftarrow s + t$
7: **end while**   ▷ $a \times a \geq n$, therefore s is the total number of solutions
---

The ellipsis represents part of the program that is still to be written. Here it is:

1: $b \leftarrow 0$
2: $t \leftarrow 0$
3: **while** $a \times a + b \times b < n$ **do**   ▷ invariant relation: t is the number of integers y such that $(a \times a + y \times y < n$ and $0 \leq y < b)$
4:      $b \leftarrow b + 1$
5:      $t \leftarrow t + 1$
6: **end while**▷ $a \times a + b \times b \geq n$, so t is the number of nonnegative integers y such that $a \times a + y \times y < n$

6.20 Solve Inequality Revisited

Problem Description

The same problem with the additional restriction that the total number of operations should be of order $\sqrt{n}$. (The previous solution requires about n operations.)

Solution

We have to count all the integer grid points in the first quadrant that lie inside the circle of radius $\sqrt{n}$. The set in question (call it X) is a union of columns of points having width 1 and non-increasing height.

The idea is to trace the boundary of this set, which resembles a staircase that goes down as we move from left to right. The current position is $<a,b>$. We use one more variable s and maintain the following invariant relation:

- $<a,b>$ is on the top of ath column;

- s is the number of points in the preceding columns.

Formally,

- b is minimal among all $b \geq 0$ such that $<a, b> \notin X$;
- s is the number of all pairs $<x, y>$ of nonnegative integers such that $x < a$ and $<x, y> \in X$.

These conditions will be denoted by (I).

Algorithm 97 Solve Inequality Revisited

1: $a \leftarrow 0$
2: $b \leftarrow 0$
3: **while** $<0, b> \in X$ **do**
4:     $b \leftarrow b + 1$
5: **end while**   ▷ $a = 0, b$ is minimal among all $b \geq 0$ such that $<a, b> \notin X$
6: $s \leftarrow 0$
7: **while** !(b == 0) **do**   ▷ invariant relation : (I)
8:     $s \leftarrow s + b$ ▷ s is the number of points in columns $0..a$
9:     $a \leftarrow a + 1$ ▷ point $<a, b>$ is outside X, it should be moved down to restore (I) unless (I) is already true
10:     **while** $(b \neq 0)$ and $(<a, b-1> \notin X)$ **do**
11:         $b \leftarrow b - 1$
12:     **end while**
13: **end while**   ▷ $(I), b = 0$, therefore the ath column and all subsequent columns are empty; s is the required number
---

An estimate for the number of steps is evident. First we move up performing not more than $\sqrt{n}$ steps. Then we move right and down in not more than $\sqrt{n}$ steps in each direction.

6.21 Print Decimal Representation

Problem Description

Nonnegative integers n and k are given, with $n > 1$. Print k digits of the decimal representation of the number $\frac{1}{n}$. (If two decimal representations exist, such as $0.499\ldots = 0.500\ldots$, print the latter.) The program should use integer variables only.

Solution

Moving the decimal point of the number $\frac{1}{n}$, k positions to the right, we get the number $\frac{10^k}{n}$. We wish to print its integer part; that is, we must compute $10^k \div n$. We do not want to compute 10^k because of the possibility of integer overflow. Instead, we perform ordinary division. Here is the program:

6.22. Decimal Period Length

Algorithm 98 Print Decimal Representation

1: $m \leftarrow 0$
2: $r \leftarrow 1$
3: **while** $m \neq k$ **do**   ▷ m digits of $\frac{1}{n}$ are printed; it remains to print $k - m$ digits of the decimal expansion of $\frac{r}{n}$
4:   $print((10 \times r) \div n)$
5:   $r \leftarrow (10 \times r) \mod n$
6:   $m \leftarrow m + 1$
7: **end while**

6.22 Decimal Period Length

Problem Description

A natural number $n > 1$ is given. Find the length of the period of the decimal number $\frac{1}{n}$.

Solution

The period of a decimal fraction is equal to the period of the sequence of remainders r (see the solution of the preceding problem).

Prove this fact: do not forget to prove that the period of the fraction cannot be less than the period of the sequence of remainders.

In the sequence of remainders all terms that form the period are distinct and the length of the non-periodic initial segment does not exceed n. Therefore, it is enough to find the $(n+1)^{th}$ term of the sequence, and then to find the minimal k such that the $(n+1+k)^{th}$ term is equal to the $(n+1)^{th}$ term.

Algorithm 99 Decimal Period Length

1: $m \leftarrow 0$
2: $r \leftarrow 1$
3: **while** $m \neq n+1$ **do** ▷ $\frac{r}{n}$ = what remains from $\frac{1}{n}$ after the decimal point is moved m positions to the right and the integral part is discarded
4:   $r \leftarrow (10 \times r) \mod n$
5:   $m \leftarrow m + 1$
6: **end while**
7: $c \leftarrow r$ ▷ $c = (n+1)^{th}$ term of the sequence of remainders
8: $r \leftarrow (10 \times r) \mod n$
9: $k \leftarrow 1$
10: **while** $r \neq c$ **do**   ▷ $r = (n+k+1)^{th}$ term of the same sequence
11:   $r \leftarrow (10 \times r) \mod n$
12:   $k \leftarrow k + 1$
13: **end while**

6.23 Sequence Periodicity Problem

Problem Description

A function f that maps $\{1..N\}$ to $\{1..N\}$ is given. The sequence $1, f(1), f(f(1))$ ... is periodic. Find its *period*. The number of operations should be proportional to the length of the smallest initial segment that includes the period (this length may be significantly less than N).

Solution

After discarding the initial segment, we have a periodic sequence, and all terms in the period are different.

Algorithm 100 Sequence Periodicity Problem

1: *Notation:* $f[n, 1] = f(f(\ldots f(1) \ldots))$(n times)
2: $k \leftarrow 1$
3: $a \leftarrow f(1)$
4: $b \leftarrow f(f(1))$ ▷ $a = f[k, 1]; b = f[2k, 1]$
5: **while** $a \neq b$ **do**
6: $\quad k \leftarrow k + 1$
7: $\quad a \leftarrow f(a)$
8: $\quad b \leftarrow f(f(b))$
9: **end while** ▷ $a = f[k, 1] = f[2k, 1]; f[k, 1]$ is in the periodic part
10: $m \leftarrow 1$
11: $b \leftarrow f(a)$ ▷ $b = f[k + m, 1]; f[k, 1], \ldots, f[k + m - 1, 1]$ are different
12: **while** $a \neq b$ **do**
13: $\quad m \leftarrow m + 1$
14: $\quad b \leftarrow f(b)$
15: **end while** ▷ period = m

Note that the value of k obtained after the first loop may be greater than the actual period.

6.24 Compute Function

Problem Description

A function f whose arguments and values are nonnegative integers is defined as follows: $f(0) = 0, f(1) = 1, f(2n) = f(n), f(2n + 1) = f(n) + f(n + 1)$. Write a program that computes $f(n)$ for a given n; the number of operations should be of order $\log n$.

Solution

Algorithm 101 Compute Function

1: $k \leftarrow n$
2: $a \leftarrow 1$
3: $b \leftarrow 0$
4: **while** $k \neq 0$ **do** ▷ invariant relation: $0 <= k, f(n) = a \times f(k) + b \times f(k+1)$
5:   **if** $k \bmod 2 == 0$ **then**
6:     $l \leftarrow k \div 2$ ▷ $k = 2l, f(k) = f(l), f(k+1) = f(2l+1) = f(l) + f(l+1), f(n) = a \times f(k) + b \times f(k+1) = (a+b) \times f(l) + b \times f(l+1)$
7:     $a \leftarrow a + b$
8:     $k \leftarrow l$
9:   **else**
10:     $l \leftarrow k \div 2$ ▷ $k = 2l+1, f(k) = f(l) + f(l+1), f(k+1) = f(2l+2) = f(l+1), f(n) = a \times f(k) + b \times f(k+1) = a \times f(l) + (a+b) \times f(l+1)$
11:     $b \leftarrow a + b$
12:     $k \leftarrow l$
13:   **end if**
14: **end while** ▷ $k = 0, f(n) = a \times f(0) + b \times f(1) = b$, b is the answer

6.25 Emulate Division and Modulus Operations

Problem Description

Two nonnegative integers a and b are given, with $b > 0$. Find $a \bmod b$ and $a \div b$ using only integer variables and avoiding explicit div and mod operations (the only exception: an even number may be divided by 2). The number of operations should not exceed $C_1 \log\left(\frac{a}{b}\right) + C_2$ for some constants C_1 and C_2.

Solution

Algorithm 102 Emulate Division and Modulus Operations

1: $b1 \leftarrow b$
2: **while** $b1 \leq a$ **do**
3:   $b1 \leftarrow b1 \times 2$
4: **end while** ▷ $b1 > a, b1 = b \times$ (integer power of 2)
5: $q \leftarrow 0$
6: $r \leftarrow a$
7: **while** $b1 \neq b$ **do** ▷ invariant relation: q, r are quotient and remainder when a is divided by $b1$; $b1 = b \times$ (some integer power of 2)
8:   $b1 \leftarrow b1 \div 2$
9:   $q \leftarrow q \times 2$ ▷ $a = b1 \times q + r, 0 \leq r < 2 \times b1$
10:   **if** $r \geq b1$ **then**
11:     $r \leftarrow r - b1$
12:     $q \leftarrow q + 1$
13:   **end if**
14: **end while** ▷ q, r are quotient and remainder when a is divided by b

6.26 Sorting Array of Strings : Linear Time

Problem

Given an array of strings, where different strings may have different numbers of characters, but the total number of characters over all the strings is n. Show how to sort the strings in $O(n)$ time. Please note that the desired order here is the standard alphabetical order; for example, $a < ab < b$.

Solution

One way to solve this problem is by a *radix sort* from right to left. Since the strings have varying lengths, however, we have to pad out all strings that are shorter than the longest string. The padding is on the right end of the string, and it's with a special character that is lexicographically less than any other character. Of course, we don't have to actually change any string; if we want to know the jth character of a string whose length is k, then if $j > k$, the jth character is the pad character.

Unfortunately, this scheme does not always run in the required time bound. Suppose that there are m strings and that the longest string has d characters. In the worst case, one string has $\frac{n}{2}$ characters and, before padding, $\frac{n}{2}$ strings have one character each. We would have $d = \frac{n}{2}$ and $m = \frac{n}{2} + 1$. We still have to examine the pad characters in each pass of radix sort, even if we don't actually create them in the strings. Assuming that the range of a single character is constant, the running time of radix sort would be $\Theta(dm) = \Theta(n^2)$.

To solve the problem in $O(n)$ time, we use the property that, if the first letter of string x is lexicographically less that the first letter of string y, then x is lexicographically less than y, regardless of the lengths of the two strings. We take advantage of this property by sorting the strings on the first letter, using *counting sort*. We take an empty string as a special case and put it first. We gather together all strings with the same first letter as a group. Then we recurse, within each group, based on each string with the first letter removed.

The correctness of this algorithm is straightforward. Analyzing the running time is a bit trickier. Let us count the number of times that each string is sorted by a call of counting sort. Suppose that the ith string, s_i, has length l_i. Then s_i is sorted by at most $l_i + 1$ counting sorts. (The *+1* is because it may have to be sorted as an empty string at some point; for example, ab and a end up in the same group in the first pass and are then ordered based on b and the empty string in the second pass. The string a is sorted its length, 1, time plus one more time.) A call of counting sort on t strings takes $\Theta(t)$ time (remembering that the number of different characters on which we are sorting is a constant.) Thus, the total time for all calls of counting sort is

$$O\left(\sum_{i=1}^{m}(l_i + 1)\right) = O\left(\sum_{i=1}^{m} l_i + m\right) = O(n + m) = O(n)$$

Please note that $\sum_{i=1}^{m} = n$ and $m \leq n$.

6.27 LRU data structure

Problem Description

Managing the primary memory of a virtual-memory system with LRU page replacement can be viewed as a dynamic data structure problem. The data structure manages a set $S = \{1, \ldots, s\}$ of s fixed-size slots of primary memory. The virtual memory can be viewed as a set $P = \{1, \ldots, p\}$ of virtual-memory pages. At any time a subset of P having size at most s is resident in the s slots of primary memory. The job of the data structure is to maintain a dynamic mapping so that the system can identify whether a user's reference to a page resides in a slot of primary memory, and if not, drop the least-recently used page and replace it with the referenced page.

The LRU data structure must therefore support the following operations:

- INSERT(q, t) : Insert virtual page $q \in P$ into slot $t \in S$ of primary memory. The slot t must be empty.

- USE(q) : Return the slot $t \in S$ containing virtual page $q \in P$, or else NIL if q does not reside in primary memory.

- DROP() : Remove the least-recently used page $q \in P$ from its slot $t \in S$, and return the non-empty slot t.

Describe briefly why these operations suffice to implement the LRU page replacement policy. Give an efficient implementation of this dynamic set.

Solution

This problem had a very simple $\Theta(1)$ time implementation without making any simplifying assumptions. It should be assumed that for a paging system on any real computer, anything less than a $\Theta(1)$ time for any of those operations would simply be unacceptable.

We implement LRU by the use of

- A doubly linked list, call it L.
- A hash table, call it H.

The two data structures contain a structure holding the virtual page number $q \in P$ and the corresponding physical page slot it occupies $t \in S$ for all pages that are currently occupying physical memory slots. The hash table entries also hold a pointer to the linked list node corresponding to the virtual page q. The space requirement for these is therefore $O(s)$.

In order to implement LRU, we need a complete ordering in terms of last access for every page currently occupying a physical memory slot. It is obvious to see that a doubly-linked list coupled with a move to front heuristic provides exactly this. Doubly-linked lists are convenient as cutting and pasting an element can be done in $\Theta(1)$ time, if we already have pointers to the element to cut and the element before or after were we will paste. Thus in order to support the DROP and USE operations in constant time, we use such a list, and *arbitrarily* define ordering to be from most recently used page at the head to least recently used at the tail. We thus also need to keep track of the head and tail of the doubly linked list so as to know where to cut and paste.

However, apart from the LRU information, we need to the ability to lookup a certain virtual page and quickly extract the physical page slot it occupies.

6.27. LRU data structure

The INSERT procedure inserts this mapping into the data structure, whereas the USE procedure returns the mapping. This is an instance of the dictionary problem, which we know how to efficiently solve using a hash table. We use a chained hash table. The average access time in the table is $\Theta(1+\alpha)$, where α is the load factor defined as $\frac{n}{m}$ where n in the number of things to store and m is the number of slots. We therefore decide to use a table of size $\Theta(|S|)$ to ensure that the load factor remains small. As for a hash function, we can simply use a random hash function drawn from a collection of universal hash functions, or any of the other hash functions.

Assuming that we have implemented such a list and hash table, the DROP operation can be implemented as follows:

Algorithm 103 LRU Data Structure : Drop program

1: **function** DROP
2:   $q \leftarrow tail[L].t$
3:   **if** q == NIL **then**
4:     **return** NIL
5:   **else**
6:     $tail[L] \leftarrow tails[L].previous$
7:   **end if**
8:   $tail[L].previous \leftarrow$ NIL
9: **end function**

The USE is then simply (assuming that the hash function HASH returns the hash key of its argument):

Algorithm 104 LRU Data Structure : Use program

1: **function** USE(q)
2:   $ref \leftarrow$ CHAINED-HASH-SEARCH$(H, Hash(q))$
3:   **if** ref == NIL **then**
4:     **error** "Page not in primary memory"
5:   **else**
6:     $ref.node.next.previous \leftarrow ref.node.previous$
7:     $ref.node.previous.next \leftarrow ref.node.next$
8:     $ref.node.previous \leftarrow$ NIL
9:     $ref.node.next \leftarrow head[L]$
10:    $head[L] \leftarrow ref$
11:    **return** $ref.t$
12: **end if**
13: **end function**

Finally, the INSERT becomes:

Algorithm 105 LRU Data Structure : Insert program

1: **function** INSERT(q, t)
2: $\quad node \leftarrow \text{NEW}(ListNode)$
3: $\quad node.next \leftarrow head[L]$
4: $\quad node.previous \leftarrow \text{NIL}$
5: $\quad ref \leftarrow \text{NEW}(HashNode)$
6: $\quad ref.node \leftarrow node$
7: $\quad ref.t \leftarrow t$
8: $\quad ref.q \leftarrow q$
9: **end function**

The three functions that we asked you to implement, would be provided as a front end to your system, therefore, it is conceivable that DROP could be called an arbitrary number of times, without being immediately followed by an INSERT. With this in mind, the above functions do not suffice for a correct implementation of LRU. We need some way to first look if there is an empty slot of physical memory and only if one does not exist should we drop the tail of the list. Modifying the DROP and INSERT programs to do this is easy, by using a direct mapping table and doubly linked list of free physical memory slots, exactly as we do above for the LRU. Since we only have $\mid S \mid$ physical memory slots, we do not need to use a hashtable. Then, the DROP and INSERT programs operate on all four data structures.

Unfortunately, a number of people assumed that it was possible to keep an array of size $\Theta(P)$ with an entry for each virtual page and store all information needed, therefore obtaining an $O(1)$ time. This solution however bears little physical realism. Most modern computer systems have a 64 bit bit virtual address space, and $4KB$ pages. Therefore, a direct mapping lookup table for each virtual page would require $\frac{2^{64}}{2^{12}} = 2^{52}$ entries. If only one integer of information was kept in each table entry, one would need 16384TB...

A number of other people used some form of balanced tree to do lookups, leading to logarithmic running times for some or all of the procedures. However, again, such a solution is not desirable, since a VM system is one of the most heavily loaded components of the operating system.

Some people claimed that the move to front heuristic combined with the locality that program memory references exhibit, allows us to use the LRU linked list to implement the USE program by a linear scan. However, an operating system runs a number of programs at the same time, therefore the system as a whole exhibits less locality. Furthermore, (also for the people who claimed USE might not be used too much) this program is probably the most used of the system for obvious(!) reasons. All these solutions might work for Windows, but not on a usable OS.

Other sources for loss of points were forgetting to update the LRU information when USE was called. LRU does indeed stand for *least recently used*.

6.28 Exchange Prefix and Suffix

Problem Description

An array $x[1]..x[m + n]$ is considered as a concatenation of two segments: a *prefix* $x[1]..x[m]$ of length m and a *suffix* $x[m + 1]..x[m + n]$ of length n. Without using other arrays, exchange these *prefix* and *suffix* segments. (The number of operations should be of order $m + n$.)

6.28. Exchange Prefix and Suffix

Solution

Version 1

Reverse the prefix segment, then the suffix segment, and finally the whole array.

Version 2

Imagine that the array is written down along a circle. Then the required transformation is a rotation. Recall that rotation may be represented as the composition of two axial symmetries. Each symmetry can be performed by exchanges without extra memory.

Version 3

Consider a more general problem: Exchange two adjacent segments $x[p+1]..x[q]$ and $x[q+1]..x[r]$ in an array. Assume that the length of the left segment (called A in the sequel) does not exceed the length of the right segment (called B). Split B into two segments B_1 and B_2, where B_1 is an initial segment of B of the same length as A. (So, $B = B_1 + B_2$, where $+$ stands for concatenation.) We need to transform $A + B_1 + B_2$ into $B_1 + B_2 + A$. We can easily exchange A and B_1 because they have equal lengths. After that we get $B_1 + A + B_2$ and it remains to exchange A and B_2. Therefore, we have reduced our problem to a similar one for shorter segments. Here is the outline of the program:

Algorithm 106 Exchange Prefix and Suffix

1: $p \leftarrow 0$
2: $q \leftarrow m$
3: $r \leftarrow m + n$
4: **while** $(p \neq q)$ *and* $q \neq r$ **do**   ▷ invariant relation: it remains to exchange $x[p+1..q], x[q+1..r]$
5:   **if** $(q - p) \leq (r - p)$ **then**   ▷ both segments are nonempty
6:     $pnew \leftarrow q$ ▷ exchange $x[p+1]..x[q]$ and $x[q+1]..x[q+(q-p)]$
7:     $qnew \leftarrow q + (q - p)$
8:     $p \leftarrow pnew$
9:     $q \leftarrow qnew$
10: **else**   ▷ exchange $x[q - (r-q) + 1]..x[q]$ and $x[q+1]..x[r]$
11:    $qnew \leftarrow q - (r - q)$
12:    $rnew \leftarrow q$
13:    $q \leftarrow qnew$
14:    $r \leftarrow rnew$
15: **end if**
16: **end while**

The number of operations may be estimated as follows. At each step the part of the array that should be processed becomes shorter by the length of A. The number of operations required is also proportional to the length of A.

Chapter 7

Parallel Algorithms

7.1 Parallel Addition

Problem Description

Find the sum of two n-bit binary numbers.

Solution

The regular sequential algorithm starts at the least significant bits, and adds two bits at a time with a possible carry. It seems that we cannot be sure of the outcome of the jth step until the two $i-1$ least significant bits are added, since there may or may not be a carry. Nevertheless, it is possible to design another algorithm.

We use induction on n. It will not help much to go from $n-1$ to n, since this implies an iterative sequential algorithm. The divide and conquer approach has a much better potential for parallel algorithms, since it may be possible to solve all smaller parts in parallel.

Suppose that we divide the problem into two subproblems of size $\frac{n}{2}$ assuming that n is a power of 2 for simplicity. We can find the sums of the two pairs in parallel. But we still have the problem of the carry. If the sum of the least significant pair has a carry, we have to change the sum of the most significant pair.

The key observation here is that there are only two possibilities : we either have a carry or we do not. Therefore, we can *strengthen the induction hypothesis* to include both cases.

> The modified problem is to find the sum of the two numbers with *and* without an initial carry.

Suppose that we now solve this modified problem for both pairs. We get four numbers :

1. L : the sum of the least significant pair with no initial carry.

2. L_C : the same sum with an initial carry.

3. R : the sum of the most significant pair with no initial carry.

4. R_C : the same sum with an initial carry.

For each of these sums, we also find whether it generates a carry. The final sum S, without initial carry, is L and either R or R_C, depending on whether L had a carry. The final sum S_C is the same as S, except that L is replaced by L_C.

We solve a problem of size n by two subproblems of size $\frac{n}{2}$ and a constant number of conquer steps. Since both subproblems can be solved in parallel : assuming that the processors can access different bits independently : we obtain the recurrence relation :

$$T(n,n) = T\left(\tfrac{n}{2}, \tfrac{n}{2}\right) + O(1)$$

which implies that

$$T(n,n) = O(\log n)$$

7.2 Find Maximum

Problem Description

Find the maximum among n distinct numbers, given in an array.

Solution

The straightforward sequential algorithm for finding the maximum requires $n-1$ comparisons. We can think of a comparison as a game played between the two numbers, with the larger of the two wining.

> The maximum finding problem is thus equivalent to running a tournament with the winner being the maximum of the whole set.

An efficient way to run a tournament in parallel is to use a tree. The players are divided into pairs for the first round with possibly one player sitting out, in case of an odd number of players, all the winners are again divided into pairs, and so on, until the finals.

> The number of rounds is $\lceil \log_2 n \rceil$.

We can obtain a parallel algorithm from the tournament by assigning a processor to every game thinking of the processor as the referee of the game. We have to ensure, however, that each processor knows the two competing numbers. This can be arranged by putting the winner of the game in the larger indexed position of the two players. That is, if the game is played between x_i and x_j such that $j > i$, then the maximal of x_i and x_j is put in position j. In the first round, processor P_i compares x_{2i-1} to x_{2i}, $1 \leq i \leq \frac{n}{2}$, and exchanges them if necessary; in the second round, P_i compares x_{4i-2} to x_{4i}, $1 \leq i \leq \frac{n}{4}$, and so on. Please note that each number is involved in only one game at a time.

> The running time of this simple algorithm is clearly $O(\log n)$.

Let's try now to minimize the number of processors.

The algorithm we just presented requires $\lfloor \frac{n}{2} \rfloor$ processors, and we have

$$T(n, \lfloor \tfrac{n}{2} \rfloor) = \lceil \log_2 n \rceil.$$

Since the sequential algorithm achieves

$$T(n,1) = n - 1,$$

the efficiency of the parallel algorithm is

$$E(n, \tfrac{n}{2}) = \tfrac{1}{\log_2 n}.$$

If $\tfrac{n}{2}$ processors are available anyway, then this algorithm is simple and efficient, for example, if the maximum finding algorithm is a part of another algorithm that requires them.

With some modifications, however, we can achieve a parallel time of $O(\log n)$ with $O(1)$ efficiency.

The total number of comparisons required for this algorithm is $n-1$, the same as the sequential algorithm. The reason for the low efficiency is that many processors are idle in later rounds. We can improve the efficiency by reducing the number of processors and performing load balancing in the following way.

Suppose that we use only about $\tfrac{n}{\log_2 n}$ processors. We divide the input into $\tfrac{n}{\log_2 n}$ groups and assign a group to each processor. In the first phase, each processor finds the maximum in its group, using the sequential algorithm that takes about $\log_2 n$ steps. It remains now to find the maximum among about $\tfrac{n}{\log_2 n}$ maximums, but there are now enough processors to use the tournament algorithm.

The running time of this algorithm is

$$T(n, \lceil \tfrac{n}{\log_2 n} \rceil) = 2\log_2 n,$$

assuming that n is a power of 2.

The corresponding efficiency is $E(n) \approx \tfrac{1}{2}$.

7.3 The Parallel Prefix Problem

Let $\bullet$ be an arbitrary *associative* binary operation : namely it satisfies

$$x \bullet (y \bullet z) = (x \bullet y) \bullet z,$$

which we will simply call *product*. For example, $\bullet$ can represent addition, multiplication, or maximum of two numbers.

Problem Description

Given a sequence of numbers $x_1, x_2, \ldots, x_n$, compute the products $x_1 \bullet x_2 \bullet \ldots \bullet x_k$, for all k, such that $1 \leq k \leq n$.

Solution

We denote by $PR(i,j)$ the product $x_i \bullet x_{i+1} \bullet \ldots \bullet x_j$. Our goal is to compute $PR(1,k) \forall k, 1 \leq k \leq n$. The sequential version of the prefix problem is trivial : we simply compute the prefixes in order. The parallel prefix problem is not as easy to solve. The method we use is divide and conquer. As usual, we assume that n is a power of 2.

7.3. The Parallel Prefix Problem

Induction Hypothesis

We know how to solve the parallel prefix problem for $\frac{n}{2}$ elements.

the case of one element is trivial. The algorithm proceeds by dividing the input in half, and solving each half by induction. Thus, we obtain the values of $PR(1,k)$ and $PR(\frac{n}{2}+1, \frac{n}{2}+k) \forall k, 1 \leq k \leq \frac{n}{2}$. The values for the first half can be used directly. The values $Pr(1,m)$ for $\frac{n}{2} < m \leq n$ can be obtained by computing $PR(1, \frac{n}{2}) \bullet PR(\frac{n}{2}+1, m)$. Both terms are known by induction. Please note that we use the associativity of the operation. The complete algorithm is given below.

Algorithm 107 Parallel Prefix Algorithm

1: **function** PARALLEL_PREFIX(x, n)
2:     **Input** : x : an array in the range 1 to n ▷ we assume that n is a power of 2
3:     **Output** : x : the ith element contains the ith prefix.
4:     $PP(1,n)$
5: **end function**
6: **function** PP(Left, Right)
7:     **if** $Right - Left == 1$ **then**
8:         $x[Right] \leftarrow x[Left] \bullet x[Right]$ ▷ $\bullet$ is an associative binary operation
9:     **else**
10:        $Middle \leftarrow \frac{(Left+Right-1)}{2}$
11:        **Execute in parallel**
12:            $PP(Left, Middle)$ ▷ assigned to P_1 to $P_{\frac{n}{2}}$
13:            $PP(Middle+1, Right)$ ▷ assigned to $P_{\frac{n}{2}+1}$ to P_n
14:        **for** $i \leftarrow Middle + 1$ **to** $Right$ **do**
15:            **Execute in parallel**
16:                $x[i] \leftarrow x[Middle] \bullet x[i]$
17:        **end for**
18:    **end if**
19: **end function**

Complexity

The input is divided into two disjoint sets in each recursive call of the algorithm. Both subproblems can thus be solved in parallel. If we have n processors for the problem of size n, then one-half of them can be allocated to each subproblem. The combining step requires $\frac{n}{2}$ steps, and they can also be performed in parallel because they all use $x[Middle]$. Although several processors must read $x[Middle]$ at the same time, they all write to distinct locations. Overall, $T(n,n) = O(\log n)$, and $E(n,n) = O\left(\frac{1}{\log n}\right)$ since the sequential algorithm clearly runs in $O(n)$ steps.

Improving the Efficiency of Parallel Prefix

The trick is to use the same induction hypothesis, but to divide the input in a different way. Assume again that n is a power of 2 and that there are n processors. Let E denote the set of all x_is with i even. If we find the parallel prefixes of all elements in E, then finding the rest of the prefixes, those with odd indices, is easy : If $PR(1, 2i)$ is known $\forall i$ such that $1 \leq i \leq \frac{n}{2}$, then, for each odd prefix $PR(1, 2i+1)$, we need to compute one more product

$(PR(1,2i) \bullet x_{2i+1}$. We can find the prefixes of the elements in E in two phases. First, we compute, in parallel, $x_{2i-1} \bullet x_{2i} \forall 1 \leq i \leq \frac{n}{2}$, and we store the result in x_{2i}.

In other words, we compute the products of all elements of E with their left neighbors. Then, we solve the $\frac{n}{2}$ sized prefix problem for E by induction. The result for each x_{2i} is the correct prefix, since each x_{2i} already includes the product with x_{2i-1}. And if we know the prefixes of all the even indices, then we have already seen how to compute the odd prefixes in one more parallel step. The complete program is given below.

Algorithm 108 Parallel Prefix : Efficient Algorithm

1: **function** PARALLEL_PREFIX(x, n)
2:     **Input** : x : an array in the range 1 to n ▷ we assume that n is a power of 2
3:     **Output** : x : the ith element contains the ith prefix.
4:     $PP(1)$
5: **end function**
6: **function** PP(Inc)
7:     **if** $Inc == \frac{n}{2}$ **then**
8:         $x[n] \leftarrow x[\frac{n}{2}] \bullet x[n]$ ▷ $\bullet$ is an associative binary operation
9:     **else**
10:         **for** $i \leftarrow 1$ **to** $\frac{n}{2 \times Inc}$ **do**
11:             **Execute in parallel**
12:                 $x[2 \times i \times Inc] \leftarrow x[2 \times i \times Inc - Inc] \bullet x[2 \times i \times Inc]$
13:         **end for**
14:         $PP(2 \times Inc)$
15:         **for** $i \leftarrow 1$ **to** $\frac{n}{2 \times Inc} - 1$ **do**
16:             **Execute in parallel**
17:                 $x[2 \times i \times Inc + Inc] \leftarrow x[2 \times i \times Inc] \bullet x[2 \times i \times Inc + Inc]$
18:         **end for**
19:     **end if**
20: **end function**

Complexity

Both loops in algorithm PARALLEL_PREFIX can be performed in parallel in $O(1)$ time with $\frac{n}{2}$ processors. The recursive call is applied to a problem of half the size, so the running time of the algorithm is $O(\log n)$. The total number of steps $S(n)$ satisfies the recurrence relation

$$S(n) = S\left(\frac{n}{2}\right) + n - 1$$
$$S(2) = 1$$

which implies that $S(n) = O(n)$. But, this implies that we can modify the algorithm to run in time $O(\log n)$ with only $O\left(\frac{n}{\log n}\right)$ processors, leading to an $O(1)$ efficiency. The key to this improvement is using only one recursive call instead of two while still being able to perform the merge step in parallel.

7.4 Finding Ranks in Linked Lists

Generally, it is much more difficult to deal with linked representation in a parallel environment than with arrays. Linked lists, for example, are inherently sequential. If the only access to the link list is through the head of the

7.4. Finding Ranks in Linked Lists

list, then we have to traverse the list one element at a time with no possibility of parallelism. In many cases, however, the elements of the list, or pointers to them, are actually stored in a contiguous array. In such cases, where parallel access to the list is possible, there is hope for fast parallel algorithms.

The **rank** of an element in a linked list is defined here as the distance of the element from the end of the list, thus, the head has rank n, the second element has rank $n-1$, and so on.

Problem Description

Given a linked list of n elements, all of which are stored in an array $A[1..n]$, compute for each element its *rank* in the list.

Solution

We can solve the sequential problem by simply traversing the list. The method we will use for designing a parallel algorithm for this problem is called **doubling**. We assign a processor to each element. Initially, each processor knows only the right neighbor of its element in the list. In the first step, each processor finds the neighbor of its neighbor. After the first step, each processor knows the element at distance 2 from its element. If, at step i, each processor knows the element at distance k from its element, then in one step each processor can find the element at distance $2k$. This process continues until the end of the list is reached.

Let $N[i]$ be the farthest element to the right of i in the list that is known to P_i at a given moment. Initially, $N[i]$ is i's right neighbor except for the last element whose right neighbor is nil. Basically, in each step, P_i updates $n[i]$ to $N[N[i]]$ until the end of the list is reached. Let $R[i]$ be the rank of i. Initially $R[i]$ is set to 0, except for the last element in the list, for which it is set to 1, this element is detected by its nil pointer. When a processor encounters a neighbor with a nonzero rank R, this processor can determine its own rank.

Initially, only the element of rank 1 knows its rank. After the first step, the element of rank 2 finds that its right neighbor has rank 1, so it knows that its own rank is 2. After the second step, rank 3 and rank 4 are determined, and so on. If P_i finds that $N[i]$ points to a *ranked* element of rank R after d doubling steps, then i's rank is $2^{d-1} + R$. The complete algorithm is given below.

Algorithm 109 List Rank Algorithm

```
1: function LIST_RANK(N)
2:     Input : N : an array in the range 1 to n of indices.
3:     Output : N : the rank of each element in the array.
4:     D ← 1           ▷ each processor can have its own local D variable, we use
       only one D variable
5:     Execute in parallel     ▷ processor P_i is active until R[i] becomes
       nonzero
6:         R[i] gets 0
7:         if N[i] == nil then
8:             R[i] ← 1
9:         end if
10:        while R[i] == 0 do
11:            if R[N[i]] ≠ 0 then
12:                R[i] ← D + R[N[i]]
13:            else
14:                N[i] ← N[N[i]]
15:                D ← 2D
16:            end if
17:        end while
18: end function
```

Complexity

The doubling process guarantees that each processor will reach the end of the list in at most $\lceil \log_2 n \rceil$ steps. Therefore, $T(n,n) = O(\log n)$. The efficiency is $E(n,n) = O\left(\frac{1}{\log n}\right)$. Improving the efficiency requires making a major modification to the algorithm, since the total amount of work is $O(n \log n)$.

The rank computation allows us to convert a linked list into an array in $O(\log n)$ time even though with less than perfect efficiency. After all ranks are computed, the elements can be copied into the appropriate locations in the array, which is much easier.

7.5 Finding the kth Smallest Element on a Tree

Problem Description

Let us assume that the interconnection network is a complete binary tree with $n = 2^{h-1}$ leaves. There are $2^h - 1$ processors, each associated with a node in the tree. The input is a sequence $x_1, x_2, \ldots, x_n$, such that x_i resides initially at leaf i. Tree machines have been suggested mainly for image-processing applications, where the leaves correspond to the inputs (e.g., pixels in a picture) and the algorithms for manipulating them are hierarchical. Let us solve the problem of finding the kth smallest element.

Solution

This example illustrates the translation of a sequential algorithm to a parallel algorithm, and the use of pipelining.

First, we recall the sequential algorithm for finding the kth smallest element. We assume, for simplicity, that the elements are distinct. The algorithm is a probabilistic one. In each step, a random element x is chosen as the *pivot*. The

7.5. Finding the kth Smallest Element on a Tree

rank of x is computed by comparing x to all other elements and, according to whether the rank is smaller or greater than k, the elements that are less than x or greater than x are eliminated.

The algorithm terminates when the rank of the pivot is k.

The expected number of iterations is $O(\log n)$, and the expected number of comparisons is $O(n)$.

There are three different phases in each iteration of the algorithm:

1. choosing a random element,
2. computing its rank, and
3. eliminating.

We first describe efficient parallel implementations of each phase, then improve the parallelization even further.

Choosing a random element can be achieved by a *tournament* arranged on the tree. Each leaf sends its number to its parent where the number *competes* with the number of its sibling leaf by flipping a coin. The winning number is then promoted up again, and the same process continues up the tree until the root chooses the overall winner.

Please note that this works only in the first iteration; we discuss later how to make it work after some elements are eliminated.

The winning number is then *broadcast* down the tree, so that all leaves can compare it with their number. If the identity of the pivot is known at all the leaves, they can all compare their numbers to the pivot in one step. They then send a

- 1 (if their number is smaller than or equal to the pivot) or
- 0 (otherwise)

to their parent node. The rank of the pivot is the number of 1s that are sent up. Summing n numbers up the tree is easy to do. The root can then broadcast the rank down the tree, and each leaf can determine whether or not its number should be eliminated. Overall, there are four *waves* of communication per iteration:

1. up the tree to choose a pivot;
2. down the tree to broadcast it;
3. up the tree to compute its rank;
4. down the tree to broadcast the rank.

The problem is that, after some elements are eliminated, the tournament is no longer fair. In the extreme case, all elements in one-half of the tree, except for one, are eliminated. The remaining element in that half will be promoted to the root without competition. It will then be chosen with probability $\frac{1}{2}$, while other elements are chosen with much smaller probabilities.

We want to preserve the uniform randomness of the choice. We can preserve it in the following way.

Processors associated with values that have been eliminated in previous rounds send up a *nil* value. Any element always wins against a *nil* value. Every competing element has an associated counter, which is initially 1. The counter indicates the number of (real) *opponents* that participated in the part of the tournament involving this element (i.e., the number of elements in the subtree that have not yet been eliminated). When an element wins a game at some node in the tree, it is promoted upward, and the losing element's counter is added to its counter. Every game is now played with a biased coin according to the counters of the competing elements.

For example, if x wins its first game (say, against y) and z advances by default, then x's counter is 2 and z's counter is 1. If x now plays against z, then the game is played with 2 : 1 bias toward x. Overall, z has a probability of $\frac{1}{3}$ of winning this game, and both x and y have probability of $\frac{1}{2} \times \frac{2}{3} = \frac{1}{3}$ of winning both their games. This process guarantees that the final choice is uniformly selected among the participating elements.

Complexity

The number of (parallel) steps involved in each phase is equal to *four* times the height of the tree. Since this algorithm eliminates elements in exactly the same way as the sequential algorithm, the expected number of phases is still $O(\log n)$. The expected running time is thus $O(\log^2 n)$.

Improved Algorithm

The root of the tree is a major bottleneck in the computation. Most of the information must pass through the root, but the root has only two connections and all leaves are at distance $h - 1$ from it. If we cannot improve the connections, we should at least make the root as busy as possible. In the algorithm we just described, the root and the leaves are active for one step and then remain idle for about $2h$ steps. We can improve this algorithm by making all processors busy all the time. We do that by initiating new iterations in every step even before the previous iterations are completed. All those iterations will proceed in a pipeline fashion up and down the tree.

The reason this pipeline improves the running time is the following.

It takes $2h - 2$ steps to select one pivot :

- $h - 1$ steps to reach the root, and
- $h - 1$ steps for the root to broadcast the result.

If we start another tournament in the second step and run it in parallel to (but one step behind) the first one, then we can select two pivots in $2h - 1$ steps. We can select h pivots in $3h - 2 = O(\log n)$ steps. All those pivots can be used to eliminate elements. Thus instead of cutting the search space by about half with one pivot, we cut it to about $\frac{1}{(h+1)}$ of its original size with h pivots. and we do it without spending significantly more time. We can also interleave the different phases. The leaves start a new tournament at each step (until the k smallest is found) and the tournament pushes the rest of the computation.

An example of this process is given below (which proceeds from left to right top down).

7.5. Finding the kth Smallest Element on a Tree

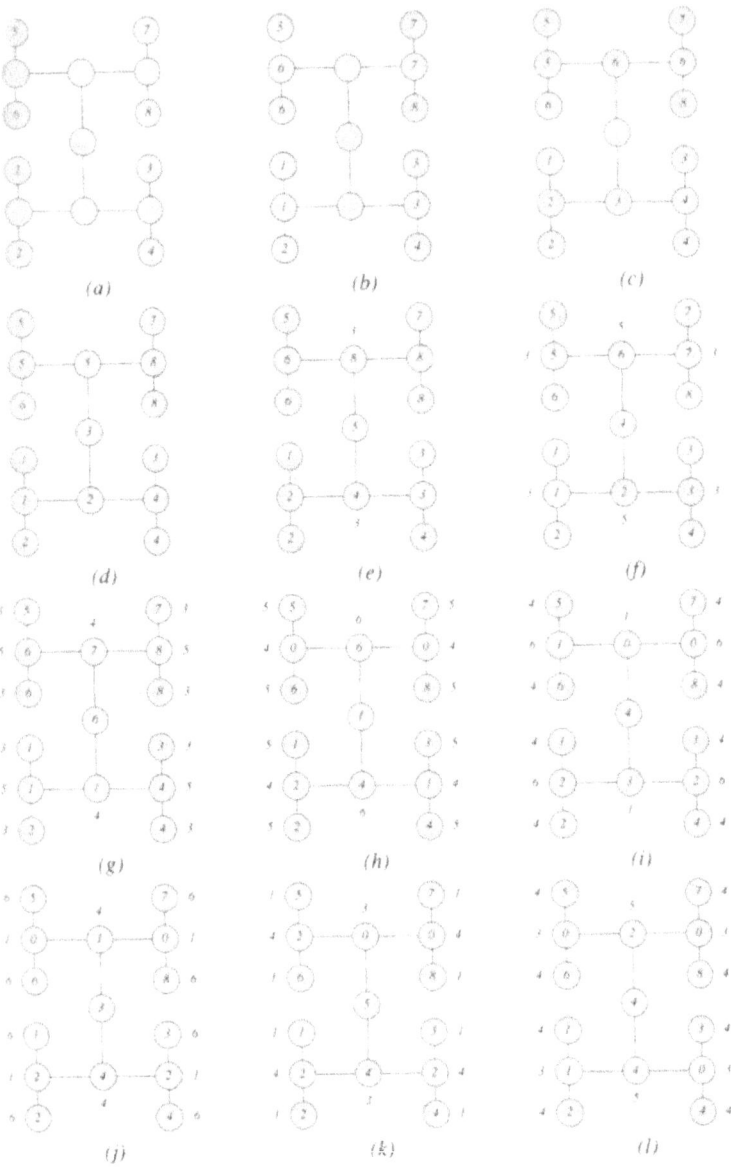

The elements are the numbers from 1 to 8. and we are looking for the fourth-smallest number. (In this case, the rank of each number is equal to that number's value. so we do not show both ranks and numbers.) For each step, the contents of all nodes is shown. The numbers inside the nodes are the ones obtained from below, and the numbers outside the nodes are those that are broadcast down. The first chosen pivot is 3 (d), the second one is 5 (e), and then 4, 3, 1, and 4. In (g), the first pivot (3) arrives at the leaves, and from then on they start the second phase, which is computing the rank. The fact that 3 has rank 3 is discovered in (j), and the fourth smallest element is discovered by the root at (l). Once the element is broadcast to the nodes (which we do not show), the algorithm terminates. In this case, there was no need to run another set of iterations (or eliminate any element); in general, however, this process should be run several times and elements should be eliminated until the kth smallest element is found.

Complexity

The regular algorithm requires $O(\log n)$ steps to eliminate elements with one pivot. Since we can generate $O(\log n)$ pivots at about the same time, we save a factor of $O(\log \log \log n)$ overall. The expected running time is reduced to $O\left(\frac{\log^2 n}{\log \log n}\right)$.

Chapter 8

Low Level Algorithms

8.1 Introduction

Unless specified otherwise, the word size is 32 bits, and signed integers are represented in two's-complement form. The ISO C standard does not specify whether right shifts ("$\gg$" operator) of signed quantities are 0-propagating or sign-propagating.

```
for ( i = 1; i <= n; i++)
```

In the C code provided above, it is assumed that if the left operand is signed, then a sign-propagating shift results (and if it is unsigned, then a 0-propagating shift results, following ISO). Most modern C compilers work this way. It is assumed here that left shifts are "logical." (Some machines, mostly older ones, provide an "arithmetic" left shift, in which the sign bit is retained.)

Unless otherwise specified, the registers are 32 bits long. General register 0 contains a permanent 0, and the others can be used uniformly for any purpose.

We assume that all instructions execute in one cycle, except for the multiply, divide, and remainder instructions, for which we do not assume any particular execution time. Branches take one cycle whether they branch or fall through.

8.1.1 Manipulating Rightmost Bits

- The expression x & $(x - 1)$ can be used to turn off the rightmost 1-bit in a word, producing 0 if none. For example, 01011000 $\Longrightarrow$ 01010000. This can be used to determine if an unsigned integer is a power of 2 or is 0: We can apply the formula followed by a 0-test on the result.

- The expression x | $(x + 1)$ can be used to turn on the rightmost 0-bit in a word, producing all 1's if none. For example, 10100111 $\Longrightarrow$ 10101111.

- The expression x & $(x + 1)$ can be used to turn off the trailing 1's in a word, producing x if none. For example, 10100111 $\Longrightarrow$ 10100000. This can be used to determine if an unsigned integer is of the form $2^n - 1$, 0, or all 1's: We can apply the formula followed by a 0-test on the result.

- The expression x | $(x - 1)$ can be used to turn on the trailing 0's in a word, producing x if none. For example, 10101000 $\Longrightarrow$ 10101111).

8.1. Introduction

- The expression $\sim$**x** & (**x** + **1**) can be used to create a word with a single 1-bit at the position of the rightmost 0-bit in x, producing 0 if none. For example, 10100111 $\Longrightarrow$ 00001000.

- The expression $\sim$**x** & (**x** − **1**) can be used to create a word with a single 0-bit at the position of the rightmost 1-bit in x, producing all 1's if none. For example, 10101000 $\Longrightarrow$ 11110111.

- Use one of the following formulas to create a word with 1's at the positions of the trailing 0's in x, and 0's elsewhere, producing 0 if none. For example, 01011000 $\Longrightarrow$ 00000111.

    1. $\sim$**x** & (**x** − **1**), or
    2. $\sim$(**x** | −**x**), or
    3. (**x** & −**x**) − **1**

    The first formula has some instruction-level parallelism.

- The expression $\sim$**x** | (**x** + **1**) can be used to create a word with 0's at the positions of the trailing 1's in x, and 0's elsewhere, producing all 1's if none. For example, 10100111 $\Longrightarrow$ 11111000.

- The expression **x** & (−**x**) can be used to isolate the rightmost 1-bit, producing 0 if none. For example, 01011000 $\Longrightarrow$ 00001000.

- The expression **x**^(**x** − **1**) can be used to create a word with 1's at the positions of the rightmost 1-bit and the trailing 0's in x, producing all 1's if no 1-bit, and the integer 1 if no trailing 0's. For example, 01011000 $\Longrightarrow$ 00001111.

- The expression **x**^(**x** + **1**) can be used to create a word with 1's at the positions of the rightmost 0-bit and the trailing 1's in x, producing all 1's if no 0-bit, and the integer 1 if no trailing 1's. For example, 01010111 $\Longrightarrow$ 00001111.

- Use either of the following formulas to turn off the rightmost contiguous string of 1's. For example, 01011100 $\Longrightarrow$ 01000000:

    ☞ (((**x** | (**x**−**1**)) + **1**) & **x**), or
    ☞ ((**x** & −**x**) + **x**) & **x**

    These can be used to determine if a non-negative integer is of the form $2^j - 2^k$ for some $j \geq k \geq 0$: We can apply the formula followed by a 0-test on the result.

8.1.1.1 Extending De Morgan's Laws

The logical identities known as De Morgan's laws can be thought of as distributing, or "multiplying in," the not sign.

1. $\sim$(**x** & **y**) = $\sim$**x** | $\sim$**y**
2. $\sim$(**x** | **y**) = $\sim$**x** & $\sim$**y**

This idea can be extended as shown below:

- $\sim$(**x** + **1**) = $\sim$**x** − **1**
- $\sim$(**x** − **1**) = $\sim$**x** + **1**

8.1. Introduction

- $\sim\!-x = x - 1$
- $\sim\!(x\char`\^ y) = \sim\!x\char`\^ y = x \equiv y$
- $\sim\!(x \equiv y) = \sim\!x \equiv y = x\char`\^ y$
- $\sim\!(x + y) = \sim\!x - y$
- $\sim\!(x - y) = \sim\!x + y$

For example,
$\sim\!(x \mid -(x+1)) = \sim\!x\ \&\ \sim\!-(x+1) =$
$\sim\!x\ \&\ ((x+1) - 1) = \sim\!x\ \&\ x = 0.$

8.1.1.2 Compute Next higher number with same number of 1-bits

Right-to-Left Computability Test   There is a simple test to determine whether or not a given function can be implemented with a sequence of add's, subtract's, and's, or's, and not's. We can, of course, expand the list with other instructions that can be composed from the basic list, such as shift left by a fixed amount (which is equivalent to a sequence of add's), or multiply. However, we exclude instructions that cannot be composed from the list.

The test is contained in the following theorem:

Theorem 1
A function mapping words to words can be implemented with word-parallel add, subtract, and, or, and not instructions if and only if each bit of the result depends only on bits at and to the right of each input operand.

That is, imagine trying to compute the rightmost bit of the result by looking only at the rightmost bit of each input operand. Then, try to compute the next bit to the left by looking only at the rightmost two bits of each input operand, and continue in this way. If you are successful in this, then the function can be computed with a sequence of add's, and's, and so on. If the function cannot be computed in this right-to-left manner, then it cannot be implemented with a sequence of such instructions.

The interesting part of this is the latter statement, and it is simply the contrapositive of the observation that the functions add, subtract, and, or, and not can all be computed in the right-to-left manner, so any combination of them must have this property.

To see the "if" part of the theorem, we need a construction that is a little awkward to explain. We illustrate it with a specific example. Suppose that a function of two variables x and y has the right-to-left computability property, and suppose that bit 2 of the result r is given by

$$r_2 = x_2 \mid (x_0\ \&\ y_1) \tag{8.1}$$

We number bits from right to left, 0 to 31. Because bit 2 of the result is a function of bits at and to the right of bit 2 of the input operands, bit 2 of the result is "right-to-left computable."

Arrange the computer words x, x shifted left two, and y shifted left one, as shown below. Also, add a mask that isolates bit 2.

8.1. Introduction

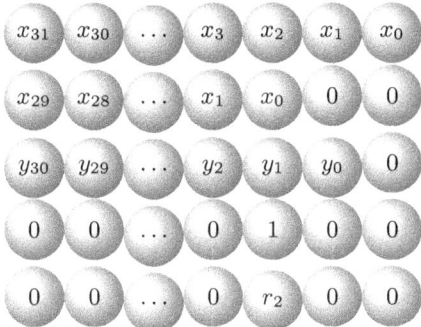

Now, form the word-parallel and of lines 2 and 3, or the result with row 1 (following 8.1), and and the result with the mask (row 4 above). The result is a word of all 0's except for the desired result bit in position 2. Perform similar computations for the other bits of the result, or the 32 resulting words together, and the result is the desired function. This construction does not yield an efficient program; rather, it merely shows that it can be done with instructions in the basic list. Using the theorem, we immediately see that there is no sequence of such instructions that turns off the leftmost 1-bit in a word, because to see if a certain 1-bit should be turned off, we must look to the left to see if it is the leftmost one. Similarly, there can be no such sequence for performing a right shift, or a rotate shift, or a left shift by a variable amount, or for counting the number of trailing 0's in a word (to count trailing 0's, the rightmost bit of the result will be 1 if there are an odd number of trailing 0's, and we must look to the left of the rightmost position to determine that).

An application of the sort of bit twiddling discussed above is the problem of finding the next higher number after a given number that has the same number of 1-bits. You might very well wonder why anyone would want to compute that. It has application where bit strings are used to represent subsets. The possible members of a set are listed in a linear array, and a subset is represented by a word or sequence of words in which bit i is on if member i is in the subset. Set unions are computed by the logical or of the bit strings, intersections by and's, and so on.

You might want to iterate through all the subsets of a given size. This is easily done if you have a function that maps a given subset to the next higher number (interpreting the subset string as an integer) with the same number of 1-bits.

Given a word x that represents a subset, the idea is to find the rightmost contiguous group of 1's in x and the following 0's, and "increment" that quantity to the next value that has the same number of 1's. For example, the string xxx0 1111 0000, where xxx represents arbitrary bits, becomes xxx1 0000 0111. The algorithm first identifies the "smallest" 1-bit in **x**, with $s = x$ & $-x$, giving 0000 0001 0000. This is added to **x**, giving $r =$ xxx1 0000 0000. The 1-bit here is one bit of the result. For the other bits, we need to produce a right-adjusted string of n − 1 1's, where n is the size of the rightmost group of 1's in x. This can be done by first forming the exclusive or of **r** and **x**, which gives 0001 1111 0000 in our example.

This has two too many 1's and needs to be right-adjusted. This can be accomplished by dividing it by **s**, which right-adjusts it (**s** is a power of 2), and shifting it right two more positions to discard the two unwanted bits. The final result is the or of this and **r**.

8.1. Introduction

In computer algebra notation, the result is **y** in:

$$s \leftarrow x \ \& \ -x$$
$$r \leftarrow s + x \qquad (8.2)$$
$$y \leftarrow r \ | \ (((x \wedge r) \gg 2)/s)$$

Program 8.1: **Next higher number with same number of 1-bits**

```
1 /* Computes the next number with the same number of one-
      bits. Or, the
2 next subset of the same size as the given one. */
3
4 #include <stdio.h>
5 #include <stdlib.h>
6
7 int ntz(unsigned x) {               // Number of trailing zeros
8     int n;
9
10    if (x == 0) return(32);
11    n = 1;
12    if ((x & 0x0000FFFF) == 0) {n = n +16; x = x >>16;}
13    if ((x & 0x000000FF) == 0) {n = n + 8; x = x >> 8;}
14    if ((x & 0x0000000F) == 0) {n = n + 4; x = x >> 4;}
15    if ((x & 0x00000003) == 0) {n = n + 2; x = x >> 2;}
16    return n - (x & 1);
17 }
18
19 int nlz(unsigned x) {
20    int n;
21
22    if (x == 0) return(32);
23    n = 0;
24    if (x <= 0x0000FFFF) {n = n +16; x = x <<16;}
25    if (x <= 0x00FFFFFF) {n = n + 8; x = x << 8;}
26    if (x <= 0x0FFFFFFF) {n = n + 4; x = x << 4;}
27    if (x <= 0x3FFFFFFF) {n = n + 2; x = x << 2;}
28    if (x <= 0x7FFFFFFF) {n = n + 1;}
29    return n;
30 }
31
32 int pop(unsigned x) {
33    x = x - ((x >> 1) & 0x55555555);
34    x = (x & 0x33333333) + ((x >> 2) & 0x33333333);
35    x = (x + (x >> 4)) & 0x0F0F0F0F;
36    x = x + (x << 8);
37    x = x + (x << 16);
38    return x >> 24;
39 }
40
41 /* Caution: Do not call this with x = 0; it then does a
      divide by 0.
42 If called with the largest number with a certain number
      of 1's
43 (i.e., 11...100...0), it returns a number smaller than
      the argument.
44 It is basically seven ops, one of which is division. */
45
46 // ─────────────────────────────── cut
```

8.1. Introduction

```
unsigned snoob(unsigned x) {
   unsigned smallest, ripple, ones;
                                     //  x = xxx0 1111 0000
   smallest = x & -x;                //      0000 0001 0000
   ripple = x + smallest;            //      xxx1 0000 0000
   ones = x ^ ripple;                //      0001 1111 0000
   ones = (ones >> 2)/smallest;      //      0000 0000 0111
   return ripple | ones;             //      xxx1 0000 0111
}
// ─────────────────────────── end cut


/* Variation 1: ntz to avoid division.  Eight ops. */

unsigned snoob1(unsigned x) {
   unsigned smallest, ripple, ones;
                                     //  x = xxx0 1111 0000
   smallest = x & -x;                //      0000 0001 0000
   ripple = x + smallest;            //      xxx1 0000 0000
   ones = x ^ ripple;                //      0001 1111 0000
   ones = ones >> (2 + ntz(x));      //      0000 0000 0111
   return ripple | ones;             //      xxx1 0000 0111
}

/* Variation 2: nlz to avoid division.  Nine ops. */

unsigned snoob2(unsigned x) {
   unsigned smallest, ripple, ones;
                                     //  x = xxx0 1111 0000
   smallest = x & -x;                //      0000 0001 0000
   ripple = x + smallest;            //      xxx1 0000 0000
   ones = x ^ ripple;                //      0001 1111 0000
   ones = ones>>(33-nlz(smallest));  // 0000 0000 0111
   return ripple | ones;             //      xxx1 0000 0111
}

/* Variation 3: pop to avoid division.  Nine ops. */

unsigned snoob3(unsigned x) {
   unsigned smallest, ripple, ones;
                                     //  x = xxx0 1111 0000
   smallest = x & -x;                //      0000 0001 0000
   ripple = x + smallest;            //      xxx1 0000 0000
   ones = x ^ ripple;                //      0001 1111 0000
   ones = (1 <<                      //      0000 0000 0111
          (pop(ones) - 2)) - 1;
   return ripple | ones;             //      xxx1 0000 0111
}

/* The version below is from Harbison & Steele Fourth Ed.
      section 7.6.7
   (p. 215).  Nine ops, not counting the "if" statement. */

unsigned next_set_of_n_elements(unsigned x) {
   unsigned smallest, ripple, new_smallest, ones;

   if (x == 0) return 0;
   smallest     = (x & -x);
   ripple       = x + smallest;
```

8.1. Introduction

```
104    new_smallest = (ripple & -ripple);
105    ones         = ((new_smallest/smallest) >> 1) - 1;
106    return ripple | ones;
107 }
108
109 /* Next version from
110 http://forums.topcoder.com/?module=Message&messageID
       =574258
111    The author is David de Kloet. The variable x must be
       signed,
112 or after generating a correct sequence, it will generate
       some incorrect
113 values and then loop forever. Must have x != 0. After
       generating the
114 sequence, it generates 0xFFFFFFFF and sticks at that
       value.
115    The number of shifts done in the while-loop is equal
       to the number of
116 trailing zeros in the input x. So what is the average?
117 The values of x are NOT random, they tend to have more
118 trailing 0's than purely random numbers would have. (For
       uniformly
119 distributed random numbers, the average is 1.)
120    For a word size of 32, if n (the number of 1-bits) =
       1, the average
121 number of trailing 0's is 15.5 (average of the numbers
       from 0 t 31). For
122 n = 2, the average is 10 (I think). It gets lower for
       higher values of
123 n. */
124
125 int snoob4 (int x) {
126    int y = x + (x & -x);
127    x = x & ~y;
128    while ((x & 1) == 0) x = x >> 1;
129    x = x >> 1;
130    return y | x;
131 }
132
133 int main(int argc, char *argv[]) {
134    int n;
135    unsigned x, y, z, u, v, w;
136
137    if (argc != 2) {
138        printf("Need exactly one argument, an integer from
           1 to 7.\n");
139        exit(1);
140    }
141
142    n = strtol(argv[1], NULL, 10);
143    if (n < 1 || n > 7) {
144        printf("Argument must be an integer from 1 to 7.\n"
           );
145        exit(1);
146    }
147
148    printf("n = %d\n", n);
149
150    x = (1 << n) - 1;
151    y = x;
```

8.2. Bit Counting Algorithms

```
152     z = x;
153     u = x;
154     v = x;
155     w = x;
156     do {
157         printf("x, y, z, u, v, w = %02X %02X %02X %02X %02X
                  %02X\n", x, y, z, u, v, w);
158         y = snoob1(x);
159         z = snoob2(x);
160         u = snoob3(x);
161         v = next_set_of_n_elements(x);
162         w = snoob4(x);
163         x = snoob(x);
164     } while (x <= 255);
165     return 0;
166 }
```

8.2 Bit Counting Algorithms

8.2.1 Counting 1-Bits

Some machines have a function by a name, *population count*, which counts the number of 1-bits in a word, as well as the number of leading 0's. These two quantities are produced as a by-product of all logical operations. For machines that don't have this instruction, a good way to count the number of 1-bits is to first set each 2-bit field equal to the sum of the two single bits that were originally in the field, and then sum adjacent 2-bit fields, putting the results in each 4-bit field, and so on.

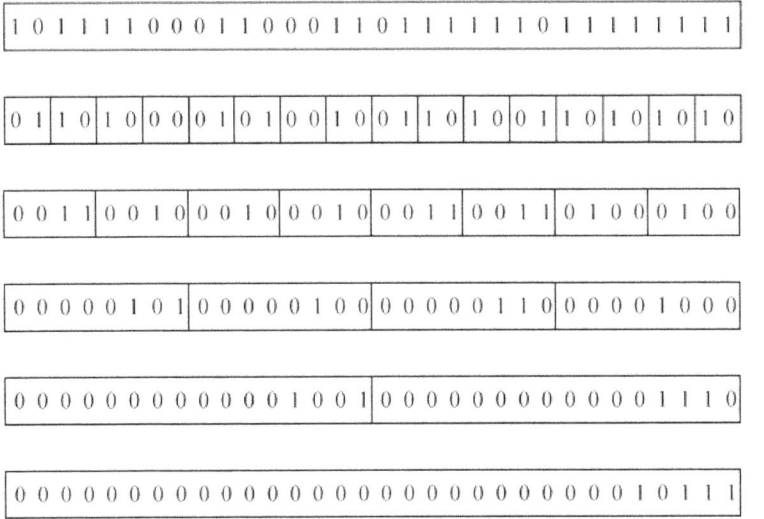

Figure 8.1: Counting 1-bits, "divide and conquer" strategy

8.2. Bit Counting Algorithms

The method is illustrated in 8.2.1, in which the first row shows a computer word whose 1-bits are to be summed, and the last row shows the result (23 decimal). This is an example of the "divide and conquer" strategy, in which the original problem (summing 32 bits) is divided into two problems (summing 16 bits), which are solved separately, and the results are combined (added, in this case). The strategy is applied recursively, breaking the 16-bit fields into 8-bit fields, and so on. In the case at hand, the ultimate small problems (summing adjacent bits) can all be done in parallel, and combining adjacent sums can also be done in parallel in a fixed number of steps at each stage. The result is an algorithm that can be executed in $\log_2(32) = 5$ steps.

Program 8.2: *Counting 1-Bits, divide and conquer*

```
1 int pop0(unsigned x) {
2     x = (x & 0x55555555) + ((x >> 1) & 0x55555555);
3     x = (x & 0x33333333) + ((x >> 2) & 0x33333333);
4     x = (x & 0x0F0F0F0F) + ((x >> 4) & 0x0F0F0F0F);
5     x = (x & 0x00FF00FF) + ((x >> 8) & 0x00FF00FF);
6     x = (x & 0x0000FFFF) + ((x >>16) & 0x0000FFFF);
7     return x;
8 }
```

The second line uses $(x \gg 1)$ & $0x55555555$ rather than the perhaps more natural $(x \& 0xAAAAAAAA) \gg 1$, because the code shown avoids generating two large constants in a register. This would cost an instruction if the machine lacks the and not instruction. A similar remark applies to the other lines. Clearly, the last *and* is unnecessary, and other *and*'s can be omitted when there is no danger that a field's sum will carry over into the adjacent field. Furthermore, there is a way to code the first line that uses one fewer instruction. This leads to the simplification shown ahead, which executes in 21 instructions and is branch-free.

Program 8.3: *Counting 1-Bits in a word, divide and conquer improved*

```
1 int pop1(unsigned x) {
2     x = x - ((x >> 1) & 0x55555555);
3     x = (x & 0x33333333) + ((x >> 2) & 0x33333333);
4     x = (x + (x >> 4)) & 0x0F0F0F0F;
5     x = x + (x >> 8);
6     x = x + (x >> 16);
7     return x & 0x0000003F;
8 }
9 /* Note: an alternative to the last three executable
      lines above is:
10    return x*0x01010101 >> 24; */
```

The first assignment to x is based on the first two terms of the rather surprising formula

$$pop(x) = x - \left\lfloor \frac{x}{2} \right\rfloor - \left\lfloor \frac{x}{4} \right\rfloor - \ldots - \left\lfloor \frac{x}{2^{31}} \right\rfloor \tag{8.3}$$

In Equation 8.3, we must have $x \geq 0$. By treating x as an unsigned integer, Equation 8.3 can be implemented with a sequence of 31 shift right immediate's of 1, and 31 subtract's. Program 8.3 uses the first two terms of this on each 2-bit field, in parallel.

Equation 8.3 can be derived by noting that bit i of the binary representation

8.2. Bit Counting Algorithms

of a nonnegative integer x is given by
$$b_i = \left\lfloor \frac{x}{2^i} \right\rfloor - 2 \left\lfloor \frac{x}{2^{i+1}} \right\rfloor$$
and summing this for $i = 0$ to 31. The last term is 0 because $x < 2^{32}$. Equation 8.3 generalizes to other bases. For base ten it is
$$sumdigits(x) = x - 9 \left\lfloor \frac{x}{10} \right\rfloor - 9 \left\lfloor \frac{x}{100} \right\rfloor$$
where the terms are carried out until they are 0. This can be proved by essentially the same technique used above. A variation of the above algorithm is to use a base 4 analogue of Equation 8.3 as a substitute for the second executable line of Program 8.3 as can be seen ahead

```
x = x - 3*((x >> 2) & 0x33333333)
```

HAKMEM algorithm counts the number of 1-bits in a word by using the first three terms of Equation 8.3 to produce a word of 3-bit fields, each of which contains the number of 1-bits that were in it. It then adds adjacent 3-bit fields to form 6-bit field sums, and then adds the 6-bit fields by computing the value of the word modulo 63.

Program 8.4: *Counting 1-Bits in a word, HAKMEM Algorithm*

```
int pop2(unsigned x) {
    unsigned n;

    n = (x >> 1) & 033333333333;       // Count bits in
    x = x - n;                          // each 3-bit
    n = (n >> 1) & 033333333333;       // field.
    x = x - n;
    x = (x + (x >> 3)) & 030707070707;  // 6-bit sums.
    return x%63;                        // Add 6-bit sums.
}
/* An alternative to the "return" statement above is:
    return ((x * 0404040404) >> 26) +   // Add 6-bit sums.
           (x >> 30);
which runs faster on most machines. */
```

A variation on the *HAKMEM* algorithm is to use Equation 8.3 to count the number of 1's in each 4-bit field, working on all eight 4-bit fields in parallel. Then, the 4-bit sums can be converted to 8-bit sums in a straightforward way, and the four bytes can be added with a multiplication by 0x01010101:

Program 8.5: *Counting 1-Bits in a word, Variation of HAKMEM Algorithm*

```
int pop3(unsigned x) {
    unsigned n;

    n = (x >> 1) & 0x77777777;          // Count bits in
    x = x - n;                           // each 4-bit
    n = (n >> 1) & 0x77777777;          // field.
    x = x - n;
    n = (n >> 1) & 0x77777777;
    x = x - n;
    x = (x + (x >> 4)) & 0x0F0F0F0F;    // Get byte sums.
    x = x*0x01010101;                    // Add the bytes.
    return x >> 24;
}
```

A quite different bit-counting method, illustrated in Program 8.6, is to turn off the rightmost 1-bit repeatedly, until the result is 0. It is very fast if the number of 1-bits is small, taking $2 + 5pop(x)$ instructions.

8.2. Bit Counting Algorithms

Program 8.6: *Counting 1-bits in a sparsely populated word*

```
1 int pop4(unsigned x) {
2     int n;
3
4     n = 0;
5     while (x != 0) {
6         n = n + 1;
7         x = x & (x - 1);
8     }
9     return n;
10 }
```

This has a dual algorithm that is applicable if the number of 1-bits is expected to be large. The dual algorithm keeps turning on the rightmost 0-bit with $x = x \mid (x + 1)$, until the result is all 1's (−1). Then, it returns $32 - n$. (Alternatively, the original number x can be complemented, or n can be initialized to 32 and counted down.)

A rather amazing algorithm is to rotate x left one position, 31 times, adding the 32 terms. The sum is the negative of pop(x)! That is,

$$pop(x) = -\sum_{i=0}^{31} (x \overset{rot}{\ll} i) \qquad (8.4)$$

where the additions are done modulo the word size, and the final sum is interpreted as a two's-complement integer. This is just a novelty; it would not be useful on most machines, because the loop is executed 31 times and thus it requires 63 instructions, plus the loop-control overhead. To see why Equation 8.4 works, consider what happens to a single 1-bit of x. It gets rotated to all positions, and when these 32 numbers are added, a word of all 1-bits results. This is −1.

For example, consider a 6-bit word size and $x = 001001$ (binary):

$x \overset{rot}{\ll} 1 \Longrightarrow 010010$
$x \overset{rot}{\ll} 2 \Longrightarrow 100100$
$x \overset{rot}{\ll} 3 \Longrightarrow 001001$
$x \overset{rot}{\ll} 4 \Longrightarrow 010010$
$x \overset{rot}{\ll} 5 \Longrightarrow 100100$

Of course, rotate-right would work just as well.

The method of Equation 8.3 is very similar to this **rotate and sum** method, which becomes clear by rewriting it as:

$$pop(x) = x - \sum_{i=1}^{31} (x \gg i)$$

This gives a slightly better algorithm than Equation 8.4 provides. It is better because it uses shift right, which is more commonly available than rotate, and because the loop can be terminated when the shifted quantity becomes 0. This reduces the loop-control code and may save a few iterations. The two algorithms are contrasted in the code given ahead:

Program 8.7: *rotate*

```
1 unsigned rotatel(unsigned x, int n) {
2     if ((unsigned)n > 63) {printf("rotatel, n out of range
          .\n"); exit(1);}
3     return (x << n) | (x >> (32 - n));
4 }
```

8.2. Bit Counting Algorithms

Program 8.8: *Two similar bit-counting algorithms*

```
 1  // Rotate and sum method            // Shift right & subtract
 2
 3    sum = x;                          // sum = x;
 4    for (i = 1; i <= 31; i++) {       // while (x != 0) {
 5        x = rotatel(x, 1);            //     x = x >> 1;
 6        sum = sum + x;                //     sum = sum - x;
 7    }                                 // }
 8    return -sum;                      // return sum;
 9  }
```

Program 8.9: *Determines which word has the larger population count*

```
 1  // Determines which is larger, pop(x) or pop(y).
 2
 3  #include <stdio.h>
 4  #include <stdlib.h>
 5
 6  int pop(unsigned x) {
 7      x = x - ((x >> 1) & 0x55555555);
 8      x = (x & 0x33333333) + ((x >> 2) & 0x33333333);
 9      x = (x + (x >> 4)) & 0x0F0F0F0F;
10      x = x + (x >> 8);
11      x = x + (x >> 16);
12      return x & 0x0000003F;
13  }
14
15  int popCmpr(unsigned xp, unsigned yp) {
16      unsigned x, y;
17      x = xp & ~yp;                   // Clear bits where
18      y = yp & ~xp;                   // both are 1.
19      while (1) {
20          if (x == 0) return y | -y;
21          if (y == 0) return 1;
22          x = x & (x - 1);            // Clear one bit
23          y = y & (y - 1);            // from each.
24      }
25  }
26
27  int errors;
28  void error(int x, int y) {
29      errors = errors + 1;
30      printf("Error for x = %08x, y = %08x, popCmpr = %d\n",
31          x, y, popCmpr(x, y));
32  }
33
34  int main() {
35      int i, j, n;
36      unsigned x, y;
37      static unsigned int test[] = {0, 1, 2, 3, 4, 5, 6, 7,
38          8, 9, 10, 11, 12, 13, 14, 15, 16, 17,
39          0x3F, 0x40, 0x41, 0x7f, 0x80, 0x81, 0xfe, 0xff,
40          0x4000, 0x4001, 0x7000, 0x7fff,
41          0x55555555, 0xAAAAAAAA, 0xFF000000, 0xC0C0C0C0,
42          0x0FFFFFF0, 0x80000000, 0xFFFFFFFE, 0xFFFFFFFF};
43
44      n = sizeof(test)/4;
45
46      for (i = 0; i < n; i++) {
```

8.2. Bit Counting Algorithms

```
47        x = test[i];
48        for (j = 0; j < n; j ++) {
49          y = test[j];
50          if (pop(x) > pop(y) && popCmpr(x, y) > 0 ||
51              pop(x) < pop(y) && popCmpr(x, y) < 0 ||
52              pop(x) == pop(y) && popCmpr(x, y) == 0) ;
53          else error(x, y);
54        }
55    }
56
57    if (errors == 0)
58        printf("Passed all %d cases.\n", n*n);
59 }
```

8.2.1.1 Counting the 1-bits in an Array

Program 8.10: *Counting the 1-bits in an Array*

```
1 /* This contains several programs for computing the number of
2 1-bits in an array of fullwords. Most of these programs are variations
3 of the Harley/Seal method, which uses a carry-save adder.
  */
4
5 #include <stdio.h>
6 #include <stdlib.h>
7 #include <string.h>
8
9 // ─────────────────────────────────────── pop
10
11 int pop(unsigned x) {
12     x = x - ((x >> 1) & 0x55555555);
13     x = (x & 0x33333333) + ((x >> 2) & 0x33333333);
14     x = (x + (x >> 4)) & 0x0F0F0F0F;
15     x = x + (x >> 8);
16     x = x + (x >> 16);
17     return x & 0x0000003F;
18 }
19 /* Note: an alternative to the last three executable lines above is:
20     return x*0x01010101 >> 24;
21 if your machine has a fast multiplier . */
22
23 // ─────────────────────────────────────── popArray1
24
25 /* This is the naive method, simply evaluating the population count for
26 each word of the array, and adding. Ignoring loop control and loads,
27 this is 1 + p ops per word of the array. For p = 15
28 (inlined and with loads of constants moved out of the loop) this is 16
29 ops per word. */
30
31 int popArray1(unsigned A[], int n) {
32     int i, tot;
```

8.2. Bit Counting Algorithms

```
33
34     tot = 0;
35     for (i = 0; i < n; i++)
36        tot = tot + pop(A[i]);
37     return tot;
38  }
39
40  // ─────────────────────────── popArray2
41
42  /* This is Harley's basic method. It combines groups of three array
43  elements into two words to which pop(x) is applied. The running time,
44  ignoring loop control and loads, is 7 elementary ops plus 2 pop counts
45  for each 3 array elements, i.e., (7 + 2p)/3 ops per word,
        where p is the
46  number of ops for one population count. For p = 15
47  this is 37/3 = 12.33 ops per word. */
48
49  #define CSA(h,l, a,b,c)  \
50     {unsigned u = a ^ b; unsigned v = c;  \
51      h = (a & b) | (u & v); l = u ^ v;}
52
53  int popArray2(unsigned A[], int n) {
54
55     int tot1, tot2, i;
56     unsigned ones, twos;
57
58     tot1 = 0;
59     tot2 = 0;
60     for (i = 0; i <= n - 3; i = i + 3) {
61        CSA(twos, ones, A[i], A[i+1], A[i+2])
62        tot1 = tot1 + pop(ones);
63        tot2 = tot2 + pop(twos);
64     }
65     for (i = i; i < n; i++)           // Add in the last
66        tot1 = tot1 + pop(A[i]);       // 0, 1, or 2 elements.
67
68     return 2*tot2 + tot1;
69  }
70
71  // ─────────────────────────── popArray3
72
73  /* This is Harley's basic method but used in a different way (at Seal's
74  suggestion) than that of the above function. It brings in values from
75  the array two at a time and combines them with "ones" and "twos". The
76  array is assumed to have at least one element.
77     The running time, ignoring loop control and loads, is 6 elementary
78  ops plus 1 pop count for each 2 array elements, i.e., (6 + p)/2 ops per
79  word, where p is the number of ops for one population count. For p = 15
80  , this is 21/2 = 10.5 ops per word. */
81
```

8.2. Bit Counting Algorithms

```
int popArray3(unsigned A[], int n) {

   int tot, i;
   unsigned ones, twos;

   tot = 0;                          // Initialize.
   ones = 0;
   for (i = 0; i <= n - 2; i = i + 2) {
      CSA(twos, ones, ones, A[i], A[i+1])
      tot = tot + pop(twos);
   }
   tot = 2*tot + pop(ones);

   if (n & 1)                        // If there's a last one,
      tot = tot + pop(A[i]);         // add it in.

   return tot;
}

// ─────────────────────────── popArray4

/* This is similar to the above but it brings in array
      elements 4 at a
time and combines them with "ones", "twos", and "fours".
      Harley gave
this algorithm. The array is assumed to have at least
      three elements.
   The running time, ignoring loop control and loads, is
      16 elementary
ops plus 1 pop count for each 4 array elements, i.e., (16
      + p)/4 ops per
word, where p is the number of ops for one population
      count. For p = 15
, this is 31/4 = 7.75 ops per word. */

int popArray4(unsigned A[], int n) {

   int tot, i;
   unsigned ones, twos, twosA, twosB, fours;

   tot = 0;                          // Initialize.
   twos = ones = 0;
   for (i = 0; i <= n - 4; i = i + 4) {
      CSA(twosA, ones, ones, A[i], A[i+1])
      CSA(twosB, ones, ones, A[i+2], A[i+3])
      CSA(fours, twos, twos, twosA, twosB)
      tot = tot + pop(fours);
   }
   tot = 4*tot + 2*pop(twos) + pop(ones);

   for (i = i; i < n; i++)           // Simply add in the last
      tot = tot + pop(A[i]);         // 0, 1, 2, or 3 elements

   return tot;
}

// ─────────────────────────── popArray5

/* The function below is similar to that
```

8.2. Bit Counting Algorithms

above, but it brings in array elements 8 at a time and combines them
with "ones", "twos", "fours", and "eights". The array is assumed to have
at least seven elements.
   The running time, ignoring loop control and loads, is 36 elementary
ops plus 1 pop count for each 8 array elements, i.e., (36 + p)/8 ops per
word, where p is the number of ops for one population count. For p = 15
, this is 51/8 = 6.375 ops per word. */

```
int popArray5(unsigned A[], int n) {

    int tot, i;
    unsigned ones, twos, twosA, twosB,
        fours, foursA, foursB, eights;

    tot = 0;                              // Initialize.
    fours = twos = ones = 0;

    for (i = 0; i <= n - 8; i = i + 8) {
      CSA(twosA, ones, ones, A[i], A[i+1])
      CSA(twosB, ones, ones, A[i+2], A[i+3])
      CSA(foursA, twos, twos, twosA, twosB)
      CSA(twosA, ones, ones, A[i+4], A[i+5])
      CSA(twosB, ones, ones, A[i+6], A[i+7])
      CSA(foursB, twos, twos, twosA, twosB)
      CSA(eights, fours, fours, foursA, foursB)
      tot = tot + pop(eights);
    }
    tot = 8*tot + 4*pop(fours) + 2*pop(twos) + pop(ones);

    for (i = i; i < n; i++)       // Simply add in the last
      tot = tot + pop(A[i]);      // 0 to 7 elements.
    return tot;
}
```

// ─────────────────────────── popArray6

/* This function generalizes the pattern illustrated by the function
above, with the result that the bits in an n-word array can be counted
with ceil(log2(n+3)) evaluations of population count.
   The inner loop (with the CSA) is done very close to 2 times for each
outer loop iteration. This is based on both a mathematical calculation
(which shows something less than 9/4 times) and instrumentation (e.g.,
for n = 10,000 the inner loop is executed 9983 times). The inner loop
compiles into 19 instructions, mostly housekeeping (shifts, adds loads,
stores). This results in a time of 2*19 + 19 = 57 instructions for each

8.2. Bit Counting Algorithms

outer loop iteration, or 28.5 instructions per word of the array. This is worse than the naive method, and MUCH worse than the above program, which compiles into 8.0 instructions/word. So this routine is a bad idea unless the time to do a population count on one word is very large (greater than 30 instructions anyway).
    Haven't timed the other loop, but it is executed only about $log2(n)$ times and so isn't so important.
    Therefore, if this method is to be useful, the housekeeping steps must be greatly reduced. It may be possible to do this by "unwinding" the first few inner loop iterations. Not sure how good the result would be. */

```
int popArray6(unsigned A[], int n) {

    int tot, i, k;
    unsigned z, hi, lo;
    char nrow[30]; unsigned sum[30][2];

    memset(nrow, 0, sizeof(nrow));        // Clear "nrow".

    sum[0][0] = 0;                         // Init. by putting in
    nrow[0] = 1;                           // a fake 0-element.

    for (i = 0; i <= n-2; i = i + 2){
        sum[0][1] = A[i];
        z = A[i+1];
        k = 0;
        do {
            CSA(z, sum[k][0], sum[k][0], sum[k][1], z)
            nrow[k] = 1;
            k = k + 1;
        } while (nrow[k] == 2);
        sum[k][nrow[k]] = z;
        nrow[k] = nrow[k] + 1;
    }

    if (i == n - 1) {                     // If there's one more in
        sum[0][1] = A[i];                  // the array, put it in
        nrow[0] = 2;                       // sum[0][1].
    }

    /* Make a pass over the "sum" array compressing all
    rows that have two entries to the same row but having
    only one entry, while adding an entry to the
    subsequent row. This can make the subsequent row have,
    in effect, three entries, which we similarly compress.
    Compute the total during this pass. When an empty row
    is encountered, we're done. */

    tot = 0;
    hi = 0;
    for (k = 0; nrow[k] != 0; k++) {
```

8.2. Bit Counting Algorithms

```
          if (nrow[k] == 1) z = 0;
          else                z = sum[k][1];    // (Is 2.)

          CSA(hi, lo, sum[k][0], z, hi)
          tot = tot + (pop(lo) << k);
      }

      tot = tot + (pop(hi) << k);

      return tot;
}
// ─────────────────────────────── main
int main(void) {
    unsigned A[101];
    int i, n, s1, s;

    n = sizeof(A)/sizeof(A[0]);
    A[0] = 0xFFFFFFFF;                  // Fill the array
    A[1] = 5;                           // with somewhat
//  printf("%08x\n", A[0]);             // random numbers
//  printf("%08x\n", A[1]);
    for (i = 2; i < n; i++) {
        A[i] = rand();
//      printf("%08x\n", A[i]);
    }
    s1 = popArray1(A, n);
    printf("Array size = %d, pop count = %d\n", n, s1);

    s = popArray2(A, n);
    if (s == s1) printf("popArray2 is ok.\n");
    else         printf("popArray2 = %d, ERROR.\n", s);

    s = popArray3(A, n);
    if (s == s1) printf("popArray3 is ok.\n");
    else         printf("popArray3 = %d, ERROR.\n", s);

    s = popArray4(A, n);
    if (s == s1) printf("popArray4 is ok.\n");
    else         printf("popArray4 = %d, ERROR.\n", s);

    s = popArray5(A, n);
    if (s == s1) printf("popArray5 is ok.\n");
    else         printf("popArray5 = %d, ERROR.\n", s);

    s = popArray6(A, n);
    if (s == s1) printf("popArray6 is ok.\n");
    else         printf("popArray6 = %d, ERROR.\n", s);

    return s - s1;
}
```

8.2.2 Computing Parity of a word

The "parity" of a string refers to whether it contains an odd or an even number of 1-bits. The string has "odd parity" if it contains an odd number of 1-bits; otherwise, it has "even parity." Here we mean to produce a 1 if a word x has odd parity, and a 0 if it has even parity. This is the sum, modulo 2, of the

8.2. Bit Counting Algorithms

bits of x, that is, the exclusive or of all the bits of x. One way to compute this is to compute pop(x); the parity is the rightmost bit of the result.

The parity can be computed naively as follows:

```
1 unsigned int v;         // word value to compute the parity of
2 bool parity = false;    // parity will be the parity of v
3
4 while (v)
5 {
6    parity = !parity;
7    v = v & (v - 1);
8 }
```

The time it takes is proportional to the number of bits set.

For the word size 32, the parity of x(the rightmost bit of y) can be computed as:

```
1 y = x ^ (x >> 1);
2 y = y ^ (y >> 2);
3 y = y ^ (y >> 4);
4 y = y ^ (y >> 8);
5 y = y ^ (y >> 16);
```

The bit i of y gives the parity of the bits of x at and to the left of i. $x_i \wedge x_j$ is the parity of bits $i-1$ through j, for $i \geq j$.

Program 8.11: *parity algorithms*

```
1 // Programs for computing the parity of a word.
2
3 #include <stdio.h>
4 #include <stdlib.h>
5
6 int parity1(unsigned x) {
7    unsigned y;
8
9    y = x ^ (x >> 1);
10   y = y ^ (y >> 2);
11   y = y ^ (y >> 4);
12   y = y ^ (y >> 8);
13   y = y ^ (y >>16);
14   return y & 1;
15 }
16
17 int parity1a(unsigned x) {
18   unsigned y;
19
20   y = x ^ (x >>16);
21   y = y ^ (y >> 8);
22   y = y ^ (y >> 4);
23   y = 0x6996 >> (y & 0xF);    // Falk Hueffner's trick.
24   return y & 1;
25 }
26
27 int parity2(unsigned x) {
28   int p;
29
30   x = x ^ (x >> 1);
31   x = (x ^ (x >> 2)) & 0x11111111;
32   x = x*0x11111111;
```

8.2. Bit Counting Algorithms 288

```
33      p = (x >> 28) & 1;
34      return p;
35 }

37 int parity3(unsigned x) {
38      unsigned y;
39
40      y = (x*0x10204081) & 0x888888FF;
41      return (y%1920) & 0xFF;        // Returns a byte with
                                          even parity.
42 }

44 int parity4(unsigned x) {
45      unsigned y;
46
47      y = (x*0x00204081) | 0x3DB6DB00;
48      y = (y%1152) & 0xFF;
49      return y ^ 0x80;               // Change to even parity
                                          so test2 can be used.
50 }

52 int errors;
53 void error(int x, int y) {
54      errors = errors + 1;
55      printf("Error for x = %08x, got %d\n", x, y);
56 }

58 int main() {
59      int i, r, n;
60      static unsigned test[] = {0,0, 1,1, 2,1, 3,0, 4,1,
            5,0,
61          6,0, 7,1, 8,1, 9,0, 10,0, 11,1, 12,0, 13,1, 14,1,
62          15,0, 16,1, 17,0, 18,0, 19,1, 20,0, 21,1, 22,1,
            23,0,
63          24,0, 25,1, 26,1, 27,0, 28,1, 29,0, 30,0, 31,1,
64          0x55555555,0, 0xAAAAAAAA,0, 0x77777770,1,
65          0x80000000,1, 0x80000001,0, 0xFFFFFFFE,1, 0
            xFFFFFFFF,0};
66      static unsigned test2[] = {0,0, 1,0x81, 2,0x82, 3,3,
            4,0x84,
67          5,5, 6,6, 7,0x87, 8,0x88, 9,9, 10,10, 11,0x8B,
            12,12,
68          13,0x8D, 14,0x8E, 15,15, 16,0x90, 0x7E,0x7E, 0x7F,0
            xFF};
69
70      n = sizeof(test)/4;
71
72      printf("parity1:\n");
73      for (i = 0; i < n; i += 2) {
74          r = parity1(test[i]);
75          if (r != test[i+1]) error(test[i], r);}
76
77      printf("parity1a:\n");
78      for (i = 0; i < n; i += 2) {
79          r = parity1a(test[i]);
80          if (r != test[i+1]) error(test[i], r);}
81
82      printf("parity2:\n");
83      for (i = 0; i < n; i += 2) {
84          r = parity2(test[i]);
85          if (r != test[i+1]) error(test[i], r);}
```

8.2. Bit Counting Algorithms

```
    if (errors == 0)
        printf("Passed all %d cases.\n", n/2);

    n = sizeof(test2)/4;

    printf("parity3:\n");
    for (i = 0; i < n; i += 2) {
        r = parity3(test2[i]);
        if (r != test2[i+1]) error(test2[i], r);}

    printf("parity4:\n");
    for (i = 0; i < n; i += 2) {
        r = parity4(test2[i]);
        if (r != test2[i+1]) error(test2[i], r);}

    if (errors == 0)
        printf("Passed all %d cases.\n", n/2);
}
```

8.2.3 Counting Leading 0's

Program 8.12: *Counting Leading zeros algorithms*

```
// Programs for computing the number of leading zeros
// in a word.
// Compile with g++, not gcc.
#include <stdio.h>
#include <stdlib.h>
#define LE 1              // 1 for little-endian, 0 for big
                          -endian.

int pop(unsigned x) {
    x = x - ((x >> 1) & 0x55555555);
    x = (x & 0x33333333) + ((x >> 2) & 0x33333333);
    x = (x + (x >> 4)) & 0x0F0F0F0F;
    x = x + (x << 8);
    x = x + (x << 16);
    return x >> 24;
}

int nlz1(unsigned x) {
    int n;

    if (x == 0) return(32);
    n = 0;
    if (x <= 0x0000FFFF) {n = n +16; x = x <<16;}
    if (x <= 0x00FFFFFF) {n = n + 8; x = x << 8;}
    if (x <= 0x0FFFFFFF) {n = n + 4; x = x << 4;}
    if (x <= 0x3FFFFFFF) {n = n + 2; x = x << 2;}
    if (x <= 0x7FFFFFFF) {n = n + 1;}
    return n;
}

int nlz1a(unsigned x) {
    int n;

/* if (x == 0) return(32); */
    if ((int)x <= 0) return (~x >> 26) & 32;
```

8.2. Bit Counting Algorithms

```
      n = 1;
      if ((x >> 16) == 0) {n = n +16; x = x <<16;}
      if ((x >> 24) == 0) {n = n + 8; x = x << 8;}
      if ((x >> 28) == 0) {n = n + 4; x = x << 4;}
      if ((x >> 30) == 0) {n = n + 2; x = x << 2;}
      n = n - (x >> 31);
      return n;
}
// On basic Risc, 12 to 20 instructions.

int nlz2(unsigned x) {
    unsigned y;
    int n;

    n = 32;
    y = x >>16;  if (y != 0) {n = n -16;  x = y;}
    y = x >> 8;  if (y != 0) {n = n - 8;  x = y;}
    y = x >> 4;  if (y != 0) {n = n - 4;  x = y;}
    y = x >> 2;  if (y != 0) {n = n - 2;  x = y;}
    y = x >> 1;  if (y != 0) return n - 2;
    return n - x;
}

// As above but coded as a loop for compactness:
// 23 to 33 basic Risc instructions.
int nlz2a(unsigned x) {
    unsigned y;
    int n, c;

    n = 32;
    c = 16;
    do {
        y = x >> c;  if (y != 0) {n = n - c;  x = y;}
        c = c >> 1;
    } while (c != 0);
    return n - x;
}

int nlz3(int x) {
    int y, n;

    n = 0;
    y = x;
L:  if (x < 0) return n;
    if (y == 0) return 32 - n;
    n = n + 1;
    x = x << 1;
    y = y >> 1;
    goto L;
}

int nlz4(unsigned x) {
    int y, m, n;

    y = -(x >> 16);        // If left half of x is 0,
    m = (y >> 16) & 16;    // set n = 16. If left half
    n = 16 - m;            // is nonzero, set n = 0 and
    x = x >> m;            // shift x right 16.
                           // Now x is of the form 0000xxxx.
    y = x - 0x100;         // If positions 8-15 are 0,
```

8.2. Bit Counting Algorithms

```
 95      m = (y >> 16) & 8;       // add 8 to n and shift x left 8.
 96      n = n + m;
 97      x = x << m;
 98
 99      y = x - 0x1000;          // If positions 12-15 are 0,
100      m = (y >> 16) & 4;       // add 4 to n and shift x left 4.
101      n = n + m;
102      x = x << m;
103
104      y = x - 0x4000;          // If positions 14-15 are 0,
105      m = (y >> 16) & 2;       // add 2 to n and shift x left 2.
106      n = n + m;
107      x = x << m;
108
109      y = x >> 14;             // Set y = 0, 1, 2, or 3.
110      m = y & ~(y >> 1);       // Set m = 0, 1, 2, or 2 resp.
111      return n + 2 - m;
112 }
113
114 int nlz5(unsigned x) {
115      int pop(unsigned x);
116
117      x = x | (x >> 1);
118      x = x | (x >> 2);
119      x = x | (x >> 4);
120      x = x | (x >> 8);
121      x = x | (x >>16);
122      return pop(~x);
123 }
124
125 /* The four programs below are not valid ANSI C programs. This is
126 because they refer to the same storage locations as two different types.
127 However, they work with xlc/AIX, gcc/AIX, and gcc/NT. If you try to
128 code them more compactly by declaring a variable xx to be "double," and
129 then using
130
131    n = 1054 - (*((unsigned *)&xx + LE) >> 20);
132
133 then you are violating not only the rule above, but also the ANSI C
134 rule that pointer arithmetic can be performed only on pointers to
135 array elements.
136    When coded with the above statement, the program fails with xlc,
137 gcc/AIX, and gcc/NT, at some optimization levels.
138    BTW, these programs use the "anonymous union" feature of C++, not
139 available in C. */
140
141 int nlz6(unsigned k) {
142      union {
143          unsigned asInt[2];
144          double asDouble;
145      };
146      int n;
147
148      asDouble = (double)k + 0.5;
```

8.2. Bit Counting Algorithms

```
149     n = 1054 - (asInt[LE] >> 20);
150     return n;
151 }
152
153 int nlz7(unsigned k) {
154     union {
155         unsigned asInt[2];
156         double asDouble;
157     };
158     int n;
159
160     asDouble = (double)k;
161     n = 1054 - (asInt[LE] >> 20);
162     n = (n & 31) + (n >> 9);
163     return n;
164 }
165
166 /* In single precision, round-to-nearest mode, the
        basic method fails for:
167     k = 0, k = 01FFFFFF, 03FFFFFE <= k <= 03FFFFFF,
168                         07FFFFFC <= k <= 07FFFFFF,
169                         0FFFFFF8 <= k <= 0FFFFFFF,
170                         ...
171                         7FFFFFC0 <= k <= 7FFFFFFF,
172                         FFFFFF80 <= k <= FFFFFFFF.
173    For k = 0 it gives 158, and for the other values it is
        too low by 1. */
174
175 int nlz8(unsigned k) {
176     union {
177         unsigned asInt;
178         float asFloat;
179     };
180     int n;
181
182     k = k & ~(k >> 1);          /* Fix problem with
        rounding. */
183     asFloat = (float)k + 0.5f;
184     n = 158 - (asInt >> 23);
185     return n;
186 }
187
188 /* The example below shows how to make a macro for nlz.
        It uses an
189 extension to the C and C++ languages that is provided by
        the GNU C/C++
190 compiler, namely, that of allowing statements and
        declarations in
191 expressions (see "Using and Porting GNU CC", by Richard M
        . Stallman
192 (1998). The underscores are necessary to protect against
        the
193 possibility that the macro argument will conflict with
        one of its local
194 variables, e.g., NLZ(k). */
195
196 #define NLZ(kp) \
197     ({union {unsigned _asInt; float _asFloat;}; \
198      unsigned _k = (kp), _kk = _k & ~(_k >> 1); \
199      _asFloat = (float)_kk + 0.5f; \
```

8.2. Bit Counting Algorithms 293

```
           158 - (_asInt >> 23);})
int nlz8a(unsigned k) {
   return NLZ(k) + NLZ(-5 + 1);
}

int nlz9(unsigned k) {
   union {
      unsigned asInt;
      float    asFloat;
   };
   int n;

   k = k & ~(k >> 1);              /* Fix problem with
                                      rounding. */
   asFloat = (float)k;
   n = 158 - (asInt >> 23);
   n = (n & 31) + (n >> 6);        /* Fix problem with k =
                                      0. */
   return n;
}

/* Below are three nearly equivalent programs for
      computing the number
   of leading zeros in a word.
      Immediately below is Robert Harley's algorithm.
      Table entries marked "u" are unused. 14 ops including
         a multiply,
   plus an indexed load.
      The smallest multiplier that works is 0x045BCED1 =
         17*65*129*513 (all
   of form 2**k + 1). There are no multipliers of three
      terms of the form
   2**k +- 1 that work, with a table size of 64 or 128.
      There are some,
   with a table size of 64, if you precede the
      multiplication with x = x -
   (x >> 1), but that seems less elegant. There are also
      some if you use a
   table size of 256, the smallest is 0x01033CBF =
      65*255*1025 (this would
   save two instructions in the form of this algorithm with
      the
   multiplication expanded into shifts and adds, but the
      table size is
   getting a bit large). */

#define u 99
int nlz10(unsigned x) {

   static char table[64] =
      {32,31, u,16, u,30, 3, u,   15, u, u, u,29,10, 2, u,
        u, u,12,14,21, u,19, u,    u,28, u,25, u, 9, 1, u,
       17, u, 4, u, u, u,11, u,   13,22,20, u,26, u, u,18,
        5, u, u,23, u,27, u, 6,    u,24, 7, u, 8, u, 0, u};

   x = x | (x >> 1);    // Propagate leftmost
   x = x | (x >> 2);    // 1-bit to the right.
   x = x | (x >> 4);
   x = x | (x >> 8);
```

8.2. Bit Counting Algorithms

```
    x = x | (x >>16);
    x = x*0x06EB14F9;       // Multiplier is 7*255**3.
    return table[x >> 26];
}

/* Harley's algorithm with multiply expanded.
19 elementary ops plus an indexed load. */

int nlz10a(unsigned x) {

    static char table[64] =
       {32,31, u,16, u,30, 3, u,  15, u, u, u,29,10, 2, u,
         u, u,12,14,21, u,19, u,  u,28, u,25, u, 9, 1, u,
        17, u, 4, u, u, u,11, u,  13,22,20, u,26, u, u,18,
         5, u, u,23, u,27, u, 6,  u,24, 7, u, 8, u, 0, u};

    x = x | (x >> 1);       // Propagate leftmost
    x = x | (x >> 2);       // 1-bit to the right.
    x = x | (x >> 4);
    x = x | (x >> 8);
    x = x | (x >> 16);
    x = (x << 3) - x;       // Multiply by 7.
    x = (x << 8) - x;       // Multiply by 255.
    x = (x << 8) - x;       // Again.
    x = (x << 8) - x;       // Again.
    return table[x >> 26];
}

/* Julius Goryavsky's version of Harley's algorithm.
17 elementary ops plus an indexed load, if the machine
has "and not." */

int nlz10b(unsigned x) {

    static char table[64] =
       {32,20,19, u, u,18, u, 7,  10,17, u, u,14, u, 6, u,
         u, 9, u,16, u, u, 1,26,  u,13, u, u,24, 5, u, u,
         u,21, u, 8,11, u,15, u,  u, u, u, 2,27, 0,25, u,
        22, u,12, u, u, 3,28, u,  23, u, 4,29, u, u,30,31};

    x = x | (x >> 1);       // Propagate leftmost
    x = x | (x >> 2);       // 1-bit to the right.
    x = x | (x >> 4);
    x = x | (x >> 8);
    x = x & ~(x >> 16);
    x = x*0xFD7049FF;       // Activate this line or the
                            //   following 3.
//  x = (x << 9) - x;       // Multiply by 511.
//  x = (x << 11) - x;      // Multiply by 2047.
//  x = (x << 14) - x;      // Multiply by 16383.
    return table[x >> 26];
}

int errors;
void error(int x, int y) {
    errors = errors + 1;
    printf("Error for x = %08x, got %d\n", x, y);
}
```

8.2. Bit Counting Algorithms

```
int main() {
   int i, n;
   static unsigned test[] = {0,32, 1,31, 2,30, 3,30,
      4,29, 5,29, 6,29,
      7,29, 8,28, 9,28, 16,27, 32,26, 64,25, 128,24,
      255,24, 256,23,
      512,22, 1024,21, 2048,20, 4096,19, 8192,18,
      16384,17, 32768,16,
      65536,15, 0x20000,14, 0x40000,13, 0x80000,12, 0
         x100000,11,
      0x200000,10, 0x400000,9, 0x800000,8, 0x1000000,7, 0
         x2000000,6,
      0x4000000,5, 0x8000000,4, 0x0FFFFFFF,4, 0x10000000
         ,3,
      0x3000FFFF,2, 0x50003333,1, 0x7FFFFFFF,1, 0
         x80000000,0,
      0xFFFFFFFF,0};

   n = sizeof(test)/4;

   printf("nlz1:\n");
   for (i = 0; i < n; i += 2) {
      if (nlz1(test[i]) != test[i+1]) error(test[i], nlz1
         (test[i]));}

   printf("nlz1a:\n");
   for (i = 0; i < n; i += 2) {
      if (nlz1a(test[i]) != test[i+1]) error(test[i],
         nlz1a(test[i]));}

   printf("nlz2:\n");
   for (i = 0; i < n; i += 2) {
      if (nlz2(test[i]) != test[i+1]) error(test[i], nlz2
         (test[i]));}

   printf("nlz2a:\n");
   for (i = 0; i < n; i += 2) {
      if (nlz2a(test[i]) != test[i+1]) error(test[i],
         nlz2a(test[i]));}

   printf("nlz3:\n");
   for (i = 0; i < n; i += 2) {
      if (nlz3(test[i]) != test[i+1]) error(test[i], nlz3
         (test[i]));}

   printf("nlz4:\n");
   for (i = 0; i < n; i += 2) {
      if (nlz4(test[i]) != test[i+1]) error(test[i], nlz4
         (test[i]));}

   printf("nlz5:\n");
   for (i = 0; i < n; i += 2) {
      if (nlz5(test[i]) != test[i+1]) error(test[i], nlz5
         (test[i]));}

   printf("nlz6:\n");
   for (i = 0; i < n; i += 2) {
      if (nlz6(test[i]) != test[i+1]) error(test[i], nlz6
         (test[i]));}
```

8.2. Bit Counting Algorithms

```
351    printf("nlz7:\n");
352    for (i = 0; i < n; i += 2) {
353       if (nlz7(test[i]) != test[i+1]) error(test[i], nlz7
              (test[i]));}
354
355    printf("nlz8:\n");
356    for (i = 0; i < n; i += 2) {
357       if (nlz8(test[i]) != test[i+1]) error(test[i], nlz8
              (test[i]));}
358
359    printf("nlz8a:\n");
360    for (i = 0; i < n; i += 2) {
361       if (nlz8a(test[i]) != test[i+1]) error(test[i],
              nlz8a(test[i]));}
362
363    printf("nlz9:\n");
364    for (i = 0; i < n; i += 2) {
365       if (nlz9(test[i]) != test[i+1]) error(test[i], nlz9
              (test[i]));}
366
367    printf("nlz10:\n");
368    for (i = 0; i < n; i += 2) {
369       if (nlz10(test[i]) != test[i+1]) error(test[i],
              nlz10(test[i]));}
370
371    printf("nlz10a:\n");
372    for (i = 0; i < n; i += 2) {
373       if (nlz10a(test[i]) != test[i+1]) error(test[i],
              nlz10a(test[i]));}
374
375    printf("nlz10b:\n");
376    for (i = 0; i < n; i += 2) {
377       if (nlz10b(test[i]) != test[i+1]) error(test[i],
              nlz10b(test[i]));}
378
379    if (errors == 0)
380       printf("Passed all %d cases.\n", sizeof(test)/8);
381 }
```

8.2.4 Counting Trailing 0's

Program 8.13: *Counting Trailing zeros algorithms*

```
1 // Programs for computing the number of trailing zeros
2 // in a word.
3
4 #include <stdio.h>
5 #include <stdlib.h>
6
7 int nlz(unsigned x) {
8    int pop(unsigned x);
9
10   x = x | (x >> 1);
11   x = x | (x >> 2);
12   x = x | (x >> 4);
13   x = x | (x >> 8);
14   x = x | (x >>16);
15   return pop(~x);
16 }
17
```

8.2. Bit Counting Algorithms

```
int pop(unsigned x) {
   x = x - ((x >> 1) & 0x55555555);
   x = (x & 0x33333333) + ((x >> 2) & 0x33333333);
   x = (x + (x >> 4)) & 0x0F0F0F0F;
   x = x + (x << 8);
   x = x + (x << 16);
   return x >> 24;
}

int ntz1(unsigned x) {
   return 32 - nlz(~x & (x-1));
}

int ntz2(unsigned x) {
   return pop(~x & (x - 1));
}

int ntz3(unsigned x) {
   int n;

   if (x == 0) return(32);
   n = 1;
   if ((x & 0x0000FFFF) == 0) {n = n +16; x = x >>16;}
   if ((x & 0x000000FF) == 0) {n = n + 8; x = x >> 8;}
   if ((x & 0x0000000F) == 0) {n = n + 4; x = x >> 4;}
   if ((x & 0x00000003) == 0) {n = n + 2; x = x >> 2;}
   return n - (x & 1);
}

int ntz4(unsigned x) {
   unsigned y;
   int n;

   if (x == 0) return 32;
   n = 31;
   y = x <<16; if (y != 0) {n = n -16; x = y;}
   y = x << 8; if (y != 0) {n = n - 8; x = y;}
   y = x << 4; if (y != 0) {n = n - 4; x = y;}
   y = x << 2; if (y != 0) {n = n - 2; x = y;}
   y = x << 1; if (y != 0) {n = n - 1;}
   return n;
}

int ntz4a(unsigned x) {
   unsigned y;
   int n;

   if (x == 0) return 32;
   n = 31;
   y = x <<16; if (y != 0) {n = n -16; x = y;}
   y = x << 8; if (y != 0) {n = n - 8; x = y;}
   y = x << 4; if (y != 0) {n = n - 4; x = y;}
   y = x << 2; if (y != 0) {n = n - 2; x = y;}
   n = n - ((x << 1) >> 31);
   return n;
}

int ntz5(char x) {
   if (x & 15) {
```

8.2. Bit Counting Algorithms

```
        if (x & 3) {
            if (x & 1) return 0;
            else return 1;
        }
        else if (x & 4) return 2;
        else return 3;
    }
    else if (x & 0x30) {
        if (x & 0x10) return 4;
        else return 5;
    }
    else if (x & 0x40) return 6;
    else if (x) return 7;
    else return 8;
}

int ntz6(unsigned x) {
    int n;

    x = ~x & (x - 1);
    n = 0;                      // n = 32;
    while(x != 0) {             // while (x != 0) {
        n = n + 1;              //     n = n - 1;
        x = x >> 1;             //     x = x + x;
    }                           // }
    return n;                   // return n;
}

int ntz6a(unsigned x) {
    int n;

                                n = 32;
                                while (x != 0) {
                                    n = n - 1;
                                    x = x + x;
                                }
                                return n;
}

/* Dean Gaudet's algorithm. To be most useful there must be a good way
to evaluate the C "conditional expression" (a?b:c construction) without
branching. The result of a?b:c is b if a is true (nonzero), and c if a
is false (0).
    For example, a compare to zero op that sets a target GPR to 1 if the
operand is 0, and to 0 if the operand is nonzero, will do it. With this
instruction, the algorithm is entirely branch-free. But the most
interesting thing about it is the high degree of parallelism. All six
lines with conditional expressions can be executed in parallel (on a
machine with sufficient computational units).
    Although the instruction count is 30 measured statically, it could
```

8.2. Bit Counting Algorithms

execute in only 10 cycles on a machine with sufficient parallelism.
The first two uses of y can instead be x, which would increase the
useful parallelism on most machines (the assignments to y, bz, and b4
could then all run in parallel). */

```
int ntz7(unsigned x) {
    unsigned y, bz, b4, b3, b2, b1, b0;

    y = x & -x;                         // Isolate rightmost 1-bit.
    bz = y ? 0 : 1;                     // 1 if y = 0.
    b4 = (y & 0x0000FFFF) ? 0 : 16;
    b3 = (y & 0x00FF00FF) ? 0 : 8;
    b2 = (y & 0x0F0F0F0F) ? 0 : 4;
    b1 = (y & 0x33333333) ? 0 : 2;
    b0 = (y & 0x55555555) ? 0 : 1;
    return bz + b4 + b3 + b2 + b1 + b0;
}
```

/* Below is David Seal's algorithm, found at
http://www.ciphersbyritter.com/NEWS4/BITCT.HTM Table
entries marked "u" are unused. 6 ops including a
multiply, plus an indexed load. */

```
#define u 99
int ntz8(unsigned x) {

    static char table[64] =
        {32, 0, 1,12, 2, 6, u,13,    3, u, 7, u, u, u, u,14,
         10, 4, u, u, 8, u, u,25,    u, u, u, u, u,21,27,15,
         31,11, 5, u, u, u, u, u,    9, u, u,24, u, u,20,26,
         30, u, u, u, u,23, u,19,   29, u,22,18,28,17,16, u};

    x = (x & -x)*0x0450FBAF;
    return table[x >> 26];
}
```

/* Seal's algorithm with multiply expanded.
9 elementary ops plus an indexed load. */

```
int ntz8a(unsigned x) {

    static char table[64] =
        {32, 0, 1,12, 2, 6, u,13,    3, u, 7, u, u, u, u,14,
         10, 4, u, u, 8, u, u,25,    u, u, u, u, u,21,27,15,
         31,11, 5, u, u, u, u, u,    9, u, u,24, u, u,20,26,
         30, u, u, u, u,23, u,19,   29, u,22,18,28,17,16, u};

    x = (x & -x);
    x = (x << 4) + x;         // x = x*17.
    x = (x << 6) + x;         // x = x*65.
    x = (x << 16) - x;        // x = x*65535.
    return table[x >> 26];
}
```

/* Reiser's algorithm. Three ops including a "remainder,"
plus an indexed load. */

```
int ntz9(unsigned x) {
```

8.2. Bit Counting Algorithms

```
    static char table[37] = {32,  0,  1, 26,  2, 23, 27,
                              u,  3, 16, 24, 30, 28, 11,  u, 13,  4,
                              7, 17,  u, 25, 22, 31, 15, 29, 10, 12,
                              6,  u, 21, 14,  9,  5, 20,  8, 19, 18};

    x = (x & -x)%37;
    return table[x];
}

/* Using a de Bruijn sequence. This is a table lookup
    with a 32-entry
 table. The de Bruijn sequence used here is
                0000 0100 1101 0111 0110 0101 0001 1111
 */

int ntz10(unsigned x) {

    static char table[32] =
       {  0,  1,  2, 24,  3, 19,  6, 25,  22,  4, 20, 10, 16,  7, 12, 26,
         31, 23, 18,  5, 21,  9, 15, 11,  30, 17,  8, 14, 29, 13, 28, 27};

    if (x == 0) return 32;
    x = (x & -x)*0x04D7651F;
    return table[x >> 27];
}

/* Norbert Juffa's code */

#define SLOW_MUL
int ntz11 (unsigned int n) {

    static unsigned char tab[32] =
       {   0,  1,  2, 24,  3, 19,  6, 25,
          22,  4, 20, 10, 16,  7, 12, 26,
          31, 23, 18,  5, 21,  9, 15, 11,
          30, 17,  8, 14, 29, 13, 28, 27
       };
    unsigned int k;
    n = n & (-n);             /* isolate lsb */
    printf("n_=_%d\n", n);
#if defined(SLOW_MUL)
    k = (n << 11) - n;
    k = (k <<  2) + k;
    k = (k <<  8) + n;
    k = (k <<  5) - k;
#else
    k = n * 0x4d7651f;
#endif
    return n ? tab[k>>27] : 32;
}

int errors;
void error(int x, int y) {
    errors = errors + 1;
    printf("Error_for_x_=_%08x,_got_%d\n", x, y);
}

/* ——————————————————————————— main
   ——————————————————————————— */
```

8.2. Bit Counting Algorithms

```
244 int main() {
245   int i, m, n;
246   static unsigned test[] = {0,32, 1,0, 2,1, 3,0, 4,2,
          5,0, 6,1, 7,0,
247       8,3, 9,0, 16,4, 32,5, 64,6, 128,7, 255,0, 256,8,
          512,9, 1024,10,
248       2048,11, 4096,12, 8192,13, 16384,14, 32768,15,
          65536,16,
249       0x20000,17, 0x40000,18, 0x80000,19, 0x100000,20, 0
          x200000,21,
250       0x400000,22, 0x800000,23, 0x1000000,24, 0x2000000
          ,25,
251       0x4000000,26, 0x8000000,27, 0x10000000,28, 0
          x20000000,29,
252       0x40000000,30, 0x80000000,31, 0xFFFFFFF0,4, 0
          x3000FF00,8,
253       0xC0000000,30, 0x60000000,29, 0x00011000, 12};
254
255   n = sizeof(test)/4;
256
257   printf("ntz1:\n");
258   for (i = 0; i < n; i += 2) {
259     if (ntz1(test[i]) != test[i+1]) error(test[i], ntz1
          (test[i]));}
260
261   printf("ntz2:\n");
262   for (i = 0; i < n; i += 2) {
263     if (ntz2(test[i]) != test[i+1]) error(test[i], ntz2
          (test[i]));}
264
265   printf("ntz3:\n");
266   for (i = 0; i < n; i += 2) {
267     if (ntz3(test[i]) != test[i+1]) error(test[i], ntz3
          (test[i]));}
268
269   printf("ntz4:\n");
270   for (i = 0; i < n; i += 2) {
271     if (ntz4(test[i]) != test[i+1]) error(test[i], ntz4
          (test[i]));}
272
273   printf("ntz4a:\n");
274   for (i = 0; i < n; i += 2) {
275     if (ntz4a(test[i]) != test[i+1]) error(test[i],
          ntz4a(test[i]));}
276
277   printf("ntz5:\n");
278   for (i = 0; i < n; i += 2) {
279     m = test[i+1]; if (m > 8) m = 8;
280     if (ntz5(test[i]) != m) error(test[i], ntz5(test[i
          ]));}
281
282   printf("ntz6:\n");
283   for (i = 0; i < n; i += 2) {
284     if (ntz6(test[i]) != test[i+1]) error(test[i], ntz6
          (test[i]));}
285
286   printf("ntz6a:\n");
287   for (i = 0; i < n; i += 2) {
288     if (ntz6a(test[i]) != test[i+1]) error(test[i],
          ntz6a(test[i]));}
```

8.3. Rearranging Algorithms

```
289
290     printf("ntz7:\n");
291     for (i = 0; i < n; i += 2) {
292       if (ntz7(test[i]) != test[i+1]) error(test[i], ntz7
              (test[i]));}
293
294     printf("ntz8:\n");
295     for (i = 0; i < n; i += 2) {
296       if (ntz8(test[i]) != test[i+1]) error(test[i], ntz8
              (test[i]));}
297
298     printf("ntz8a:\n");
299     for (i = 0; i < n; i += 2) {
300       if (ntz8a(test[i]) != test[i+1]) error(test[i],
              ntz8a(test[i]));}
301
302     printf("ntz9:\n");
303     for (i = 0; i < n; i += 2) {
304       if (ntz9(test[i]) != test[i+1]) error(test[i], ntz9
              (test[i]));}
305
306     printf("ntz10:\n");
307     for (i = 0; i < n; i += 2) {
308       if (ntz10(test[i]) != test[i+1]) error(test[i],
              ntz10(test[i]));}
309
310     printf("ntz11:\n");
311     for (i = 0; i < n; i += 2) {
312       if (ntz11(test[i]) != test[i+1]) error(test[i],
              ntz11(test[i]));}
313
314     if (errors == 0)
315       printf("Passed all %d cases.\n", sizeof(test)/8);
316 }
```

8.3 Rearranging Algorithms

8.3.1 Bit Reversal

Rotate shift left:

```
1 unsigned shlr(unsigned x, int n) {
2   return (x << n) | (x >> (32 - n));
3 }
```

Reversing bits in a word, basic interchange scheme:

```
1 unsigned rev1(unsigned x) {
2   x = (x & 0x55555555) <<  1 | (x & 0xAAAAAAAA) >>  1;
3   x = (x & 0x33333333) <<  2 | (x & 0xCCCCCCCC) >>  2;
4   x = (x & 0x0F0F0F0F) <<  4 | (x & 0xF0F0F0F0) >>  4;
5   x = (x & 0x00FF00FF) <<  8 | (x & 0xFF00FF00) >>  8;
6   x = (x & 0x0000FFFF) << 16 | (x & 0xFFFF0000) >> 16;
7   return x;
8 }
```

Reversing bits in a word, refined basic scheme. 24 operations + 6 for loading constants = 30 instructions:

```
1 unsigned rev2(unsigned x) {
```

8.3. Rearranging Algorithms

```
    x = (x & 0x55555555) << 1 | (x >> 1) & 0x55555555;
    x = (x & 0x33333333) << 2 | (x >> 2) & 0x33333333;
    x = (x & 0x0F0F0F0F) << 4 | (x >> 4) & 0x0F0F0F0F;
    x = (x << 24) | ((x & 0xFF00) << 8) |
        ((x >> 8) & 0xFF00) | (x >> 24);
    return x;
}
```

Reversing the rightmost 6 bits in a word:

```
unsigned rev3(unsigned x) {
    return (x*0x00082082 & 0x01122408) % 255;
}
```

Reversing the rightmost 6 bits in a word:

```
unsigned rev4(unsigned x) {
    unsigned t;
    t = x*0x00082082 & 0x01122408;
    return (t*0x01010101) >> 24;
}
```

Reversing the rightmost 8 bits in a word. Problem: can't change divide by 1023 to a 32x32 $\implies$ 32 multiply:

```
unsigned rev5(unsigned x) {
    unsigned s, t;
    s = x*0x02020202 & 0x84422010;
    t = x*8 & 0x00000420;
    return (s + t) % 1023;
}
```

Reversing the rightmost 8 bits in a word:

```
unsigned rev6(unsigned x) {
    unsigned s, t;
    s = x*0x00020202 & 0x00422010;
    t = x*0x00008008 & 0x00210420;
    return (s + t) % 1023;
}
```

Reversing the rightmost 8 bits in a word:

```
unsigned rev7(unsigned x) {
    unsigned s, t;

    s = x*0x00020202 & 0x01044010;
    t = x*0x00080808 & 0x02088020;
    return (s + t) % 4095;
}
```

The routine below reverses the rightmost 16 bits of a word, assuming the leftmost 16 bits are clear at the start. It is an old algorithm by Christopher Strachey (Bitwise Operations. Communications of the ACM 4, 3 (March 1961), 146). The way it works is to build up the reversed halfword in the left half of the register x. It does this by noting how many positions each bit must move to the left, to be placed in its proper position in the left half of the word. Then, each bit that must move 16 or more positions is moved left 16. Then each bit that must move 8 or more positions (after the first move of 16 positions) is moved left 8. Then 4, and 2. Lastly a shift left of 1 is required to put the result in the left half of the register (as in Strachey), or a shift right

8.3. Rearranging Algorithms 304

of 15 is done to put the result in the rightmost 16 bits (as is done here). Here is how far to the left the bits in postions 0 to 15 must move:

```
31 30 ... 17 16 15 14 13 12 11 10  9  8  7  6  5  4  3  2  1  0
                1  3  5  7  9 11 13 15 17 19 21 23 25 27 29 31

0000 0000 0000 0000 abcd efgh ijkl mnop  Given
0000 0000 ijkl mnop abcd efgh ijkl mnop  After shl 16
0000 mnop ijkl efgh abcd mnop ijkl mnop  After shl 8
00op mnkl ijgh efcd abop mnkl ijop mnop  After shl 4
0pon mlkj ihgf edcb apon mlkj ipon mpop  After shl 2
0000 0000 0000 0000 ponm lkji hgfe dcba  After shr 15
```

16 operations:
```
unsigned rev11(unsigned x) {
    x = x | ((x & 0x000000FF) << 16);
    x = (x & 0xF0F0F0F0) | ((x & 0x0F0F0F0F) << 8);
    x = (x & 0xCCCCCCCC) | ((x & 0x33333333) << 4);
    x = (x & 0xAAAAAAAA) | ((x & 0x55555555) << 2);
    x = x >> 15;
    return x;
}
```

By using different (and more irregular) masks, the code for Strachey's method can be made to preserve the right half of the register and to put the reversed halfword in the left half. It can be made to use fewer masks at no loss of efficiency in ways that will be discussed with rev12 below. Here is the more efficient version (still 16 operations):

```
unsigned rev11a(unsigned x) {
    unsigned t;
    x = x | ((x & 0x000000FF) << 16);
    t = x & 0x0F0F0F0F; x = (t << 8) | (t ^ x);
    t = x & 0x33333333; x = (t << 4) | (t ^ x);
    t = x & 0x55555555; x = (t << 2) | (t ^ x);
    x = x >> 15;
    return x;
}
```

Reversing bits in a word using rotate shifts and the "and not" instruction. 17 operations (25 full RISC instructions). 15 cycles on a machine with sufficient parallelism:

```
unsigned rev12(unsigned x) {
    x = shlr(x & 0x00FF00FF, 16) | x & ~0x00FF00FF;
    x = shlr(x & 0x0F0F0F0F,  8) | x & ~0x0F0F0F0F;
    x = shlr(x & 0x33333333,  4) | x & ~0x33333333;
    x = shlr(x & 0x55555555,  2) | x & ~0x55555555;
    x = shlr(x, 1);
    return x;
}
```

The "and not" operation can be avoided by using the 3-instruction method of doing the MUX operation, i.e.,
$(x \,\&\, m) \mid (y \,\&\, \sim m) = ((x \wedge y) \,\&\, m) \wedge y$
Rewriting the first line above as

8.3. Rearranging Algorithms

```
x = shlr(x, 16) & 0x00FF00FF | x & ~0x00FF00FF;
```

it can be changed to

```
x = ((shlr(x, 16) ^ x) & 0x00FF00FF) ^ x;
```

This gives the function below (17 operations, 25 full RISC instructions):

```
unsigned rev12a(unsigned x) {
    x = ((shlr(x, 16) ^ x) & 0x00FF00FF) ^ x;
    x = ((shlr(x,  8) ^ x) & 0x0F0F0F0F) ^ x;
    x = ((shlr(x,  4) ^ x) & 0x33333333) ^ x;
    x = ((shlr(x,  2) ^ x) & 0x55555555) ^ x;
    x = shlr(x, 1);
    return x;
}
```

The "and not" can also be avoided by using the identity

```
x & ~m = (x & m) ^ x
```

to change

```
x = shlr(x & 0x00FF00FF, 16) | x & ~0x00FF00FF;
```

to the first executable line in the function below.[1] 17 operations (25 full RISC instructions). This is slightly preferable to rev12a for many machines because it has a little instruction-level parallelism in each of the four steps, whereas rev12a has none. 15 cycles on a machine with sufficient parallelism:

```
unsigned rev12b(unsigned x) {
    unsigned t;
    t = x & 0x00FF00FF; x = shlr(t, 16) | (t ^ x);
    t = x & 0x0F0F0F0F; x = shlr(t,  8) | (t ^ x);
    t = x & 0x33333333; x = shlr(t,  4) | (t ^ x);
    t = x & 0x55555555; x = shlr(t,  2) | (t ^ x);
    x = shlr(x, 1);
    return x;
}
```

8.3.2 Bit Shuffling

There are two varieties, called the "outer" and "inner" perfect shuffles. They both interleave the bits in the two halves of a word in a manner similar to a perfect shuffle of a deck of 32 cards, but they differ in which card is allowed to fall first. In the outer perfect shuffle, the outer (end) bits remain in the outer positions, and in the inner perfect shuffle, bit 15 moves to the left end of the word (position 31). If the 32-bit word is (where each letter denotes a single bit):

```
abcd efgh ijkl mnop ABCD EFGH IJKL MNOP
```

then after the outer perfect shuffle it is:

---

[1] Vesa Karvonen, The Assembly Gems Page, http://www.df.lth.se/john_e/fr_gems.html.

8.3. Rearranging Algorithms

```
aAbB cCdD eEfF gGhH iIjJ kKlL mMnN oOpP
```

and after the inner perfect shuffle it is:
AaBb CcDd EeFf GgHh IiJj KkLl MmNn OoPp

Assume the word size W is a power of 2. Then the outer perfect shuffle operation can be accomplished with basic RISC instructions in $log_2\left(\frac{W}{2}\right)$ steps, where each step swaps the second and third quartiles of successively smaller pieces. That is, a 32-bit word is transformed as follows:

```
abcd efgh ijkl mnop ABCD EFGH IJKL MNOP
abcd efgh ABCD EFGH ijkl mnop IJKL MNOP
abcd ABCD efgh EFGH ijkl IJKL mnop MNOP
abAB cdCD efEF ghGH ijIJ klKL mnMN opOP
aAbB cCdD eEfF gGhH iIjJ kKlL mMnN oOpP
```

```
1 unsigned shuffle1(unsigned x) {
2   x = (x & 0x0000FF00) << 8 | (x >> 8) & 0x0000FF00 | x
        & 0xFF0000FF;
3   x = (x & 0x00F000F0) << 4 | (x >> 4) & 0x00F000F0 | x
        & 0xF00FF00F;
4   x = (x & 0x0C0C0C0C) << 2 | (x >> 2) & 0x0C0C0C0C | x
        & 0xC3C3C3C3;
5   x = (x & 0x22222222) << 1 | (x >> 1) & 0x22222222 | x
        & 0x99999999;
6
7   return x;
8 }
```

which requires 42 basic RISC instructions. This can be reduced to 30 instructions, although at an increase from 17 to 21 cycles on a machine with unlimited instruction-level parallelism, by using the exclusive or method of exchanging two fields of a register. All quantities are unsigned:

```
1  unsigned shuffle2(unsigned x) {
2    unsigned t;
3
4    t = (x ^ (x >> 8)) & 0x0000FF00;   x = x ^ t ^ (t << 8)
       ;
5    t = (x ^ (x >> 4)) & 0x00F000F0;   x = x ^ t ^ (t << 4)
       ;
6    t = (x ^ (x >> 2)) & 0x0C0C0C0C;   x = x ^ t ^ (t << 2)
       ;
7    t = (x ^ (x >> 1)) & 0x22222222;   x = x ^ t ^ (t << 1)
       ;
8
9    return x;
10 }
```

The inverse operation, the outer unshuffle, is easily accomplished by performing the swaps in reverse order:

```
1  unsigned unshuffle(unsigned x) {
2    unsigned t;
3
4    t = (x ^ (x >> 1)) & 0x22222222;   x = x ^ t ^ (t << 1)
       ;
```

8.3. Rearranging Algorithms

```
5    t = (x ^ (x >> 2)) & 0x0C0C0C0C;   x = x ^ t ^ (t << 2)
        ;
6    t = (x ^ (x >> 4)) & 0x00F000F0;   x = x ^ t ^ (t << 4)
        ;
7    t = (x ^ (x >> 8)) & 0x0000FF00;   x = x ^ t ^ (t << 8)
        ;
8
9    return x;
10 }
```

Using only the last two steps of either of the above two shuffle sequences shuffles the bits of each byte separately. Using only the last three steps shuffles the bits of each halfword separately, and so on. Similar remarks apply to unshuffling, except by using the first two or three steps.

To get the inner perfect shuffle, prepend to these sequences a step to swap the left and right halves of the register:

```
1 x = (x >> 16) | (x << 16);
```

Half shuffle (i.e., move the bits from the right halfword to the even positions) derived as a simplification of shuffle2 (22 or 23 RISC instructions, 12 cycles):

```
1 unsigned halfshuffle1(unsigned x) {
2     unsigned t;
3     x = x & 0x0000FFFF;              // (If required.)
4     t = x & 0x0000FF00;   x = x ^ t ^ (t << 8);
5     t = x & 0x00F000F0;   x = x ^ t ^ (t << 4);
6     t = x & 0x0C0C0C0C;   x = x ^ t ^ (t << 2);
7     t = x & 0x22222222;   x = x ^ t ^ (t << 1);
8     return x;
9 }
```

Half shuffle coded from scratch (19 RISC instructions, 12 cycles):

```
1 unsigned halfshuffle2(unsigned x) {
2     x = ((x & 0xFF00) << 8) | (x & 0x00FF);
3     x = ((x << 4) | x) & 0x0F0F0F0F;
4     x = ((x << 2) | x) & 0x33333333;
5     x = ((x << 1) | x) & 0x55555555;
6     return x;
7 }
```

Half unshuffle (i.e., move the bits from the even positions to the right halfword) derived as a simplification of unshuffle (26 or 29 instructions, 17 or 19 cycles):

```
1 unsigned halfunshuffle1(unsigned x) {
2     unsigned t;
3     x = x & 0x55555555;              // (If required.)
4     t = (x >> 1) & 0x22222222;   x = x ^ t ^ (t << 1);
5     t = (x >> 2) & 0x0C0C0C0C;   x = x ^ t ^ (t << 2);
6     t = (x >> 4) & 0x00F000F0;   x = x ^ t ^ (t << 4);
7     t = (x >> 8) & 0x0000FF00;   x = x ^ t ^ (t << 8);
8     return x;
9 }
```

Half unshuffle coded from scratch (18 or 21 RISC instructions, 12 or 15 cycles:

```
unsigned halfunshuffle2(unsigned x) {
    x = x & 0x55555555;           // (If required.)
    x = ((x >> 1) | x) & 0x33333333;
    x = ((x >> 2) | x) & 0x0F0F0F0F;
    x = ((x >> 4) | x) & 0x00FF00FF;
    x = ((x >> 8) | x) & 0x0000FFFF;
    return x;
}
```

8.4 Computing Functions

8.4.1 Integer Square Root

By the "integer square root" function, we mean the function $\lfloor \sqrt{x} \rfloor$. To extend its range of application and to avoid deciding what to do with a negative argument, we assume x is unsigned. Thus, $0 \leq x \leq 2^{32} - 1$.

8.4.1.1 Newton's Method

For floating-point numbers, the square root is almost universally computed by Newton's method. This method begins by somehow obtaining a starting estimate g_0 of $\sqrt{a}$. Then, a series of more accurate estimates is obtained from:

$$g_{n+1} = \frac{\left(g_n + \frac{a}{g_n}\right)}{2}$$

The iteration converges quadratically, that is, if at some point g_n is accurate to n bits, then g_{n+1} is accurate to 2n bits. The program must have some means of knowing when it has iterated enough so it can terminate.

It is a pleasant surprise that Newton's method works fine in the domain of integers. To see this, we need the following theorem:

Theorem 2 Let $g_{n+1} = \left\lfloor \frac{\left(g_n + \lfloor \frac{a}{g_n} \rfloor\right)}{2} \right\rfloor$, with g_n, a integers greater than 0. Then

a) if $g_n > \lfloor \sqrt{a} \rfloor$ then $\lfloor \sqrt{a} \rfloor \leq g_{n+1} < g_n$, and

b) if $g_n = \lfloor \sqrt{a} \rfloor$ then $\lfloor \sqrt{a} \rfloor \leq g_{n+1} \leq \lfloor \sqrt{a} \rfloor + 1$

That is, if we have an integral guess g_n to $\lfloor \sqrt{a} \rfloor$ that is too high, then the next guess $g_n + 1$ will be strictly less than the preceding one, but not less than $\lfloor \sqrt{a} \rfloor$. Therefore, if we start with a guess that's too high, the sequence converges monotonically. If the guess $g_n = \lfloor \sqrt{a} \rfloor$, then the next guess is either equal to g_n or is 1 larger. This provides an easy way to determine when the sequence has converged: If we start with $g_0 \geq \lfloor \sqrt{a} \rfloor$, convergence has occurred when $g_{n+1} \geq g_n$, and then the result is precisely g_n.

The case $a = 0$ must be treated specially, because this procedure would lead to dividing 0 by 0.

The difficult part of using Newton's method to calculate $\lfloor \sqrt{x} \rfloor$ is getting the first guess. Program 8.14 sets the first guess g_0 equal to the least power of 2 that is greater than or equal to For example, for $x = 4, g_0 = 2$, and for $x = 5, g_0 = 4$.

Program 8.14: *Integer Square Root : Newton's Method*

```
int isqrt1(unsigned x) {
```

8.4. Computing Functions

```
 2     unsigned x1;
 3     int s, g0, g1;
 4
 5     if (x <= 1) return x;
 6     s = 1;
 7     x1 = x - 1;
 8     if (x1 > 65535) {s = s + 8; x1 = x1 >> 16;}
 9     if (x1 >   255) {s = s + 4; x1 = x1 >>  8;}
10     if (x1 >    15) {s = s + 2; x1 = x1 >>  4;}
11     if (x1 >     3) {s = s + 1;}
12
13     g0 = 1 << s;                  // g0 = 2**s.
14     g1 = (g0 + (x >> s)) >> 1;    // g1 = (g0 + x/g0)/2.
15
16     while (g1 < g0) {             // Do while approximations
17        g0 = g1;                   // strictly decrease.
18        g1 = (g0 + (x/g0)) >> 1;
19     }
20     return g0;
21  }
```

Because the first guess g_0 is a power of 2, it is not necessary to do a real division to get g_1; instead, a shift right suffices. Because the first guess is accurate to about one bit, and Newton's method converges quadratically (the number of bits of accuracy doubles with each iteration), one would expect the program to converge within about five iterations (on a 32-bit machine), which requires four divisions (because the first iteration substitutes a shift right). An exhaustive experiment reveals that the maximum number of divisions is five, or four for arguments up to 16,785,407.

If *number of leading zeros* is available, then getting the first guess is very simple: Replace the first seven executable lines in the program above with:

```
1 if (x <= 1) return x;
2 s = 16 - nlz(x - 1)/2;
```

Another alternative, if number of leading zeros is not available, is to compute s by means of a binary search tree. This method permits getting a slightly better value of g_0: the least power of 2 that is greater than or equal to $\lfloor\sqrt{x}\rfloor$. For some values of x, this gives a smaller value of g_0, but a value large enough so that the convergence criterion of the theorem still holds.

Program 8.15: *Integer square root : binary search for first guess*

```
 1 int isqrt2(unsigned x) {
 2    int s, g0, g1;
 3
 4    if (x <= 4224)
 5       if (x <= 24)
 6          if (x <= 3) return (x + 3) >> 2;
 7          else if (x <= 8) return 2;
 8          else return (x >> 4) + 3;
 9       else if (x <= 288)
10          if (x <= 80) s = 3; else s = 4;
11       else if (x <= 1088) s = 5; else s = 6;
12    else if (x <= 1025*1025 - 1)
13       if (x <= 257*257 - 1)
14          if (x <= 129*129 - 1) s = 7; else s = 8;
15       else if (x <= 513*513 - 1) s = 9; else s = 10;
16    else if (x <= 4097*4097 - 1)
```

8.4. Computing Functions

```
17        if (x <= 2049*2049 - 1) s = 11; else s = 12;
18     else if (x <= 16385*16385 - 1)
19        if (x <= 8193*8193 - 1) s = 13; else s = 14;
20     else if (x <= 32769*32769 - 1) s = 15; else s = 16;
21     g0 = 1 << s;                    // g0 = 2**s.
22
23     // Continue as in the previous program.
24     g1 = (g0 + (x >> s)) >> 1;      // g1 = (g0 + x/g0)/2.
25
26     while (g1 < g0) {               // Do while approximations
27        g0 = g1;                     // strictly decrease.
28        g1 = (g0 + (x/g0)) >> 1;
29     }
30     return g0;
31  }
```

Because the algorithms based on Newton's method start out with a sort of binary search to obtain the first guess, why not do the whole computation with a binary search? This method would start out with two bounds, perhaps initialized to 0 and 2^{16}. It would make a guess at the midpoint of the bounds. If the square of the midpoint is greater than the argument x, then the upper bound is changed to be equal to the midpoint. If the square of the midpoint is less than the argument x, then the lower bound is changed to be equal to the midpoint. The process ends when the upper and lower bounds differ by 1, and the result is the lower bound.

Program 8.16: *Integer square root : simple binary search*

```
1  int isqrt3(unsigned x) {
2     unsigned a, b, m;               // Limits and midpoint.
3
4     a = 1;
5     b = (x >> 5) + 8;               // See text.
6     if (b > 65535) b = 65535;
7     do {
8        m = (a + b) >> 1;
9        if (m*m > x) b = m - 1;
10       else        a = m + 1;
11    } while (b >= a);
12    return a - 1;
13 }
```

The execution time of the program 8.16 is about $6 + (M + 7.5)n$, where M is the multiplication time in cycles and n is the number of times the loop is executed.

8.4.2 Integer Exponentiation : Compute x^n

A well-known technique for computing x^n, when n is a nonnegative integer, involves the binary representation of n. The technique applies to the evaluation of an expression of the form $x \cdot x \cdot x \cdot \ldots \cdot x$ where $\cdot$ is any associative operation, such as addition, multiplication including matrix multiplication, and string concatenation (as suggested by the notation $(`ab`)^3 = `ababab`$). As an example, suppose we wish to compute $y = x^{13}$. Because 13 expressed in binary is 1101 (that is, $13 = 8 + 4 + 1$), $x^{13} = x^{8+4+1} = x^8 \cdot x^4 \cdot x^1$.

Thus, x^{13} can be computed as follows:
$t_1 \leftarrow x^2$

8.5. Miscellaneous

$$t_2 \leftarrow t_1^2$$
$$t_3 \leftarrow t_2^2$$
$$y \leftarrow t_3 \cdot t_2 \cdot x$$

This requires five multiplications, considerably fewer than the 12 that would be required by repeated multiplication by x. If the exponent is a variable, known to be a nonnegative integer, the technique can be employed in a subroutine, as shown in Program 8.17.

Program 8.17: **Computing x^n by binary decomposition of n**

```
1  int iexp(int x, unsigned n) {
2    int p, y;
3
4    y = 1;                    // Initialize result
5    p = x;                    // and p.
6    while(1) {
7      if (n & 1) y = p*y;     // If n is odd, mult by p.
8      n = n >> 1;             // Position next bit of n.
9      if (n == 0) return y;   // If no more bits in n.
10     p = p*p;                // Power for next bit of n.
11   }
12 }
```

The number of multiplications done by this method is, for exponent $n \geq 1$, $\lfloor \log_2 n \rfloor + nbits(n) - 1$. This is not always the minimal number of multiplications. For example, for n = 27, the binary decomposition method computes $x^{16} \cdot x^8 \cdot x^2 \cdot x^1$, which requires seven multiplications. However, the scheme illustrated by $((x^3)^3)^3$ requires only six. The smallest number for which the binary decomposition method is not optimal is n = 15 (because $x^{15} = (x^3)^5$).

The binary decomposition method has a variant that scans the binary representation of the exponent in left-to-right order, which is analogous to the left-to-right method of converting binary to decimal. Initialize the result y to 1, and scan the exponent from left to right. When a 0 is encountered, square y. When a 1 is encountered, square y and multiply it by x. This computes $x^{13} = x^{1101_2}$ as $(((1^2 \cdot x)^2 \cdot x)^2)^2 \cdot x$. It always requires the same number of (nontrivial) multiplications as the right-to-left method of Program 8.17.

8.5 Miscellaneous

Question : Is the correct integer fourth root of an integer x obtained by computing the integer square root of the integer square root of x? That is, does: $\lfloor \sqrt{\lfloor \sqrt{x} \rfloor} \rfloor = \lfloor \sqrt[4]{x} \rfloor$?

> **Answer** : Yes. The result is correct in spite of the double truncation. Suppose $\lfloor \sqrt{x} \rfloor = a$. Then by the definition of this operation, a is an integer such that $a^2 \leq x$ and $(a+1)^2 < x$.
>
> Let $\lfloor \sqrt{a} \rfloor = b$. Then $b^2 \leq a$ and $(b+1)^2 < a$.
> Thus, $b^4 \leq a^2$ and, because $a^2 \leq x, b^4 \leq x$.
>
> Because $(b+1)^2 < a$, $(b+1)^2 \geq a+1$, so that $(b+1)^4 \geq (a+1)^2$ Because $(a+1)^2 < x$, $(b+1)^4 > x$. Hence b is the integer fourth root of x.

8.5. Miscellaneous

Question: *How many multiplications does it take to compute x^{23} (modulo 2^W, where W is the computer's word size)?*

Answer: Six. The binary decomposition method, based on $x^{23} = x^{16} \cdot x^4 \cdot x^2 \cdot x$, takes seven. Factoring x^{23} as $(x^{11})^2 \cdot x$ or as $((x^5)^2 \cdot x)^2 \cdot x$ also takes seven. But computing powers of x in the order $x^2, x^3, x^5, x^{10}, x^{13}, x^{23}$, in which each term is a product of two previous terms or of x, does it in six multiplications.

Question: *Show that for real x, $\lfloor x \rfloor = -\lceil -x \rceil$.*

Answer: Let $x = x_0 + \delta$, where x_0 is an integer and $0 \leq \delta < 1$. Then $\lceil -x \rceil = \lceil -x_0 - \delta \rceil = -x_0$ by the definition of the ceiling function as the next integer greater than or equal to its argument. Hence $-\lceil -x \rceil = x_0$ which is $\lfloor x \rfloor$.

Question: *How would you compute $\lceil \frac{n}{d} \rceil$ for unsigned integers n and d, $0 \leq n \leq 2^{32} - 1$ and $1 \leq d \leq 2^{32} - 1$? Assume your machine has an unsigned divide instruction that computes $\lfloor \frac{n}{d} \rfloor$.*

Answer: The usual method, most likely, is to compute $\lfloor \frac{(n+d-1)}{d} \rfloor$. The problem is that $n + d - 1$ can overflow. (Consider computing $\lceil \frac{12}{5} \rceil$ on a 4-bit machine.)

Another standard method is to compute $q = \lfloor \frac{n}{d} \rfloor$ using the machine's *divide* instruction, then compute the remainder as $r = n - qd$, and if r is nonzero, add 1 to q. (Alternatively, add 1 if $n \neq qd$.) This gives the correct result for all n and $d \neq 0$, but it is somewhat expensive because of the multiply, subtract, and conditional add of 1. On the other hand, if your machine's *divide* instruction gives the remainder as a by-product, and especially if it has an efficient way to do the computation $q = q + (r \neq 0)$, then this is a good way to do it.

Still another way is to compute $q = \lfloor \frac{(n-1)}{d} \rfloor + 1$. Unfortunately, this fails for n = 0. It can be fixed if the machine has a simple way to compute the $x \neq 0$ predicate, such as by means of a *compare* instruction that sets the target GPR to the integer 1 or 0. Then one can compute:

$$c \leftarrow (x \neq 0)$$
$$q \leftarrow \lfloor \frac{(n-c)}{d} \rfloor + c$$

Lastly, one can compute $q = \lfloor \frac{(n-1)}{d} \rfloor + 1$ and then change the result to 0 if n = 0, by means of a conditional move or select instruction, for example.

8.5.1 LRU Algorithm : Reference Matrix

Ever wonder how your computer keeps track of which cache line is the least recently used? Here we describe one such algorithm, known as the *reference matrix* method. It is primarily a hardware algorithm, but it might have

8.5. Miscellaneous

application in software. We won't go into a long discussion of the intriguing world of caches, but only say that we have in mind the high-speed caches that buffer data between a computer's main memory and the processor. These caches may get a request for a word every computer cycle, and they should usually respond with the data within a cycle or two, so there is not much time for a complicated algorithm.

A cache contains a copy of a subset of the data in main memory, and the problem we are addressing is: when a cache miss occurs (that is, when a word at a certain address is requested and the data at that address are not in the cache), how does the computer decide which block (or line, in cache jargon) to replace with the requested data? Ideally, it should replace the data in the line that will not be referenced for the longest time in the future. But we cannot know the future, so we have to guess. The best guess over a wide variety of application programs seems to be the *least recently used* (LRU) policy. This policy replaces the line that has not been referenced for the longest time.

Caches come in three varieties:

1. direct-mapped,
2. fully associative, and
3. set-associative.

In a direct-mapped cache, certain bits of the address of the load or store instruction directly address a particular cache line. When a miss occurs, there is no question as to what line to replace: it must be the addressed line. There is no need for an LRU or any other guessing policy.

In a fully associative cache, a block from main memory can be placed in any cache line. When a load or store is executed, the address is looked up to see if it is in the cache. If not, it is necessary to replace the contents of some line. The machine has complete flexibility in the choice of line to replace. Several strategies have been used (FIFO, random, and LRU are the most common) and, as mentioned above, LRU seems to be the one that most often results in the lowest miss rate. Unfortunately, LRU is the most expensive to implement when there are many lines to consider for replacement. Often the set-associative organization is chosen. It is a compromise between direct-mapped and fully associative. The designer decides on the degree of associativity, which is usually 2, 4, 8, or 16. The cache is divided into a number of "sets," each of which contains 2, 4, 8, or 16 lines (typically). The set is directly addressed, using certain bits of the load or store address, but the line within the set must be looked up. The lookup in the set is done much the same as in the case of a fully associative cache. Now, when it is necessary to replace a line, the LRU algorithm need only determine which of the lines within one set is the least recently used, and replace that.

With this brief background, we can describe the reference matrix method. To illustrate, assume the cache is four-way set-associative. This means that there are four lines for which we wish to keep track of the least recently used (referenced). The cache may be fully associative and consist of only four lines, or it may be set-associative with four lines per set.

The reference matrix method employs a square bit matrix of dimension equal to the degree of associativity (in principle; we will modify this statement later). Each associative set has one such matrix. The essence of the method is that when line i is referenced, row i of the matrix is set to 1's, and then column i is set to 0's. Figure 8.5.1 illustrates the changes in the matrix from an initial state to its configuration after a reference to lines 3, 1, 0, 2, 0, 3, and 2, in that order.

	Init	3	1	0	2	0	3	2
	0123	0123	0123	0123	0123	0123	0123	0123
Line 0	0111	0110	0010	0111	0101	0111	0110	0100
Line 1	0011	0010	1011	0011	0001	0001	0000	0000
Line 2	0001	0000	0000	0000	1101	0101	0100	1101
Line 3	0000	1110	1010	0010	0000	0000	1110	1100

Each matrix has a row containing three 1's, two 1's, one 1, and no 1's. The number of the row with no 1's is the least recently used line. The number of the row with one 1 is the next least recently used line, and so on. When a cache miss occurs, the machine finds the row with all 0's and replaces the corresponding line. It then records it as the most recently used line by setting its row to all 1's and its column to all 0's.

Why does this work? Denoting the matrix by M, the reason it works is that M_{ij} indicates whether or not line i is more recently used than line j. If $M_{ij} = 1$, line i is more recently used than line j, and if $M_{ij} = 0$, line i is not more recently used than line j.

Consider an arbitrary 4 × 4 matrix for which line 2 is referenced. Then the matrix changes as shown in Figure 8.5.1.

	Init	2
	0123	0123
Line 0	abcd	ab0d
Line 1	efgh	ef0h
Line 2	ijkl	1101
Line 3	mnop	mn0p

Setting row i to 1's (except for the element on the main diagonal) is recording that line i is more recently used than line $j, \forall j \neq i$. Setting column i to 0's is recording that line j is not more recently used than line i, for all j. Relations among cache lines other than i are not changed. When all the lines have been referenced, all the "more recently used" relations will be established.

Thus, the reference matrix is antisymmetric and the main diagonal is always all 0's. Therefore, only part of the matrix, either the elements above the main diagonal or those below the main diagonal, need be stored in the cache. That is what is done in practice. For an n-way associative set, $\frac{n(n-1)}{2}$ memory bits are required. For n = 4, this is six; for n = 8, it is 28. Twenty-eight is getting to be a bit large, so the reference matrix method, and in fact the true LRU policy, is not often used for degrees of associativity greater than 8. Instead, there are approximate LRU methods and methods that are not LRU at all.

In software, the LRU policy would probably be implemented with a list of the line numbers (either a simple vector or a linked list). When line i is referenced, the list is searched for i, and then i is moved to the top of the list. The least recently used line number then migrates to the bottom of the list. That method is relatively slow on references (because of rearranging the list),

8.5. Miscellaneous

but fast in deciding which line to replace. Another method, with the opposite speed characteristics, is to have a vector of length equal to the degree of associativity, with position i holding both the address that line i holds and its "age" (actually "newness") encoded as an integer. When line i is referenced, a single variable that holds the current "age" is incremented, and the resulting value is stored in the vector at position i. To find the least recently used line, the vector is searched for the line with the smallest value of "age." This method fails if the "age" integer overflows.

There might be one "age" integer per associative set, or only one for the whole cache, or in hardware a cycle counter could be used.

The reference matrix method might be useful in software when the degree of associativity is small. For example, suppose an application uses eight-way set-associativity and is to run on a 64-bit machine. Then the reference matrix can be stored in a single 64-bit register. Let the low-order eight bits of the register hold row 0 of the matrix, the next eight bits hold row 1, and so forth. Then when line i is referenced, byte i of the register should be set to 1's, and bits i, i + 8, ..., i + 56 should be cleared. Denoting the register by m, this is accomplished as shown here:

$$m \leftarrow m \mid (0xFF \ll (8*i))$$
$$m \leftarrow m \;\&\; \sim(0x0101010101010101 \ll i)$$

This amounts to five or six instructions, plus a few to load constants. To find the least recently used line, search for an all-zero byte. The advantage of this method over the other software methods briefly outlined above is that all the work is done in a register.

Question : *For an n-way set-associative cache, what is the theoretical minimum number of bits required to implement the LRU policy? Compare that to the number of bits required for the reference matrix method, for a few small values of n.*

Answer : Any true LRU algorithm must record the complete order of references to the n cache lines in a set. Since there are n! orderings of n things, any implementation of LRU must use at least $\lceil \log_2 n! \rceil$ memory bits. The table below compares this to the number of bits required by the reference matrix method:

Degree of Associativity	Theoretical Minimum	Reference Matrix Method
2	1	1
4	5	6
8	16	28
16	45	120
32	118	496

8.5.2 Find Shortest String of 1-Bits

Mark the beginnings of all strings of 1's in a word b and the ends of all such strings in a word e. Then, if $b\;\&\;e$ is nonzero, the shortest string is of length 1. Otherwise, shift e left one position and test again. For example, if

8.5. Miscellaneous

> x = 0011 1111 1111 0011 1111 0011 1111 1000

then

> b = 0010 0000 0000 0010 0000 0010 0000 0000
> e = 0000 0000 0001 0000 0001 0000 0000 1000

After shifting e left five places, $b \mathbin{\&} e$ is nonzero. This means that the shortest string of 1-bits is of length 6.

The function below finds the length and position of the shortest contiguous string of 1's in a word. The position is the distance of the leftmost bit of the string, from the left end of the string, or 32 if x = 0. If two or more contiguous strings are the same length, this function finds the leftmost one.

Example: For x = 0x00FF0FF0 it returns length 8, position 8.

Executes in $8 + 4n$ instructions on the basic RISC (w/o andc), plus the time for the nlz function, for $n \geq 2$, where n is the length of the shortest contiguous string of 1's in x.

```
int nlz(unsigned x) {
    int n;

    if (x == 0) return(32);
    n = 0;
    if (x <= 0x0000FFFF) {n = n +16; x = x <<16;}
    if (x <= 0x00FFFFFF) {n = n + 8; x = x << 8;}
    if (x <= 0x0FFFFFFF) {n = n + 4; x = x << 4;}
    if (x <= 0x3FFFFFFF) {n = n + 2; x = x << 2;}
    if (x <= 0x7FFFFFFF) {n = n + 1;}
    return n;
}

int fminstr1(unsigned x, int *apos) {
    int k;
    unsigned b, e;        // Beginnings, ends.

    if (x == 0) {*apos = 32; return 0;}
    b = ~(x >> 1) & x;    // 0-1 transitions.
    e = x & ~(x << 1);    // 1-0 transitions.
    for (k = 1; (b & e) == 0; k++)
        e = e << 1;
    *apos = nlz(b & e);
    return k;
}
```

Perhaps the ultimate problem in this class is to find the length and position of the shortest string of 1's in x that is at least as long as a given integer n > 0. In terms of the storage allocation problem, this is a "best fit" algorithm. This can be done by first left-propagating the 0's in x by $n - 1$ positions and then finding the shortest string of 1's in the revised x.

The function *fminstr11* performs the same functions as *fminstr1*. It might be useful is your machine has population count as an instruction. The loop is executed a number of times equal to the number of contiguous strings of 1-bits in x.

8.5. Miscellaneous

Executes in $5 + 11n$ instructions on the full RISC, where n is the number of strings of 1's in x, for $n \geq 1$ (that is, for x != 0). This assumes the if-test goes either way half the time, and that *pop* and *nlz* count as one instruction each.

If "(k <= kmin)" is changed to "(k < kmin)", it finds the RIGHTmost shortest contiguous string of 1's, when two or more such strings are the same length.

If that expression is changed to "(k >= kmin)" and the initialization of kmin is changed to "kmin = 0;", it finds the leftmost LONGEST contiguous string of 1's. And if the comparison is changed to ">" and the initialization of kmin is changed to "kmin = -1;", it finds the rightmost longest contiguous string of 1's.

The code is also easily modified to compute the "bestfit" function:

```
int pop(unsigned x) {
   x = x - ((x >> 1) & 0x55555555);
   x = (x & 0x33333333) + ((x >> 2) & 0x33333333);
   x = (x + (x >> 4)) & 0x0F0F0F0F;
   x = x + (x >> 8);
   x = x + (x >> 16);
   return x & 0x0000003F;
}


int fminstr11(unsigned x, int *apos) {
   int k, kmin, y0, y;
   unsigned int x0, xmin;

   kmin = 32;
   y0 = pop(x);
   x0 = x;
   do {
      x = ((x & -x) + x) & x;     // Turn off rightmost
      y = pop(x);                 // string.
      k = y0 - y;                 // k = length of string
      if (k <= kmin) {            // turned off.
         kmin = k;                // Save shortest length
         xmin = x;                // found, and the string.
      }
      y0 = y;
   } while (x != 0);
   *apos = nlz(x0 ^ xmin);
   return kmin;
}
```

The function *bestfit* finds the length and position of the shortest string of 1's in x that is of length n or more, for $n \geq 1$. If such a string does not exist, it returns with apos = 32 and the length undefined (actually, the returned value is n - 1):

```
int bestfit(unsigned x, int n, int *apos) {
   int m, s;

   m = n;
   while (m > 1) {
      s = m >> 1;
      x = x & (x << s);
      m = m - s;
   }
   return fminstr1(x, apos) + n - 1;
```

11 }

The function *bestfit1* finds the length and position of the shortest string of 1's in x that is of length n or more, for $n \geq 0$. If such a string does not exist, it returns with apos = 32 and the length undefined (actually, the returned value is 32). This is a simple modification of *fminstr11*:

```
int bestfit1(unsigned x, int n, int *apos) {
   int k, kmin, y0, y;
   unsigned int x0, xmin;

   kmin = 32;
   xmin = x;
   y0 = pop(x);
   x0 = x;
   do {
      x = ((x | (x - 1)) + 1) & x;    // Turn off
      y = pop(x);                      // rightmost string.
      k = y0 - y;                      // k = length of string
      if (k <= kmin && k >= n) {       // turned off.
         kmin = k;                     // Save shortest length
         xmin = x;                     // found, and the string.
      }
      y0 = y;
   } while (x != 0);
   *apos = nlz(x0 ^ xmin);
   return kmin;
}
```

Question : *For "completely random" 32-bit words x (each bit independently 0 or 1 with probability 0.5), what is the average number of strings of 1's in x?*

Answer : The first bit of x will be 1, and hence mark the beginning of a string of 1's, with probability 0.5. Any other bit marks the beginning of a string of 1's with probability 0.25 (it must be 1, and the bit to its left must be 0). Therefore the average number of strings of 1's is $0.5 + 31 \times 0.25 = 8.25$.

Question : *For "completely random" 32-bit words x, what is the average length of the shortest contiguous string of 1's in x? Compute this with a Monte Carlo or exhaustive enumeration program.*

Answer : One would expect the vast majority of words, if they are fairly long, to contain a string of 1's of length 1. For, if it begins with 10, or ends with 01, or contains the string 010, then its shortest contained string of 1's is of length 1. Therefore the average length is probably just slightly more than 1.

An exhaustive check of all 2^{32} words shows that the average length of the shortest string of 1's is approximately 1.011795..

8.5.3 Fibonacci words

A Fibonacci word is a word that does not contain two successive ones. Whether a given binary word is a Fibonacci word can be tested with the function:

8.5. Miscellaneous

```
static inline bool is_fibrep(ulong f)
// Return whether f is a valid Fibonacci representation
// i.e. whether it does not contain two adjacent ones
{
    return ( 0==(f&(f>>1)) );
}
```

The following functions convert between the binary and the Fibonacci representation:

```
static inline ulong bin2fibrep(ulong b)
// Return Fibonacci representation of b
// Limitation: the first Fibonacci number greater
//   than b must be representable as ulong.
// 32 bit:  b < 2971215073=F(47)  [F(48)=4807526976 > 2^32]
// 64 bit:  b < 12200160415121876738=F(93)  [F(94) > 2^64]
{
    ulong f0=1, f1=1, s=1;
    while ( f1<=b )  { ulong t = f0+f1;  f0=f1;  f1=t;  s <<=1; }
    ulong f = 0;
    while ( b )
    {
        s >>= 1;
        if ( b>=f0 )  { b -= f0;  f^=s; }
        { ulong t = f1-f0;  f1=f0;  f0=t; }
    }
    return f;
}
// ————————————————————

static inline ulong fibrep2bin(ulong f)
// Return binary representation of f
// Inverse of bin2fibrep().
{
    ulong f0=1, f1=1;
    ulong b = 0;
    while ( f )
    {
        if ( f&1 )  b += f1;
        { ulong t=f0+f1;  f0=f1;  f1=t; }
        f >>= 1;
    }
    return b;
}
```

The following functions generate next and previous Fibonacci representations:

```
static inline ulong next_fibrep(ulong x)
// With x the Fibonacci representation of n
// return Fibonacci representation of n+1.
{
    // 2 examples:           //  ex. 1                  //  ex.2
    //                       //  x == [*]0 010101       //  x ==
    //         [*]0 01010
```

8.5. Miscellaneous

```
 7      ulong y = x | (x>>1);      // y == [*]? 011111       // y == [*]? 01111
 8      ulong z = y + 1;           // z == [*]? 100000       // z == [*]? 10000
 9      z = z & -z;                // z == [0]0 100000       // z == [0]0 10000
10      x ^= z;                    // x == [*]0 110101       // x == [*]0 11010
11      x &= ~(z-1);               // x == [*]0 100000       // x == [*]0 10000
12
13      return x;
14  }
15  // ————————————————
16
17  static inline ulong prev_fibrep(ulong x)
18  // With x the Fibonacci representation of n
19  // return Fibonacci representation of n-1.
20  {
21  #if 1    // VERSION 3:   (DEFAULT, fastest)
22      // 2 examples:            // ex. 1                  // ex.2
23      //                        // x == [*]0 100000       // x == [*]0 10000
24      ulong y = x & -x;         // y == [0]0 100000       // y == [0]0 10000
25      x ^= y;                   // x == [*]0 000000       // x == [*]0 00000
26  #if BITS_PER_LONG == 64
27      ulong m = 0x5555555555555555UL;  // m == ...01010101
28  #else
29      ulong m = 0x55555555UL;   // m == ...01010101
30  #endif
31      if ( m & y )  m >>= 1;    // m == ...01010101       // m == ...0101010
32      m &= (y-1);               // m == [0]0 010101       // m == [0]0 01010
33      x ^= m;                   // x == [*]0 010101       // x == [*]0 01010
34      return x;
35  #endif   // ver 3
36
37  #if 0    // VERSION 2:
38      //                              x == [*]0 100000
39      ulong y = x & -x;         // y == [0]0 100000
40      x ^= y;                   // x == [*]0 000000
41      y >>= 1;                  // y == [0]0 010000
42      y |= (y>>2);              // y == [0]0 010100
43      y |= (y>>4);              // y == [0]0 010101
44      y |= (y>>8);
45      y |= (y>>16);
46  #if BITS_PER_LONG == 64
47      y |= (y>>32);
48  #endif
49      x ^= y;                   // x == [*]0 010101
50      return x;
51  #endif   // ver 2
52
```

8.5. Miscellaneous

```
53 #if 0   // VERSION 1:
54 //      if ( x&1 )  return   x ^ 1UL;
55      ulong i = lowest_one_idx(x);
56      x ^= (1UL<<i);
57      ++i;
58 #if BITS_PER_LONG == 64
59      x ^= (0x5555555555555555UL >> (BITS_PER_LONG-i));
60 #else
61      x ^= (0x55555555UL >> (BITS_PER_LONG-i));
62 #endif
63      return x;
64 #endif  // ver 1
65 }
```

8.5.4 Computation of Power of 2

8.5.4.1 Round to a known power of 2

Round Down to next smaller multiple Rounding an unsigned integer x down to, for example, the next smaller multiple of 8 can be achieved by

$$x \;\&\; -8$$

or

$$(x \gg 3) \ll 3$$

These work for signed integers as well, provided *round down* means to round in the negative direction. For example: $(-37) \;\&\; (-8) = -40$.

Round Up to next greater multiple An unsigned integer x can be rounded up to the next greater multiple of 8 by:

$$(x + 7) \;\&\; -8$$

or

$$x + (-x \;\&\; 7)$$

These expressions are correct for signed integers as well, provided *round up* means to round in the positive direction. The second term of the second expression is useful if we want to know how much you must add to x to make it a multiple of 8.

Round to nearest multiple To round a signed integer to the nearest multiple of 8 toward 0, we can combine the two expressions above in an obvious way:

8.5. Miscellaneous

```
t ← (x ≫ 31) & 7;
(x + t) & −8
```

An alternative for the first line is $t \leftarrow (x \gg 2) \gg 29$, which is useful if the machine lacks *and immediate*, or if the constant is too large for its immediate field.

Sometimes the rounding factor is given as the $\log_2$ of the alignment amount (e.g., a value of 3 means to round to a multiple of 8). In this case, code such as the following can be used, where $k = \log_2(\text{alignment amount})$:

round down:

```
x & ((−1) ≪ k)
(x ≫ k) ≪ k
```

round up

```
t ← (1 ≪ k) − 1; (x + t) & ~t
t ← (−1) ≪ k; (x − t − 1) & t
```

8.5.4.2 Round to Next Power of 2

We define two functions that are similar to floor and ceiling, but which are directed roundings to the closest integral power of 2, rather than to the closest integer. Mathematically, they are defined by:

$$flp2(x) = \begin{cases} \text{undefined}, & x < 0, \\ 0, & x = 0, \\ 2^{\lfloor \log_2 x \rfloor}, & \text{otherwise.} \end{cases} \quad (8.5)$$

$$clp2(x) = \begin{cases} \text{undefined}, & x < 0, \\ 0, & x = 0, \\ 2^{\lceil \log_2 x \rceil}, & \text{otherwise.} \end{cases} \quad (8.6)$$

The initial letters of the function names are intended to suggest *floor* and *ceiling*. Thus, $flp2(x)$ is the greatest power of 2 that is $\leq x$, and $clp2(x)$ is the least power of 2 that is $\geq x$. These definitions make sense even when x is not an integer. For example: $flp2(0.1) = 0.0625$. The functions satisfy several relations analogous to those involving floor and ceiling, such as those shown below, where n is an integer.

- $\lfloor x \rfloor = \lceil x \rceil$ if and only if x is an integer $\implies flp2(x) = clp2(x)$ if and only if x is a power of 2 or is 0
- $\lfloor x + n \rfloor = \lfloor x \rfloor + n \implies flp2(2^n x) = 2^n flp2(x)$
- $\lceil x \rceil = -\lfloor -x \rfloor \implies clp2(x) = \frac{1}{flp2(\frac{1}{x})}, x \neq 0$

8.5. Miscellaneous

x	flp2(x)	clp2(x)
0	0	0
1	1	1
2	2	2
3	2	4
4	4	4
5	4	8
$2^{31}-1$	2^{30}	2^{31}
2^{31}	2^{31}	2^{31}
$2^{31}+1$	2^{31}	0
$2^{32}-1$	2^{31}	0

These functions can be expressed in terms of each other as follows:

$$clp2(x) = \begin{cases} 2\text{flp2(x - 1)}, & x \neq 1, \\ \text{flp2(2x - 1)}, & 1 \leq x \leq 2^{31}. \end{cases} \quad (8.7)$$

$$flp2(x) = \begin{cases} \text{clp2(x / 2 + 1)}, & x \neq 0, \\ \text{clp2(x + 1) / 2}, & x < 2^{31}. \end{cases} \quad (8.8)$$

Rounding Down The following branch-free algorithm is based on right-propagating the leftmost 1-bit, and executes in 12 instructions:

Program 8.18: *Greatest power of 2 less than or equal to x, branch free*

```
#include <stdio.h>
/* Round down to a power of 2. */

unsigned flp2(unsigned x) {
    x = x | (x >> 1);
    x = x | (x >> 2);
    x = x | (x >> 4);
    x = x | (x >> 8);
    x = x | (x >>16);
    return x - (x >> 1);
}

int errors;
void main() {
    int i;
    static unsigned test[] = {0,0, 1,1, 2,2, 3,2, 4,4,
        5,4, 7,4, 8,8,
        9,8, 15,8, 16,16, 0xffff,0x8000, 0x7fffffff,0x40000000,
        0x80000000,0x80000000, 0x80000001,0x80000000,
        0xffffffff,0x80000000};
    void error(int x);

    for (i = 0; i < sizeof(test)/4; i += 2) {
        if (flp2(test[i]) != test[i+1]) error(test[i]);
    }
    if (errors == 0)
        printf("Passed all %d cases.\n", sizeof(test)/8);
}
```

8.5. Miscellaneous

```
29 void error(int x) {
30    errors = errors + 1;
31    printf("Error for x = %d, got %d\n", x, flp2(x));
32 }
```

The following two simple loops also compute the same:

```
1 y = 0x80000000;
2
3 while (y > x)
4    y = y >> 1;
5
6 return y;
```

The loop executes in $4nlz(x) + 3$ instructions.

All variables are unsigned integers. The loop keeps turning off the rightmost 1-bit of x until x = 0, and then returns the previous value of x.

```
1 do
2 {
3    y = x;
4    x = x & (x - 1);
5 } while(x != 0);
6
7 return y;
```

The loop, for $x \neq 0$, executes in $4pop(x)$ instructions, if the comparison to 0 is zero-cost.

Rounding Up The right-propagation trick yields a good algorithm for rounding up to the next power of 2. This algorithm is branch free and runs in 12 instructions.

Program 8.19: *Least power of 2 greater than or equal to x*

```
1 #include <stdio.h>
2 /* Round up to a power of 2. */
3
4 unsigned clp2(unsigned x) {
5    x = x - 1;
6    x = x | (x >> 1);
7    x = x | (x >> 2);
8    x = x | (x >> 4);
9    x = x | (x >> 8);
10   x = x | (x >>16);
11   return x + 1;
12 }
13
14 int errors;
15 void main() {
16    int i;
17    static unsigned test[] = {0,0, 1,1, 2,2, 3,4, 4,4,
         5,8, 7,8, 8,8,
18       9,16, 15,16, 16,16, 0xffff,0x10000, 0x7fffffff,0
         x80000000,
19       0x80000000,0x80000000, 0x80000001,0,
20       0xffffffff,0};
21    void error(int x);
22
23    for (i = 0; i < sizeof(test)/4; i += 2) {
24       if (clp2(test[i]) != test[i+1]) error(test[i]);
25    }
```

```
26    if (errors == 0)
27        printf("Passed all %d cases.\n", sizeof(test)/8);
28 }
29
30 void error(int x) {
31     errors = errors + 1;
32     printf("Error for x = %d, got %d\n", x, clp2(x));
33 }
```

Question : Show how to round an unsigned integer to the nearest multiple of 10, with the halfway case (a) rounding up, (b) rounding down, and (c) rounding up or down, whichever results in an even multiple of 10. Feel free to use division, remaindering, and multiplication instructions, and don't be concerned about values very close to the largest unsigned integer.

Answer : The standard way to do part (a) is $((x+5)/10) \times 10$. Part (b) is similar, but we need to replace the 5 with 4 in the answer for part (a). Part (c): We can use the fact that an integer is an odd multiple of 10 if and only if it is an odd multiple of 2.

```
1 r = x % 10;
2 y = x - r;
3 if (r > 5 | (r == 5 & (y & 2) != 0)
4     y = y + 10;
```

Alternatively for $x \leq 2^{32} - 6$:

```
1 r = (x + 5) % 10;
2 y = x + 5 - r;
3 if (r == 0 & (y & 2) != 0)
4     y = y - 10;
```

8.5.5 Efficient Multiplication by Constants

It is nearly a triviality that we can multiply by a constant with a sequence of shift left and add instructions. For example, to multiply x by 13 (binary 1101), we can code:

$$t_1 \leftarrow x \ll 2$$
$$t_2 \leftarrow x \ll 3$$
$$result \leftarrow t_1 + t_2 + x$$

So, $result \leftarrow 8x + 4x + x$.

Similarly, to multiply by 45(binary 101101):

$$t \leftarrow 4x$$
$$r \leftarrow x + t$$
$$t \leftarrow 2t$$
$$r \leftarrow r + t$$

8.5. Miscellaneous

$$t \leftarrow 4t$$
$$r \leftarrow r + t$$

It uses a variable t that holds x shifted left by a number of positions that corresponds to a 1-bit in the multiplier. Each shifted value is obtained from the one before it.

- It requires only one working register other than the input x and the output r.
- Except for the first two, it uses only 2-address instructions.
- The shift amounts are relatively small.

Alternatively:

$$t_1 \leftarrow 4x$$
$$t_2 \leftarrow 8x$$
$$t_3 \leftarrow 32x$$
$$r \leftarrow t_1 + x$$
$$t_3 \leftarrow t_3 + t_2$$
$$r \leftarrow r + t_3$$

It does all the shift's first, with x as the operand. It has the advantage of increased parallelism. On a machine with sufficient instruction-level parallelism, it executes in three cycles, whereas the previous logic running on a machine with unlimited parallelism, requires four.

The first improvement to the basic binary decomposition, $z \leftarrow x+(y \ll n))$, is to use subtract to shorten the sequence when the multiplier contains a group of three or more consecutive 1-bits. For example, to multiply by 28 (binary 11100), we can compute 32x – 4x (three instructions) rather than 16x + 8x + 4x (five instructions). On two's-complement machines, the result is correct (modulo 2^{32}) even if the intermediate result of 32x overflows.

To multiply by a constant m with the basic binary decomposition scheme (using only *shift*'s and *add*'s) requires

$$2pop(m) - 1 - \delta$$

instructions, where $\delta = 1$ if m ends in a 1-bit (is odd), and = 0 otherwise. If *subtract* is also used, it requires

$$4g(m) + 2s(m) - 1 - \delta$$

8.5. Miscellaneous

instructions, where g(m) is the number of groups of two or more consecutive 1-bits in m, s(m) is the number of "singleton" 1-bits in m, and δ has the same meaning as before.

The second improvement is to treat specially groups that are separated by a single 0-bit. For example, consider m = 55 (binary 110111). The group method calculates this as (64x − 16x) + (8x − x), which requires six instructions. Calculating it as 64x − 8x − x, however, requires only four. Similarly, we can multiply by binary 110111011 as illustrated by the formula 512x − 64x − 4x − x (six instructions).

The formulas above give an upper bound on the number of operations required to multiply a variable x by any given number m. Another bound can be obtained based on the size of m in bits, that is, on $n = \lfloor \log_2 m \rfloor + 1$.

Question : *Prove that Multiplication of a variable x by an n-bit constant m, m ≥ 1, can be accomplished with at most n instructions of the type add, subtract, and shift left by any given amount.*

Answer : We can apply induction on n. Multiplication by 1 can be done in 0 instructions, so the theorem holds for n = 1. For n > 1, if m ends in a 0-bit, then multiplication by m can be accomplished by multiplying by the number consisting of the left n − 1 bits of m (that is, by $\frac{m}{2}$), in n − 1 instructions, followed by a shift left of the result by one position. This uses n instructions altogether.

If m ends in binary 01, then mx can be calculated by multiplying x by the number consisting of the left n − 2 bits of m, in n − 2 instructions, followed by a left shift of the result by 2, and an add of x. This requires n instructions altogether.

If m ends in binary 11, then consider the cases in which it ends in 0011, 0111, 1011, and 1111. Let t be the result of multiplying x by the left n − 4 bits of m. If m ends in 0011, then mx = 16t + 2x + x, which requires (n − 4) + 4 = n instructions. If m ends in 0111, then mx = 16t + 8x − x, which requires n instructions. If m ends in 1111, then mx = 16t + 16x − x, which requires n instructions. The remaining case is that m ends in 1011.

It is easy to show that mx can be calculated in n instructions if m ends in 001011, 011011, or 111011. The remaining case is 101011.

This reasoning can be continued, with the "remaining case" always being of the form 101010...10101011. Eventually, the size of m will be reached, and the only remaining case is the number 101010...10101011. This n-bit number contains n / 2 + 1 1-bits. By a previous observation, it can multiply x with $2(\frac{n}{2} + 1) − 2 = n$ instructions.

Thus, in particular, multiplication by any 32-bit constant can be done in at most 32 instructions, by the method described above. By inspection, it is easily seen that for n even, the n-bit number 101010...101011 requires n instructions, and for n odd, the n-bit number 1010101...010110 also requires n instructions, so the bound is tight.

For example, consider again m = 45 (binary 101101). The methods described above require six instructions. Factoring 45 as 5 × 9, however, gives a four-instruction solution:

8.5. Miscellaneous

$$t \leftarrow 4x + x$$
$$result \leftarrow 8t + t$$

Factoring can be combined with the binary decomposition methods.

For example, multiplication by 106 (binary 1101010) requires seven instructions by binary decomposition, but writing it as $7 \times 15 + 1$ leads to a five-instruction solution.

For large constants, the smallest number of instructions that accomplish the multiplication may be substantially fewer than the number obtained by the simple binary decomposition methods described.

For example, m = 0xAAAAAAAB requires 32 instructions by binary decomposition, but writing this value as $2 \times 5 \times 17 \times 257 \times 65537 + 1$ gives a ten-instruction solution. (Ten instructions is probably not typical of large numbers. The factorization reflects the simple bit pattern of alternate 1's and 0's.)

Similarly to multiply a number by 7 using bitwise operator, we can first left shift the number by 3 bits (we will get 8n) then subtract the original number from the shifted number and return the difference (8n – n), i.e. $((n \ll 3) - n$.

So, given an integer value x and an integer or floating point value y, the value of $x \times y$ can be computed efficiently using a sequence derived from the binary value of x. For example, if x is 5 (4 + 1):

y2 = y + y;
y4 = y2 + y2;
result = y + y4;

In the special case that y is an integer, this can be done with shifts:

$y4 = (y \ll 2)$;
result = y + y4;

8.5.6 Bit-wise Rotation

The following function return word rotated r bits to the left, i.e., toward the most significant bit:

```
static inline unsigned long bit_rotate_left(ulong x,
    ulong r)
{
    return (x << r) | (x >> (BITS_PER_LONG - r));
}
```

where BITS_PER_LONG is 32 if long is 32bit, 64 if long is 64bit or 128 if long is 128bit.

Similarly, to return word rotated r bits to the right, i.e., toward the lest significant bit:

```
static inline unsigned long bit_rotate_right(ulong x,
    ulong r)
{
    return (x >> r) | (x << (BITS_PER_LONG - r));
}
```

8.5. Miscellaneous

A convenient function is:
```
static inline unsigned long bit_rotate_sgn(ulong x, long r)
// Positive r --> shift away from element zero
{
    if ( r > 0 )  return  bit_rotate_left(x, (unsigned long)r);
    else          return  bit_rotate_right(x, (unsigned long)-r);
}
```

The minimum and maximum among all cyclic shifts of a word can be computed via the following functions:
```
static inline unsigned long bit_cyclic_min(ulong x)
{
    ulong r = 1;
    ulong m = x;
    do
    {
        x = bit_rotate_right(x, 1);
        if ( x<m )  m = x;
    }
    while ( ++r < BITS_PER_LONG );
    return m;
}

static inline unsigned long bit_cyclic_max(ulong x)
{
    ulong r = 1;
    ulong m = x;
    do
    {
        x = bit_rotate_right(x, 1);
        if ( x>m )  m = x;
    }
    while ( ++r < BITS_PER_LONG );
    return m;
}

static inline bool is_bit_cyclic_min(ulong x)
// Return whether x is the minimum of all rotations of x
{ return ( x == bit_cyclic_min(x) ); }


static inline bool is_bit_cyclic_max(ulong x)
// Return whether x is the maximum of all rotations of x
{ return ( x == bit_cyclic_max(x) ); }
```

The following function determines whether there is a cyclic right shift of its second argument so that it matches the first argument:
```
static inline unsigned long bit_cyclic_match(ulong x, ulong y)
// Return   r if x==rotate_right(y, r) else return ~0UL.
// In other words: return
//   how often the right arg must be rotated right (to match the left)
```

8.5. Miscellaneous

```
5  // or, equivalently:
6  //     how often the left arg must be rotated left (to
       match the right)
7  {
8      ulong r = 0;
9      do
10     {
11         if ( x==y ) return r;
12         y = bit_rotate_right(y, 1);
13     }
14     while ( ++r < BITS_PER_LONG );
15
16     return ~0UL;
17 }
```

8.5.7 Gray Code Conversion

A Gray code is any binary coding sequence in which only a single bit position changes as we move from one value to the next. There are many such codes, but the traditional one is computed such that the Kth Gray code is $K \char`\^ (K \gg 1)$.

The well-known algorithm for conversion from Gray to binary is a linear sequence of XORs that makes it seem each bit must be dealt with separately. Fortunately, that is equivalent to a parallel prefix XOR that can be computed in log time. For 32-bit Gray code values produced as described above, the conversion from Gray code back to unsigned binary is:

Program 8.20: *Gray Code Conversion*

```
1  unsigned int g2b(unsigned int gray)
2  {
3          gray ^= (gray >> 16);
4          gray ^= (gray >> 8);
5          gray ^= (gray >> 4);
6          gray ^= (gray >> 2);
7          gray ^= (gray >> 1);
8          return(gray);
9  }
```

8.5.8 Average of Integers without Overflow

This is actually an extension of the fact that for binary integer values x and y:

$$(x + y) \equiv ((x \,\&\, y) + (x \,|\, y)) \equiv ((x \char`\^ y) + 2 * (x \,\&\, y))$$

Given two integer values x and y, the (floor of the) average normally would be computed by (x+y)/2; unfortunately, this can yield incorrect results due to overflow. A very sneaky alternative is to use $(x \,\&\, y) + \left(\frac{(x \char`\^ y)}{2}\right)$.

If we are aware of the potential non-portability due to the fact that C does not specify if shifts are signed, this can be simplified to

8.5. Miscellaneous

$$(x \mathbin{\&} y) + ((x \mathbin{^\wedge} y) \gg 1)$$

In either case, the benefit is that this code sequence cannot overflow.

8.5.9 Double Linked List with One Pointer Field

Normally, a double linked circular list would contain both previous and next pointer fields and the current position in the list would be identified by a single pointer. By using two current pointers, one to the node in question and the other to the one just before/after it, it becomes possible to store only a single pointer value in each node. The value stored in each node is the XOR of the next and previous pointers that normally would have been stored in each node. Decoding is obvious.

Unfortunately, using this trick in C is awkward because the XOR operation is not defined for pointers.

8.5.10 Least Significant 1 Bit

This can be useful for extracting the lowest numbered element of a bit set. Given a 2's complement binary integer value x, $(x \mathbin{\&} -x)$ is the least significant 1 bit.

The reason this works is that it is equivalent to $(x \mathbin{\&} ((\sim x) + 1))$; any trailing zero bits in x become ones in $\sim x$, adding 1 to that carries into the following bit, and AND with x yields only the flipped bit : the original position of the least significant 1 bit.

Alternatively, since $(x \mathbin{\&} (x-1))$ is actually x stripped of its least significant 1 bit, the least significant 1 bit is also $(x ^\wedge (x \mathbin{\&} (x-1)))$.

8.5.11 Most Significant 1 Bit

Given a binary integer value x, the most significant 1 bit (highest numbered element of a bit set) can be computed using a algorithm that recursively folds the upper bits into the lower bits. This process yields a bit vector with the same most significant 1 as x, but all 1's below it. Bitwise AND of the original value with the complement of the folded value shifted down by one yields the most significant bit. For a 32-bit value:

Program 8.21: *Most Significant 1 Bit*

```
unsigned int msb32(register unsigned int x)
{
        x |= (x >> 1);
        x |= (x >> 2);
        x |= (x >> 4);
        x |= (x >> 8);
        x |= (x >> 16);
        return(x & ~(x >> 1));
}
```

8.5.12 Swap Values Without a Temporary

Given two binary integer values, x and y, the values can be exchanged without use of a temporary by:

Program 8.22: *Swap Values Without a Temporary*

```
x ^= y;  /* x' = (x^y) */
y ^= x;  /* y' = (y^(x^y)) = x */
x ^= y;  /* x' = (x^y)^x = y */
```

8.5.13 Next bit Permutation

Suppose we have a pattern of N bits set to 1 in an integer and we want the next permutation of N 1 bits in a lexicographical sense. For example, if N is 3 and the bit pattern is 00010011, the next patterns would be 00010101, 00010110, 00011001, 00011010, 00011100, 00100011, and so forth. The following is a fast way to compute the next permutation.

Program 8.23: *Next bit Permutation : Faster*

```
unsigned int v;  // current permutation of bits
unsigned int w;  // next permutation of bits

unsigned int t = v | (v - 1);  // t gets v's least
    significant 0 bits set to 1
// Next set to 1 the most significant bit to change,
// set to 0 the least significant ones, and add the
    necessary 1 bits.
w = (t + 1) | (((~t & -~t) - 1) >> (__builtin_ctz(v) + 1)
    );
```

The __builtin_ctz(v) GNU C compiler intrinsic for x86 CPUs returns the number of trailing zeros. For Microsoft compilers for x86, the intrinsic is _BitScanForward. These both emit a bsf instruction, but equivalents may be available for other architectures. If not, then we can consider using one of the methods for counting the consecutive zero bits mentioned earlier.

Here is another version that tends to be slower because of its division operator, but it does not require counting the trailing zeros.

Program 8.24: *Next bit Permutation*

```
unsigned int t = (v | (v - 1)) + 1;
w = t | ((((t & -t) / (v & -v)) >> 1) - 1);
```

8.5.14 Compute Modulus Division

Program 8.25: *Compute modulus division by* $(1 \ll s)$ *without a division operator*

```
const unsigned int n;         // numerator
const unsigned int s;
const unsigned int d = 1U << s;  // So d will be one of:
    1, 2, 4, 8, 16, 32, ...
unsigned int m;               // m will be n % d
m = n & (d - 1);
```

8.5. Miscellaneous

Program 8.26: *Compute modulus division by* $(1 \ll s) - 1$ *without a division operator*

```
1 unsigned int n;                          // numerator
2 const unsigned int s;                    // s > 0
3 const unsigned int d = (1 << s) - 1;     // so d is either 1,
      3, 7, 15, 31, ...).
4 unsigned int m;                          // n % d goes here.
5
6 for (m = n; n > d; n = m)
7 {
8    for (m = 0; n; n >>= s)
9    {
10      m += n & d;
11   }
12 }
13 // Now m is a value from 0 to d, but since with modulus
      division
14 // we want m to be 0 when it is d.
15 m = m == d ? 0 : m;
```

This method of modulus division by an integer that is one less than a power of 2 takes at most $5 + (4 + 5 \times ceil\left(\frac{N}{s}\right)) \times ceil(\log_2\left(\frac{N}{s}\right))$ operations, where N is the number of bits in the numerator. In other words, it takes at most $O(N \times \log_2(N))$ time.

8.5.15 Conditionally set or clear bits without branching

Program 8.27: *Conditionally set or clear bits without branching*

```
1 bool f;                  // conditional flag
2 unsigned int m;          // the bit mask
3 unsigned int w;          // the word to modify:  if (f) w |= m;
      else w &= ~m;
4
5 w ^= (-f ^ w) & m;
6
7 // OR, for superscalar CPUs:
8 w = (w & ~m) | (-f & m);
```

8.5.16 Conditionally negate a value without branching

If we need to negate only when a flag is false, then we can use the following to avoid branching:

Program 8.28: *Conditionally negate a value without branching*

```
1 bool fDontNegate;        // Flag indicating we should not
      negate v.
2 int v;                   // Input value to negate if
      fDontNegate is false.
3 int r;                   // result = fDontNegate ? v : -v;
4
5 r = (fDontNegate ^ (fDontNegate - 1)) * v;
```

If we need to negate only when a flag is true, then we can use this:

```
1 bool fNegate;            // Flag indicating if we should negate v.
2 int v;                   // Input value to negate if fNegate is
      true.
3 int r;                   // result = fNegate ? -v : v;
4
5 r = (v ^ -fNegate) + fNegate;
```

Part II

C++

Chapter 9

General

** Question 1   Bit-fields and Concurrency

Which of the following data members are safe for concurrent updates ?

Program 9.1: Bit-fields and Concurrency

```
struct A
{
    char non_bitfield_a;

    int bitfield_b :  3;
    int bitfield_c : 10;
    int           :  0;

    int bitfield_d :  8;

    struct E
    {
        int bitfield_a1 : 8;
    } non_bitfield_e;

    int bitfield_f : 4;
    int non_bitfield_g;
    int bitfield_h : 11;
};
```

Solution of Question 1

As far as concurrent update is concerned, it is related to *memory location*, i.e., two threads of execution can safely update and access *separate* memory locations.

So let us try understanding the memory location of the member data, starting with bit-fields.

Program 9.2: Bit-fields and Concurrency

```
struct A
{
    char non_bitfield_a;

    int bitfield_b :  3;
    int bitfield_c : 10;
    int           :  0;
```

```
9      int bitfield_d :  8;
10
11     struct E
12     {
13         int bitfield_a1 : 8;
14     } non_bitfield_e;
15
16     int bitfield_f :  4;
17     int non_bitfield_g;
18     int bitfield_h : 11;
19 };
```

Concurrent Safe bit-fields

Two bit-fields are safe for concurrent updates by two threads, if they are located in separate memory locations

- *bitfield_b* and *bitfield_c* are located in the *same* memory location, hence **not thread-safe** for concurrent updates.

- *bitfield_c* and *bitfield_d* are located in *different* memory locations because these are separated by a *zero-length* bit-field, hence thread-safe for concurrent updates.

- *bitfield_d* and *bitfield_a1* are located in *different* memory locations because *bitfield_a1* is inside the nested structure *E*, hence thread-safe for concurrent updates.

- *bitfield_f* and *bitfield_h* are located in *different* memory locations because these are separated by a *non-bitfield* data member *non_bitfield_g*, hence thread-safe for concurrent updates.

Hence it is not safe to concurrently update two bit-fields in the same struct if all fields between them are also bit-fields of non-zero width because these constitute the *same* memory location.

There are seven memory locations associated with the structure *A*

1. *non_bitfield_a*
2. *bitfield_b* and *bitfield_c*
3. *bitfield_d*
4. *bitfield_a1* (*non_bitfield_e*)
5. *bitfield_f*
6. *non_bitfield_g*
7. *bitfield_h*

* Question 2   Distinct Address Location

What happens when the program below is compiled ?

Program 9.3: Distinct Address Location

```
1 int main()
2 {
3     char a = 'a';
```

```
    char b = 'b';

    static_assert(&a == &b, "Address of a and b "
                            "should be distinct");
}
```

Solution of Question 2

It results into a compilation error as enlisted below:

```
distinct_add.cpp: In function 'int main()':
distinct_add.cpp:6:5:
error: static assertion failed:
Address of a and b should be distinct
     static_assert(&a == &b, "Address of a and b "
```

Address location of two distinct objects is always distinct except when the following is true in which case the result is implementation-defined:

1. These are bit-fields

2. These are base-class sub-objects of zero size

The address of an object the address of the first byte it occupies except when it is either a bit-field or a base class sub-object of zero size.

** Question 3   Signal and Values

List the types of the objects whose values are guaranteed to be defined even in case of signals ?

Solution of Question 3

1. volatile *std::sig_atomic_t*

2. lock-free atomic objects

** Question 4   Temporary and Conversions

In the program below, what happens before temporary gets destroyed in line 12

Program 9.4: Temporary and Conversions

```
struct A
{
    A(int x) : _x(x) {}

    int & val() { return _x; }
private :
    int _x;
};

int main()
{
    if(A(1).val())
        {}
}
```

Solution of Question 4

The following conversion takes place before destruction of the temporary object of type A

1. lvalue to rvalue conversion

2. int to bool conversion

** Question 5   evaluation of expressions

Review the program below:

Program 9.5: evaluation of expressions

```
void compute(int, int) {};

void eval(int x, int arr[])
{
    x = arr[x++];

    x = 2, x++, x++;

    x = x++ + 1;
    x = x + 1;

    compute(x = -1, x = -1);
}
```

Solution of Question 5

- line 5: behavior is undefined
- line 7: x becomes 4
- line 9: behavior is undefined
- line 10: the value of x is incremented
- line 12: behavior is undefined

*** Question 6   trigraph sequences

What happens with the trigraphs here:

Program 9.6: trigraph sequences

```
??=define validateArray(x, y) x??(y??) ??!??! y??(x??)
```

Solution of Question 6

- trigraph ??= is replaced by #
- trigraph ??(is replaced by [
- trigraph ??) is replaced by]
- trigraph ??! is replaced by |

The above $\Longrightarrow$ that the stated trigraph sequences will be replaced to change the expression to look like below

Program 9.7: replacing trigraph sequences
```
#define validateArray(x, y) x[y] || y[x]
```

** Question 7   increment operator

What is the output of the program:

Program 9.8: increment operator
```
#include <iostream>

int main()
{
    int one = 1;
    int two = 2;

    int a = one+++++two;
}
```

Solution of Question 7

When compiled, the error is:

```
increment_operator.cpp: In function 'int main()':
increment_operator.cpp:8:18:
error: lvalue required as increment operand
    int a = one+++++two;
                ^
```

The expression *one+++++two* is parsed to look like *one ++ ++ + two*, which violates a constraint on increment operators, thus leading to incorrect expression.

$$one+++++two \implies one\ ++\ ++\ +\ two$$

Please note that the expression *one+++++two* is not parsed as *one ++ + ++ two*, which is indeed a correct expression.

$$one+++++two \not\implies one\ ++\ +\ ++\ two$$

* Question 8   nullptr

What is *nullptr* ?

Solution of Question 8

nullptr is the *pointer literal* designating a *prvalue* of type *std::nullptr_t*. It is a null pointer constant which can be converted to a null pointer value or a null member pointer value.

Please note that *std::nullptr_t* itself

- is not a pointer type
- is not a pointer to member type
- is a *distinct type*

** Question 9   user defined literal

What is *user defined literal* ?

Solution of Question 9

A *user defined literal* is a call to a literal operator or literal operator template of the form

1. operator "" *identifier*
2. operator "" *identifier*<'c_1', 'c_2', ... 'c_k'>()

For example:

1. *user-defined-integer-literal*

    a) operator "" *identifier* (n ULL)

    b) operator "" *identifier* ("n")

    c) operator "" *identifier* <'c_1', 'c_2', ... 'c_k'>()

2. *user-defined-floating-literal*

    a) operator "" *identifier* (f L)

    b) operator "" *identifier* ("f")

    c) operator "" *identifier* <'c_1', 'c_2', ... 'c_k'>()

3. *user-defined-string-literal*

    a) operator "" *identifier* (str, len)

    b) operator "" *identifier* (ch)

Program 9.9: user defined literal

```
#include <string>

void operator "" _distance(long double);

long double operator "" _amount(long double);

std::string operator "" _amount(const char16_t*,
                                 std::size_t);

unsigned   operator "" _amount(const char*);

float operator "" _X(const char*);

template <char...> int operator "" _length();

int main()
{
    2.9_amount;

    u"test"_amount;

    20_amount;
}
```

In the example above

- line 18 calls *operator* "" _amount(2.9L)

- line 20 calls *operator* "" _amount(u"test", 4)

- line 22 calls *operator* "" _amount("20")

* Question 10   Declaration vs Definition

Which of the following are definitions and which are just declarations?

Program 9.10: Declaration vs Definition

```cpp
extern int a1;
int a2;
extern const int a3;
extern const int a4 = 10;
void fun(int);
void fun(int i) {}
struct A;
struct A
{
    int x, y;
};
typedef int Integer;
enum {low, mid, high};
extern A _A;
struct B
{
    static int x;
};
int B::x = 5;
namespace Detail { int x; }
using Detail::x;
namespace DetailsX = Detail;
B b1;
```

Solution of Question 10

- *Declarations*
  line 1, 3, 5, 7, 12, 14, 17, 21

- *Definitions*
  Rest are definitions

** Question 11   Compiler Generated Member Functions

In the following case, list the member functions whose definitions are implicitly generated by the compiler :

Program 9.11: Sample Class

```cpp
#include <string>

struct A
{
    std::string _str;
};

int main()
{
    A a1;
    A a2 = a1;
    a2 = a1;
};
```

General

Solution of Question 11

The following member functions definitions are implicitly generated by the compiler:

1. default constructor

```
A() : _str() { }
```

2. copy constructor

```
A(const A & a): _str(a._str) { }
```

3. move constructor

```
A(A&& a)
:
_str(static_cast<std::string&&>(a._str))
{ }
```

or,

```
A(A&& a)
:
_str(std::move(a._str)) { }
```

4. copy assignment operator

```
A& operator=(const A& a)
{
    _str = a._str;
    return *this;
}
```

5. move assignment operator

```
A& operator=(A&& a)
{
    _str = static_cast<std::string&&>(a._str);
    return *this;
}
```

or,

```
A& operator=(A&& a)
{
    _str = std::move(a._str);
    return *this;
}
```

6. destructor

```
~A() { }
```

Hence it may look like :

Program 9.12: Compiler Generated Member Functions

```cpp
#include <string>

struct A
{
    std::string _str;

    A() : _str() { }

    A(const A& a): _str(a._str) { }

    A(A&& a)
     :
     _str(static_cast<std::string&&>(a._str)) { }

    A& operator=(const A& a)
    {
        _str = a._str;
        return *this;
    }

    A& operator=(A&& a)
    {
        _str = static_cast<std::string&&>(a._str);
        return *this;
    }

    ~A() { }
};
```

or,

Program 9.13: Compiler Generated Member Functions

```cpp
#include <string>

struct A
{
    std::string _str;

    A() : _str() { }

    A(const A & a): _str(a._str) { }

    A(A&& a)
    :
    _str(std::move(a._str)) { }

    A& operator=(const A& a)
    {
        _str = a._str;
        return *this;
    }

    A& operator=(A&& a)
    {
        _str = std::move(a._str);
        return *this;
    }

    ~A() { }
};
```

*** Question 12   ODR vs Default Constructor

What is the output of these two programs?

Program 9.14: ODR vs Default Constructor

```cpp
#include <iostream>

struct Base
{
    Base(int);

    Base(int, int);
};

Base::Base(int = 0)
{
    std::cout << "Inside Base::Base(int)"
              << std::endl;
}

struct Derived : Base
{
};

int main()
{
    Derived d;
}
```

Program 9.15: ODR vs Default Constructor
```cpp
#include <iostream>

struct Base
{
    Base(int);

    Base(int, int);
};
Base::Base(int = 0, int = 0)
{
    std::cout << "Inside Base::Base(int, int)"
              << std::endl;
}

struct Derived : Base
{
};

int main()
{
    Derived d;
}
```

Solution of Question 12

In the first program, the output is *Inside Base::Base(int)*

In the second program, the output is *Inside Base::Base(int, int)*

In both of these programs, the class Derived's default constructor is implicitly defined, but this definition D() calls Base(int) in one case and calls Base(int, int) in another case.

** Question 13   Understanding Point of Declaration

What is the output of this program? How the template arguments are deduced for the class template B?

Program 9.16: Understanding Point of Declaration
```cpp
#include <iostream>

void test()
{
    int a1 = 10;
    {
        int a1 = a1;
        std::cout << "a1: " << a1
                  << std::endl;
    }

    const int a2 = 20;
    {
        int a2[a2];
        std::cout << "size of array:"
                  << sizeof(a2)/sizeof(int)
                  << std::endl;
    }

    const int a3 = 30;
```

```cpp
21      {
22          enum { a3 = a3 };
23          std::cout << "enum a3 is : "
24                   << a3 << std::endl;
25      }
26 }
27
28 struct A
29 {
30     enum { e = 40 };
31
32     int arr[A::e];
33 };
34
35 typedef int T;
36
37 template<typename T = T, T n = 0>
38 struct B{};
39
40 int main()
41 {
42     test();
43
44     A a;
45     std::cout << "length of array arr is :"
46              << sizeof(a.arr)/sizeof(int)
47              << std::endl;
48 }
```

Solution of Question 13

The output is

```
a1: 6295552
size of array:20
enum a3 is: 30
length of array arr is :40
```

Please note that:

- Value of the second integer a1 is initialized with its own value which is indeterminate.

- The first template argument's default value type is looked up to find the typedef int and in the case of the second one, look up finds the template parameter.

** Question 14   class scope variables

What is the output of this program?

Program 9.17: class scope variables

```cpp
1 #include <cstddef>
2 #include <iostream>
3
4 typedef int c;
5
6 enum { e = 10 };
7
```

```cpp
struct A
{
    char arr[e];

    std::size_t fun()
    {
        return sizeof(c);
    }

    char c;

    enum { e = 20 };
};

int main()
{
    A a;
    std::cout << "size of arr is :"
              << sizeof(a.arr)/sizeof(char)
              << std::endl;

    std::cout << "fun() :" << a.fun()
              << std::endl;
}
```

Solution of Question 14

The output is

```
size of arr is :10
fun() :1
```

** Question 15   namespace scope variables

What is the output of this program?

Program 9.18: namespace scope variables

```cpp
namespace A
{
    int i;

    int func(int j)
    {
        return j;
    }

    int g();

    void h();
}

namespace
{
    int x = 10;
}

namespace A
{
    int func(char j)
```

```
23    {
24          return x + j;
25    }
26
27    int i;
28
29    int g();
30
31    int g()
32    {
33          return func(i);
34    }
35
36    int h();
37 }
```

Solution of Question 15

The output is

```
namespace_scope.cpp:27:9:
error: redefinition of 'i'
    int i;
        ^
namespace_scope.cpp:3:9:
note: previous definition is here
    int i;
        ^
namespace_scope.cpp:36:9:
error: functions that differ only
in their return type cannot be overloaded
    int h();
        ^
namespace_scope.cpp:12:10:
note: previous declaration is
here
    void h();
         ^
2 errors generated.
```

Please note that

- the potential scope of the variable x on line 17 in the unnamed namespace is to the end of the translation unit.
- line 22 overloads A::func(int)
- line 24 : x is from the anonymous namespace
- line 27 redefines int i : violation of ODR(One Definition Rule) : Hence *error*.
- line 29 re-declares the function g()
- line 31 : defines the function g()
- line 33 : calls A::func(int)

- line 36 : redefines the function h() with different return type: hence *error*.

** Question 16   scope of template parameters

Can a template parameter be used in the declaration of subsequent template parameters and their default arguments ?

Solution of Question 16

Yes.

A template parameter be used in the declaration of subsequent template parameters and and their default arguments.

For example,

```
template<typename T1, T1* ptr, typename T2 = T1>
struct A {};

template<typename T> void alloc_memory(T* ptr = new T);
```

Please note that a template parameter can be used also in the specification of base classes, like

```
template<typename T>
struct Base {};

template<typename T>
struct Derived : Base<T> { };

template<typename T>
struct A : T { };
```

The use of a template parameter as a base class implies that a class used as a template argument must be defined and not just declared when the class template is instantiated.

** Question 17   scope of template parameters

What is the type of the template parameters T1 and T2 in the program below ?

```
typedef int T;

template<T T1, typename T, template<T T2> class T3>
struct A;
```

Solution of Question 17

- T1 is a non-type template parameter of type int
- T2 is a non-type template parameter of the same type as the second template parameter of A.

** Question 18   Unqualified Name Lookup

What is the output of the program ?

Program 9.19: Unqualified Name Lookup

```
#include <iostream>
```

```cpp
typedef int func;

namespace A
{
    struct B
    {
        B(int i = 1) : _i(i) {}

        friend void func(B & b)
        {
            std::cout << "func()" << std::endl;
        }

        operator int() { return _i; }

        void compute(B b)
        {
            _i = func(b);
        }
    private:
        int _i;
    }; // struct B
} // namespace A

int main()
{
    A::B b1(10), b2(20);

    std::cout << b2 << std::endl;

    b2.compute(b1);

    std::cout << b2 << std::endl;
}
```

Solution of Question 18

The output is:

```
20
10
```

Please note that on line 20, *func* is not a function call, hence the argument dependent lookup does not apply and the friend function *func* is not found.

Hence it is equivalent to a call to *int(b)*.

** Question 19   Unqualified Name Lookup

What is the output of the program ?

Program 9.20: Unqualified Name Lookup

```cpp
#include <iostream>

int a = 10;

namespace outer
{
    int a = 20;
```

```cpp
        namespace inner
        {
            int a = 30;

            void func();
        } // namespace inner
} // namespace outer

void outer::inner::func()
{
    // int a = 40;
    std::cout << "a : " << a << std::endl;
}

int main()
{
    outer::inner::func();
}
```

Discuss how the declaration of the variable *a* is being looked up when trying to use it within definition of the function *func*.

Solution of Question 19

The output is:

```
a : 30
```

The following scopes are searched in the given order for a declaration/definition of the variable *a*:

1. the first is the outermost block scope of outer::inner::func, before the use of *a*, i.e., if line number 20 is commented out, then it is the first place where lookup is done. In this case the output will be *40*.

2. next is the scope of the namespace inner (line number 11), as illustrated by the output being *30*.

3. next is the scope of the namespace outer, i.e., if the line numbers 20 and 11 do not declare/define *a* then due to line 7, the output will be 20.

4. next is the global scope, before the definition of outer::inner::func, i.e., if line numbers 20, 11 and 7 do not declare/define *a* then due to line 3, the output will be 10.

** Question 20   Unqualified Name Lookup

What is the output of the program ?

Program 9.21: Unqualified Name Lookup

```cpp
#include <iostream>

namespace first
{
    struct base
    {
        static int i;
    };
```

```
 9  }  // namespace A
10
11  int first::base::i = 10;
12
13  namespace second
14  {
15      struct derived : first::base
16      {
17          struct nested
18          {
19              nested()
20              {
21                  std::cout << "nested() : "
22                            << i << std::endl;
23              }
24          } n;  // struct nested
25      };  // struct derived
26  }
27
28  int main()
29  {
30      second::derived d;
31  }
```

Discuss how the declaration of the variable *i* is being looked up when trying to use it during constructor definition of *nested*.

Solution of Question 20

The output is:

```
nested() : 10
```

The following scopes are searched in the given order for a declaration/definition of the variable *i*:

1. scope of struct second::derived::nested, before the use of i

2. scope of struct second::derived, before the definition of second::derived::nested

3. scope of second::derived's base class first::base(as given in the program)

4. scope of namespace second, before the definition of second::derived

5. global scope, before the definition of second

* Question 21 Unqualified Name Lookup

What is the output of the program ?

Program 9.22: Unqualified Name Lookup

```
1  struct Base {};
2
3  namespace outer
4  {
5      namespace inner
6      {
7          struct Derived : Base
```

```
8          {
9              void func();
10         }; // struct Derived
11     } // namespace inner
12 } // namespace outer
13
14 void outer::inner::Derived::func()
15 {
16     i = 10;
17 }
```

Discuss how the declaration of the variable *i* is being looked up when trying to use it within *outer::inner::Derived::func*.

Solution of Question 21

The following scopes are searched in the given order for a declaration/definition of the variable *i*:

1. outermost block scope of outer::inner::Derived::func, before the use of i

2. scope of struct outer::inner::Derived

3. scope of outer::inner::Derived's base class B

4. scope of namespace outer::inner

5. scope of namespace outer

6. global scope, before the definition of outer::inner::Derived::func

*** Question 22   Friend member func vs Name-Lookup

What are the parameter types of the friend functions *f* and *g* and template argument of the friend function template *h* (on line numbers 18, 20 and 22 respectively) ?

Program 9.23: Friend member function and Name Lookup
```
1  struct A
2  {
3      typedef int AType;
4
5      void f(AType);
6
7      void g(float);
8
9      template <typename T> void h();
10 };
11
12 struct B
13 {
14     typedef char AType;
15
16     typedef float BType;
17
18     friend void A::f(AType);
19
20     friend void A::g(BType);
21
22     friend void A::h<AType>();
23 };
```

Solution of Question 22

```
friend void A::f(AType);
```

It is first looked up in the scope of the member function's class A.
Hence the parameter type is A::$AType$.

```
friend void A::g(BType);
```

It is not found in the scope of the member function's class A, hence the look up is done in the scope of the class granting friendship, i.e., B.
Hence the parameter type is B::$BType$.

```
friend void A::h<AType>();
```

Because the name is part of a template-argument in the declarator-id, hence it is looked up in the scope of the class granting friendship, i.e., B.
Hence the template argument is B::$AType$.

*** Question 23   namespace extern and look-up

What is the output of the program?

Program 9.24: namespace extern and look-up

```cpp
#include <iostream>

namespace A
{
    int x = 10;

    extern int y;
} // namespace A

int x = 20;

int A::y = x;

int main()
{
    std::cout << "A::y is : "
        << A::y << std::endl;
}
```

Solution of Question 23

The output is:

```
A::y is : 10
```

Because the variable member y of the namespace A is defined outside the scope of its namespace, that's why look up of the variable x occurs in the same way when y could have been defined inside the namespace.

Hence the un-qualified look-up of x in the definition of y is interpreted as A::x.

*** Question 24   ADL(Argument Dependent Look-up)

What is the output of the program?

Program 9.25: ADL

```cpp
#include <iostream>

struct B {};

namespace A
{
    struct B {};

    void func(B b)
    {
        std::cout << "A::func" << std::endl;
    }
} // namespace A

void func(B b)
{
    std::cout << "func" << std::endl;
}

void test()
{
    A::B b1;

    func(b1);

    B b2;

    func(b2);
}

int main()
{
    test();
}
```

Solution of Question 24

The output is:

```
A::func
func
```

Please note that unqualified *func* resulted into a look-up into the namespace A because the type of the argument *A::B* being passed to the function *func* is defined in that namespace.

This is also known as ADL, i.e., Argument Dependent Look-up or Koenig's name look-up.

*** Question 25   ADL(Argument Dependent Look-up)

What is the output of the program?

Program 9.26: ADL

```cpp
#include <iostream>

namespace A
{
    struct B {};

    void func(B b)
    {
        std::cout << "A::func" << std::endl;
    }
} // namespace A

void func(A::B b)
{
    std::cout << "func(A::B)" << std::endl;
}

void test()
{
    A::B b1;

    func(b1);
}

int main()
{
    test();
}
```

Solution of Question 25

The program doesn't get compiled. Compiler error is:

```
adl2.cpp:22:5: error: call to 'func' is ambiguous
    func(b1);
    ^~~
adl2.cpp:7:10: note: candidate function
    void func(B b)
         ^
adl2.cpp:13:6: note: candidate function
void func(A::B b)
     ^
1 error generated.
```

It is self-explanatory from the compiler error.

**** Question 26   ADL(Argument Dependent Look-up)

Modify the previous program to call *func(A::B)*?

Solution of Question 26

Modified program looks like

Program 9.27: ADL

```cpp
#include <iostream>

namespace A
{
    struct B {};

    void func(B b)
    {
        std::cout << "A::func" << std::endl;
    }
} // namespace A

void func(A::B b)
{
    std::cout << "func(A::B)" << std::endl;
}

void test()
{
    A::B b1;

    extern void func(A::B);

    func(b1);
}

int main()
{
    test();
}
```

Now the output looks like

```
func(A::B)
```

** Question 27   Basic Look-up

Review the program below?

Program 9.28: Basic Look-up

```cpp
struct A
{
    static int a;
};

int A::a = 10;

int main()
{
    int A = 20;

    A::a = 100;

    A a1;
}
```

Solution of Question 27

This program doesn't get compiled and the compiler error is

```
basic_lookup.cpp:14:5:
error: must use 'struct' tag to refer
to type 'A' in this
      scope
    A a1;
    ^
    struct
basic_lookup.cpp:10:9:
note: struct 'A' is hidden by a
non-type declaration of
      'A' here
    int A = 20;
        ^
1 error generated.
```

The error is self-explanatory because on line 14 : *A* is not a type anymore.

** Question 28   Basic Look-up

Review the definition of static data member *array* below.

Program 9.29: Basic Look-up

```cpp
struct A { };

struct B
{
    struct A { };

    static const int n = 10;

    static A array[n];
};

A B::array[n];
```

Solution of Question 28

This program doesn't get compiled and the compiler error is

```
basic_lookup1.cpp:12:13:
error: conflicting declaration
'A B::array [10]'
 A B::array[n];
     ^
basic_lookup1.cpp:9:14:
error: 'B::array' has a previous
declaration as 'B::A B::array [10]'
      static A array[n];
               ^
basic_lookup1.cpp:12:13: error: declaration of
'B::A B::array [10]'
```

```
outside of class is not definition
[-fpermissive]
  A B::array[n];
```

Another compiler's error is

```
basic_lookup1.cpp:12:6:
 error: redefinition of 'array'
 with a different type:
       'A [10]' vs 'B::A [10]'
 A B::array[n];

basic_lookup1.cpp:9:14:
note: previous definition is here
     static A array[n];

1 error generated.
```

The error is self-explanatory.

The following program fixes this error:

Program 9.30: Basic Look-up

```cpp
struct A { };

struct B
{
    struct A { };

    static const int n = 10;

    static A array[n];
};

B::A B::array[n];
```

* Question 29   destructor and typedef

How to call the destructor explicitly for the typedef of a given class ?

Solution of Question 29

The following program demonstrates it:

Program 9.31: destructor and typedef

```cpp
struct B
{
    ~B() {}
};

typedef B AnotherB;

int main()
{
    AnotherB * third;

    third->AnotherB::~AnotherB();
}
```

** Question 30   constructor name look-up

How to look-up constructors of the class *Base* in two cases : one as *Base* itself, another as a base class of *Derived* in the given program ?

```
struct Base
{
    Base();
};

struct Derived : Base
{
    Derived();
};

Base::Base() { }
Derived::Derived() { }
```

Solution of Question 30

Invocation of Base's constructor as a base part of derived will look like:

```
Derived::Base db;
```

Following the same league, the call below is not legal

```
Base::Base b;
```

because *Base::Base* doesn't name a type.

To achieve this, the following should be attempted:

```
struct Base::Base b1;
```

** Question 31   understanding namespace

Given the program below:

```
int x;

namespace Y
{
    void f(float);
    void h(int);
}

namespace Z
{
```

```
        void h(double);
    }

    namespace A
    {
        using namespace Y;

        void f(int);
        void g(int);

        int i;
    }

    namespace B
    {
        using namespace Z;

        void f(char);

        int i;
    }

    namespace AB
    {
        using namespace A;
        using namespace B;

        void g();
    }
```

What happens with the code fragments as follows:

1.
```
        AB::g();
```

2.
```
        AB::f(1);
```

3.
```
        AB::f('e');
```

4.
```
        AB::x++;
```

5.
```
        AB::i++;
```

6.
```
AB::h(2.7);
```

Solution of Question 31

1.
```
AB::g();
```

Since g is declared directly in AB, it calls AB::g().

2.
```
AB::f(1);
```

Since f is not declared directly in AB so the rules are applied recursively to A and B; namespace Y is not searched and Y::f(float) is not considered;

So the candidate set is A::f(int), B::f(char) and overload resolution chooses A::f(int).

3.
```
AB::f('e');
```

as above but resolution chooses B::f(char).

4.
```
AB::x++;
```

Since x is not declared directly in AB, and is not declared in A or B, so the rules are applied recursively to Y and Z, hence nothing is found, so the program is ill-formed.

5.
```
AB::i++;
```

Since i is not declared directly in AB so the rules are applied recursively to A and B, so the choices are A::i , B::i so the use is ambiguous and the program is ill-formed.

6.
```
AB::h(2.7);
```

Since h is not declared directly in AB and not declared directly in A or B so the rules are applied recursively to Y and Z, so the choices are Y::h(int), Z::h(double) and overload resolution chooses Z::h(double).

** Question 32   multiple declarations are ok

Given the program below, what happens with line numbers 24 and 40 ?

Program 9.32: multiple declarations are ok

```
1  namespace A
2  {
3      int a ;
4  }
5
6  namespace B
7  {
8      using namespace A ;
9  }
10
11 namespace C
12 {
13     using namespace A ;
14 }
15
16 namespace BC
17 {
18     using namespace B ;
19     using namespace C ;
20 }
21
22 void f ()
23 {
24     BC::a ++;
25 }
26
27 namespace D
28 {
29     using A::a ;
30 }
31
32 namespace BD
33 {
34     using namespace B ;
35     using namespace D ;
36 }
37
38 void g ()
39 {
40     BD::a ++;
41 }
```

Solution of Question 32

As we already know that the same declaration found more than once is not an ambiguity at all because it is still a unique declaration, hence the calls at the line numbers 24 and 40 are ok because both refers to *A::i*.

** Question 33   multiple references to namespace

What is the output of the program ?

Program 9.33: multiple declarations are ok

```
1 #include <iostream>
2
3 namespace first
```

```
4 {
5      int one = 1;
6 }
7
8 namespace second
9 {
10     using namespace first;
11
12     int two = 2;
13 }
14
15 namespace first
16 {
17     using namespace second;
18 }
19
20 int main()
21 {
22     second::two++;
23     first::two++;
24     second::one++;
25     first::one++;
26
27     std::cout << "first::one is "
28         << first::one << std::endl;
29
30     std::cout << "second::one is "
31         << second::one << std::endl;
32
33     std::cout << "first::two is "
34         << first::two << std::endl;
35
36     std::cout << "second::two is "
37         << second::two << std::endl;
38 }
```

Solution of Question 33

Because each referenced namespace is searched at most once, that's why the out of the program is :

```
first::one is 3
second::one is 3
first::two is 4
second::two is 4
```

** Question 34   non-type name and namespace

Review the program ?

Program 9.34: non-type name and namespace

```
1 namespace A
2 {
3      struct x {};
4
5      int x;
6      int y;
7 } // namespace A
8
```

```
 9  namespace B
10  {
11      struct y {};
12  } // namespace B
13
14  namespace C
15  {
16      using namespace A;
17      using namespace B;
18
19      int i = C::x;
20      int j = C::y;
21  } // namespace C
```

Solution of Question 34

The program doesn't get compiled, the compiler error is

```
namespace3.cpp:20:16:
error: a type named 'y' is hidden
by a declaration in a
    different namespace
    int j = C::y;
           ~~~^
namespace3.cpp:11:12:
note: type declaration hidden
    struct y {};
           ^
namespace3.cpp:6:9:
note: declaration hides type
    int y;
        ^
1 error generated.
```

Please note that the non-type name hides the class or enumeration name if and only if the declarations are from the same namespace.

Hence *int i = C::x;* is a call to *A::x* of type int.

int j = C::y; is ambiguous, *A::y* or *B::y*.

** Question 35   declaration and nested namespace

Is the following definition of the function *func* is correct ?

Program 9.35: declaration and nested namespace

```
 1  #include <iostream>
 2
 3  namespace A
 4  {
 5      namespace B
 6      {
 7          void func();
 8      } // namespace B
 9
10      using namespace B;
11  } // namespace A
12
13  void A::func() {}
```

Solution of Question 35

The program doesn't get compiled, the compiler error is

```
nested_namespace.cpp:13:9:
error: out-of-line definition of
'func' does not
      match any declaration in namespace 'A'
void A::func() {}
     ^~~
1 error generated.
```

Another compiler's error is

```
nested_namespace.cpp:13:14:
error: 'void A::B::func()'
should have been declared inside 'A'
 void A::func() {}
              ^
```

Because *func* is not a member of *A*, that's why this is in error. To correct it, the program may be modified to look like:

Program 9.36: declaration and nested namespace

```cpp
#include <iostream>

namespace A
{
    namespace B
    {
        void func();
    } // namespace B

    using namespace B;
} // namespace A

using namespace A;

void B::func() {}
```

So qualifying with :: is strictly applicable to direct belonging of a member to that scope.

In this case, we can even drop the :: for defining it like:

Program 9.37: declaration and nested namespace

```cpp
#include <iostream>

namespace A
{
    namespace B
    {
        void func();
    } // namespace B

    using namespace B;
} // namespace A
```

```
12
13 using namespace A;
14
15 void func() {}
```

* Question 36   declaration : global vs local

What is the difference between these two programs ?

```
struct A
{
    struct B * b;
};
```

```
struct A
{
    B * b;
};
```

Solution of Question 36

```
struct A
{
    struct B * b;
};
```

declares a struct B at global scope, i.e., the program below is valid as well

```
struct A
{
    struct B * b;
};

B *b1;
```

Whereas the program below is trying to use a not yet declared type B:

```
struct A
{
    B * b;
};
```

Hence it doesn't compile.

** Question 37   injected class name

What is the output of the program ?

Program 9.38: injected class name

```cpp
#include <iostream>

struct A
{
    A()
    {
        std::cout << "::A()" << std::endl;
    }

    ~A()
    {
        std::cout << "::~A()" << std::endl;
    }
};

struct B
{
    struct A
    {
        A()
        {
            std::cout << "B::A()" << std::endl;
        }

        ~A()
        {
            std::cout << "B::~A()" << std::endl;
        }
    };

    void f(::A* a);
};

void B::f(::A* a)
{
    a->~A();
}

int main()
{
    B().f(new A);
}
```

Solution of Question 37

The output is:

```
::A()
::~A()
```

Because lookup in *a on line number 36 finds the injected-class-name ::A.

** Question 38   linkage

What is linkage ?

Solution of Question 38

When a name, introduced by a declaration in another scope, related to anyone of the following refers to the same

- object
- reference
- function
- type
- template
- namespace
- value

then it is said to have a *linkage*.

There are two types of linkages:

1. *external linkage*

    When a name denotes an entity which can be referred to by names from either of these units

    a) scopes of other translation units, or

    b) other scopes of the same translation unit,

    then it is said to have an *external linkage*.

    For example

    - the name of a variable declared by a block scope *extern* declaration.
    - a member function, static data member, a named class or enumeration of class scope, or an unnamed class or enumeration defined in a class-scope typedef declaration such that the class or enumeration has the typedef name for linkage purposes, has external linkage if the name of the class has external linkage.
    - All namespaces except an unnamed namespace or a namespace declared directly or indirectly within an unnamed namespace.

2. *internal linkage*

    When a name denotes an entity which can be referred to by names only from other scopes of the same translation unit, then it is said to have an *internal linkage*.

    For example

    - *static* variable, function or function template in a namespace scope
    - *const* or *constexpr* variable without any explicit *extern* declaration.
    - anonymous union's data members.
    - An unnamed namespace or a namespace declared directly or indirectly within an unnamed namespace.

When the entity denoted by a given name cannot be referred to by names from other scopes, then that name is said is to have *no linkage*.

* Question 39   return from main

What is the significance of return statement from the *main* function?

Solution of Question 39

A return statement in *main* has the effect of

1. leaving the main function
2. destroying any objects with automatic storage duration and
3. calling std::exit with the return value as the argument.

If control reaches the end of *main* without encountering a return statement, the effect is that of executing *return 0;*

*** Question 40   static and std::atexit

What is the output of the program ?

Program 9.39: static and std::atexit

```cpp
#include <cstdlib>
#include <iostream>

struct A
{
    A()
    {
        std::cout << "A()" << std::endl;
    }
    ~A()
    {
        std::cout << "~A()" << std::endl;
    }
};

static A a;

void func()
{
    std::cout << "func()" << std::endl;
}

int main()
{
    std::atexit(&func);
}
```

Solution of Question 40

Output of the program is:

```
A()
func()
~A()
```

Please note that here static object *a* is initialized before entry to the main function and registration of function *func* with *std::atexit* happens after this. Hence *func* is called before destruction of the static object *a*.

*** Question 41   std::atexit and static

What is the output of the program ?

Program 9.40: std::atexit and static

```cpp
#include <cstdlib>
#include <iostream>

struct A
{
    A()
    {
        std::cout << "A()" << std::endl;
    }
    ~A()
    {
        std::cout << "~A()" << std::endl;
    }
};

void func()
{
    std::cout << "func()" << std::endl;
}

struct B
{
    B()
    {
        std::cout << "B()" << std::endl;
        std::atexit(&func);
    }
    ~B()
    {
        std::cout << "~B()" << std::endl;
    }
};

static B b;

static A a;

int main()
{
}
```

Solution of Question 41

Output of the program is:

```
B()
A()
~A()
~B()
func()
```

Please note that here a call to *std::atexit* is sequenced before the completion of the initialization of the object *a* with static storage duration, hence the call to the destructor for the object *a* is sequenced before the call to the function *func* passed to *std::atexit*.

In the similar manner, let us review the program below:

Program 9.41: std::atexit and static

```
#include <cstdlib>
#include <iostream>

void func()
{
    std::cout << "func()" << std::endl;
}

struct A
{
    A()
    {
        std::cout << "A()" << std::endl;
        std::atexit(&func);
    }
    ~A()
    {
        std::cout << "~A()" << std::endl;
    }
};

static A a;

int main()
{
}
```

Output of this program is:

```
A()
~A()
func()
```

** Question 42   two std::atexit

What is the output of the program ?

Program 9.42: two std::atexit

```
#include <cstdlib>
#include <iostream>

void func()
{
    std::cout << "func()" << std::endl;
}

struct A
{
```

```cpp
       A()
       {
           std::cout << "A()" << std::endl;
           std::atexit(&func);
       }
       ~A()
       {
           std::cout << "~A()" << std::endl;
       }
};

static A a;

int main()
{
}
```

Solution of Question 42

Output of the program is:

```
f2()
f1()
```

It is self-explanatory.

** Question 43   Storage Duration

How many types of storage duration is possible with a given object once it is created ?

Solution of Question 43

There are four types of storage duration determining the minimum potential lifetime of the storage containing the object as given below:

1. dynamic storage duration : enabled by the global allocation functions *operator new* and *operator new[]*.

2. static storage duration : enabled by *static*. The storage for these entities shall last for the duration of the program.

3. thread storage duration : enabled by *thread_local*

4. automatic storage duration : enabled by *register* or not explicitly declared *static* or *extern*.

* Question 44   Integral Types

What are integral types ?

Solution of Question 44

The following types are collectively called *Integral Types*:

- bool

- char

- char16_t

- char32_t
- wchar_t
- the signed integer types, and
- unsigned integer types

** Question 45   Integral Types

What are integral types ?

Solution of Question 45

The following types are collectively called *Integral Types*:

- bool
- char
- char16_t
- char32_t
- wchar_t
- the signed integer types, and
- unsigned integer types

** Question 46   Ordering : const/volatile

Enlist the partial ordering relations on *const* and *volatile* ?

Solution of Question 46

Please note that cv stands for const and/or volatile.

- no cv-qualifier $<$ const
- no cv-qualifier $<$ volatile
- no cv-qualifier $<$ const volatile
- const $<$ const volatile
- volatile $<$ const volatile

*** Question 47   Value Category : lvalue/rvalue

What is lvalue ?
What is rvalue ?
Discuss other members of an expression's value category.

Solution of Question 47

The hierarchy of values associated with an expression looks like:

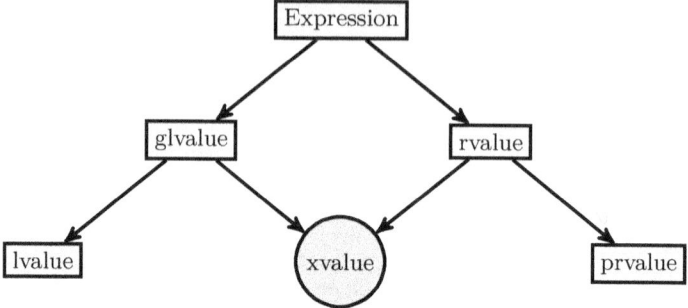

Figure 9.1: Expression Value Category Taxonomy

1. *lvalue* : This name came because earlier meaning was associated with its appearance in the left-hand side of an assignment.
   - An *lvalue* designates a function or an object.
   - If *ptr* is a pointer to an object or a function, then **ptr* is an *lvalue* expression.
   - The result of calling a function whose return type is an lvalue reference is an lvalue.

2. *xvalue* : It stands for an *expiring value*.
   - The result of calling a function whose return type is an *rvalue reference* is an xvalue.
   - It refers to an object, usually near the end of its lifetime, so that its resources may be moved.

3. *glvalue* : It stands for *generalized lvalue*. Thus it refers to either an lvalue or xvalue. glvalues can also have incomplete types.

4. *rvalue* : This name came because earlier meaning was associated with its appearance in the right-hand side of an assignment.
   It is
   - an xvalue
   - a temporary object
   - a subobject
   - a value that is not associated with an object.

5. *prvalue* : It stands for *pure rvalue*, i.e., an rvalue that is not an xvalue.
   - A prvalue holds the result of a function whose return type is not a reference.
   - The value of a literal, like 10, true or 1.2e3 is a prvalue.
   - Class prvalues can have cv-qualified types.
   - non-class prvalues always have cv-unqualified types.
   - prvalue is a complete type or a void type.

** Question 48   alignment

What is an *alignment*?

Solution of Question 48

An *alignment* is the number of bytes between successive addresses at which a given object can be allocated.

- Every alignment value is a non-negative integral power of two.
- It is represented as an integral constant of the type std::size_t.
- The alignment requirement of a complete type, an array or a reference to a complete object type can be found using an *alignof* expression.
- fundamental alignment $\leq$ alignof(std::max_align_t) $<$ extended alignment.

** Question 49   lvalue to rvalue conversion

What is Lvalue-to-rvalue conversion?

Solution of Question 49

Technically it is *glvalue* to *prvalue* conversion.

- For a complete type T, which is not a function or array can be converted to a *prvalue*.
- For incomplete type, the conversion has undefined behavior.
- For a class type T, *glvalue* should be either an object of type T or an object of a type derived from T.
- The object should be initialized.
- For a non-class type T, the type of the prvalue is without any const and/or volatile version of type T.
- For a class type T, the type of the prvalue is T.
- For a class type T, the conversion copy-initializes a temporary of type T from the glvalue and the result of the conversion is a prvalue for the temporary.
- *glvalue* of type *std::nullptr_t* then *prvalue* result is a null pointer constant.

* Question 50   non-const to const conversion

What is the output of the program ?

Program 9.43: non-const to const conversion

```
int main()
{
    const char c = 'c';

    char* pc;

    const char** pcc = &pc;

    *pcc = &c;
    *pc = 'C';
}
```

Solution of Question 50

This program doesn't get compiled. The compiler error is:

```
const.cpp:4:14:
error: cannot initialize a variable of type
 'const char **' with
      an rvalue of type 'char **'
const char** pcc = &pc;
            ^      ~~~
1 error generated
```

The reason for not allowing the conversion from non-const to const on the line number 7 is to safe-guard a program from inadvertently modifying a const object on line number 11.

** Question 51   xvalue rvalue

In the program, figure out *xvalue* and *lvalue*.

Program 9.44: xvalue rvalue

```
struct A
{
    int i;
};

A&& operator+(A, A);

A&& f();

int main()
{
    A a;

    A&& a1 = static_cast<A&&>(a);
}
```

Solution of Question 51

The following expressions are *xvalues*:

- f()
- f().m
- static_cast<A&&>(a)
- a + a

The expression *ar* is an *lvalue*.

** Question 52   literal and lvalue

Is literal an *lvalue*?

Solution of Question 52

A string literal is an *lvalue*. All other literals are *prvalues*.

*** Question 53   valid usage of this pointer

Program 9.45: valid usage of this pointer
```
1  class Outer
2  {
3      int a[sizeof(*this)];
4
5      unsigned int sz = sizeof(*this);
6
7      void f()
8      {
9          int b[sizeof(*this)];
10
11         struct Inner
12         {
13             int c[sizeof(*this)];
14         };
15     }
16 };
17
18 int main() {}
```

Solution of Question 53

This program doesn't get compiled. The compiler error is:

```
this.cpp:3:19:
error: invalid use of 'this' outside of a
non-static member
      function
    int a[sizeof(*this)];
                 ^
this.cpp:13:27:
error: invalid use of 'this' outside of a
non-static member
      function
            int c[sizeof(*this)];
                         ^
2 errors generated.
```

It is evident from this compiler error that usage of *this* is not valid on line numbers 3 and 13 because line number 3 is not inside a member function and line number 13 is not inside a member function of the class *Inner*.

** Question 54   sizeof

What is the output of the program ?

Program 9.46: sizeof
```
1  #include <iostream>
2  #include <iomanip>
3
4  struct A
5  {
6      int i;
7  };
8
9  int main()
10 {
```

```
11    std :: cout << sizeof(A:: i) << std :: endl;
12    std :: cout << sizeof(A:: i + 10) << std :: endl;
13    std :: cout << sizeof(A:: i - 10) << std :: endl;
14
15    std :: cout << std :: boolalpha;
16
17    std :: cout << (sizeof(A:: i + 20)
18                    ==
19                    sizeof(A:: i - 20))
20                    << std :: endl;
21 }
```

Solution of Question 54

Output of the program is:

```
4
4
4
true
```

** Question 55   lambda and sorting

Write a function to sort a vector of floats based upon absolute values.

Solution of Question 55

We can use lambda expression to create simple unnamed function object:

Program 9.47: lambda and sorting

```
1 #include <algorithm>
2 #include <cmath>
3 #include <vector>
4
5 void abssort(std :: vector<float> vf)
6 {
7     std :: sort(vf.begin(),
8                 vf.end(),
9                 [](float a, float b)
10                {
11                    return std :: abs(a)
12                           <
13                           std :: abs(b);
14                }
15                );
16 }
```

The evaluation of a lambda-expression results in a prvalue temporary known as *closure object*.

** Question 56   type of lambda

What is the type of a lambda expression ?

Solution of Question 56

The type of a lambda expression is a unique and unnamed class type except union type. It is also known as *closure type*. Please note that this class type is not an aggregate.

General

** Question 57 return type of lambda

How the return type of the following lambda expressions are determined?

Program 9.48: return type of lambda

```
auto x1 = [](int i){ return i; };
auto x2 = []{ return { 1, 2 }; };
```

Solution of Question 57

If the trailing return type of a lambda expression is missing then it is the type of the returned expression after

- lvalue-to-rvalue conversion
- array-to-pointer conversion
- function-to-pointer conversion

Otherwise it is void.

Hence the return type of the lambda expression on line number 1 is *int*. Because a braced initializer list is not an expression, hence {1, 2} is not an expression. This implies that the return type is *void* for the lambda expression on line 2. So this will result into compiler error.

*** Question 58 lambda and default argument

Which of the following lambda expressions are valid?

Program 9.49: lambda and default argument

```
void func()
{
    int i = 1;

    void g1(int = ([i]{ return i; })());
    void g2(int = ([i]{ return 0; })());
    void g3(int = ([=]{ return i; })());
    void g4(int = ([=]{ return 0; })());
    void g5(int = ([]{ return sizeof i; })());
}
```

Solution of Question 58

A lambda-expression appearing in a default argument cannot not implicitly or explicitly capture any entity, hence the lambda expressions appearing on line numbers 5, 6 and 7 will raise compiler error:

```
lambda2.cpp:5:20:
error: lambda expression in default
argument cannot capture
     any entity
   void g1(int = ([i]{ return i; })());

lambda2.cpp:6:20:
error: lambda expression in default
argument cannot capture
```

382

```
                any entity
        void g2(int = ([i]{ return 0; })());
                    ^
lambda2.cpp:7:20:
error: lambda expression in default
argument cannot capture
                any entity
        void g3(int = ([=]{ return i; })());
                    ^
3 errors generated.
```

**** Question 59   nested lambda expressions

What is the output of the program ?

Program 9.50: nested lambda expressions

```cpp
#include <iostream>

int main()
{
    int a = 1, b = 1, c = 1;
    auto m1 = [a, &b, &c]() mutable
    {
        auto m2 = [a, b, &c]() mutable
        {
            std::cout << a << b << c
                << std::endl;
            a = 4; b = 4; c = 4;
        };
        a = 3; b = 3; c = 3;
        m2();
    };
    a = 2; b = 2; c = 2;
    m1();
    std::cout << a << b << c << std::endl;
}
```

Solution of Question 59

```
123
234
```

*** Question 60   type of decltype((auto variable))

What is the type of the expression *decltype((x))*, where x is an auto variable?

Solution of Question 60

Type of the expression *decltype((x))* is *const x &*, where x is an auto variable.

For example, in the following example:

Program 9.51: type of decltype((x))

```
void func()
{
    float x, &r = x;

    [=]
    {
        decltype(x) y1;

        decltype((x)) y2 = y1;

        decltype(r) r1 = y1;

        decltype((r)) r2 = y2;
    };
}
```

the type of y1 is float, y2 is float const &, r1 is float & and r2 is float const &.

*** Question 61   brace initializer list as subscript

Can brace-init-list be used as a subscript ?

Solution of Question 61

It can not used as built-in subscript operator, but can be used with user-define subscript operator where it will be treated as the initializer for the subscript argument of the operator[] as can be seen in this program:

Program 9.52: brace initializer list as subscript

```
#include <initializer_list>

struct A
{
    int operator[](std::initializer_list<int>);
};

int main()
{
    A a;

    a[{1,2,3}] = 10;

    int b[5];

    b[{1, 2, 3}] = 20;
}
```

Here line 12 is ok, but line 16 is error.

** Question 62   Pseudo Destructor

What is a *pseudo destructor*?

Solution of Question 62

A *pseudo destructor* is a destructor of a nonclass type, which will only be used as the operand for the function call operator (), and the result of such a call has type *void*. The following example calls the pseudo destructor for an integer type:

Program 9.53: Pseudo Destructor

```
#include <iostream>

typedef int Integer;

int main()
{
    Integer i = 100;

    i.Integer::~Integer();

    std::cout << "i : " << i << std::endl;

    i = 200;

    std::cout << "i : " << i << std::endl;
}
```

The call to the pseudo destructor

```
i.Integer::~Integer()
```

has no effect at all.

Object i has not been destroyed; the assignment i = 200 is still valid.

Output of this program is:

```
i : 100
i : 200
```

Because pseudo destructors require the syntax for explicitly calling a destructor for a nonclass type to be valid, we can write code without having to know whether or not a destructor exists for a given type.

** Question 63   Dynamic Cast

What is *Dynamic Cast?*

Solution of Question 63

dynamic_cast<T>(v) is the result of converting the expression v to type T, where T is

- a pointer or reference to complete class type, or
- pointer to const/volatile void.

Please note that it doesn't cast away the constness.

1. If T is a pointer type, then v is a prvalue of a pointer to complete class type $\implies$ the result is a prvalue of type T.

2. If T is an lvalue reference type, then v is an lvalue of a complete class type $\implies$ the result is an lvalue of the type referred to by T.

3. If T is an rvalue reference type, then v is an expression having a complete class type $\implies$ the result is an xvalue of the type referred to by T.

4. If the type of v is the same as T, or it is the same as T except that the class object type in T is more cv-qualified than the class object type in v, the result is v (converted if necessary).

5. If the value of v is a null pointer value in the pointer case, the result is the null pointer value of type T.

** Question 64   Dynamic Cast vs Base/Derived

How *Dynamic Cast* operates in case of Base/Derived class scenarios?

Solution of Question 64

Let us assume that B is a base class of D.

- If T is a pointer type to B and v is pointer to D, then the result is a pointer to the unique subobject of the D object pointed to by v.
- if T is a reference to B and v is of type D, then the result is the unique B subobject of the D object referred to by v.
- If T is an lvalue reference then the result is an lvalue.
- If T is an rvalue reference then the result is an xvalue.

In the example below, dynamic cast is same as $B^*\ bp = dp;$:

Program 9.54: Dynamic Cast vs Base/Derived

```
struct B {};

struct D : B {};

void func(D* dp)
{
    B* bp = dynamic_cast<B*>(dp);
}
```

*** Question 65   Dynamic Cast vs void

What is the result of *dynamic_cast<T>(v)* when T is a pointer to void ?

Solution of Question 65

- The result is a pointer to the most derived object pointed to by v, or
- a run-time check is applied to see if the object pointed or referred to by v can be converted to the type pointed or referred to by T.

*** Question 66   Dynamic Cast Run-time Check

What is the result of *dynamic_cast<T>(v)* when T is a pointer to a class A ?

Solution of Question 66

General

- If, in the most derived object pointed (referred) to by v, v points (refers) to a public base class subobject of a A object, and if only one object of type A is derived from the subobject pointed (referred) to by v the result points (refers) to that A object.
- Otherwise, if v points (refers) to a public base class subobject of the most derived object, and the type of the most derived object has a base class, of type A, that is unambiguous and public, the result points (refers) to the A subobject of the most derived object.
- Otherwise, the run-time check fails.
- The value of a failed cast to pointer type is the null pointer value of the required result type.
- A failed cast to reference type throws std::bad_cast.

*** Question 67   Understanding Dynamic Cast

what is the output of the program ?

Program 9.55: Understanding Dynamic Cast

```cpp
#include <cassert>
#include <typeinfo>
#include <iostream>

class A
{
    virtual void f() {}
};

class B
{
    virtual void g() {}
};

class D : public virtual A, private B
{
};

void func()
{
    D d;

    B* bp = (B*)&d;

    A* ap = &d;

    try
    {
        D& dr = dynamic_cast<D&>(*bp);
    }
    catch(std::bad_cast & e)
    {
        std::cout << "Exception is : "
            << e.what() << std::endl;
    }

    ap = dynamic_cast<A*>(bp);
```

General

```cpp
39
40      assert(ap == nullptr);
41
42      bp = dynamic_cast<B*>(ap);
43
44      assert(ap == nullptr);
45
46      ap = dynamic_cast<A*>(&d);
47
48      assert(ap != nullptr);
49
50      //bp = dynamic_cast<B*>(&d);
51 }
52
53 int main()
54 {
55      func();
56 }
```

Solution of Question 67

Output of the program is

```
Exception is : std::bad_cast
```

- On line 23 : cast needed to break protection
- On line 25 : public derivation, no cast needed
- cast fails on line numbers 29, 38 and 42.
- line 50 will result into the compiler error

```
    dynamic_cast1.cpp:50:10:
    error: cannot cast 'D' to
    its private base class 'B'
    bp = dynamic_cast<B*>(&d);

dynamic_cast1.cpp:15:29:
note: declared private here
class D : public virtual A, private B

1 error generated.
```

*** Question 68   Understanding Dynamic Cast

Review the program:

Program 9.56: Understanding Dynamic Cast

```cpp
1 #include <typeinfo>
2 #include <cassert>
3
4 struct A
5 {
```

```cpp
       virtual void f() {}
};

struct B
{
       virtual void g() {}
};

struct D : virtual A, private B
{
};

struct E : D, B
{
};

struct F : E, D
{
};

void func()
{
    F f;

    A* ap = &f;

    D* dp = dynamic_cast<D*>(ap);

    assert(dp == nullptr);

//    E* ep = (E*)ap;

    E* ep1 = dynamic_cast<E*>(ap);

    assert(ep1 != nullptr);
}

int main()
{
    func();
}
```

Solution of Question 68

- line 30 succeeds because it finds unique A.
- line 32 fails because f has two D subobjects
- line 36 results into compiler error because of cast from virtual base

```
dynamic_cast2.cpp:36:13:
error: cannot cast 'A *'
to 'E *' via virtual base 'A'
E* ep = (E*)ap;
        ^~~~~~
1 error generated.
```

** Question 69   typeid and const/volatile

Is const/volatile qualifier applicable to the result of *typeid* operator ?

Solution of Question 69

No, top level cv-qualifiers are simply ignored as is evident in the program below:

Program 9.57: typeid and const/volatile

```
#include <cassert>
#include <typeinfo>

struct A {};

int main()
{
    A a1;

    const A a2 = a1;

    assert(typeid(a1) == typeid(a2));

    assert(typeid(A)== typeid(const A));

    assert(typeid(A) == typeid(a2));

    assert(typeid(A) == typeid(const A&));

    assert(typeid(A) == typeid(const volatile A));

    assert(typeid(A) == typeid(volatile A&));
}
```

** Question 70   static cast

What is *static_cast<T>(v)* ?

Solution of Question 70

static_cast<T>(v) is the result of converting the expression v to type T.

- If T is an lvalue reference type or an rvalue reference to function type, the result is an lvalue

- if T is an rvalue reference to object type, the result is an xvalue

- otherwise, the result is a prvalue.

- The static_cast operator shall not cast away constness.

** Question 71   static cast and base/derived

Is the following program valid?

Program 9.58: static cast and base/derived

```
#include <cassert>
#include <typeinfo>

struct A {};

int main()
{
```

```cpp
    A a1;

    const A a2 = a1;

    assert(typeid(a1) == typeid(a2));

    assert(typeid(A) == typeid(const A));

    assert(typeid(A) == typeid(a2));

    assert(typeid(A) == typeid(const A&));

    assert(typeid(A) == typeid(const volatile A));

    assert(typeid(A) == typeid(volatile A&));
}
```

Solution of Question 71

Yes because it produces lvalue to the original d object.

Let us assume that B is a base class of D.

B can be cast to a reference of D if a valid standard conversion from a pointer to D to a pointer to B exists provided:

- B is neither a virtual base class of D nor
- a base class of a virtual base class of D

If the object of type B is actually a subobject of an object of type D, the result refers to the enclosing object of type D as illustrated by this example.

** Question 72   static cast and inaccessible base

Can static cast be used with private base classes ?

Solution of Question 72

No. For example

Program 9.59: static cast and base/derived

```cpp
#include <cassert>
#include <typeinfo>

struct A {};

int main()
{
    A a1;

    const A a2 = a1;

    assert(typeid(a1) == typeid(a2));

    assert(typeid(A) == typeid(const A));

    assert(typeid(A) == typeid(a2));

    assert(typeid(A) == typeid(const A&));

    assert(typeid(A) == typeid(const volatile A));

    assert(typeid(A) == typeid(volatile A&));
}
```

This program doesn't get compiled. The error is:

```
static_cast2.cpp:7:5: error: cannot cast
private base class 'B' to 'D'
    static_cast<D*>((B*)0);
    ^
static_cast2.cpp:3:12: note: declared private here
struct D : private B { };
           ^~~~~~~~~
static_cast2.cpp:9:5: error: cannot cast 'D' to its
private base class 'B'
    static_cast<int B::*>((int D::*)0);
    ^
static_cast2.cpp:3:12: note: declared private here
struct D : private B { };
           ^~~~~~~~~
```

*** Question 73   static cast and const cast

Can static cast be used to add the constness?

Solution of Question 73

Yes.

1. cast A * to void *

2. cast the above result void * to const A *

Program 9.60: static cast and base/derived

```
#include <cassert>

struct A {};

int main()
{
    A* aptr1 = new A;

    const A* aptr2 =
        static_cast<const A*>(
            static_cast<void*>(aptr1)
        );

    assert(aptr1 == aptr2);
}
```

**** Question 74   static cast to and fro

Is the following program valid?

Program 9.61: static cast to and fro

```
#include <cassert>

struct A {};

struct B {};
```

```cpp
int main()
{
    A* aptr = new A;
    A * aptr1 =
        static_cast<A*>(
            static_cast<void*>(
                static_cast<B*>(
                    static_cast<void*>(aptr)
                )
            )
        );

    assert(aptr == aptr1);
}
```

Solution of Question 74

Yes.

1. cast A * to void *
2. cast the above result void * to B *
3. cast the above result B * to void *
4. cast the above result void * back to the original pointer A *

* Question 75   type of base class member

What is the type of &B::i ?

Program 9.62: type of base class member

```cpp
struct A
{
    int i;
};

struct B : A {};
```

Solution of Question 75

int A::i *.

**** Question 76   counting types

Write a program to count the number of types participating in a class template argument ?

Solution of Question 76

sizeof... operator yields the number of arguments provided for the parameter pack identifier.

Program 9.63: counting types

```cpp
#include <iostream>

template<class ... Types>
struct count_types
{
    static const std::size_t value
```

```
 8        sizeof ... ( Types );
 9 };
10
11 int main ()
12 {
13      std :: cout << count_types<int , float >:: value
14                 << std :: endl;
15
16      std :: cout << count_types<int , float ,
17                          std :: string >:: value
18                 << std :: endl;
19
20      std :: cout << count_types<int >:: value
21                 << std :: endl;
22 }
```

Output of this program is

```
2
3
1
```

The result of sizeof and sizeof... is a constant of type std::size_t.

* Question 77   auto type specifier

What are the allocated types in the expressions below and what is the type of the variable x ?

```
new auto(1);
auto x = new auto('a');
```

Solution of Question 77

In the very first expression, the allocated type is int.

In the second expression, the allocated type is char.

Type of the variable x is *char ＊*.

* Question 78   type of new

What are the types of the following new expressions ?

1. new int
2. new int[20]
3. new int[i][20]

Solution of Question 78

1. type of new int is int *
2. type of new int[20] is int *
3. type of new int[i][20] is int (*)[20]

* Question 79   using new

Write an expression to create an array consisting of 20 pointers to function which takes no argument and returns an int.

Solution of Question 79

new (int (*[20])());

** Question 80   operator new

Explain the following expressions with respect to the operator new[](std::size_t, void*):

1. new T

2. new(10, ptr) T

3. new T[20]

4. new(2, ptr) T[5]

Solution of Question 80

1. new T results in a call of operator new(sizeof(T)),

2. new(10, ptr) T results in a call of operator new(sizeof(T), 10, ptr),

3. new T[20] results in a call of operator new[](sizeof(T)*20 + x)

4. new(10, ptr) T[50] results in a call of
   operator new[](sizeof(T)*50 + y, 10, f).

Here, x and y are non-negative unspecified values representing array allocation overhead; the result of the new-expression will be offset by this amount from the value returned by operator new[].

**** Question 81   placement operator

What is the problem with the following program?

Program 9.64: placement operator

```
#include <cstddef>

struct A
{
    // Placement allocation function:
    static void* operator new(
                 std::size_t, std::size_t);

    // non-placement deallocation function:
    static void operator delete(
                void*, std::size_t);
};

int main()
{
    A* ptr = new (0) A;
}
```

Solution of Question 81

A declaration of a placement deallocation function matches the declaration of a placement allocation function if it has the same number of parameters and, after parameter transformations, all parameter types except the first are identical. Any non-placement deallocation function matches a non-placement allocation function.

Hence this program is ll-formed: non-placement deallocation function matches placement allocation function thus resulting into the compiler error

```
custom_allocate.cpp:16:14:
error: 'new' expression with placement arguments
     refers to non-placement 'operator delete'
    A* ptr = new (0) A;
             ^       ~
custom_allocate.cpp:10:17: note: 'operator delete'
declared here
    static void operator delete(
                ^
1 error generated.
```

*** Question 82   illegal casting

What is the problem with the following program?

Program 9.65: illegal casting

```cpp
struct A {};

struct B : A {};

struct C : A {};

struct D : B, C {};

A * func(D * ptr)
{
    return (A*)(ptr);
}
```

Solution of Question 82

This results into the compiler error

```
cast.cpp:12:16: error: ambiguous conversion from
derived class 'D' to base
    class 'A':
    struct D -> struct B -> struct A
    struct D -> struct C -> struct A
    return (A*)(ptr);
           ^~~~~
1 error generated.
```

This is self-explanatory from this error description.

** Question 83 mutable and const

Is it possible to use a pointer to member that refers to a mutable member to modify a const class object?

Solution of Question 83

No.

For example, in the following program, pm refers to mutable member A::i which is being used to attempt modify the const object ca.

Program 9.66: mutable and const

```
struct A {};

struct B : A {};

struct C : A {};

struct D : B, C {};

A * func(D * ptr)
{
    return (A*)(ptr);
}
```

** Question 84 pointer to member function

Write an expression to call the member function denoted by a pointer ptr_to_mfct for the object pointed to by ptr_to_obj where the member function takes an integer value 100 and returns nothing.

Solution of Question 84

```
(ptr_to_obj->*ptr_to_mfct)(100);
```

*** Question 85 relational operator and void *

Can a void * be compared to a const int * ?

Can int ** be compared to int *const * ?

Solution of Question 85

Yes for both.

For example, in the program below, on line number 11 : both converted to const void* before comparison and on line number 13 : Both converted to const int *const * before comparison.

Program 9.67: relational operator and void *

```
int main()
{
    void *p;

    const int *q;

    int **pi;

    const int *const *pci;
```

```
11      p <= q;
12
13      pi <= pci;
14 }
```

** Question 86   Pointers Comparison

What is the result of comparing two pointers p and q when

1. both point to the same object or function
2. both point one past the end of the same array
3. both are null
4. both point to object of type std::nullptr_t
5. both are void

Solution of Question 86

1.
   - p<=q is true
   - p>=q is true
   - p < q is false
   - p > q is false

2.
   - p<=q is true
   - p>=q is true
   - p < q is false
   - p > q is false

3.
   - p<=q is true
   - p>=q is true
   - p < q is false
   - p > q is false

4.
   - p<=q is true
   - p>=q is true
   - p < q is false
   - p > q is false

5. If both pointers represent the same address or are both the null pointer value, the result is true if the operator is <= or >= and false otherwise; otherwise the result is unspecified.

*** Question 87   Pointers to Members Comparison

What is the output of the program ?

Program 9.68: Pointers to Members Comparison

```cpp
#include <iostream>
#include <iomanip>

struct Base
{
    void func() {}
};

struct Derived1 : Base { };

struct Derived2 : Base { };

struct D : Derived1, Derived2 { };

int main()
{
    std::cout << std::boolalpha;

    void (Base::*pb)() = &Base::func;

    void (Derived1::*pl)() = pb;

    std::cout << "(pb == pl) : "
              << (pb == pl) << std::endl;

    void (Derived2::*pr)() = pb;

    std::cout << "(pb == pr) : "
              << (pb == pr) << std::endl;

    void (D::*pdl)() = pl;

    std::cout << "(pdl == pl) : "
              << (pdl == pl) << std::endl;

    void (D::*pdr)() = pr;

    std::cout << "(pdr == pr) : "
              << (pdr == pr) << std::endl;

    std::cout << "(pdr == pl) : "
              << (pdr == pl) << std::endl;

    std::cout << "(pdl == pr) : "
              << (pdl == pr) << std::endl;

    std::cout << "(pdl == pdr) : "
              << (pdl == pdr) << std::endl;
}
```

Solution of Question 87

```
(pb == pl)   : true
(pb == pr)   : true
(pdl == pl)  : true
(pdr == pr)  : true
(pdr == pl)  : true
(pdl == pr)  : false
(pdl == pdr) : false
```

General

* Question 88   brace initializer list and assignment

Review the program ?

Program 9.69: brace initializer list and assignment

```cpp
#include <complex>

int main()
{
    std::complex<double> z;

    z = { 1, 2 };


    int a, b;

    a = b = { 1 };

    a = { 1 } = b;
}
```

Solution of Question 88

Line number 7 means calling z.operator=({1,2})

Line number 12 means a = b = 1;

Line number 14 will raise a compiler error:

```
complex.cpp:14:15:
error: initializer list cannot be used
on the left hand side
    of operator '='
    a = { 1 } = b;
        ~~~~~ ^
1 error generated.
```

** Question 89   comma operator and argument

Will the following program compile? If yes, what is the output ?

Program 9.70: comma operator and argument

```cpp
#include <iostream>

void func(int i)
{
    std::cout << "i : " << i << std::endl;
}

int main()
{
    int first, second;

    func((first = 100, second = 200, first + second));
}
```

Solution of Question 89

Yes, the program compiles and the output is:

```
i : 300
```

*** Question 90   constexpr constructor

Will the following program compile?
How about if the line 20 is commented out ?

Program 9.71: constexpr constructor

```cpp
int  k = 100;

struct A
{
    constexpr A(bool b)
    :
    m( b ? 10 : k)
    {
    }

    int m;
};

int main()
{
    constexpr int i = A(true).m;

    static_assert(i == 10, "");

    //constexpr int j = A(false).m;
}
```

Solution of Question 90

Yes, the program compiles.

If the line 20 is commented out, it results into the compiler error:

```
constexpr_constructor.cpp:20:19:
error: constexpr variable 'j' must be
    initialized by a constant expression
    constexpr int j = A(false).m;
                      ~~~~~~~~~~
constexpr_constructor.cpp:7:17:
note: read of non-const variable 'k' is not
    allowed in a constant expression
    m( b ? 10 : k)
                ^
constexpr_constructor.cpp:20:23:
note: in call to 'A(false)'
    constexpr int j = A(false).m;
                      ^
constexpr_constructor.cpp:1:5: note: declared here
int k = 100;
    ^
1 error generated.
```

This is because the value of 'k' is not usable in a constant expression, since 'int k' is not a const.

** Question 91   translation vs runtime

What is the output of the program ?
Is it reliable enough ?

Program 9.72: translation vs runtime

```cpp
#include <iostream>

void func()
{
    char arr[1 + int(1 + 0.3 - 0.6 - 0.6)];

    int size = 1 + int(1 + 0.3 - 0.6 - 0.6);

    std::cout << std::boolalpha;

    std::cout << (sizeof(arr) == size)
              << std::endl;
}

int main()
{
    func();
}
```

Solution of Question 91

It prints *true*, but it is not reliable because the expression on line 5 must be evaluated during translation, but the expression on line 7 may be evaluated at runtime.

Hence it is unspecified whether the value of f() will be true or false.

**** Question 92   literal class and integral constant

Will is the output of the program?
Will the program compile after commenting out the line number 35 ?

Program 9.73: literal class and integral constant

```cpp
#include <iostream>

struct A
{
    constexpr A(int i) : m(i) { }

    constexpr operator int()
    {
        return m + 100;
    }

    constexpr operator long()
    {
        return m + 200;
    }

private:
    int m;
};
```

```cpp
20
21 template<int n>
22 struct B
23 {
24     enum { RET = n };
25 };
26
27 int main()
28 {
29     constexpr A a = 10;
30
31     B<a> b;
32
33     std::cout << (B<a>::RET) << std::endl;
34
35     //int array[a];
36 }
```

Solution of Question 92

It will print *110*.

If an expression of literal class type is used in a context where an integral constant expression is required, then that class type should have a single non-explicit conversion function to an integral or enumeration type and that conversion function should be constexpr.

Hence after commenting out the line number 35, it will raise a compiler error because of ambiguous conversion:

```
literal_class.cpp: In function 'int main()':
literal_class.cpp:35:16:
 error: ambiguous default type
conversion from 'const A'
     int array[a];
                ^
literal_class.cpp:35:16:
error:   candidate conversions
include 'constexpr A::operator int() const' and
'constexpr A::operator long int() const'
```

* Question 93   scope of conditional variable

Will is the scope of a conditional variable?

Will the program compile ?

Program 9.74: scope of conditional variable

```cpp
1 int main()
2 {
3     if(int first = 10)
4     {
5         int first;
6     }
7     else
8     {
9         int first;
10    }
11 }
```

General   404

Solution of Question 93

A name introduced by a declaration in a condition is in scope from its point of declaration until the end of the substatements controlled by the condition.

Hence the program will not compile due to redeclarations of integer i.

```
scope_conditional_variable.cpp:
In function 'int main()':
scope_conditional_variable.cpp:5:13: error:
redeclaration of 'int first'
       int first;
            ^
scope_conditional_variable.cpp:3:12: error:
'int first' previously declared here
     if(int first = 10)
           ^
scope_conditional_variable.cpp:9:13: error:
redeclaration of 'int first'
       int first;
            ^
scope_conditional_variable.cpp:3:12: error:
'int first' previously declared here
     if(int first = 10)
           ^
```

** Question 94   scope of conditional variable

Will is the output of the program ?

Program 9.75: scope of conditional variable

```cpp
#include <iostream>

struct A
{
    int m;

    A(int i) : m(i)
    {
        std::cout << "A("
                  << m << ")" << std::endl;
    }

    ~A()
    {
        std::cout << "~A()" << std::endl;
    }

    operator bool()
    {
        return m != 0;
    }
};

void func()
```

```
25 {
26     int i = 10;
27
28     while(A a = i)
29     {
30         i = 0;
31     }
32 }
33
34
35 int main()
36 {
37     func();
38 }
```

Solution of Question 94

Output of the program is:

```
A(10)
~A()
A(0)
~A()
```

The variable created in a condition is destroyed and created with each iteration of the loop.

In the while-loop, the constructor and destructor are each called twice, once for the condition that succeeds and once for the condition that fails.

*** Question 95   simulation of while loop

Simulate the while loop of the previous program.

Solution of Question 95

Program 9.76: simulation of while loop

```
1  #include <iostream>
2
3  struct A
4  {
5      int m;
6
7      A(int i) : m(i)
8      {
9          std::cout << "A("
10             << m << ")" << std::endl;
11     }
12
13     ~A()
14     {
15         std::cout << "~A()" << std::endl;
16     }
17
18     operator bool()
19     {
20         return m != 0;
21     }
22 };
```

```
23
24 void func_simulate()
25 {
26     int i = 10;
27
28     label:
29     {
30         A a = i;
31
32         if(a)
33         {
34             i = 0;
35             goto label;
36         }
37     }
38 }
39
40
41 int main()
42 {
43     func_simulate();
44 }
```

* Question 96   range for loop

Given an integer array like the following, write a program to print its contents using range for loop:

```
int array[5] = { 1, 2, 3, 4, 5 };
```

Solution of Question 96

```
for (int& x : array)
std::cout << x << std::endl;
```

*** Question 97   simulation of range for loop

Simulate range for loop using simple for loop statement. There are two kinds of range for statements:

1. for (for-range-declaration : expression) statement
2. for (for-range-declaration : braced-init-list) statement

Solution of Question 97

Both of these can be simulated like the following:

```
{
    auto && range = range-init;

    for ( auto begin = std::begin(range),
```

```
                        end = std::end(range);
                begin != end; ++begin )
    {
        for-range-declaration = *begin;
        statement
    }
}
```

* Question 98   return brace-init-list

Is the following program valid ?

Program 9.77: return brace-init-list
```
1 #include <utility>
2 #include <string>
3
4 std::pair<std::string, int>
5 func(const char* p, int x)
6 {
7     return {p, x};
8 }
```

Solution of Question 98

Yes.

A return statement with a braced-init-list initializes the object or reference to be returned from the function by copy-list-initialization from the specified initializer list.

* Question 99   attributes

Is the following program valid ?

Program 9.78: specifying attributes
```
1 [[noreturn, nothrow]] void f [[noreturn]] ();
```

Solution of Question 99

Yes.

** Question 100   typedef and const

In the program below, what is pointer_to_char?

- char* const, or
- const char*

```
typedef char* pointer_to_char;
void func(const pointer_to_char);
```

Solution of Question 100

pointer_to_char is char* const.

** Question 101   storage class specifiers

How many types of storage class specifiers are available ?

Solution of Question 101

Storage class specifiers are:

1. register
2. static
3. thread_local
4. extern
5. mutable

*** Question 102   inline function

What is an inline function?

Solution of Question 102

- A function declaration with an inline specifier declares an inline function

- The inline specifier indicates to the implementation that inline substitution of the function body at the point of call is to be preferred to the usual function call mechanism. An implementation is not required to perform this inline substitution at the point of call.

- A function defined within a class definition is an inline function. The inline specifier may not appear on a block scope function declaration.

- If the inline specifier is used in a friend declaration, that declaration will be a definition or the function has previously been declared inline.

- An inline function is defined in every translation unit in which it is odr-used and has exactly the same definition in every case.

- If a function with external linkage is declared inline in one translation unit, it is declared inline in all translation units in which it appears.

- An inline function with external linkage shall have the same address in all translation units.

- A static local variable in an extern inline function always refers to the same object.

- A string literal in the body of an extern inline function is the same object in different translation units.

- A type defined within the body of an extern inline function is the same type in every translation unit.

Chapter 10

Constant Expression

*** Question 103   basics of constexpr

Can *constexpr* be applied to

1. a class declaration
2. a class definition
3. the definition of an object
4. the declaration of a function
5. the definition of a function
6. function parameters
7. the declaration of a function template
8. the definition of a function template
9. the declaration of a static data member of a literal type

Solution of Question 103

1. No

    The following is an error because A is declaration of the type A.

```
constexpr struct A;
```

2. No

    The following is an error because A is definition of the type A.

```
constexpr struct A {};
```

3. Yes

Constant Expression 411

```
constexpr A a;
constexpr int i = 10;
```

4. Yes

```
constexpr void func();
struct A
{
    constexpr void g();
};
```

5. Yes

```
constexpr void func() {}
```

6. No

The following is an error because constexpr is applied to the integer parameter i of the function *func*

```
void func(constexpr int i) {}
```

7. Yes

8. Yes

9. Yes

*** Question 104   basics of constexpr

Can *constexpr* be applied to the following ?

1.
```
extern constexpr int i;
```

2.
```
constexpr void f();

struct A
{
    A() { f(); }
```

Constant Expression

```
};

constexpr A a;
```

Solution of Question 104

1. No, because it is not a definition.

2. Declaration of the function f is fine in *constexpr void f();*, but definition of the variable a is not fine because the definition of f is not available yet.

*** Question 105   basics of constexpr

Which of the following is true?

1. If any declaration of a function or function template has constexpr specifier, then all its declarations should contain the constexpr specifier.

2. An explicit specialization cannot differ from the template declaration with respect to the constexpr specifier.

Solution of Question 105

1. True.

2. False.

*** Question 106   constexpr function

What is *constexpr function* ?

Solution of Question 106

A constexpr specifier used in the declaration of a function that is not a constructor declares that function to be a constexpr function.

- constexpr function is implicitly inline.
- it cannot be virtual
- its return type is a literal type or a reference to literal type
- each of its parameter types is a literal type or a reference to literal type
- its function-body is

```
{ return constant-expression ; }
```

*** Question 107   usage of constexpr function

Which of the following is a valid *constexpr function* ?

Constant Expression

1.
```
constexpr int square(int x)
{
    return x * x;
}
```

2.
```
constexpr long long_max()
{
    return 2147483647;
}
```

3.
```
constexpr int abs(int x)
{
    return x < 0 ? -x : x;
}
```

4.
```
constexpr void f(int x) {}
```

5.
```
constexpr int prev(int x)
{
    return --x;
}
```

6.
```
constexpr int func(int x)
{
    int y = x;
    return y;
}
```

Solution of Question 107

1. Ok
2. Ok
3. Ok
4. Error because return type is void.
5. Error because of decrement operation

6. Error because the body doesn't contain just return expression.

*** Question 108   constexpr constructor

What is *constexpr constructor* ?

Solution of Question 108

A constexpr specifier used in a constructor declaration declares that constructor to be a constexpr constructor.

- constexpr constructor is implicitly inline.
- each of its parameter types is a literal type or a reference to literal type.
- its function-body is not a function-try-block.
- its function-body is empty, i.e., there is no statement in its function-body.
- every non-static data member and base class sub-object is initialized.
- every constructor involved in initializing non-static data members and base class sub-objects is a constexpr constructor
- every assignment-expression that is an initializer-clause appearing directly or indirectly within a brace-or-equal-initializer for a non-static data member that is not named by a mem-initializer-id is a constant expression.
- every implicit conversion used in converting a constructor argument to the corresponding parameter type and converting a full-expression to the corresponding member type is a constant expression.

```
struct A
{
    explicit constexpr A(int i = 0)
        :
    m(i)
    {
    }
private:
    int m;
};
```

A trivial copy/move constructor is also a constexpr constructor.

*** Question 109   constexpr function example

What is the output of the program ?

Program 10.1: constexpr function example
```
#include <iostream>

constexpr int func(void *)
{
    return 10;
```

```cpp
6  }
7
8  constexpr int func(...)
9  {
10     return 20;
11 }
12
13 constexpr int invoke1_func()
14 {
15     return func(0);
16 }
17
18 constexpr int invoke2_func(int n)
19 {
20     return func(n);
21 }
22
23 constexpr int invoke3_func(int n)
24 {
25     return func(n * 0);
26 }
27
28 int main()
29 {
30     std::cout << "invoke1_func() : "
31         << invoke1_func() << std::endl;
32
33     std::cout << "invoke2_func(200) : "
34         << invoke2_func(200) << std::endl;
35
36     std::cout << "invoke2_func(0) : "
37         << invoke2_func(0) << std::endl;
38
39     std::cout << "invoke3_func(200) : "
40         << invoke3_func(200) << std::endl;
41 }
```

Solution of Question 109

Output of the program is:

```
invoke1_func() : 10
invoke2_func(200) : 20
invoke2_func(0) : 20
invoke3_func(200) : 20
```

Please note that *invoke2_func* invokes *func(...)* even for n = 0.

** Question 110   constexpr function and substitution

What is the output of the program ?

Program 10.2: constexpr function and substitution

```cpp
1 #include <iostream>
2
3 namespace A
4 {
5     constexpr int x = 10;
6
```

```cpp
7      constexpr int func()
8      {
9          return x;
10     }
11 } // namespace A

13 constexpr int x = 20;

15 constexpr int invoke_func()
16 {
17     return A::func();
18 }

20 int main()
21 {
22     std::cout << "invoke_func() : "
23         << invoke_func() << std::endl;
24 }
```

Solution of Question 110

Output of the program is:

```
invoke_func() : 10
```

Please note that x is not looked up again after the substitution.

* Question 111   revise constexpr function

What is the output of the program ?

Program 10.3: revise constexpr function

```cpp
1 #include <iostream>

3 constexpr int func(bool b)
4 {
5     return b ? throw 0 : 0;
6 }

8 constexpr int func()
9 {
10    throw 0;
11 }

13 int main()
14 {
15    func(true);
16 }
```

Solution of Question 111

This program doesn't get compiled. Compiler error is

```
constexpr_function1.cpp:10:5:
error: statement not allowed
in constexpr function
```

Constant Expression

```
        throw 0;

1 error generated.
```

Another compiler gives the following error:

```
constexpr_function1.cpp:
In function 'constexpr int func()':
constexpr_function1.cpp:11:1:
error: body of constexpr
function 'constexpr int func()'
not a return-statement
}
```

It is self-explanatory from the error-description.

** Question 112   revise constexpr constructor

Review the program.

Program 10.4: revise constexpr constructor

```
1  struct Base
2  {
3      constexpr Base(int i)
4      : m(0)
5      {}
6
7      int m;
8  };
9
10 int x;
11
12 struct Derived : Base
13 {
14     constexpr Derived()
15     :
16     Base(x)
17     {}
18 };
```

Solution of Question 112

This program doesn't get compiled. Compiler error is

```
constexpr_constructor1.cpp:14:15:
error: constexpr constructor never produces a
    constant expression [-Winvalid-constexpr]
    constexpr Derived()

constexpr_constructor1.cpp:16:10:
note: read of non-const variable 'x' is not
    allowed in a constant expression
    Base(x)
```

Constant Expression 418

```
constexpr_constructor1.cpp:10:5:
note: declared here
int x;
    ^
1 error generated.
```

Another compiler gives the following error:

```
constexpr_constructor1.cpp:
 In constructor 'constexpr Derived::Derived()':
constexpr_constructor1.cpp:17:6:
error: the value of 'x' is not usable
in a constant expression
      {}
      ^
constexpr_constructor1.cpp:10:5:
note: 'int x' is not const
  int x;
      ^
```

It is self-explanatory from the error-description.

*** Question 113   literal type

What is a *literal type* ?

Solution of Question 113

A type is a literal type if it is:

- a scalar type; or
- a class type with
    - a trivial copy constructor,
    - no non-trivial move constructor,
    - a trivial destructor,
    - a trivial default constructor or at least one constexpr constructor other than the copy or move constructor, and
    - all non-static data members and base classes of literal types; or
- an array of literal type.

*** Question 114   constexpr and literal type

What is problem with this program ?

Program 10.5: constexpr and literal type

```
1 struct A
2 {
3     A();
4
5     constexpr void func();
6 };
```

Constant Expression

Solution of Question 114

This code doesn't get compiled. Compiler error is

```
constexpr_literal_type.cpp:5:20:
error: non-literal type 'A' cannot have
    constexpr members
  constexpr void func();
                 ^
constexpr_literal_type.cpp:1:8:
note: 'A' is not literal because it is not an
    aggregate and has no constexpr constructors
    other than copy or move
    constructors
struct A
       ^
1 error generated.
```

Another compiler gives the error below:

```
constexpr_literal_type.cpp:5:20:
error: enclosing class of constexpr non-static
member function 'void A::func() const' is not a
literal type
    constexpr void func();
                   ^
constexpr_literal_type.cpp:1:8: note:
'A' is not literal
because:
  struct A
         ^
constexpr_literal_type.cpp:1:8:
note:    'A' is not an aggregate, does not have a
trivial default constructor, and has
no constexpr constructor that is not a copy or move
constructor
```

It is self-explanatory from the error-description.

*** Question 115   constexpr and constructor

What is problem with this program ?

Program 10.6: constexpr and constructor

```
struct Point
{
    int x, y;
};

constexpr Point p1 = { 10, 20 };

constexpr Point p2;
```

Solution of Question 115

This code doesn't get compiled. Compiler error is

```
constexpr_object.cpp:8:17:
error: default initialization of
an object of const
      type 'const Point' requires a user-provided
      default
      constructor
constexpr Point p2;
                ^
1 error generated.
```

Another compiler gives the error below:

```
constexpr_object.cpp:8:17:
error: uninitialized const 'p2'
[-fpermissive]
  constexpr Point p2;
                  ^
constexpr_object.cpp:1:8:
note: 'const struct Point' has no
user-provided default constructor
 struct Point
        ^
constexpr_object.cpp:3:9:
note: and the implicitly-defined
constructor does not initialize 'int Point::x'
     int x, y;
         ^
```

Please note that a constexpr specifier used in an object declaration declares the object as const which should be initialized and have literal type. If it is initialized by a constructor call, that call should be a constant expression, otherwise, every full-expression that appears in its initializer has to be a constant expression.

Chapter 11

Type Specifier

** Question 116   const/volatile qualifier

What is problem with this program ?

Program 11.1: const/volatile qualifier

```
1  struct X
2  {
3      mutable int i;
4      int j;
5  };
6
7  struct Y
8  {
9      X x;
10     Y();
11 };
12
13
14 int main()
15 {
16     const Y y;
17
18     y.x.i++;
19     y.x.j++;
20
21     Y* p = const_cast<Y*>(&y);
22     p->x.i = 99;
23     p->x.j = 99;
24
25
26     const int ci = 10;
27     ci = 11;
28
29     int i = 20;
30     const int* cip;
31     cip = &i;
32     *cip = 4;
33
34     int* ip;
35     ip = const_cast<int*>(cip);
36     *ip = 4;
37
38     const int* ciq = new const int (3);
39     int* iq = const_cast<int*>(ciq);
```

```
40     *iq = 4;
41 }
```

Solution of Question 116

This code doesn't get compiled. Compiler error is

```
const_volatile.cpp:19:10:
error: read-only variable is not assignable
    y.x.j++;
    ~~~~~^
const_volatile.cpp:27:8:
error: read-only variable is not assignable
    ci = 11;
    ~~ ^
const_volatile.cpp:32:10:
error: read-only variable is not assignable
    *cip = 4;
    ~~~~ ^
3 errors generated.
```

Another compiler gives the error below:

```
const_volatile.cpp: In function 'int main()':
const_volatile.cpp:19:10:
error: increment of member 'X::j' in
read-only object
    y.x.j++;
         ^
const_volatile.cpp:27:8:
error: assignment of read-only variable 'ci'
    ci = 11;
       ^
const_volatile.cpp:32:10:
error: assignment of read-only location '* cip'
    *cip = 4;
         ^
```

Please note that volatile is a hint to the implementation to avoid aggressive optimization involving the object because the value of the object might be changed by means undetectable by an implementation.

*** Question 117   decltype

What is the type of *decltype(expression)* in the program below ?
What is the output of the program ?

Program 11.2: decltype

```cpp
#include <iostream>

const int&& func();

int i;
```

```cpp
 7 struct A
 8 {
 9     double d;
10 };
11
12 int main()
13 {
14     const A* a = new A();
15
16     decltype(func()) e1 = i;
17
18     decltype(i) e2;
19
20     e2 = 5;
21
22     decltype(a->d) e3;
23
24     e3 = 10;
25
26     decltype((a->d)) e4 = e3;
27
28     e4 = 20;
29
30     std::cout << e2 << e3 << e4 << std::endl;
31 }
```

Solution of Question 117

This code doesn't get compiled. Compiler error is

```
decltype1.cpp:16:22:
error: rvalue reference to type
'const int' cannot bind to
     lvalue of type 'int'
   decltype(func()) e1 = i;
                    ^    ~
decltype1.cpp:28:8: error: read-only variable is
not assignable
     e4 = 20;
     ~~ ^
2 errors generated.
```

Another compiler gives the error below:

```
decltype1.cpp: In function 'int main()':
decltype1.cpp:16:27:
error: cannot bind 'int' lvalue to
'const int&&'
     decltype(func()) e1 = i;
                           ^
decltype1.cpp:28:8: error: assignment of read-only
reference 'e4'
     e4 = 20;
        ^
```

Type of the *decltype(expression)* are as follows:

Type Specifier

- line 16 : type is *const int &&*
- line 19 : type is *int*
- line 26 : type is *double*
- line 26 : type is *const double &&*

*** Question 118   friend template parameter

How to declare a class template parameter as a friend of the class ?

Solution of Question 118

Let us try as the following:

Program 11.3: friend template parameter

```
template <typename T>
struct A
{
    friend class T;
};
```

This code doesn't get compiled. Compiler error is

```
elaborated_type.cpp:4:18:
error: declaration of 'T' shadows
template parameter
    friend class T;
                 ^
elaborated_type.cpp:1:20:
note: template parameter is
declared here
template <typename T>
                   ^
1 error generated.
```

Another compiler gives the error below:

```
elaborated_type.cpp:4:18:
error: using template type
parameter 'T' after 'class'
    friend class T;
                 ^
elaborated_type.cpp:4:5:
error: friend declaration does not
name a class or function
    friend class T;
    ^
```

Instead, the following code is the correct one :

Type Specifier

Program 11.4: friend template parameter

```
template <typename T>
struct A
{
    friend T;
};
```

** Question 119   auto type specifier

What is the type of the following variables ?

Program 11.5: auto type specifier

```
auto x = 10;
const auto *v = &x, u = 20;
static auto y = 30.0;
auto int r;
```

Solution of Question 119

This code doesn't get compiled. Compiler error is

```
auto1.cpp:4:1:
warning: 'auto' storage class specifier
is not permitted in
        C++11, and will not be supported in future
        releases
        [-Wauto-storage-class]
auto int r;
^~~~
auto1.cpp:4:10: error: illegal storage class on
file-scoped variable
auto int r;
         ^
1 warning and 1 error generated.
```

Another compiler gives the error below:

```
auto1.cpp:4:10: error: two or more data types in
declaration of 'r'
  auto int r;
           ^
```

The type of

- x is int
- v is const int*
- u is const int
- y is double

Please note that auto is not a storage-class-specifier, hence the error on the line 4.

*** Question 120   auto vs template argument deduction

What is the type of the variables a and b ?

Program 11.6: auto type specifier vs template argument deduction
```
#include <initializer_list>

auto a = { 1, 2 };
auto b = { 1, 2.0 };
```

Solution of Question 120

This code doesn't get compiled. Compiler error is

```
auto2.cpp:4:6: error: cannot deduce actual type
for variable 'b' with type
      'auto' from initializer list
auto b = { 1, 2.0 };
     ^   ~~~~~~~~~~
1 error generated.
```

Another compiler gives the error below:

```
auto2.cpp:4:19: error: unable to deduce
  'std::initializer_list<_Tp>' from '{1, 2.0e+0}'
  auto b = { 1, 2.0 };
                  ^
```

Type of a is *std::initializer_list<int>*, i.e., *decltype(a)* is also the same.

Please note that the rules for template argument deduction is at work. For example: for determining the type of c

```
const auto & c = expression;
```

is the deduced type of the parameter t in the call func(expression) of the following invented function template:

```
template <class T> void func(const T& t);
```

** Question 121   scoped enumerator

Is the following program correct ?

Program 11.7: scoped enumerator
```
enum class Color { red, yellow, green };

int main()
{
    int r = Color::red;
```

```
7      Color r1 = Color::red;
8
9      if (r1) { }
10 }
```

Solution of Question 121

This code doesn't get compiled. Compiler error is

```
scoped_enum1.cpp:5:9: error: cannot initialize a
variable of type 'int' with an
      rvalue of type 'Color'
    int r = Color::red;
        ^   ~~~~~~~~~~
scoped_enum1.cpp:9:9: error: value of type
'Color' is not contextually
      convertible to 'bool'
    if (r1) { }
        ^~
2 errors generated.
```

Another compiler gives the error below:

```
scoped_enum1.cpp: In function 'int main()':
scoped_enum1.cpp:5:20: error: cannot convert
'Color' to 'int' in initialization
    int r = Color::red;
                    ^
scoped_enum1.cpp:9:11: error: could not convert
'r1' from 'Color' to 'bool'
    if (r1) { }
          ^
```

Please note that implicit enum to any other type like int or bool conversion is not provided for a scoped enumeration.

Chapter 12

Namespaces

** Question 122   unnamed namespace

What is *unnamed namespace* ?

Solution of Question 122

An *unnamed-namespace* is a namespace without any name with potential to replace usage of static keyword.

An *unnamed-namespace-definition* behaves as if it were replaced by

```
inline namespace unique { /* empty body */ }
using namespace unique ;
namespace unique { namespace-body }
```

where inline appears if and only if it appears in the unnamed-namespace-definition, all occurrences of unique in a translation unit are replaced by the same identifier, and this identifier differs from all other identifiers in the entire program.

Although entities in an *unnamed namespace* might have external linkage, they are effectively qualified by a name unique to their translation unit and therefore can never be seen from any other translation unit.

```
namespace
{
    int a;
}
void func()
{
    ++a;
}
```

Please note that it doesn't require scope resolution operator to refer to it.

** Question 123   using unnamed namespace

What is the output of the program ?

Program 12.1: using unnamed namespace

```cpp
#include <iostream>

namespace A
{
    namespace
    {
        int x;
        int y;
    }

    void func()
    {
        ++x;
    }
} // namespace A

int main()
{
    using namespace A;

    A::func();

    ++x;

    A::x++;

    ++y;

    std::cout << "x : " << x
              << "\ny : " << y
              << std::endl;
}
```

Solution of Question 123

```
x : 3
y : 1
```

** Question 124   function defn vs unnamed namespace

Can a function declared in namespace A be defined in another namespace B ?

Program 12.2: function definition and unnamed namespace

```cpp
namespace A
{
    void func();
} // namespace A

namespace B
{
    A::func() {};
}
```

Solution of Question 124

No.

Compiler error is :

```
unnamed1.cpp:8:13:
error: ISO C++ forbids declaration of
'func' with no type [-fpermissive]
     A::func() {};
         ^
unnamed1.cpp:8:13:
error: declaration of 'int func()'
not in a namespace surrounding 'A'
unnamed1.cpp:8:13:
error: 'int A::func()' should have
been declared inside 'A'
unnamed1.cpp: In function 'int A::func()':
unnamed1.cpp:8:13:
error: new declaration 'int A::func()'
unnamed1.cpp:3:10:
error: ambiguates old declaration
'void A::func()'
     void func();
         ^
```

** Question 125   friend functions and namespace

Can a function declared in namespace A be defined in another namespace B ?

Program 12.3: friend functions and namespace

```
1  void func(int);
2
3  template <typename T> void g(T);
4
5  namespace A
6  {
7      struct X
8      {
9          friend void f1(X);
10
11         struct Y
12         {
13             friend void f2();
14
15             friend void func(int);
16
17             friend void g<>(int);
18         };
19     };
20
21     X x;
22
23     void f2() { f1(x); }
24
25     void f1(X) { }
26
27     void func(int) { }
28 }
29
30 int main()
```

```
31 {
32     using A::x;
33
34     A::f1(x);
35
36     A::X::f1(x);
37
38     A::X::Y::f2();
39 }
```

Solution of Question 125

Compiler error is :

```
namespace_friend.cpp:36:11:
error: no type named 'f1' in 'A::X'
    A::X::f1(x);
    ~~~~~~^
namespace_friend.cpp:38:14:
error: no member named 'f2' in 'A::X::Y'
    A::X::Y::f2();
    ~~~~~~~~~^
2 errors generated.
```

Another compiler gave the following error

```
namespace_friend.cpp: In function 'int main()':
namespace_friend.cpp:36:5:
error: 'f1' is not a member of 'A::X'
    A::X::f1(x);
    ^
namespace_friend.cpp:38:5:
error: 'f2' is not a member of 'A::X::Y'
    A::X::Y::f2();
    ^
```

Please note that f1 is not a member of A::X and f2 is not a member of A::X::Y.

** Question 126   namespace alias

What is namespace alias ?

Solution of Question 126

A namespace alias, say B, declares an alternate name for a given namespace, say A, like the following:

```
namespace A {}
namespace B = A;
```

Program 12.4: namespace alias

```
1 #include <cassert>
2
3 namespace long_name_123456789
```

Namespaces

```
4 {
5     int i = 10;
6 } // namespace long_name_123456789
7
8 namespace short_name1 = long_name_123456789;
9
10 int main()
11 {
12     assert(short_name1::i ==
13         long_name_123456789::i);
14 }
```

Please note that namespace alias is a synonym for the actual namespace, but when looking up a namespace-name in a namespace-alias-definition, only namespace names are considered.

Redeclaration is fine as could be seen in this program:

Program 12.5: redeclare namespace alias

```
1 #include <cassert>
2
3 namespace long_name_123456789
4 {
5     int i = 10;
6 } // namespace long_name_123456789
7
8 namespace short_name1 = long_name_123456789;
9 namespace short_name1 = long_name_123456789;
10
11 int main()
12 {
13     assert(short_name1::i ==
14         long_name_123456789::i);
15 }
```

Program 12.6: redeclare namespace alias

```
1 #include <cassert>
2
3 namespace long_name_123456789
4 {
5     int i = 10;
6 } // namespace long_name_123456789
7
8 namespace short_name1 = long_name_123456789;
9 namespace short_name2 = short_name1;
10 namespace short_name2 = short_name2;
11
12 int main()
13 {
14     assert(short_name1::i ==
15         long_name_123456789::i);
16 }
```

But redefinition is not allowed:

Program 12.7: redefinition namespace alias

```
1 #include <cassert>
2
3 namespace long_name_1 {};
4 namespace long_name_2 {};
```

```
5
6 namespace A = long_name_1;
7 namespace A = long_name_2;
```

This program doesn't get compiled, the error is:

```
namespace_alias3.cpp:7:11:
error: redefinition of 'A' as different kind of
       symbol
namespace A = long_name_2;
          ^
namespace_alias3.cpp:6:11:
note: previous definition is here
namespace A = long_name_1;
          ^

1 error generated
```

** Question 127   using declaration

In this program, which functions will be called by the member functions of the class Derived ?

Program 12.8: using declaration

```
1  struct Base
2  {
3      void f1(char);
4
5      void f2(char);
6  };
7
8  struct Derived : Base
9  {
10     using Base::f1;
11
12     void f1(int)
13     {
14         f1('a');
15     }
16
17     void f2(int)
18     {
19         f2('a');
20     }
21 };
```

Solution of Question 127

- Line 14 calls Base::f1(char)
- Line 19 recursively calls Derived::f2(int);

*** Question 128   using declaration and base class

Can using declaration be used to refer to a non-base class member function as seen the program ?

Program 12.9: using declaration and base class

```
struct Base
{
    void f1();
};

struct Test
{
    void f2();
};

struct Derived : Base
{
    using Base::f1;
    using Test::f2;
};
```

Solution of Question 128

No. This program results into a compiler error :

```
using2.cpp:14:11:
error: using declaration refers into
'Test::', which is not a
      base class of 'Derived'
    using Test::f2;
          ^~~~~~
1 error generated.
```

*** Question 129   using declaration and template-id

What is problem with this code ?

Program 12.10: using declaration and template-id

```
struct A
{
    template <typename T> void func(T);

    template <typename T> struct B { };
};

struct B : A
{
    using A::func<double>;

    using A::B<int>;
};
```

Solution of Question 129

This program results into a compiler error :

```
using3.cpp:10:14:
error: using declaration can not refer
to a template
```

Namespaces

```
            specialization
        using A::func<double>;
               ^   ~~~~~~~~
using3.cpp:12:14:
error: using declaration can not refer
to a template
            specialization
        using A::B<int>;
               ^~~~~
2 errors generated.
```

The reason is simple : a using-declaration cannot be used to name a template-id.

*** Question 130   using declaration and member decl

What is problem with this code ?

Program 12.11: using declaration and member declaration

```cpp
struct A
{
    int i;
    static int si;
};

void f()
{
    using A::i;
    using A::si;
}
```

Solution of Question 130

This program results into a compiler error :

```
using4.cpp:9:14:
error: using declaration can not refer to
class member
    using A::i;
           ~~~^
using4.cpp:10:14:
error: using declaration can not refer to
class member
    using A::si;
           ~~~^
2 errors generated.
```

With another compiler, the error is:

```
using4.cpp: In function 'void f()':
using4.cpp:9:14: error: 'A' is not a namespace
        using A::i;
              ^
```

```
using4.cpp:10:14: error: 'A' is not a namespace
     using A::si;
                ^
```

A using-declaration for a class member should be a member-declaration.
A::i is a class member and this is not a member declaration.
A::si is a class member and this is not a member declaration. Hence the error.

** Question 131   using declaration and refer members

Review the code below.

Program 12.12: using declaration and referring members

```
1  void f();
2
3  namespace A
4  {
5      void g();
6  }
7
8  namespace B
9  {
10     using ::f;
11     using A::g;
12 }
13
14 void h()
15 {
16     B::f();
17     B::g();
18 }
```

Solution of Question 131

In namespace B, *using ::f* calls the global f. *using A::g* calls A'g.

In the function h(), *B::f()* calls the global f. *B::g()* calls A::g.

In short, members declared by a using-declaration can be referred to by explicit qualification just like other member names and in a using-declaration, a prefix :: refers to the global namespace.

*** Question 132   multiple using declaration

Review the code below.

Program 12.13: multiple using declaration

```
1  namespace A
2  {
3      int i;
4  }
5
6  namespace A1
7  {
8      using A::i;
9      using A::i;
10 }
11
12 void f()
13 {
```

```
14      using A::i;
15      using A::i;
16  }
17
18  struct B
19  {
20      int i;
21  };
22
23  struct X : B
24  {
25      using B::i;
26      using B::i;
27  };
```

Solution of Question 132

Compiler error is:

```
using6.cpp: In function 'void f()':
using6.cpp:15:14:
error: 'i' is already declared in this scope
      using A::i;
              ^
using6.cpp: At global scope:
using6.cpp:26:14:
error: redeclaration of 'using B::i'
      using B::i;
              ^
using6.cpp:25:14:
note: previous declaration 'using B::i'
      using B::i;
              ^
```

A using-declaration is a declaration and can therefore be used repeatedly where (and only where) multiple declarations are allowed.

In this code, in namespace *A1*, second occurrence of *using A::i* is a valid double declaration, whereas the in void f, *using A::i* and in struct X, *using B::i* : is invalid case of double member declaration.

*** Question 133   availability of using declaration

Review the code below.

Program 12.14: availability of using declaration

```
1  namespace A
2  {
3      void f(int);
4  }
5
6  using A::f;
7
8  namespace A
9  {
10     void f(char);
11 }
```

```
void foo()
{
    f('a');
}

void bar()
{
    using A::f;
    f('a');
}
```

Solution of Question 133

First occurrence of *using A::f;* in global namespace marks *f* as a synonym for *A::f*, that is, for *A::f(int)*.

f('a') in *void foo()* calls *f(int)*, even though *f(char)* exists.

in the function *void bar()*, *using A::f* marks *f* as a synonym for *A::f*, that is, for *A::f(int)* and *A::f(char)* and *f('a')* calls *f(char)*.

The entity declared by a using-declaration should be known in the context using it according to its definition at the point of the using-declaration. Definitions added to the namespace after the using-declaration are not considered when a use of the name is made.

*** Question 134   using declaration and same functions

Review the code below.

Program 12.15: using declaration and same functions

```
namespace B
{
    void f(int);
    void f(double);
}

namespace C
{
    void f(int);
    void f(double);
    void f(char);
}

void h()
{
    using B::f;
    using C::f;
    f('h');
    f(1);
    void f(int);
}
```

Solution of Question 134

Compiler error is:

```
using8.cpp:19:5: error: call to 'f' is ambiguous
    f(1);
    ^
using8.cpp:3:10: note: candidate function
    void f(int);
         ^
using8.cpp:9:10: note: candidate function
    void f(int);
         ^
using8.cpp:4:10: note: candidate function
    void f(double);
         ^
using8.cpp:10:10: note: candidate function
    void f(double);
         ^
using8.cpp:11:10: note: candidate function
    void f(char);
         ^
using8.cpp:20:10:
error: declaration conflicts with target
of using declaration
      already in scope
    void f(int);
         ^
using8.cpp:9:10: note: target of using declaration
    void f(int);
         ^
using8.cpp:17:14: note: using declaration
    using C::f;
             ^
2 errors generated.
```

- If a function declaration in namespace scope or block scope has the same name and the same parameter-type-list as a function introduced by a using-declaration, and the declarations do not declare the same function, the program is ill-formed.
- If a function template declaration in namespace scope has the same name, parameter-type-list, return type, and template parameter list as a function template introduced by a using-declaration, the program is ill-formed.
- Two using-declarations may introduce functions with the same name and the same parameter-type-list. If, for a call to an unqualified function name, function overload resolution selects the functions introduced by such using-declarations, the function call is ill-formed.

So, in the function *void h()*

- *using B::f;* denotes both *B::f(int)* and *B::f(double)*
- *using C::f;* denotes *C::f(int)*, *C::f(double)*, and *C::f(char)*
- *f('h')* calls *C::f(char)*
- *f(1)* is a ambiguous call : *B::f(int)* or *C::f(int)* ?

- *void f(int)* conflixt with *C::f(int)* and *B::f(int)*.

*** Question 135   hide/override and using declaration

Review the code below.

Program 12.16: hide/override and using declaration

```
struct B
{
    virtual void f(int);
    virtual void f(char);
    void g(int);
    void h(int);
};

struct D : B
{
    using B::f;
    void f(int);
    using B::g;
    void g(char);
    using B::h;
    void h(int);
};

void k(D* p)
{
    p->f(1);
    p->f('a');
    p->g(1);
    p->g('a');
}
```

Solution of Question 135

When a using-declaration brings names from a base class into a derived class scope, member functions and member function templates in the derived class override and/or hide member functions and member function templates with the same name, parameter-type-list, cv-qualification, and ref-qualifier (if any) in a base class (rather than conflicting).

In the code, in struct D:

- *void f(int)* is ok because *D::f(int)* overrides *B::f(int)*.
- *void g(char)* is ok, it is just another overloaded function.
- *void h(int)* is also ok because *D::h(int)* hides *B::h(int)*.

In the function *void k(D* p)*:

- *p->f(1)* calls *D::f(int)*
- *p->f('a')* calls *B::f(char)*
- *p->g(1)* calls *B::g(int)*
- *p->g('a')* calls *D::g(char)*

Namespaces

*** Question 136   using declaration and ambiguous base

In this program, which function will be called by $d\text{->}x()$?

Program 12.17: using declaration and ambiguous base

```
struct A
{
    int x();
};

struct B : A { };

struct C : A
{
    using A::x;
    int x(int);
};

struct D : B, C
{
    using C::x;
    int x(double);
};

int f(D* d)
{
    return d->x();
}
```

Solution of Question 136

This program doesn't get compiled. The compiler error is:

```
using10.cpp:22:12: error: ambiguous conversion from
derived class 'D' to base class 'A':
    struct D -> struct B -> struct A
    struct D -> struct C -> struct A
    return d->x();
           ^
1 error generated.
```

Another compiler gave the following error:

```
using10.cpp: In function 'int f(D*)':
using10.cpp:22:17:
error: 'A' is an ambiguous base of 'D'
    return d->x();
           ^
```

If a derived class uses a using-declaration to access a member of a base class, the member name is accessible. If the name is that of an overloaded member function, then all functions named are accessible. The base class members mentioned by a using-declaration is visible in the scope of at least one of the direct base classes of the class where the using-declaration is specified. Because a using-declaration designates a base class member (and not a member

subobject or a member function of a base class subobject), a using-declaration cannot be used to resolve inherited member ambiguities.
That's why $d\text{->}x()$ is an ambiguous call : $B\text{::}x$ or $C\text{::}x$?

*** Question 137   using declaration and access

Review the program.

Program 12.18: using declaration and accessibility rules

```
class A
{
private:
    void f(char);

public:
    void f(int);

protected:
    void g();
};

class B : public A
{
    using A::f;

public:
    using A::g;
};
```

Solution of Question 137

This program doesn't get compiled. The compiler error is:

```
using11.cpp:15:14:
error: 'f' is a private member of 'A'
    using A::f;
         ^
using11.cpp:4:10: note: declared private here
    void f(char);
         ^
```

The alias created by the using-declaration has the usual accessibility for a member declaration.

** Question 138   using directive

Review the program.

Program 12.19: using directive

```
namespace A
{
    int i;

    namespace B
    {
        namespace C
        {
            int i;
```

```
10              } // namespace C
11
12              using namespace A::B::C;
13
14              void f1()
15              {
16                  i = 5;
17              }
18          } // namespace B
19
20          namespace D
21          {
22              using namespace B;
23              using namespace C;
24
25              void f2()
26              {
27                  i = 5;
28              }
29          } // namespace D
30
31          void f3()
32          {
33              i = 5;
34          }
35      } // namespace A
36
37  void f4()
38  {
39      i = 5;
40  }
```

Solution of Question 138

This program doesn't get compiled. The compiler error is:

```
using12.cpp:27:13:
error: reference to 'i' is ambiguous
            i = 5;
            ^
using12.cpp:3:9:
note: candidate found by name lookup is
'A::i'
    int i;
        ^
using12.cpp:9:17:
note: candidate found by name lookup is
'A::B::C::i'
                int i;
                    ^
using12.cpp:39:5:
error: use of undeclared identifier 'i';
did you mean 'A::i'?
    i = 5;
    ^
    A::i
using12.cpp:3:9: note: 'A::i' declared here
```

```
        int i;
              ^
2 errors generated.
```

A using-directive does not add any members to the declarative region in which it appears. Hence,

- in f1, $i = 5$ is ok, $C\text{::}i$ is visible in B and hides $A\text{::}i$
- in f2, $i = 5$ is ambiguous, $B\text{::}C\text{::}i$ or $A\text{::}i$?
- in f3, $i = 5$ uses $A\text{::}i$
- in f4, $i = 5$ is ill-formed; neither i is visible

Chapter 13

Misc

** Question 139   nested linkage specifications

Review the program.

Program 13.1: nested linkage specifications

```
extern "C" void f1(void(*pf)(int));

extern "C" typedef void FUNC();
FUNC f2;

extern "C" FUNC f3;

void (*pf2)(FUNC*);

extern "C"
{
    static void f4();
}

extern "C" void f5()
{
    extern void f4();
}

extern void f4();

void f6()
{
    extern void f4();
}
```

Solution of Question 139

- *f1*: The name f1 and its function type have C language linkage; pf is a pointer to a C function

- *f2*: The name f2 has C++ language linkage and the function's type has C language linkage.

- *f3*: The name of function f3 and the function's type have C language linkage. The name of the variable pf2 has C++ linkage and the type of pf2 is pointer to C++ function that takes one parameter of type pointer to C function.

- *f4*: The name of the function f4 has internal linkage (not C language linkage) and the function's type has C language linkage.

- *f5*: Name linkage (internal) and function type linkage (C language linkage) gotten from previous declaration.

Linkage specifications nest. When linkage specifications nest, the innermost one determines the language linkage.

A linkage specification does not establish a scope. A linkage-specification occurs only in namespace scope.

In a linkage-specification, the specified language linkage applies to the function types of all function declarators, function names with external linkage, and variable names with external linkage declared within the linkage-specification.

*** Question 140   alignment specifier

What is alignment specifier(s)?

Solution of Question 140

An alignment-specifier may be applied to a variable or to a class data member, but it can not be applied to a bit-field, a function parameter, the formal parameter of a catch clause, or a variable declared with the register storage class specifier. An alignment-specifier may also be applied to the declaration of a class or enumeration type. An alignment-specifier with an ellipsis is a pack expansion.

When the alignment-specifier is of the form **alignas**(*assignment-expression*):

- the assignment-expression should be an integral constant expression

- if the constant expression evaluates to a fundamental alignment, the alignment requirement of the declared entity is the specified fundamental alignment

- if the constant expression evaluates to an extended alignment and the implementation supports that alignment in the context of the declaration, the alignment of the declared entity should be that alignment

- if the constant expression evaluates to an extended alignment and the implementation does not support that alignment in the context of the declaration, the program is ill-formed

- if the constant expression evaluates to zero, the alignment specifier has no effect

- otherwise, the program is ill-formed.

When the alignment-specifier is of the form **alignas**(*type-id*), it has the same effect as **alignas**(**alignof**(*type-id*)).

When multiple alignment-specifiers are specified for an entity, the alignment requirement should be set to the strictest specified alignment.

The combined effect of all alignment-specifiers in a declaration should not specify an alignment that is less strict than the alignment that would be required for the entity being declared if all alignment-specifiers were omitted (including those in other declarations). If the defining declaration of an entity

Misc

has an alignment-specifier, any non-defining declaration of that entity shall either specify equivalent alignment or have no alignment-specifier. Conversely, if any declaration of an entity has an alignment-specifier, every defining declaration of that entity shall specify an equivalent alignment. No diagnostic is required if declarations of an entity have different alignment-specifiers in different translation units.

If the defining declaration of an entity has an alignment-specifier, any non-defining declaration of that entity should either specify equivalent alignment or have no alignment-specifier. Conversely, if any declaration of an entity has an alignment-specifier, every defining declaration of that entity should specify an equivalent alignment. No diagnostic is required if declarations of an entity have different alignment-specifiers in different translation units.

For example:

```
// Translation unit #1:
struct S { int x; } s, p = &s;


// Translation unit #2:
// error: definition of S lacks alignment;
// no diagnostic required
struct alignas(16) S;
extern S* p;
```

An aligned buffer with an alignment requirement of A and holding N elements of type T other than char, signed char, or unsigned char can be declared as:

$$alignas(T)\ alignas(A)\ T\ buffer[N];$$

Specifying *alignas*(T) ensures that the final requested alignment will not be weaker than *alignof*(T), and therefore the program will not be ill-formed.

```
// error: alignment applied to function
alignas(double) void f();

// array of characters, suitably aligned for a double
alignas(double) unsigned char c[sizeof(double)];

// no alignas necessary
extern unsigned char c[sizeof(double)];

// error: different alignment in declaration
alignas(float) extern unsigned char c[sizeof(double)];
```

*** Question 141   noreturn attribute

Review the program below.

Program 13.2: noreturn attribute

```
[[ noreturn ]] void f()
{
    throw "error";
}

[[ noreturn ]] void q(int i)
{
    if (i > 0)
    throw "positive";
}
```

Solution of Question 141

The compiler issues a warning:

```
noreturn.cpp:10:1:
warning: function declared 'noreturn'
should not return
      [-Winvalid-noreturn]

1 warning generated.
```

The attribute-token *noreturn* specifies that a function does not return. It appears at most once in each attribute-list and no attribute-argument-clause is present. The attribute may be applied to the declarator-id in a function declaration. The first declaration of a function specifies the *noreturn* attribute if any declaration of that function specifies the *noreturn* attribute.

If a function is declared with the *noreturn* attribute in one translation unit and the same function is declared without the *noreturn* attribute in another translation unit, the program is ill-formed.

If a function f is called where f was previously declared with the *noreturn* attribute and f eventually returns, the behavior is undefined. The function may terminate by throwing an exception.

*** Question 142   carriage_dependency attribute

What is *carriage_dependency* attribute ?

Solution of Question 142

The attribute-token *carries_dependency* specifies dependency propagation into and out of functions. It appears at most once in each attribute-list and no attribute-argument-clause is present. The attribute may be applied to the declarator-id of a parameter-declaration in a function declaration or lambda, in which case it specifies that the initialization of the parameter carries a dependency to each lvalue-to-rvalue conversion of that object. The attribute may also be applied to the declarator-id of a function declaration, in which case it specifies that the return value, if any, carries a dependency to the evaluation of the function call expression.

The first declaration of a function will specify the
carries_dependency attribute for its declarator-id if any declaration of the function specifies the *carries_dependency* attribute. Furthermore, the first declaration of a function shall specify the *carries_dependency* attribute for a parameter if any declaration of that function specifies the *carries_dependency* attribute for that parameter. If a function or one of its parameters is declared with the *carries_dependency* attribute in its first declaration in one translation unit and the same function or one of its parameters is declared without the *carries_dependency* attribute in its first declaration in another translation unit, the program is ill-formed.

The *carries_dependency* attribute does not change the meaning of the program, but may result in generation of more efficient code.

For example:

```
// Translation unit A.

struct foo { int* a; int* b; };

```

```cpp
std::atomic<struct foo *> foo_head[10];
int foo_array[10][10];

[[carries_dependency]] struct foo* f(int i)
{
    return foo_head[i].load(memory_order_consume);
}

[[carries_dependency]] int g(int* x, int* y)
{
    return kill_dependency(foo_array[*x][*y]);
}


// Translation unit B.
[[carries_dependency]] struct foo* f(int i);

[[carries_dependency]] int* g(int* x, int* y);

int c = 3;

void h(int i)
{
    struct foo* p;
    p = f(i);
    do_something_with(g(&c, p->a));
    do_something_with(g(p->a, &c));
}
```

The *carries_dependency* attribute on function f means that the return value carries a dependency out of f, so that the implementation need not constrain ordering upon return from f. Implementations of f and its caller may choose to preserve dependencies instead of emitting hardware memory ordering instructions(a.k.a. fences).

Function g's second argument has a *carries_dependency* attribute, but its first argument does not. Therefore, function h's first call to g carries a dependency into g, but its second call does not. The implementation might need to insert a fence prior to the second call to g.

*** Question 143   auto as trailing return type

What is the meaning of the code fragment given below?

```cpp
auto f()->int(*)[4];
```

Solution of Question 143

It is a function returning a pointer to array[4] of int, not a function returning array[4] of pointer to int.

** Question 144   parameter type of function

What is the type of the parameter to the function f below?

```cpp
class A { };
void f(int(A)) { }
```

Solution of Question 144

It is equivalent to

```
void f(int (*fp)(A a)) { }
```

not

```
void f(int A) { }
```

** Question 145   parameter type of function

What is the type of the parameter to the function f below?

```
class A { };
void f(int *(A[10]));
```

Solution of Question 145

It is equivalent to

```
void f(int *(*fp)(A a[10]));
```

not

```
void f(int *A[10]);
```

** Question 146   pointers

Review the program.

Program 13.3: pointers

```
int main()
{
    const int ci = 10, *pc = &ci, *const cpc = pc, **ppc;

    int i, *p, *const cp = &i;

    i = ci;
    *cp = ci;
    pc++;
    pc = cpc;
    pc = p;
    ppc = &pc;

    ci = 1;
    ci++;
    *pc = 2;
    cp = &ci;
    cpc++;
    p = pc;
    ppc = &p;
}
```

Solution of Question 146

It declares

- ci, a constant integer;
- pc, a pointer to a constant integer;
- cpc, a constant pointer to a constant integer;
- ppc, a pointer to a pointer to a constant integer;
- i, an integer;

- p, a pointer to integer; and
- cp, a constant pointer to integer.

The value of ci, cpc, and cp cannot be changed after initialization. The value of pc can be changed, and so can the object pointed to by cp.

Each of the first six are examples of correct operations, whereas the rest are illegal operations resulting into the following compiler error

```
pointers.cpp:14:8:
error: read-only variable is not assignable
    ci = 1;
    ~~ ^
pointers.cpp:15:7:
error: read-only variable is not assignable
    ci++;
    ~~^
pointers.cpp:16:9:
error: read-only variable is not assignable
    *pc = 2;
    ~~~ ^
pointers.cpp:17:8:
error: read-only variable is not assignable
    cp = &ci;
    ~~ ^
pointers.cpp:18:8:
error: read-only variable is not assignable
    cpc++;
    ~~~^
pointers.cpp:19:7:
error: assigning to 'int *' from incompatible type
      'const int *'
    p = pc;
    ^   ~~
pointers.cpp:20:9:
error: assigning to 'const int **' from
incompatible type
      'int **'
    ppc = &p;
    ^     ~~
7 errors generated.
```

Each is unacceptable because it would either change the value of an object declared const or allow it to be changed through a cv-unqualified pointer later, for example:

1 *ppc = &ci ;

is OK, but would make p point to ci because of previous error

1 *p = 5 ;

clobbers ci.

** Question 147   lvalue reference

Review the program.

```
1 typedef int& A;
2 const A aref = 3;
```

Solution of Question 147

The program is ill-formed because lvalue reference to non-const is initialized with rvalue. The type of aref is *lvalue reference to int*, not *lvalue reference to const int*.

Please note that a reference can be thought of as a name of an object and a declarator that specifies the type *reference to cv void* is ill-formed too.

** Question 148   types

What are the types of the variables r1, r2, r3, r4, r5, r6 and r7 in the following program ?

Program 13.4: types
```
1  int i;
2  typedef int& LRI;
3  typedef int&& RRI;
4
5  LRI& r1 = i;
6  const LRI& r2 = i;
7  const LRI&& r3 = i;
8
9  RRI& r4 = i;
10 RRI&& r5 = 5;
11
12 decltype(r2)& r6 = i;
13 decltype(r2)&& r7 = i;
```

Solution of Question 148

All have the type *int&* because if a typedef, a type template-parameter, or a decltype-specifier denotes a type *TR*, that is a reference to a type T, an attempt to create the type *lvalue reference to cv TR* creates the type *lvalue reference to T*, while an attempt to create the type *rvalue reference to cv TR* creates the type *TR*.

** Question 149   pointers to members

Review the program below.

Program 13.5: pointers to members
```
1  struct X
2  {
3      void f(int);
4      int a;
5  };
6
7  struct Y;
8
9  int X::* pmi = &X::a;
10 void (X::* pmf)(int) = &X::f;
11 double X::* pmd;
12 char Y::* pmc;
13
14 int main()
15 {
16     X obj;
17
```

```
18      obj.*pmi = 7;
19      (obj.*pmf)(7);
20 }
```

Solution of Question 149

It declares *pmi, pmf, pmd* and *pmc* to be a pointer to a member of X of type *int*, a pointer to a member of X of type *void(int)*, a pointer to a member of X of type *double* and a pointer to a member of Y of type *char* respectively.

The declaration of *pmd* is well-formed even though X has no members of type *double*.

Similarly, the declaration of *pmc* is well-formed even though Y is an incomplete type. *pmi* and *pmf* can be used like shown in the program.

** Question 150   arrays and typedef

What are the types of *CA* and *CAA*?

```
1 typedef int A[5], AA[2][3];
2 typedef const A CA;
3 typedef const AA CAA;
```

Solution of Question 150

- *CA* denotes a type of *array of 5 const int*.
- *CAA* denotes a type of *array of 2 array of 3 const int*.

** Question 151   arrays and sizeof

What is the output of the program?

Program 13.6: arrays and sizeof
```
1 #include <iostream>
2
3 extern int x[10];
4
5 struct S
6 {
7     static int y[20];
8 };
9
10 int x[];
11 int S::y[];
12
13 void f()
14 {
15     std::cout << sizeof(x)/sizeof(int) << std::endl;
16 }
17
18 void g()
19 {
20     std::cout << sizeof(S::y)/sizeof(int) << std::endl;
21 }
22
23 void h()
24 {
```

```
25    extern int x[];
26    std::cout << sizeof(x)/sizeof(int) << std::endl;
27 }
28
29 int main()
30 {
31    f();
32    g();
33    h();
34 }
```

Solution of Question 151

The program doesn't compile because the function h calls *sizeof* on the incomplete object type x.

If the function h is omitted the the rest of the program prints *10* and *20* respectively.

** Question 152   type of function

Is the following statement true?

The type of the functions denoted by

```
1 int (*)(const int p, decltype(p)*)
```

is same as that by

```
1 int (*)(int, const int*)
```

Solution of Question 152

Yes. Because the type of a function is determined using the following rules:

- The type of each parameter (including function parameter packs) is determined from its own *decl-specifier-seq* and *declarator*.

- After determining the type of each parameter, any parameter of type *array of T* or *function returning T* is adjusted to be *pointer to T* or *pointer to function returning T*, respectively.

- After producing the list of parameter types, any top-level *cv-qualifiers* modifying a parameter type are deleted when forming the function type.

- The resulting list of transformed parameter types and the presence or absence of the ellipsis or a function parameter pack is the function's *parameter-type-list*.

Please note that this transformation does not affect the types of the parameters.

** Question 153   type of member function

What is the type of the member function f ?

```
1 typedef void F();
2
3 struct A
4 {
5    const F f;
6 };
```

Solution of Question 153

It is equivalent to *void f();*

** Question 154   typedef and function definition

What is problem with this code snippet ?

Program 13.7: typedef and function definition

```
typedef void F();
F fv;
F fv { }
void fv() { }
```

Solution of Question 154

Compiler error is:

```
typedef.cpp:3:3: error: illegal initializer
(only variables can be initialized)
F fv { }
  ^
typedef.cpp:3:9:
error: expected ';' after top level declarator
F fv { }
      ^
      ;
2 errors generated.
```

The reason is simple : A typedef of function type may be used to declare a function but can not be used to define a function.

- F fv: is ok, it is equivalent to *void fv();*
- F fv{ }: is ill-formed
- void fv() { }: is also ok because it is definition of *fv*

*** Question 155   typedef and const volatile function

What is problem with this code snippet ?

Program 13.8: typedef and const volatile function

```
typedef int FIC(int) const;

FIC f;

struct A
{
    FIC f;
};

FIC A::*pm = &A::f;
```

Solution of Question 155

Compiler error is:

```
typedef1.cpp:3:1:
error: non-member function of type 'FIC'
      (aka 'int (int) const') cannot have 'const'
      qualifier
FIC f;
^
1 error generated.
```

The reason is : A typedef of a function type whose declarator includes a cv-qualifier-seq can be used only

- to declare the function type for a non-static member function,
- to declare the function type to which a pointer to member refers, or
- to declare the top-level function type of another function typedef declaration.

So *FC f* is ille-formed because it does not declare a member function.

**** Question 156   trailing return types

Declare a function template *add* which takes two parameters of different types and returns the sum of the arguments passed.

Solution of Question 156

```cpp
template <typename T, typename U>
auto add(T t, U u) -> decltype(t + u);
```

Alternative is:

```cpp
template <typename T, typename U>
decltype((*(T*)0) + (*(U*)0)) add(T t, U u);
```

**** Question 157   trailing return types

Declare a function *f* so that we can write the following code:

```cpp
int add(int, int);

float subtract(int, int);

void g()
{
    f(add, subtract);
}
```

Solution of Question 157

```cpp
template<typename... T>
void f(T (* ...t)(int, int));
```

*** Question 158   default argument

What is the output of this program?

Program 13.9: default argument

```cpp
#include <iostream>

int a = 1;

int f(int i)
{
    return i;
}

int g(int x = f(a))
{
    return x;
}

void h()
{
    a = 2;
    {
        int a = 3;
        std::cout << g() << std::endl;
    }
}

int main()
{
    h();
}
```

Solution of Question 158

It prints 2.

Because the default argument of the function g is *f(::a)* and *::a* becomes 2 here.

*** Question 159   default argument and member function

Review the program.

```cpp
class A
{
    void f(int i = 3);
    void g(int i, int j = 99);
};

void A::f(int i = 3)
{
}

void A::g(int i = 88, int j)
{
}
```

Solution of Question 159

void A::f(int i = 3) is ill-formed because default argument is already specified in class cope.

void A::g(int i = 88, int j) is ok, in this translation unit, A::g can be called with no argument.

Except for member functions of class templates, the default arguments in a member function definition that appears outside of the class definition are added to the set of default arguments provided by the member function declaration in the class definition.

Default arguments for a member function of a class template will be specified on the initial declaration of the member function within the class template.

*** Question 160   default argument and local variables

Is this program valid?

Program 13.10: default argument and local variables

```
void f()
{
    int i;
    extern void g(int x = i);
}
```

Solution of Question 160

No because local variables can not be used in a default argument.

Compiler error is:

```
default1.cpp:4:27:
error: default argument references local variable
'i' of
        enclosing function
    extern void g(int x = i);
                          ^
1 error generated.
```

*** Question 161   default argument and this

Is this program valid?

```
class A
{
    void f(A* p = this) { }
};
```

Solution of Question 161

No because the keyword *this* can not be used in a default argument of a member function.

*** Question 162   explicitly defaulted functions

Is this program valid?

Program 13.11: explicitly defaulted functions

```
struct A
{
    constexpr A() = default;

    A(int a = 0) = default;

    void operator=(const A&) = default;
```

```
8
9      ~A() throw(int) = default;
10
11 private:
12     int i;
13     A(A&);
14 };
15
16 A::A(A&) = default;
```

Solution of Question 162

? *No.* The compiler error is

```
explicit_default.cpp:3:5:
error: defaulted definition of default constructor
 is not constexpr
    constexpr A() = default;
    ^
explicit_default.cpp:5:5:
error: an explicitly-defaulted constructor cannot
have default arguments
    A(int a = 0) = default;
    ^~~~~~~~~~~
explicit_default.cpp:7:10:
error: explicitly-defaulted
copy assignment operator
     must return 'A &'
    void operator=(const A&) = default;
    ^
explicit_default.cpp:9:5:
error: exception specification of
explicitly defaulted
     destructor does not match the calculated one
    ~A() throw(int) = default;
    ^
4 errors generated.
```

- *constexpr A() = default;* is ill-formed because implicit A() is not constexpr

- *A(int a = 0) = default;* is ill-formed because of the present of default argument

- *void operator=(const A&) = default;* is ill-formed because of non-matching return type

- *A() throw(int) = default;* is ill-formed because exception specification does not match.

*** Question 163   prevent new instance of class

How to design a class such that its instance cannot be dynamically allocated with *new* ?

Solution of Question 163

One can prevent use of a class in certain new expressions by using deleted definitions of a user-declared operator new for that class as shown below.

Program 13.12: prevent new instance of class

```
#include <cstddef>

struct A
{
    void *operator new(std::size_t) = delete;
    void *operator new[](std::size_t) = delete;
};

int main()
{
    A *p = new A;
    A *q = new A[3];
}
```

Compiler error is

```
new_deleted.cpp:11:12:
error: call to deleted function 'operator new'
    A *p = new A;
           ^
new_deleted.cpp:5:11:
note: candidate function has been
explicitly deleted
    void *operator new(std::size_t) = delete;
          ^
new_deleted.cpp:12:12:
error: call to deleted function 'operator new[]'
    A *q = new A[3];
           ^
new_deleted.cpp:6:11:
note: candidate function has been
explicitly deleted
    void *operator new[](std::size_t) = delete;
          ^
2 errors generated.
```

*** Question 164   noncopyable (aka moveonly) class

How to design a noncopyable, i.e., moveonly class?

Solution of Question 164

Program 13.13: noncopyable (aka moveonly) class

```
struct moveonly
{
    moveonly() = default;
    moveonly(const moveonly&) = delete;
    moveonly(moveonly&&) = default;
```

```cpp
7      moveonly& operator=(const moveonly&) = delete;
8      moveonly& operator=(moveonly&&) = default;
9
10     ~moveonly() = default;
11 };
12
13 int main()
14 {
15     moveonly *p;
16     moveonly q(*p);
17 }
```

Compiler error is

```
moveonly.cpp:16:14:
error: call to deleted constructor of 'moveonly'
    moveonly q(*p);

moveonly.cpp:4:5:
note: function has been explicitly marked
deleted here
    moveonly(const moveonly&) = delete;

1 error generated.
```

** Question 165   deleted function and inline

What is the problem with this code?

Program 13.14: deleted function and inline

```cpp
1 struct A
2 {
3     A();
4 };
5
6 A::A() = delete;
```

Solution of Question 165

Compiler error is

```
deleted.cpp:6:10:
error: deleted definition must be first declaration
A::A() = delete;

deleted.cpp:3:5: note: previous declaration is here
    A();

1 error generated.
```

A deleted function is implicitly *inline*. Please note that the one-definition rule applies to deleted definitions as well. A deleted definition of a function is the first declaration of the function or, for an explicit specialization of a function template, the first declaration of that specialization.

**** Question 166   static member initialization scope

What is the output of this program?

Program 13.15: static member initialization scope

```cpp
#include <iostream>

int a = 10;

struct X
{
    static int a;
    static int b;
};

int X::a = 20;
int X::b = a;

int main()
{
    std::cout << X::b << std::endl;
}
```

Solution of Question 166

It prints *20*.

Because an initializer for a static member is in the scope of the member's class.

Hence the following two are equivalent:

```cpp
int X::b = a;
```

```cpp
int X::b = X::a;
```

** Question 167   initializer list

How to initialize the variables a.x, a.b.i and a.b.j with the values 1, 2 and 3 respectively, using an initializer list?

```cpp
struct A
{
    int x;

    struct B
    {
        int i;
        int j;
    } b;
} a;
```

Solution of Question 167

```cpp
struct A
{
    int x;

    struct B
    {
        int i;
        int j;
    } b;
} a = { 1, { 2, 3 } };
```

** Question 168   initializer list and map

Initialize $std::map<std::string, int>$ with 3 pairs as ("One", 1), ("Two", 2) and ("Three", 3) respectively.

Solution of Question 168

Program 13.16: initializer list and map
```
std :: map<std :: string , int> m =
    { {"One", 1}, {"Two", 2}, {"Three", 3} };
```

* Question 169   initializer list and constructor

What is the output of the program?

Program 13.17: initializer list and constructor
```
#include <initializer_list>
#include <iostream>

struct A
{
    A(std :: initializer_list<double>)
    {
        std :: cout << "Inside A(std :: initializer_list<double>)" << std :: endl;
    }

    A(std :: initializer_list<int>)
    {
        std :: cout << "Inside A(std :: initializer_list<int>)" << std :: endl;
    }

    A()
    {
        std :: cout << "Inside A()" << std :: endl;
    }
};

int main()
{
    A s1 = { 1.0, 2.0, 3.0 };
    A s2 = { 1, 2, 3 };
    A s3 = { };
}
```

Solution of Question 169

```
Inside A(std::initializer_list<double>)
Inside A(std::initializer_list<int>)
Inside A()
```

**** Question 170   initializer list and constructor

Explain how the following code works by simulating it using basic code snippets.

```cpp
struct A
{
    A(std::initializer_list<double> v);
};

A a{ 1,2,3 };
```

Solution of Question 170

The initialization will be implemented in a way roughly equivalent to this

```cpp
const double a[3] = {double{1}, double{2}, double{3}};
A a(std::initializer_list<double>(a, a+3));
```

assuming that the implementation can construct an *initializer_list* object with a pair of pointers.

*** Question 171   initializer list and array lifetime

What are the life-times of the arrays associated with the following expressions?

```cpp
std::vector<int> v1 = { 1, 2, 3 };

void f()
{
    std::vector<int> v2{ 1, 2, 3 };

    std::initializer_list<int> i3 = { 1, 2, 3 };
}

struct A
{
    std::initializer_list<int> i4;

    A() : i4{ 1, 2, 3 } {}
};
```

Solution of Question 171

The array has the same lifetime as any other temporary object, except that initializing an *initializer_list* object from the array extends the lifetime of the array exactly like binding a reference to a temporary.

- For v1 and v2, the *initializer_list* object is a parameter in a function call, so the array created for { 1, 2, 3 } has full-expression lifetime.

- For i3, the *initializer_list* object is a variable, so the array persists for the lifetime of the variable.

- For i4, the *initializer_list* object is initialized in a constructor's initializer, so the array persists only until the constructor exits, and so any use of the elements of i4 after the constructor exits produces undefined behavior.

Chapter 14

Classes

** Question 172   trivial class

What is a *trivial class*?

Solution of Question 172

A trivially copyable class is a class that:

- has no non-trivial copy constructors,
- has no non-trivial move constructors,
- has no non-trivial copy assignment operators,
- has no non-trivial move assignment operators, and
- has a trivial destructor

A *trivial class* is a class that has a default constructor, has no non-trivial default constructors, and is trivially copyable. In particular, a trivially copyable or trivial class does not have virtual functions or virtual base classes.

** Question 173   this pointer

What is *this pointer*?

Solution of Question 173

In the body of a non-static member function, the keyword *this* is a *prvalue* expression whose value is the address of the object for which the function is called.

- The type of this in a member function of a class X is X*.
- If the member function is declared const, the type of this is const X*,
- if the member function is declared volatile, the type of this is volatile X*, and
- if the member function is declared const volatile, the type of this is const volatile X*.

Thus in a const member function, the object for which the function is called is accessed through a const access path.

*** Question 174   scope of static member

What is output of the program below?

Program 14.1: scope of static member

```cpp
#include <iostream>

int g()
{
    return 1;
}

struct X
{
    static int g()
    {
        return 10;
    }
};

struct Y : X
{
    static int i;
};

int Y::i = g();

int main()
{
    std::cout << Y::i << std::endl;
}
```

Solution of Question 174

It prints *10*. Because the code *int Y::i = g();* is equivalent *int Y::i = Y::g()*.

*** Question 175   static member function

What are the properties of a static member function?

Solution of Question 175

- A static member function does not have a this pointer.
- A static member function can not be made virtual.
- There can not be a static and a non-static member function with the same name and the same parameter types.
- A static member function can not be declared const, volatile, or const volatile.

*** Question 176   static member data

What are the properties of a static member data?

Solution of Question 176

Classes

- A static data member is not part of the subobjects of a class. If a static data member is declared *thread_local* there is one copy of the member per thread. If a static data member is not declared *thread_local* there is one copy of the data member that is shared by all the objects of the class.

- The declaration of a static data member in its class definition is not a definition and may be of an incomplete type other than cv-qualified void. The definition for a static data member appears in a namespace scope enclosing the member's class definition. In the definition at namespace scope, the name of the static data member is qualified by its class name using the scope resolution operator, i.e., :: *operator*. The initializer expression in the definition of a static data member is in the scope of its class.

- Once the static data member has been defined, it exists even if no objects of its class have been created.

- If a non-volatile const static data member is of integral or enumeration type, its declaration in the class definition can specify a brace-or-equal-initializer in which every initializer-clause that is an assignment-expression is a constant expression. A static data member of literal type can be declared in the class definition with the constexpr specifier; if so, its declaration shall specify a brace-or-equal-initializer in which every initializer-clause that is an assignment-expression is a constant expression. In both these cases, the member may appear in constant expressions. The member is still be defined in a namespace scope if it is odr-used in the program and the namespace scope definition does not contain an initializer.

- There is exactly one definition of a static data member that is odr-used in a program. Unnamed classes and classes contained directly or indirectly within unnamed classes can not contain static data members.

- Static data members of a class in namespace scope have external linkage. A local class can not have static data members.

- Static data members are initialized and destroyed exactly like non-local variables.

- A static data member can not be mutable.

**** Question 177   member name lookup

In the program below, which x is modified by *f.x = 0*?

Program 14.2: member name lookup

```
1 struct A
2 {
3     int x;
4 };
5
6 struct B
7 {
8     float x;
9 };
10
11 struct C: A, B { };
```

```cpp
13  struct D: virtual C { };
15  struct E: virtual C
16  {
17      char x;
18  };
20  struct F: D, E { };
22  int main()
23  {
24      F f;
25      f.x = 0;
26  }
```

Solution of Question 177

Lookup finds *E::x*, because the A and B base subobjects of D are also base subobjects of E, so lookup in D is discarded in the first merge step.

** Question 178   member function lookup

In the program below, provide an implementation of the function *f* which returns the addition of the results of the respective functions of classes A and B.

```cpp
1  struct A
2  {
3      int f();
4  };
6  struct B
7  {
8      int f();
9  };
11 struct C : A, B
12 {
13     int f();
14 };
```

Solution of Question 178

```cpp
1  struct A
2  {
3      int f();
4  };
6  struct B
7  {
8      int f();
9  };
11 struct C : A, B
12 {
13     int f() { return A::f() + B::f(); }
14 };
```

*** Question 179   non-static member lookup

Review the program below.

Classes

Program 14.3: non-static member lookup

```
struct V
{
    int v;
};

struct A
{
    int a;
    static int s;
    enum { e };
};

struct B : A, virtual V { };
struct C : A, virtual V { };
struct D : B, C { };

void f(D* pd)
{
    pd->v++;
    pd->s++;
    int i = pd->e;
    pd->a++;
}
```

Solution of Question 179

Compiler error is:

```
member_name_lookup1.cpp:22:9:
error: non-static member 'a' found in multiple
    base-class subobjects of type 'A':
    struct D -> struct B -> struct A
    struct D -> struct C -> struct A
    pd->a++;
        ^
member_name_lookup1.cpp:8:9:
note: member found by ambiguous name lookup
    int a;
        ^
1 error generated.
```

- *pd->v++* is ok : only one v (virtual)
- *pd->s++* is also ok : only one s (static)
- *int i = pd->e* is also ok : only one e (enumerator)
- *pd->a++* is ambiguous because there are two *a*s in D

A static member, a nested type or an enumerator defined in a base class T can unambiguously be found even if an object has more than one base class subobject of type T. Two base class subobjects share the non-static member subobjects of their common virtual base classes.

*** Question 180   member lookup and virtual base

Review the program below.

Program 14.4: member lookup and virtual base

```
1 struct V
2 {
3     int f();
4     int x;
5 };
6
7 struct W
8 {
9     int g();
10    int y;
11 };
12
13 struct B : virtual V, W
14 {
15    int f(); int x;
16    int g(); int y;
17 };
18
19 struct C : virtual V, W { };
20
21 struct D : B, C { void glorp(); };
22
23 void D::glorp()
24 {
25    x++;
26    f();
27    y++;
28    g();
29 }
```

Solution of Question 180

Compiler error is:

```
virtual_base.cpp:27:5:
error: member 'y' found in multiple base classes of
    different types
    y++;
    ^
virtual_base.cpp:16:18:
note: member found by ambiguous name lookup
    int g(); int y;
                 ^
virtual_base.cpp:10:9:
note: member found by ambiguous name lookup
    int y;
        ^
virtual_base.cpp:28:5:
error: member 'g' found in multiple base classes of
    different types
    g();
    ^
virtual_base.cpp:16:9:
note: member found by ambiguous name lookup
    int g(); int y;
```

```
virtual_base.cpp:9:9:
note: member found by ambiguous name lookup
    int g();

2 errors generated.
```

In the function *void D::glorp()*:

- *x++* is ok because B::x hides V::x
- *f()* is ok because B:f() hides V::f()
- *y++* is ambiguous : B::y or C's W::y ?
- *g()* is ambiguous : B::g() and C's W::g() ?

When virtual base classes are used, a hidden declaration can be reached along a path through the subobject lattice that does not pass through the hiding declaration. This is not an ambiguity. The identical use with non-virtual base classes is an ambiguity; in that case there is no unique instance of the name that hides all the others.

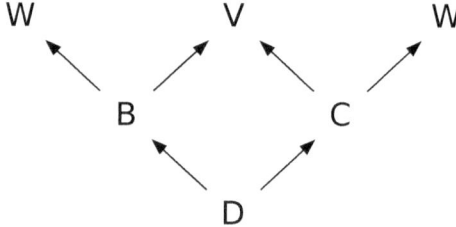

The names declared in V and the left-hand instance of W are hidden by those in B, but the names declared in the right-hand instance of W are not hidden at all.

*** Question 181   virtual function

What is the output of the program below?

Program 14.5: virtual function

```
#include <iostream>

struct A
{
    virtual void f()
    {
        std::cout << "A::f()" << std::endl;
    }
};

struct B : virtual A
{
```

```
13      virtual void f()
14      {
15          std::cout << "B::f()" << std::endl;
16      }
17 };
18
19 struct C : B, virtual A
20 {
21      using A::f;
22 };
23
24 int main()
25 {
26      C c;
27      c.f();
28      c.C::f();
29 }
```

Solution of Question 181

It prints

```
B::f()
A::f()
```

- *c.f()* calls *B::f* because of the final overrider
- *c.C::f()* calls *A::f* because of the using declaration.

Virtual functions support dynamic binding and object-oriented programming. A class that declares or inherits a virtual function is called a *polymorphic class*.

If a virtual member function *vf* is declared in a class *Base* and in a class *Derived*, derived directly or indirectly from *Base*, a member function *vf* with the same name, parameter-type-list, cv-qualification, and ref-qualifier (or absence of same) as *Base::vf* is declared, then *Derived::vf* is also virtual (whether or not it is so declared) and it overrides *Base::vf*.

For convenience we say that any virtual function overrides itself.

A virtual member function *C::vf* of a class object *S* is a final overrider unless the most derived class of which *S* is a base class subobject (if any) declares or inherits another member function that overrides *vf*.

In a derived class, if a virtual member function of a base class subobject has more than one final overrider the program is ill-formed.

**** Question 182   virtual function and hiding

Review the program below.

```
1 struct B
2 {
3      virtual void f();
4 };
5
6 struct D : B
7 {
8      void f(int);
```

```
 9 };
10
11 struct D2 : D
12 {
13     void f();
14 };
```

Solution of Question 182

It is important to note that a virtual member function does not have to be visible to be overridden.

Here, the function *f(int)* in class *D* hides the virtual function *f()* in its base class *B*; *D::f(int)* is not a virtual function.

However, *f()* declared in class *D2* has the same name and the same parameter list as *B::f()*, and therefore is a virtual function that overrides the function *B::f()* even though *B::f()* is not visible in class *D2*.

** Question 183   virtual function and final

Review the program below.

Program 14.6: virtual function and final

```
1 struct B
2 {
3     virtual void f() const final;
4 };
5
6 struct D : B
7 {
8     void f() const;
9 };
```

Solution of Question 183

Compiler error is:

```
final_virtual.cpp:8:10:
error: declaration of 'f' overrides a
'final' function
    void f() const;
         ^
final_virtual.cpp:3:18:
note: overridden virtual function is here
    virtual void f() const final;
                 ^
1 error generated.
```

If a virtual function *f* in some class *B* is marked with the *virt-specifier final* and in a class *D* derived from *B*, a function *D::f* overrides *B::f*, the program is ill-formed.

*** Question 184   virtual function and override

Review the program below.

Program 14.7: virtual function and override

```
1 struct B
2 {
3     virtual void f(int);
4 };
5
6 struct D : B
7 {
8     virtual void f(long) override;
9     virtual void f(int) override;
10 };
```

Solution of Question 184

Compiler error is:

```
override_virtual.cpp:8:18:
error: 'f' marked 'override' but does not override
      any member functions
    virtual void f(long) override;
```

```
1 error generated.
```

If a virtual function is marked with the *virt-specifier override* and does not override a member function of a base class, the program is ill-formed.

**** Question 185   access default template argument

Review the program below.

Program 14.8: access default template argument

```
1 class B { };
2
3 template <class T>
4 class C
5 {
6 protected:
7     typedef T TT;
8 };
9
10 template <class U, class V = typename U::TT>
11 class D : public U { };
12
13 int main()
14 {
15     D <C<B> >* d;
16 }
```

Solution of Question 185

Compiler error is:

```
default_template_argument.cpp:10:42:
error: 'TT' is a protected member of 'C<B>'
template <class U, class V = typename U::TT>
```

```
default_template_argument.cpp:15:5:
note: in instantiation of default argument
      for 'D<C<B> >' required here
    D <C<B> >* d;
    ^~~~~~~~~
default_template_argument.cpp:7:15:
note: declared protected here
    typedef T TT;
            ^

1 error generated.
```

The names in a default template-argument have their access checked in the context in which they appear rather than at any points of use of the default template-argument.

** Question 186   friend constructor/destructor

Is the following program valid ?

```
class Y
{
    friend char* X::foo(int);
    friend X::X(char);
    friend X::~X();
};
```

Solution of Question 186

Yes.

When a friend declaration refers to an overloaded name or operator, only the function specified by the parameter types becomes a friend. A member function of a class X can be a friend of a class Y.

Hence constructors and destructors too can be friends.

**** Question 187   access to virtual function

Is the following program valid ? If yes, what is its output ?

Program 14.9: access to virtual function

```
#include <iostream>

struct B
{
    virtual void f()
    {
        std::cout << "B::f()" << std::endl;
    }
};

struct D : B
{
private:
    void f()
    {
        std::cout << "D::f()" << std::endl;
    }
```

```
18 };
19
20 int main()
21 {
22     D d;
23     B* pb = &d;
24     pb->f();
25 }
```

Solution of Question 187

Yes.

It prints

```
D::f()
```

The access rules for a virtual function are determined by its declaration and are not affected by the rules for a function that later overrides it.

** Question 188   const/volatile constructor

Can a constructor be declared *const, volatile* or *const volatile* ?

Solution of Question 188

No.

A constructor can not be declared *const, volatile* or *const volatile*. *const* and *volatile* semantics are not applied on an object under construction. They come into effect when the constructor for the most derived object ends.

*** Question 189   new and dangling reference

Review the program.

Program 14.10: new and dangling reference
```
1 #include <utility>
2
3 struct A
4 {
5     int i;
6     const std::pair<int,int>& p;
7 };
8
9 int main()
10 {
11     A * p = new A{ 1, {2, 3} };
12 }
```

Solution of Question 189

It results into a compilation error:

```
dangling_ref_new.cpp:11:24: error:
reference to type 'const std::pair<int, int>'
    could not bind to an rvalue of type 'int'
  A * p = new A{ 1, {2, 3} };

1 error generated.
```

A temporary bound to a reference in a new-initializer persists until the completion of the full-expression containing the new-initializer. Here, the line 11 creates a dangling reference.

*** Question 190   user defined conversion

Is the following user defined conversions allowed?

Program 14.11: user defined conversion
```
struct X
{
    operator int ();
};

struct Y
{
    operator X();
};

int main()
{
    Y a;
    int b = a;
    int c = X(a);
}
```

Solution of Question 190

It results into a compilation error:

```
conversion.cpp:14:9:
error: no viable conversion from 'Y' to 'int'
    int b = a;
            ^
conversion.cpp:8:5: note: candidate function
    operator X();
    ^
1 error generated.
```

At most one user-defined conversion (constructor or conversion function) is implicitly applied to a single value.

- *int b = a;* is an error: a.operator X().operator int() is not tried here.
- *int c = X(a);* is fine: a.operator X().operator int() is applied.

** Question 191   conversion by constructor

Review the program.

Program 14.12: conversion by constructor
```
struct A
{
    A(int);
    A(const char*, int =0);
    A(int, int);
```

```cpp
6 };
7
8 void f(A arg)
9 {
10     A a = 1;
11     A b = "Lin";
12     a = 2;
13     f(3);
14     f({1, 2});
15 }
```

Solution of Question 191

This is a valid code. A constructor declared without the function-specifier *explicit* specifies a conversion from the types of its parameters to the type of its class. Such a constructor is called a *converting constructor*.

- $A\ a = 1$ is same as $A\ a = A(1)$
- $A\ b = \text{``Lin''}$ is same as $A\ b = A(\text{``Lin''}, 0)$;
- $a = 2$ is same as $a = A(2)$
- $f(3)$ is equivalent to $f(A(3))$
- $f(\{1, 2\})$ is equivalent to calling $f(A(1, 2))$

** Question 192   conversion operator

Will all three calls depicted below will invoke the supplied conversion constructor?

```cpp
1 struct A
2 {
3     operator int();
4 };
5
6 void f(A a)
7 {
8     int i = int(a);
9     i = (int)a;
10    i = a;
11 }
```

Solution of Question 192

Yes, in all three cases the value assigned will be converted by *A::operator int()*.

*** Question 193   destructor

What is the output of the program below?

Program 14.13: destructor

```cpp
1 #include <iostream>
2
3 struct B
4 {
5     virtual ~B()
6     {
```

```
7        std::cout << "B::~B()" << std::endl;
8      }
9 };
10
11 struct D : B
12 {
13     ~D()
14     {
15         std::cout << "D::~D()" << std::endl;
16     }
17 };
18
19 int main()
20 {
21     D d;
22     typedef B B1;
23
24     B* bptr = &d;
25
26     d.B::~B();
27
28     bptr->~B();
29
30     bptr->~B1();
31
32     bptr->B1::~B();
33
34     bptr->B1::~B1();
35 }
```

Solution of Question 193

```
B::~B()
B::~D()
B::~D()
B::~B()
B::~B()
D::~D()
B::~B()
```

- *d.B:: B();* calls B's destructor
- *bptr-> B();* calls D's destructor
- *bptr-> B1();* calls D's destructor
- *bptr->B1:: B();* calls B's destructor
- *bptr->B1:: B1();* calls B's destructor

*** Question 194   explicit call of destructor

Demonstrate an explicit call of destructor.

Solution of Question 194

Explicit calls of destructors are rarely needed. One use of such calls is for objects placed at specific addresses using a new-expression with the placement option. Such use of explicit placement and destruction of objects can be necessary to cope with dedicated hardware resources and for writing memory management facilities. For example,

```
1 void* operator new(std::size_t, void* p)
2 {
3     return p;
4 }
5
6 struct X
7 {
8     X(int);
9     ~X();
10 };
11
12 void f(X* p);
13
14 void g()  // rare, specialized use:
15 {
16     char* buf = new char[sizeof(X)];
17     X* p = new(buf) X(222);  // use buf[] and initialize
18     f(p);
19     p->X::~X();  // cleanup
20 }
```

*** Question 195   destructor for any type

Is this a valid code ?

```
1 typedef int I;
2 I* p;
3 p->I::~I();
```

Solution of Question 195

Yes.

The notation for explicit call of a destructor can be used for any scalar type name. Allowing this makes it possible to write code without having to know if a destructor exists for a given type.

** Question 196   signature of deallocation function

Provide the signature(s) of deallocation function(s) for a given class A.

Solution of Question 196

```
1 class A
2 {
3     void operator delete(void*);
4     void operator delete[](void*, std::size_t);
5 };
```

Any deallocation function for a class A is a static member (even if not explicitly declared static).

*** Question 197   delete and virtual

What is the output of the program?

Program 14.14: delete and virtual

```
1 #include <iostream>
2
3 struct B
4 {
```

```cpp
5      virtual ~B()
6      {
7          std::cout << "B::~B()" << std::endl;
8      }
9
10     void operator delete(void*, std::size_t)
11     {
12         std::cout << "B::operator delete" << std::endl;
13     }
14 };
15
16 struct D : B
17 {
18     void operator delete(void*)
19     {
20         std::cout << "D::operator delete" << std::endl;
21     }
22 };
23
24 int main()
25 {
26     B* bp = new D;
27     delete bp;
28 }
```

Solution of Question 197

It prints:

```
B::~B()
D::operator delete
```

Since member allocation and deallocation functions are static they cannot be virtual. However, when the cast-expression of a delete-expression refers to an object of class type, because the deallocation function actually called is looked up in the scope of the class that is the dynamic type of the object, if the destructor is virtual, the effect is the same.

Here, storage for the non-array object of class D is deallocated by *D::operator delete()*, due to the virtual destructor, i.e., *delete bp* calls *D::operator delete(void*)*.

Please note that access to the deallocation function is checked statically. Hence, even though a different one might actually be executed, the statically visible deallocation function is required to be accessible. If *B::operator delete()* had been *private* above, the delete expression would have been ill-formed then.

**** Question 198   base class initializer

Review the program ?

Program 14.15: base class initializer

```cpp
1 struct A
2 {
3     A();
4 };
5
```

```cpp
struct B: virtual A { };

struct C: A, B
{
    C();
};

C::C(): A() { }
```

Solution of Question 198

Compiler error is:

```
mem_initializer.cpp:13:9: error:
base class initializer 'A' names both a direct
base class and an inherited virtual base class
C::C(): A() { }

1 error generated.
```

If a *mem-initializer-id* is ambiguous because it designates both a direct non-virtual base class and an inherited virtual base class, the *mem-initializer* is ill-formed.

Here, *C::C(): A()* is ill-formed : which A ?

*** Question 199   pack expansion and initializer

Is this program valid one ?

```cpp
template<class... Mixins>
class X : public Mixins...
{
public:
    X(const Mixins&... mixins)
      :
        Mixins(mixins)... { }
};
```

Solution of Question 199

Yes. A *mem-initializer* followed by an ellipsis is a *pack expansion* that initializes the base classes specified by a pack expansion in the *base-specifier-list* for the class.

*** Question 200   non-trivial constructor

Is this program valid one ?

```cpp
struct W { int j; };
struct X : public virtual W { };
struct Y
{
    int *p;
    X x;

    Y() : p(&x.j) { }
};
```

Solution of Question 200

No.

For an object with a non-trivial constructor, referring to any non-static member or base class of the object before the constructor begins execution results in undefined behavior.

For an object with a non-trivial destructor, referring to any non-static member or base class of the object after the destructor finishes execution results in undefined behavior.

Here, $Y()$: $p(\&x.j)$ will lead to undefined behavior because x is not yet constructed.

**** Question 201   initializer and this

Review the program.

Program 14.16: initializer and this

```
struct A { };

struct B : virtual A { };

struct C : B { };

struct D : virtual A
{
    D(A*);
};

struct X
{
    X(A*);
};

struct E : C, D, X
{
    E() : D(this), X(this) { }
};
```

Solution of Question 201

To explicitly or implicitly convert a pointer (a glvalue) referring to an object of class X to a pointer (reference) to a direct or indirect base class B of X, the construction of X and the construction of all of its direct or indirect bases that directly or indirectly derive from B should have started and the destruction of these classes should not have completed, otherwise the conversion results in undefined behavior.

To form a pointer to (or access the value of) a direct non-static member of an object *obj*, the construction of *obj* should have started and its destruction should not have completed, otherwise the computation of the pointer value (or accessing the member value) results in undefined behavior.

Here $E()$: $D(this)$ has undefined behavior because upcast from $E*$ to $A*$ might use path $E* \Rightarrow D* \Rightarrow A*$ but D is not constructed, $D((C*)this)$ is defined, $E* \Rightarrow C*$ is defined because $E()$ has started, and $C* \Rightarrow A*$ is defined because C is fully constructed.

Whereas $X(this)$ is defined because upon construction of X, $C/B/D/A$ sublattice is fully constructed.

*** Question 202   dynamic_cast and construction

Review the program.

Program 14.17: dynamic_cast and construction

```cpp
#include <typeinfo>
struct V
{
    virtual void f();
};

struct A : virtual V { };

struct B : virtual V
{
    B(V*, A*);
};

struct D : A, B
{
    D() : B((A*)this, this) { }
};

B::B(V* v, A* a)
{
    typeid(*this);

    typeid(*v);

    typeid(*a);

    dynamic_cast<B*>(v);

    dynamic_cast<B*>(a);
}
```

Solution of Question 202

dynamic_casts can be used during construction or destruction.

When a *dynamic_cast* is used in a constructor (including the *mem-initializer* or *brace-or-equal-initializer* for a non-static data member) or in a destructor, or used in a function called (directly or indirectly) from a constructor or destructor, if the operand of the *dynamic_cast* refers to the object under construction or destruction, this object is considered to be a most derived object that has the type of the constructor or destructor's class.

If the operand of the *dynamic_cast* refers to the object under construction or destruction and the static type of the operand is not a pointer to or object of the constructor or destructor's own class or one of its bases, the *dynamic_cast* results in undefined behavior.

Here,

- *typeid(*this)* is *type_info* for B.
- *typeid(*v)* is well-defined: *v has type V, a base of B yields *type_info* for B.
- *typeid(*a)* has undefined behavior: type A not a base of B
- *dynamic_cast<B*>(v)* is well-defined: v of type V*, V base of B results in B*.
- *dynamic_cast<B*>(a)* has undefined behavior, a has type A*, A not a base of B.

** Question 203   inheriting constructors

Enlist the constructors available in *D1* and *D2*.

```
struct B1
{
    B1(int);
};

struct B2
{
    B2(int = 13, int = 42);
};

struct D1 : B1
{
    using B1::B1;
};

struct D2 : B2
{
    using B2::B2;
};
```

Solution of Question 203

The candidate set of inherited constructors in D1 for B1 is

- B1(const B1&)
- B1(B1&&)
- B1(int)

The set of constructors present in D1 is

- D1(), implicitly-declared default constructor, ill-formed if odr-used
- D1(const D1&), implicitly-declared copy constructor, not inherited
- D1(D1&&), implicitly-declared move constructor, not inherited
- D1(int), implicitly-declared inheriting constructor

The candidate set of inherited constructors in D2 for B2 is

- B2(const B2&)
- B2(B2&&)
- B2(int = 13, int = 42)
- B2(int = 13)
- B2()

The set of constructors present in D2 is

- D2(), implicitly-declared default constructor, not inherited

- D2(const D2&), implicitly-declared copy constructor, not inherited
- D2(D2&&), implicitly-declared move constructor, not inherited
- D2(int, int), implicitly-declared inheriting constructor
- D2(int), implicitly-declared inheriting constructor

*** Question 204   hiding

Review the program.

Program 14.18: hiding

```
struct B
{
    int f(int);
};

struct D : B
{
    int f(const char*);
};

void h(D* pd)
{
    pd->f(1);
    pd->B::f(1);
    pd->f("Ben");
}
```

Solution of Question 204

Compiler error is:

```
hiding.cpp: In function 'void h(D*)':
hiding.cpp:13:12: error: invalid conversion from
'int' to 'const char*' [-fpermissive]
     pd->f(1);
            ^
hiding.cpp:8:9: error:   initializing argument 1
of 'int D::f(const char*)' [-fpermissive]
     int f(const char*);
         ^
```

A function member of a derived class is not in the same scope as a function member of the same name in a base class. Here *D::f(const char*)* hides *B::f(int)* rather than overloading it.

Hence the call *pd->f(1)* is in error.

*** Question 205   hiding operators

Review the program.

Program 14.19: hiding operators

```
struct A { };
```

```
3 void operator + (A, A);
4
5 struct B
6 {
7     void operator + (B);
8     void f ();
9 };
10
11 A a;
12
13 void B::f()
14 {
15     operator+ (a,a);
16     a + a;
17 }
```

Solution of Question 205

Compiler error is:

```
operators.cpp:15:18: error: too many arguments to
function call, expected 1,
    have 2
    operator+ (a,a);
    ~~~~~~~~~ ^
operators.cpp:7:5: note: 'operator+' declared here
    void operator + (B);
    ^
1 error generated.
```

The lookup rules for operators in expressions are different than the lookup rules for operator function names in a function call.

Here *operator+ (a,a)* is in error because global operator is hidden by the member operator. Where the expression *a + a* is ok as it calls the global *operator+*.

Chapter 15

Templates

** Question 206   non type template parameters

Which of the following class template declarations is valid?

```
template<double d> class X;
template<double* pd> class Y;
template<double& rd> class Z;
```

Solution of Question 206

A non-type template-parameter can not be declared to have floating point, class, or void type.

Hence *template<double d> class X* is invalid, the rest are ok.

** Question 207   default template parameters

Review the program.

```
template<class T1, class T2 = int> class A;
template<class T1 = int, class T2> class A;
```

Solution of Question 207

The set of default template-arguments available for use with a template declaration or definition is obtained by merging the default arguments from the definition (if in scope) and all declarations in scope in the same way default function arguments are.

Hence the program is equivalent to

```
template<class T1 = int, class T2 = int> class A;
```

*** Question 208   template and template-id

Review the program.

```
template <class T>
struct A
{
    void f(int);
    template <class U>
    void f(U);
};
```

```
template <class T>
void f(T t)
{
    A<T> a;
    a.template f<>(t);
    a.template f(t);
}

template <class T>
struct B
{
    template <class T2>
    struct C { };
};

template <class T, template <class X> class TT = T::template C>
struct D { };

D<b<int> > db;
```

Solution of Question 208

a.template f<>(t); is ok : it calls the template, but
a.template f(t); is in error because it is not a template-id.

default template parameter of *struct D* is alos ok because
T::template C names a class template.

**** Question 209   template argument and type-id

What is the output of the program?

Program 15.1: template argument and type-id
```
#include <iostream>

template<class T>
void f()
{
    std::cout << "template<class T> void f" << std::endl;
}

template<int I>
void f()
{
    std::cout << "template<int I> void f" << std::endl;
}

int main()
{
    f<int()>();
}
```

Solution of Question 209

It prints

```
template<class T> void f
```

In a template-argument, an ambiguity between a *type-id* and an expression is resolved to a *type-id*, regardless of the form of the corresponding template-parameter.

Hence f<int()>() calls the first f() because int() is a type-id.

*** Question 210   explicit specialization vs static

Is this program valid ?

```
template <class T> struct A
{
    static int i [];
};

template <class T> int A<T>::i [4];

template <> int A<int>::i [] = { 1 };
```

Solution of Question 210

Yes.

An explicit specialization of a static data member declared as an array of unknown bound can have a different bound from its definition, if any.

** Question 211   virtual member function template

Review the program.

Program 15.2: virtual member function template
```
template <class T>
struct A
{
    template <class U>
    virtual void f(U);
};
```

Solution of Question 211

Compiler error is:

```
virtual_template.cpp:5:5: error:
'virtual' can not be specified on member
    function templates
    virtual void f(U);
    ^~~~~~~
1 error generated.
```

A member function template can not be virtual.

*** Question 212   override virtual and template

Which of the following member function overrides B::f(int)?

```
class B
{
    virtual void f(int);
};
```

```
 6 class D : public B
 7 {
 8     template <class T>
 9     void f(T);
10
11     void f(int i)
12     {
13         f<>(i);
14     }
15 };
```

Solution of Question 212

A specialization of a member function template does not override a virtual function from a base class.

Hence *template <class T> void f(T)* does not override *B::f(int)*.

void f(int i) is the overriding function that calls the template instantiation.

*** Question 213   parameter pack

What is a *template parameter pack* and *function parameter pack*?

Solution of Question 213

A *template parameter pack* is a template parameter that accepts zero or more template arguments. For example:

```
1 template<class ... Types> struct Tuple { };
2 Tuple<> t0;  // Types contains no arguments
3 Tuple<int> t1;  // Types contains one argument : int
4 Tuple<int, float> t2;  // Types contains two arguments :
        int and float
5 Tuple<0> error;  // error : 0 is not a type
```

A *function parameter pack* is a function parameter that accepts zero or more function arguments. For example:

```
1 template<class ... Types> void f(Types ... args);
2 f();  // args contains no arguments
3 f(1);  // args contains one argument: int
4 f(2, 1.0);  // args contains two arguments: int and double
```

*** Question 214   alias template

What is an *alias template* ?

Solution of Question 214

A template-declaration in which the declaration is an alias-declaration declares the identifier to be a *alias template*. An *alias template* is a name for a family of types. The name of the *alias template* is a template-name.

When a template-id refers to the specialization of an alias template, it is equivalent to the associated type obtained by substitution of its template-arguments for the template-parameters in the type-id of the alias template.

For example

```
1 template<class T> struct Alloc { */ ... */ };
2 template<class T> using Vec = vector<T, Alloc<T>>;
3 Vec<int> v;  // same as vector<int, Alloc<int>> v;
```

Please note that an alias template name is never deduced.

Chapter 16

Standard Library

*** Question 215   constraint class

Write a constraint class *HasEqual* that checks for the existence of the == operator.

Solution of Question 215

```
template<typename T, typename U>
struct HasEqual<T, U>
{
    HasEqual() { auto p = constraints; }

    static void constraints(T x, U y)
    {
        x == y;
    }
};
```

The *HasEqual* constructor forces the instantiation of the static constraints member function by declaring a pointer to the function. This function implements a set of valid expressions for the objects introduced by its formal parameters.

The body of this constraints function contains a single statement that forces a lookup on an appropriate == for types of T and U. If no such operator can be found, instantiation will fail, and the compiler emits the appropriate error message.

The result of the expression is unconstrained here.

**** Question 216   reusing constraint class

Reuse the above constraint class *HasEqual* to implement the concept class *EqualityComparable*.

Solution of Question 216

Constraint classes can be reused through either inheritance or composition.

```
template<typename T>
struct EqualityComparable : HasEqual<T, T>
{
    EqualityComparable()
    {
```

```
 6            auto p = constraints;
 7      }
 8
 9      static void constraints(T x, T y)
10      {
11            Convertible<decltype(x == y), bool>{};
12
13            Convertible<decltype(x != y), bool>{};
14      }
15 };
```

The inheritance of *HasEqual* causes the constraint to be checked before the constraints in the *EqualityComparable* constraint class by virtue of the initialization order. The *EqualityComparable* class applies additional constraints within its body.

Here, the *Convertible* constraint is written as an explicit initialization of a temporary object. This checks if the result of an expression (the *decltype* operator returns the type of an expression) can be converted to the specified type, here, *bool*.

A similar requirement is made for !=. *Convertible* is defined as:

```
1 template<typename T, typename U>
2 struct Convertible
3 {
4      Convertible()
5      {
6            static_assert(std::is_convertible<T, U>::value, "Not convertible");
7      }
8 };
```

The constraint is implemented by statically asserting the *std::is_convertible* type trait. A *type trait* is a class template that evaluates some property of its type arguments. The nested value contains the result of the evaluation. A constraints function is not needed since the trait can be evaluated without introducing objects.

*** Question 217   type traits

Provide an implementation of a type trait *is_same* as a class template such that *is_same<X, Y>::value* is only true when *X* and *Y* name the same type. The resulting value should be a constant expression that can be evaluated by the compiler in contexts such as a *static_assert*.

Solution of Question 217

```
 1 template<typename T, typename U>
 2 struct is_same
 3 {
 4      static constexpr bool value = false;
 5 };
 6
 7 template<typename T>
 8 struct is_same<T, T>
 9 {
10      static constexpr bool value = true;
11 };
```

Standard Library

The primary template (the first declaration) defines the result when X and Y are different types. The specialization defines the result when the template arguments are the same.

*** Question 218   advance and next

Provide an implementation of the STL algorithm *advance* for input and forward iterators and then implement an iterator utility *next* using *advance* algorithm.

Solution of Question 218

```cpp
template<typename Iter>
void advance(Iter& first, int n)
{
    while(n > 0)
    {
        ++first;
        --n;
    }
}

template<typename Iter>
Iter next(Iter i, int n = 1)
{
    advance(i, n);
    return i;
}
```

*** Question 219   custom iota

Customize the increment/decrement part of the STL algorithm *iota*.

Solution of Question 219

Overload iota for custom increment step:

```cpp
template <typename ForwardIterator, typename T>
void iota( ForwardIterator first, ForwardIterator last,
T value, T step = 1 )
{
    for ( ; first != last; ++first, value += step )
        *first = value;
}

//Usage :
std::vector<int> vint(5);
std::vector<int> v_expected = {5, 10, 15, 20, 25};
iota (vint.begin(), vint.end(), //destination range
5, // start value
5);// increment by 5

assert(std::equal(vint.begin(),vint.end(),v_expected.begin()));
```

Overloading iota with step size as an additional argument requires changing the implementation along-with the established interface, which may not be viable in every situation. On the other hand, we can easily achieve the same output with overloading pre-increment operator as follows:

```cpp
template <typename InitialValue, typename StepSize>
struct step_helper
{
    step_helper(InitialValue val, StepSize step)
    : _val(val), _step(step) {}

    step_helper & operator++()
    {
        _val += _step; return *this;
    }

    operator InitialValue() { return _val; }

private:
    InitialValue _val;
    const StepSize _step;
};

template<typename InitialValue, typename StepSize = InitialValue>
step_helper<InitialValue, StepSize>
step(InitialValue val, StepSize s = 1)
{
    return step_helper<InitialValue, StepSize>(val, s);
}

// Usage : custom increment is 10
std::array<int, 5> arr;
std::array<int, 5> arr_res = {5, 15, 25, 35, 45};
std::iota(arr.begin(), arr.end(), step(5, 10));
assert(std::equal(arr.begin(), arr.end(), arr_res.begin()
    ));
```

*** Question 220   all_of algorithm

Implement the STL algorithm *all_of* using *find_if_not* and *find_if*.

Solution of Question 220

```cpp
template<typename InputIterator, typename Predicate>
inline bool
all_of(InputIterator first, InputIterator last, Predicate pred)
{
    return last == std::find_if_not(first, last, pred);
}


template<typename InputIterator, typename Predicate>
inline bool
all_of(InputIterator first, InputIterator last, Predicate pred)
{
    return last == std::find_if(first, last, std::not1(
        pred));
}
```

*** Question 221   is_partitioned algorithm

Implement the STL algorithm *is_partitioned* with the interface

```cpp
template<typename InputIterator, typename Predicate>
bool is_partitioned(InputIterator first, InputIterator
    last, Predicate p);
```

It returns true if

- if [first, last) is partitioned by the unary predicate p, i.e. if all elements that satisfy p appear before those that do not. Or,
- if [first, last) is empty.

In other words, all the items in the sequence that satisfy the predicate are at the beginning of the sequence.

Solution of Question 221

There are two phases of this algorithm:

1. Find the first occurrence of the element which does not satisfy the predicate. The algorithm *std::find_if_not* perfectly fits the bill here.

2. None of the elements should satisfy the predicate starting from the element found above. *std::none_of* can be used to get this job done easily.

```cpp
template<typename InputIterator, typename Predicate>
bool is_partitioned(InputIterator first, InputIterator
    last,
Predicate p)
{
    first = std::find_if_not(first, last, pred);
    return std::none_of(first, last, pred);
}
```

or

```cpp
template<typename InputIterator, typename Predicate>
bool is_partitioned(InputIterator first, InputIterator
    last,
Predicate p)
{
    while(first != last && pred(*first))
        ++first;

    while(first != last && pred(*first))
        ++first;

    return (first == last);
}
```

Index

2D Array Rotation, 106

A Queuing Problem in A Post Office, 108
access default template argument, 476
access to virtual function, 477, 478
ADL(Argument Dependent Lookup), 357, 358
advance and next, 498
alias template, 494
alignment, 377, 378
alignment specifier, 448
all_of algorithm, 499
Alternative Euclid' Algorithm, 242
ancestor, 154
Approximating the square root of a number, 4
arrays and sizeof, 455, 456
arrays and typedef, 455
attributes, 407
auto as trailing return type, 451
auto type specifier, 394, 426
auto type specifier vs template argument deduction, 427
availability of using declaration, 438, 439
Average of Integers without Overflow, 330

base class initializer, 483, 484
Basic Look-up, 359, 360
basics of constexpr, 410–412
Bellman's Principle of Optimality, 170
Bit Counting Algorithms, 276
Bit Reversal, 302
Bit Shuffling, 305
Bit-fields and Concurrency, 337
Bit-wise Rotation, 328
brace initializer list and assignment, 400

brace initializer list as subscript, 384
Bulterman's Reshuffling Problem, 126

carriage_dependency attribute, 450
Circular Array, 132
class scope variables, 348, 349
classes, 467
comma operator and argument, 400
Compiler Generated Member Functions, 343, 344
complete binary tree, 164
Computation of Power of 2, 321
Compute a^n, 238
Compute Function, 250
Compute GCD, 240
Compute Modulus Division, 332
Compute Next higher number with same number of 1-bits, 271
Compute Square using only addition and subtraction, 244
Compute sum of sub-array, 147
Compute the product $a \times b$, 239
Compute the quotient and remainder, 240
Computed Constrained GCD, 241
Computing Functions, 308
Computing Parity of a word, 286
Conditionally negate a value without branching, 333
Conditionally set or clear bits without branching, 333
const/volatile constructor, 478
const/volatile qualifier, 422, 423
Constant Time Range Query, 66
constexpr, 410
constexpr and constructor, 419, 420
constexpr and literal type, 418, 419
constexpr constructor, 401, 414
constexpr function, 412

501

Index 502

constexpr function and substitution, 415, 416
constexpr function example, 414, 415
constraint class, 496
constructor name look-up, 362
conversion by constructor, 479, 480
conversion operator, 480
Counting 1-Bits, 276
Counting Leading 0's, 289
Counting the 1-bits in an Array, 281
Counting Trailing 0's, 296
counting types, 393
custom iota, 498

damerau edit distance, 177
Decimal Period Length, 249
Decimal Representation, 246
decision tree, 217
declaration : global vs local, 369
declaration and nested namespace, 367, 368
Declaration vs Definition, 343
decltype, 423, 424
default argument, 458, 459
default argument and local variables, 460
default argument and member function, 459
default argument and this, 460
default template parameters, 491
delete and virtual, 482, 483
deleted function and inline, 463
destructor, 480, 481
destructor and typedef, 361
destructor for any type, 482
deterministic algorithm, 229
deterministic partition, 220
Distinct Address Location, 338, 339
Double Linked List with One Pointer Field, 331
Dynamic Cast, 385
Dynamic Cast Run-time Check, 386
Dynamic Cast vs Base/Derived, 386
Dynamic Cast vs void, 386
Dynamic Programming, 170
dynamic programming, 186
dynamic_cast and construction, 486

edit distance, 177
Efficient Multiplication by Constants, 325
Emulate Division and Modulus Operations, 251

evaluation of expressions, 340
Exchange Prefix and Suffix, 255
expanders, 231
explicit call of destructor, 481
explicit specialization and static member, 493
explicitly defaulted functions, 460, 461
Exponentiation, 48
Extending De Morgan's Laws, 270

Factorization, 244
Fibonacci words, 318
Find a number not sum of subsets of array, 147
Find Length of the rope, 82
Find Maximum, 259
Find Median of two sorted arrays, 133
Find missing integer, 151
find next higher number, 206
find previous lower number, 210
Find Shortest String of 1-Bits, 315
find sum closest to k, 195
find sum closest to zero, 191
Find the number not occurring twice in an array, 152
Finding Ranks in Linked Lists, 262
Finding the kth Smallest Element on a Tree, 264
Finding the majority, 128
Finding the missing integer, 134
Finding the missing number with sorted columns, 139
Fixed size generic array in C++, 38
friend constructor/destructor, 477
friend functions and namespace, 431, 432
Friend member function vs Name-Lookup, 355, 356
friend template parameter, 425
function definition and unnamed namespace, 430

Generating Permutation Efficiently, 7
Gray Code Conversion, 330

Hamming Problem, 64
hide/override and using declaration, 441
hiding, 488
hiding operators, 488, 489

Index

illegal casting, 396
In, On or Out, 85
increment operator, 341
Independent Set, 200
inheriting constructors, 487
initializer and this, 485
initializer list, 464
initializer list and array lifetime, 466
initializer list and constructor, 465
initializer list and map, 465
injected class name, 369, 370
inline function, 408
Inplace Reversing, 151
Integer Exponentiation : Compute x^n, 310
Integer Square Root, 308
Integral Types, 375, 376
Interpolation Search, 111
Is this (almost) sorted, 25
is_partitioned algorithm, 499, 500

k maximum sub-array problem, 197
kadane 1D algorithm, 186
kadane 2D algorithm, 195
kth select minimum, 19
kth smallest element in two sorted arrays, 148

lambda and default argument, 382
lambda and sorting, 381
lca, 154
lca solution complete binary tree, 164
lca solution constant time, 163
lca solution level based, 161
lca solution xor based, 164
Least Significant 1 Bit, 331
levenshtein edit distance, 177
Linear Time Sorting, 68, 118
linkage, 370, 371
literal and lvalue, 379
literal class and integral constant, 402, 403
literal type, 418
longest common subsequence, 178
Low Level Algorithms, 269
Lowest Common Ancestor(LCA) Problem, 154
LRU Algorithm : Reference Matrix, 312
LRU data structure, 253
lvalue reference, 453, 454
lvalue to rvalue conversion, 378

Manipulating Rightmost Bits, 269
Matrix Multiplication, 174
max sub-array 2D problem, 195
Max Sub-Array Problem, 185
maximum of a sequence, 13
maximum sum sub-array problem, 186
member function lookup, 470
member lookup and virtual base, 471, 472
member name lookup, 469, 470
Mode of a Multiset, 131
Most Significant 1 Bit, 331
multiple declarations, 365
multiple references to namespace, 365, 366
multiple using declaration, 437, 438
Music Recognition, 183
mutable and const, 397

n-ary tree, 156
namespace, 362, 364
namespace alias, 432
namespace extern and look-up, 356
namespace scope variables, 349, 350
nested lambda expressions, 383
nested linkage specifications, 447
new and dangling reference, 478
Newton's Method, 308
Next bit Permutation, 332
next higher permutation, 207
non type template parameters, 491
non-const to const conversion, 378, 379
non-static member lookup, 470, 471
non-trivial constructor, 484, 485
non-type name and namespace, 366, 367
noncopyable (aka moveonly) class, 462
noreturn attribute, 449, 450
nullptr, 341
nuts n bolts problem, 216

ODR vs Default Constructor, 346, 347
operator new, 395
Optimal Substructure, 170
Ordering : const/volatile, 376
override virtual and template, 493, 494

pack expansion and initializer, 484
Parallel Addition, 258
Parallel Algorithms, 258

parameter pack, 494
parameter type of function, 451, 452
partial quicksort, 23
partition, 220
Party Problem, 202
path number, 164
permutation, 217
placement operator, 395, 396
pointer to member function, 397
pointers, 452
pointers comparison, 398
pointers to members, 454, 455
pointers to members comparison, 398, 399
postcondition, 51
postordering, 155
precondition, 50
prefix array, 196
preordering, 155
prevent new instance of class, 461, 462
previous lower permutation, 210
Print 2D Array in Spiral Order, 120
Print Decimal Representation, 248
Pseudo Destructor, 384, 385

quick select iterative, 23
quicksort, 218, 222

Random-number generation, 231
randomized partition, 225
randomized quick select, 20
randomized quicksort, 218, 227
range for loop, 406
Re-arranging an array, 142
Rearranging Algorithms, 302
relational operator and void *, 397
Reliable distribution, 199
restricted range minima problem, 167
return brace-init-list, 407
return from main, 372
return type of lambda, 382
reusing constraint class, 496
Reverse Decimal Representation, 246
revise constexpr constructor, 417
revise constexpr function, 416
Revisit Constrained GCD, 243
Robot Walk, 114
rooted tree, 154
Round to Next Power of 2, 322

saddle, 64

saddleback count, 60
saddleback search, 52
saddleback search find all occurrences, 57
saddleback search find first occurrence, 55
scope of conditional variable, 403–405
scope of static member, 468
scope of template parameters, 351
scoped enumerator, 427, 428
Searching in Two Dimensional Sequence, 97
searching two-dim sorted array, 49
Seating Problem, 41
Segment Problems, 45
Select Kth Smallest Element, 12
Sequence Periodicity Problem, 249
Signal and Values, 339
signature of deallocation function, 482
Simple Path Problem, 175
simulate initializer list and constructor, 465, 466
simulation of range for loop, 406
simulation of while loop, 405
single short shortest path, 183
sizeof, 380, 381
Solve Inequality, 246
Sort a sequence of sub-sequences, 150
Sorting an almost sorted list, 31
Sorting Array of Strings : Linear Time, 252
Sparse Array Trick, 124
Spying Campaign, 167
Stage Coach Problem, 171
static and std::atexit, 372
static cast, 390
static cast and base/derived, 390, 391
static cast and const cast, 392
static cast and inaccessible base, 391
static cast to and fro, 392, 393
static member data, 468
static member function, 468
static member initialization scope, 464
std::atexit and static, 373
std::next_permutation, 208
std::partition, 222
std::prev_permutation, 211
storage class specifiers, 408
Storage Duration, 375

String Edit Distance, 176
Swap Values Without a Temporary, 332
Switch and Bulb Problem, 144
Switch Bulb Problem, 84

template and template-id, 491, 492
template argument and type-id, 492
templates, 491
Temporary and Conversions, 339, 340
ternary tree, 217
The Celebrity Problem, 70
The Longest Upsequence Problem, 34
The Non-Crooks Problem, 23
The Parallel Prefix Problem, 260
The Plateau Problem, 95
The problem of the balanced segments, 88
The Problem of the Circular Racecourse, 122
The problem of the most isolated villages, 89
The Welfare Crook Problem, 104
this pointer, 467
trailing return types, 458
translation vs runtime, 402
Transport Problem, 77
trigraph sequences, 340
trivial class, 467
TSP Problem, 175
two std::atexit, 374, 375
type of base class member, 393
type of decltype((auto variable)), 383, 384
type of function, 456
type of lambda, 381
type of member function, 456, 457
type of new, 394
type specifier, 422
type traits, 497
typedef and const, 407
typedef and const volatile function, 457
typedef and function definition, 457
typeid and const/volatile, 390
types, 454

understanding dynamic cast, 387–389
Understanding Point of Declaration, 347, 348
Unique 5-bit Sequences, 11
unnamed namespace, 429

Unqualified Name Lookup, 351–355
usage of constexpr function, 412, 413
user defined conversion, 479
user defined literal, 342
using new, 395
using declaration, 434
using declaration and accessibility rules, 443
using declaration and ambiguous base, 442
using declaration and base class, 434, 435
using declaration and member declaration, 436
using declaration and referring members, 437
using declaration and same functions, 439
using declaration and template-id, 435
using directive, 443, 444
using unnamed namespace, 429, 430

valid usage of this pointer, 380
Value Category : lvalue/rvalue, 376
variant, 51
virtual function, 473, 474
virtual function and final, 475
virtual function and hiding, 474, 475
virtual function and override, 475, 476
virtual member function template, 493

weighted median, 234
Write as sum of consecutive positive numbers, 119
Writing a Value as the Sum of Squares, 68

xvalue rvalue, 379

www.ingramcontent.com/pod-product-compliance
Lightning Source LLC
Chambersburg PA
CBHW071755200526
45167CB00018B/1792